Statebuilding from the Margins

AMERICAN GOVERNANCE:
POLITICS, POLICY, AND PUBLIC LAW

Series Editors:
Richard Valelly, Pamela Brandwein, Marie Gottschalk, Christopher Howard

A complete list of books in the series is available from the publisher.

Statebuilding from the Margins

Between Reconstruction and the New Deal

Edited by
Carol Nackenoff and Julie Novkov

PENN

UNIVERSITY OF PENNSYLVANIA PRESS

PHILADELPHIA

Published by
University of Pennsylvania Press
Philadelphia, Pennsylvania 19104-4112
www.upenn.edu/pennpress

Printed in the United States of America
on acid-free paper

10 9 8 7 6 5 4 3 2 1

Library of Congress Cataloging-in-Publication Data

Statebuilding from the margins : between Reconstruction and the New Deal / edited by Carol Nackenoff and Julie Novkov. — 1st ed.

p. cm. — (American governance: politics, policy, and public law)

Includes bibliographical references and index.

ISBN 978-0-8122-4571-4 (hardcover : alk. paper)

1. Progressivism (United States politics) 2. United States—Politics and government—1865–1933. 3. United States—Social policy. 4. United States—History—1865–1921. 5. United States—History—1919–1933. I. Nackenoff, Carol. II. Novkov, Julie, 1966– III. Series: American governance.

E661.S76 2014

973.8—dc23 2013031257

Contents

Introduction

Statebuilding in the Progressive Era: A Continuing Dilemma in American Political Development

This volume addresses statebuilding in the Progressive Era, and the years leading up to and immediately following it, by considering institutions, policy areas, reformers, and sites of development that have largely evaded the analytical gaze of researchers who explore the roots of the modern American state. In doing so, this book hopes to add to the richness and complexity of the literature concerning development in this era by bringing forward new cases for consideration. More fundamentally, though, these cases reveal themselves as crucial sites of statebuilding—the making of black and monogamous citizens in the postbellum years, the racial and personal politics of Georgia's adoption of prohibition, the rise of public waste management, the incorporation of animal management into the welfare state, the initiation of state and federal wildlife management, the creation of public juvenile courts, and the involvement of women's groups in the creation of U.S. housing policy. They were locations where boundaries between public and private shifted, where models for state "borrowing" of private capacity were piloted, where new hybrid institutions were sometimes forged, where a variety of policy entrepreneurs used creative techniques to get results through informal and formal politics, and where institutions and their development can be understood in structural, cultural, and ideological terms.

The Progressive Era was a particularly fertile moment because of the shifting boundaries between public and private. Much of this shift, and the incorporation of new issues into the regulatory reach of the public sphere, relate to a broadening vision of women's sphere as women successfully interjected themselves into the world of politics as caretakers, advocates, and policy entrepreneurs.[1] But even beyond the striking growth of middle-class women's political and policymaking capacity, the other issues these chapters discuss were increasingly framed as problems in which the state should take a direct interest in the betterment of society. Considering this process at this time with regard to these issues presents a picture of active growth of state capacity and the development of new institutions—defined not just as material structures but also through the ideological frameworks that animated them.[2] Whereas our curiosity about these individual issues drove our initial inquiries, bringing them together raises larger related questions about development, institutions, and statebuilding.

Project Origins

Over the last five years, some of the authors represented in this volume began to realize a set of shared and overlapping interests as we studied politics and policy developments during the years from the end of the Civil War to the New Deal. Many of us had done archival work on particular Progressive Era issues we found provocative, and exchanges, conference panels, and collaborations followed. We found ourselves talking, at various times, to law and courts scholars; to race, gender, and ethnicity scholars; and, quite often, with scholars of American political development (henceforth, APD) as we developed these ideas and research projects. The coeditors of this volume began thinking about bringing these authors together and we identified additional fellow travelers.

Several elements drew our research together and made it worthwhile to put our projects more directly in conversation with each other. We all saw the decades between the end of the Civil War and the beginning of the New Deal as dynamic and formative years for American political development. This period is too often treated as the raw material from which (and against which) the modern nation-state is forged. We rejected readings of these post-Civil War decades as ones in which partisanship was intense but governance was largely absent, save for urban machines.[3] We found the view, often expressed by comparativists, that America in this period lacked what could reasonably be called a "state," highly problematic and even counterproductive for studying this period.[4] We found unacceptable Hartzian arguments contending that atomistic individualism prevented significant statebuilding until the 1930s, and likewise arguments that political development took lengthy "time-outs" in certain sections of the country.[5] We rejected the idea that the struggles and institutional changes that took place during these years were superseded or overwritten entirely by subsequent institutional developments, especially those of the New Deal era.

We found changes occurring that were neither linear nor simply incremental, and that even studies incorporating intercurrence (the layering of multiple orders at the same time in institutional development) did not fully capture the dynamics we observed. Searching for and studying American political development, we encountered various processes and changes best described as "statebuilding"—whether at the local, state, or national level.

Our different projects all fundamentally interrogate statebuilding. Statebuilding as a focus emphasizes the questions we all have about how states at these different levels accrue both policy agendas and the institutional capacity to carry them out. We are called upon to think about how regulation becomes legalized, and whether legalization is essential to a state's embrace, or to the legitimation, of a new regulatory agenda.

We are likewise challenged to think about periodization in political development. With a number of chapters focused on the subnational level, we see that trajectories in statebuilding can vary by policy arena and that sometimes state and municipal trajectories differ. Although these observations relate to intercurrence, they raise additional questions through the incorporation of considerations about both ideology and the significance of reformers who actively seek out opportunities within different arenas of the state to achieve their agendas. There are provocative questions about whether statebuilding at the federal level parallels statebuilding at the state/municipal level, or whether there are interesting mismatches. Accepting that statebuilding is not simply linear prompts us to consider whether different patterns are merely evidence of survivals (e.g., common law), or whether many different patterns can coexist for long periods of time. Is statebuilding always simply muddled and fragmented, as Elisabeth Clemens's image of the Rube Goldberg state suggests? What, if anything, makes the Progressive Era distinctive when we think about statebuilding? And what, of the things we have learned about Progressive Era statebuilding, pushes us to rethink later developmental trajectories?

Our findings led us to reconsider some key assumptions and debates among scholars of American political development, and sometimes to suggest alternatives. In particular, the chapters largely begin from Clemens's portrayal of fragmented and contradictory processes to challenge the more structurally based vision of development articulated by Karen Orren and

Stephen Skowronek, and the more ordered vision favored by Theda Skocpol and Paul Pierson.

APD scholarship has taken many of its cues from efforts to bring the state back in to what had, for a previous generation of scholars, generally been society-, group-, class-, and social movement-centered analyses of political change. In *Bringing the State Back In*, Peter Evans, Dietrich Rueschemeyer, and Theda Skocpol reinserted and foregrounded the state as an agent and an institution that shapes political and social processes through its actions and policies.[6] In this project, Skocpol also emphasized state autonomy—the capacity of states to formulate and implement goals that are not simply reflective of demands and interests of social groups and that can be implemented even against opposition. In the aftermath, many important studies of the development of the American state have been state-centered. For Dan Carpenter, for instance, statebuilding in this period is driven by bureaucratic entrepreneurs, involved in "the incremental selling of new program ideas through experimentation and piecemeal coalition building."[7]

The state-centric approach is somewhat tempered in Skocpol's *Protecting Soldiers and Mothers*, where an organization such as the General Federation of Women's Clubs was able to play a major role in generating important welfare-state provisions when administrative agencies had not come to dominate the playing field.[8] She argues that patterns of bureaucratic development shape possibilities for social groups to "do things" by public authority, a point we would not contest.[9] Taking processes of state formation seriously, as Skocpol counseled, however, the authors of the chapters in this volume find that understanding state formation often requires looking outside the state. Political activities and activists were not just conditioned by institutions, structures, and previous social policies;[10] they also forged alliances that were instrumental in the creation of new public powers and administrative capacities. Their historically and institutionally contextualized visions of what the state *should* be sometimes shaped what the state *would* be. A number of chapters emphasize the ways in which these reformers envisioned, modeled, helped generate, shared, and sometimes passed on institutions and administrative capacities.

For historian Paula Baker, women in the Progressive Era who pressed the state to seek to solve, and even prevent, social problems that were too big for charitable and voluntary action contributed significantly to the domestication of politics. Several chapters in this volume argue that women helped generate this vision of the liberal state (Susan Pearson and Kimberly Smith,

Carol Nackenoff and Kathleen Sullivan, Anne-Marie Szymanski). However, while Baker sees women "passing on" and giving over their voluntary work to government in the form of social policy in the Progressive period,[11] this volume suggests that this is only one possible model for the cooperation between women's organizations and the state. Sometimes, collaboration continued, with hybrid and complex lines of public-private interaction.

Skowronek's *Building a New American State*, while critical to our understanding of statebuilding in the Progressive Era, focused the attention of American political development scholars on a particular locus for this process. This work, tending toward the Weberian tradition, characterized the turn-of-the-century period—a period long recognized as "a watershed in the development of American government"—as the "emergence of an administrative rationality based on principles of hierarchy and professionalism."[12] Skowronek sees this transition as a struggle for institutional power; it is also a struggle over controlling class conflict.[13] The move toward the administrative state was chiefly about building national state capacity. The state of courts and parties ultimately yielded because "Modern American state building successfully negotiated a break with an outmoded organization of state power"; incremental and politically contingent reforms reconstructed a nation-state with national administrative procedures and forms.[14]

Skowronek's analysis emphasizes the growth and rhetorical mobilization of an intellectual elite coming from the professional sector and the "burgeoning university sector" who, with a strong interest in policymaking, constituted the statebuilding vanguard.[15] Some chapters in this volume highlight the role of some of these same elites. In Skowronek's account, their new policymaking agenda faced significant challenges; the need for broader administrative power and capacity clashed with an old-order state of courts and parties, which resisted dismantling.[16] By his account, a conscious struggle emerged in which administrative reformers actively sought to change how government worked, contributing to the emergence of new statebuilding coalitions. As the coalitions began to have an impact on the hardened institutional structures they challenged, "they instigated a scramble for power and position throughout the governmental apparatus. The bureaucratic realm was instantly politicized."

Skowronek also emphasizes the growth of national state institutions, bureaucracies, and governing capacity in the transition to the modern state in the late nineteenth and early twentieth centuries, and does so with a specific focus on institutions as mechanisms constituted by the sum of their material practices.[17] However, states and municipalities frequently developed institutions and capacities during this period as well, and the role of reformers in the process cannot be ignored. The contributors to this volume account for state development by considering a wider variety of actors within and outside the formal confines of the state, and they consider the ideological as well as material components of institutions.

Dominant narratives of Progressive Era statebuilding in the American political development literature may reflect the types of political issues scholars have chosen for investigation, and changing the focus can change the narratives. If we acknowledge Paula Baker's argument that political spheres, issues, and agendas were gendered throughout most of the nineteenth century, that partisan politics reflected men's issues, and that organized women tended to concern themselves with issues involving children, dependents, poverty, and social problems,[18] then bringing issues of concern to women more thoroughly into an examination of statebuilding will very likely change what we see. It is possible that narratives excluding some of the kinds of issues women helped bring to the table find more nationalization and absorption of policymaking than we find in some of our case studies in this volume. It is also quite possible that patterns of statebuilding vary instead with the mix of federal, state, and local responses that are appropriate to specific issues. The cases in this volume show that there *are* different patterns, and that organized interests outside the state play important roles in building the American state.

The developmental trajectories these chapters trace are thus quite different from Skowronek's, describing some of these processes of statebuilding as substantially less self-conscious and subject to multiple driving forces within and outside of the state. James Greer's chapter shows the Better Homes in America (BHA) movement actually arguing during the 1920s against those who would have government more directly and immediately involved in housing. Ironically, however, in the Roosevelt administration's responses to the aftermath of 1929, the vision and standards the BHA formulated ended up in the National Housing Act of 1934, which established the parameters for what housing would be eligible for mortgage insurance. In these chapters, state institutional actors often seem to be less self-conscious, goal-directed, or bent on developing state power than some of the activists with whom they developed connections; in a few of our studies, the state actors charged with implementing new programs had to be goaded into action and investment. In some of our cases, activists at the state level transitioned into positions in the bureaucracies of the federal government, taking charge themselves of the policies they had successfully championed. But the authors generally do not see these conflicts as monumental struggles between forward-thinking elite bureaucratic innovators and upholders of traditional state organizations and functions.[19] Rather than a structural, largely two-sided struggle, we see a muddled mix of local, state, national, public, and private interests in policies, and a range of actors seeking leverage on policy in any ways and through any arenas where they could find it.

One way to conceptualize the difference is to compare the two approaches directly. Skowronek's approach looks from the top down and largely confines itself to state actions and development as driven through and by the state. It is typical of the large-scale narratives about political development that emphasize institutions and their involvement in the production of change. Professionals are significant, though their significance is largely tied to their professional roles rather than their individual entrepreneurial engagements. In light of this, Skowronek does not attend much to the rhetoric, framing, or ideology that drove reform, preferring to consider concrete structural changes. And his analysis largely focuses on transformations in law that led to bureaucratization as the main manifestation of institution-building.

In contrast, the chapters in this volume consider the agency and interactions among different types of actors seeking change. Some were elite state actors, but others did their work as private actors and began their campaigns outside of or alongside the state. These reformers and activists look like policy entrepreneurs; the chapters attend carefully to the choices they made about where to focus their energies, and also to how they advocated for and built change. These analyses lead the authors to address more comprehensively the role of emotional appeals and ideological frames in the process of statebuilding. And addressing these processes by highlighting the agency of reformers demonstrates how statebuilding sometimes begins outside of the state, prior to the development of legal structures for its implementation.

Some of the complexity in processes of statebuilding is captured well by Brian Balogh, who pinpoints the final decades of the nineteenth century as opening a new period of the "intermingling of state and private means of extending public authority" in the United States, with the scope often becoming national.[20] For Balogh, during this vibrant period of group development, collective and associational solutions to various social problems were advanced as superior to and more ethically advanced than individualistic or laissez-faire approaches.[21] Groups advocating for reform turned to the nation-state as one association among many—but an association with special advantages. Balogh frequently depicts the federal government as parceling out power to organizations to do state work. This is a case of mixed public-private authority, to be sure, but we find other patterns for such public-private collaborations.

Understanding state complexity is also nicely enhanced by William Novak, who recognizes a long tradition in American politics of achieving public interests through use of the private sphere.[22] Rejecting as myth the notion that the American state was historically weak, Novak instead finds continuous construction of new forms of state power. Insisting that "American power has long been distributed among a series of individuals, groups, parties, associations, organizations, and institutions not readily designated as wholly *either* public *or* private," Novak admonishes scholars to attend more closely to the "interpenetration of public and private spheres—the convergence of public and private authority in everyday policymaking."[23] He also challenges scholars to consider whether instances of public-private collaboration signal transitions or rather exhibit patterns that are chronic in the history of the American state. This volume treats these insights seriously.

The chapters in this volume are on the whole closer to accounts of state development and state complexity offered by Balogh, Novak, and Clemens than to those of Orren, Skowronek, Pierson, and Skocpol. Even so, the authors raise additional concerns and attack the problem of development from a different angle than these scholars.

Elisabeth Clemens argues against claims for the functional, rational design of institutions: "To the extent that institutions appear to 'work,' it is because they have been made to work by being implicated in ongoing practices or projects, by the selective erosion and elaboration of time."[24] She describes governance as quite tangled and disorderly. This is not simply a residue of past legacies or of unintended consequences; not all tangles are "equally durable or prone to institutionalization."[25] As she notes, "political initiatives and policy decisions have increased fragmentation while also massively complicating relations of agency, fiscal dependency, and accountability that crosscut the boundaries of agencies and formal jurisdictions."[26] Clemens finds that the state consists of "complex and hybridized arrangements." State legislatures and state officials operate in an environment with "many existing organizations, many of which were already embedded in collaborative arrangements with public agencies."[27] The federal system further complicates arrangements. These tangles of indirect governance are, for Clemens, a recurring and significant pattern in American political development.[28]

Clemens offers three different possibilities to explain the Rube Goldberg state. The first is that formal state institutions attempt to borrow state capacity from nongovernmental actors: "episodes of collaborative or delegated governance should be expected whenever political projects seek to significantly increase the reach of governmental institutions."[29] In what she terms a "life-stage" explanation, "states first rely on collaboration with private organizations to deliver publicly funded programs and then develop institutional capacity to deliver these programs through public institutions."[30] These arrangements can vary across policy domains.

Her second explanation is one of "dependence and predation"—which she calls the "political-dependence explanation."[31] A government subsidy to a charity could be designed to make the charity dependent on the goodwill of legislators, who control the purse strings; political reformers in the early twentieth century were sensitive to this possibility of co-optation and imposition of party discipline. The important question for this model is when and where this kind of dependence produces the effective delivery of public services or a growth in state capacity.

A final explanation highlights what Clemens calls "collaborative relationships as expressions of power."[32] The existing institutional framework divides and separates powers, creating incentives for creation of a "dense tangle of governance arrangements" requiring reformers and others seeking power to work by indirection. "Within a political culture suspicious of governmental power, action through collaboration might well be less costly than the construction of explicitly public state capacity." This final approach is especially at odds with Skowronek and Carpenter on forging bureaucratic autonomy both because it configures development as nonlinear and not fully rationalized and because of the significance of the actions of political entrepreneurs, who seek entrée into the system at multiple and at times contradictory locations, leading to the tangle Clemens portrays.[33]

In all three arguments, the strategic choices of political actors, ranging from state agents to individuals completely outside the state, loom large as factors in how development unfolds. Yet each of these three arguments produces different expectations, Clemens explains. In the first (borrowing capacity), the expectation would be that indirect governance was more frequent earlier than later in U.S. political history; the second (political dependence) would be expected in particularly venal or corrupt periods or locales, where party bosses and legislators provide particularistic benefits in order to cement political loyalties; the third argument "identifies a quite different set of key actors, public bureaucrats who pursue expansive agendas in a context that constrains their legitimate exercise of power. Thus, complexity and interdependence should increase with projects of state-building."[34]

The chapters in this volume corroborate all three of Clemens's explanations to different degrees, depending on the policy issue at hand. For Ann-Marie Szymanski, following Clemens, the Rube Goldberg state is a muddle/fragmentation of government and the mix of national, state, local, and private actors involved. Szymanski finds that the state tends to borrow capacity from private actors and organizations until it develops sufficiently. This is also partially what Kathleen Sullivan and Patricia Strach find when urban machines rely on and provide inducements to business interests to build and operate expensive new garbage-reduction facilities. Nackenoff and Sullivan, studying the juvenile court movement in Illinois, see the creation of hybrid institutions in which public and private activity were imbricated continually, but in a dynamic relationship. Not only was the state borrowing capacity at the outset but there were reasons to maintain collaborative arrangements. Greer's discussion of the Better Homes of America and General Federation of Women's Clubs involvement in developing standards to judge adequate housing highlights the ways that the development of national administrative capacity relied on their work.

But the chapters also focus on how important moments in development often begin outside the state and persist alongside the state. Authors show how new ideas emerged in this era through engagements with, alongside, and outside the formal boundaries of the state. Instead of seeing statebuilding as driven by bureaucratic entrepreneurs, as Carpenter does, or by elected officials, as even Clemens does, we see a kind of statebuilding from the margins. A number of us see organized activists pushing the state to take on new jobs and pressing agendas on state officials who need to be persuaded or pressured to act, at times offering their own privately developed capacity to bolster the state's capability to achieve their desired policy outcomes.

Organized women are often involved in our narratives, extending to a number of cases the important role of organized women in the development of social policy that Skocpol examined. Armed with experience and a capacity to speak authoritatively about particular kinds of social and economic ills, from which gendered roles and identities did not bar them, women in charitable and civic organizations contributed to statebuilding. Several of the chapters deepen Paula Baker's analysis of how women's political activity shifted in the late nineteenth century and into the Progressive Era as "new perceptions about the function of the state and a transformed vision of society came out of the experience of the war."[35] The political work of women was increasingly influenced by "the methods and language of social science—data collection, detached observation, and an emphasis on prevention."[36] This appeal to social scientific methods, and not just experience, provided women with claims to expertise that facilitated their claims for public response as the state itself increasingly favored objective, scientific administration and approaches to social problems. Baker contends that the vision of women's groups at the turn of the century was highly compatible with emerging visions of the liberal state as activist, bureaucratic, efficient, and with an emphasis on social responsibility.[37] A number of authors in this volume argue that women were vital contributors to the generation of this vision of the liberal state.[38]

While Baker finds women giving over their voluntary work to the state because the problems they were addressing had become too big for charitable efforts, leading to "the devaluation of voluntary work and . . . the relinquishment of social policy to experts in governmental bureaucracies,"[39] the chapters by Nackenoff and Sullivan, Szymanski, Pearson and Smith, and Greer outline a more complicated process of engagement than the linear bureaucratic rationalization Baker describes. The authors demonstrate that this is only one possible model for the cooperation between women's organizations and the state. In a number of instances, organizations and groups involved in developing specific policy ideas and agendas continued to collaborate with formal state institutions and actors. Hybrid and complex lines of public-private interaction were not unusual.

Not only is gender salient as an identity and performative aspect of reformers, but a number of authors in this book also examine sites of struggle defined by race, class, or gender classifications. Notions of proper civic behavior are raced, classed, and gendered. Julie Novkov, for instance, shows how federal prosecutors reinforced the rights of manly citizenship for freedmen and then turned to imposing appropriate gendered relations among Latter-day Saints; Marek Steedman emphasizes the uses of race in mobilizing energy behind the drive for prohibition.

Some authors also consider sites of legal contestation—for example, over competing conceptions of rights. Here, we can productively reflect on the role of traditional or common law powers in promoting or challenging statebuilding. When a formerly legal offense is transformed into a social problem (juvenile delinquency), or what was previously considered private or discretionary is now considered a matter for public regulation (alcohol consumption, treatment of animals, marriage relations), we seek to learn from the terms in which the struggles take place. The nature of legal contestation we describe differs somewhat from the struggles Skowronek identifies. In his analysis, contestation moves to legal terrains as resisters to reform rely on embedded legal formulations to maintain the social order; he describes the challenges that elite, technocratic state reformers launched to build and transform institutions in the face of this resistance. For many of our authors, law is more malleable and ambiguous in the way it weaves through the statebuilding process, reinforcing, reflecting, and transforming different ideologies.

This understanding of law enables a more robust consideration of how ideologies play into institutional transformations. Pamela Brandwein recently reminded scholars that "law must be disaggregated as a category of analysis" and that "law does not work in a unified way" in the service of particular institutions or ideologies.[40] She criticizes Skowronek's approach in part because he and those who follow him separate institutions from ideology and discount the role of ideology as a component of institutions. In their consideration of law, the chapters in this volume avoid this problem, relating how struggles on legal terrain weave ideology into the material process of institutional development. Some chapters show how reformers mobilized traditional or common law concepts to ground transformation. Others argue that contestation occurred around ideological struggles that played out across legal terrains. In all these cases, such sites of contestation provide rich opportunities for learning about statebuilding, its complexities, and its challenges. Understanding these efforts and ways to statebuilding should be ongoing scholarly projects.

The Book's Organization and Chapters

Historically, the chapters span from Julie Novkov's juxtaposition of post-Civil War efforts to extend rights for freedmen and freedwomen and those undertaken to suppress polygamy to James Greer's analysis of the development in the 1920s and 1930s of a national system of mortgage insurance based significantly on the work of the Better Homes of America and the Federation of Women's Clubs to define acceptable middle-class housing. While several themes cut across most or all of the chapters, the chapters themselves fall into smaller groupings based on the substantive issues they discuss. Julie Novkov and Marek Steedman both consider race and gender in different contexts, addressing anxieties about civic performances of racialized and gendered identities. Both chapters highlight how anxieties about citizens and proper civic behavior grounded new forms of state action and growth in state capacity. The chapters by Susan Pearson and Kim Smith and by Ann-Marie Szymanski critically consider how advocacy to regulate domestic animals and animal welfare and to promote wildlife conservation provided the impetus for change in state and federal agendas and in regulatory authority. Finally, chapters by Kathleen Sullivan and Patricia Strach, Carol Nackenoff and Kathleen Sullivan, and James Greer all address the building of regulatory authority and capacity outside or alongside the state, asking what happens when the state attempts to borrow, appropriate, or support and legitimate capacity.

Julie Novkov's chapter juxtaposes two large-scale legal campaigns to define, control, and enforce the meaning of citizenship. Between the end of the Civil War and the early 1870s, the national government sought to define and enforce citizenship rights for freedmen. The energy behind this campaign dissipated as the national government invested statebuilding resources in the campaign to suppress polygamy among Latter-day Saints in the Utah Territory. Analyzed together, these efforts reveal how committed Republicans, backed by dedicated activists, remade the national government in the wake of the Civil War's upheaval of longstanding understandings of federalism. They argued for greater latitude for national action to resolve local issues. But to leverage these arguments, they articulated visions of citizenship that reconfigured the meaning of civic membership and its associated rights. The ill-defined category of "citizen," which, with only a few exceptions, the antebellum national government had left to the states to define, grounded the expansion of federalism. Suits brought under new laws defined and enforced the rights of citizens, leveraging action through a public concern about citizens and their proper relationship to the nation. These campaigns responded to advocacy groups' promotion of gendered visions of citizenship. They also generated and institutionalized growth in state capacity to define and manage citizenship among those perceived to be problematic or marginal citizens.

Most accounts of prohibition as a movement around the turn of the century focus on the Anti-Saloon League and pressure politics, but this League had little presence in the South and was not a major factor in the rise of prohibition and its passage in Georgia, the first southern state ever to adopt statewide prohibition and the only one to do so for more than two decades. The Woman's Christian Temperance Union (WCTU) and local evangelical groups had been active in crusading for prohibition for more than a decade with not especially more success in Georgia than in other southern states, but the issue abruptly acquired more traction in Georgia after the turn of the century. Marek Steedman seeks to explain Georgia's outlier status in adopting prohibition in 1907. Why would this southern state turn, at this moment, to centralized, statewide regulation in light of a pronounced traditional preference for individual liberty and local self-governance? While Richard Bensel's explanation, framed in terms of political economy, helps to explain the emergence of strong state structures in the South while states based more in private competition developed in the North, his analysis does not address the timing issue or fully explain the political leverage engendering this shift in Georgia.[41] For Steedman, an important part of the answer is the role of independent newspapers and their editors, especially the editor of the *Atlanta Georgian*. The paper disseminated information about upcoming meetings, reproduced the content of speeches there, editorialized against antiprohibitionist officials, identified leaders in favor of prohibition, and encouraged political organization and mobilization in support of prohibition. Newspaper editors were political entrepreneurs, embedded in partisan politics, and capable of influencing policy in Georgia. But the explanation for why Georgia and why then is demonstrably steeped in race, especially the Atlanta race riot the previous year, with the newspapers blaming assaults and riots on saloons selling cheap whiskey. Newspaper coverage likewise shaped and stoked fears in the events leading up to the riot, running sensationalist headlines and pressing the supposed link between sexual assaults on white women and saloons. Prohibition, Steedman argues, was a policy linked to the political project of a white supremacist but nevertheless progressive state. In reshaping the discourse of prohibition, newspapers at this time helped generate a new narrative of state responsibility for racial order—a narrative in which prohibition and Jim Crow moved in tandem.

Focusing on waste management offers a novel window onto processes of statebuilding in the Progressive Era, as Kathleen Sullivan and Patricia Strach demonstrate. By the 1890s, larger American cities looked for alternatives to dumping trash or feeding it to swine. Of the ninety-three cities for which the authors have data, only thirteen were using new garbage-reduction technology in 1900; but by 1909 seventy-nine cities had garbage-reduction plants. Almost all were owned by private parties because cities lacked funds to invest in and operate reduction plants. Not all cities, however, were successful in employing this new and expensive technology. Examining two cities that tried reduction near the turn of the century, the authors find that Pittsburgh was successful in its efforts to build and use a reduction plant whereas New Orleans was not. The difference between the two lies in the stability of the political machine and the security of ties between the machine and the businessmen with whom the city partnered to build the reduction plant. Mere recognition of sanitary problems by reformers, merchants, new health professionals, and concerned citizens did not bring about lasting changes in garbage disposal. Since public works project collaborations with businessmen required expectations of stable revenue to launch successfully, machine dynamics and political corruption ensured the certainty of public services through public-private contracts. Political machines thus played an important role as sources of municipal state capacity and political development. Sullivan and Strach recognize the importance of the agency of policy entrepreneurs, but note that the structure of politics defined the room that these entrepreneurs had to achieve their ends, and show how corruption could produce the necessary stability to facilitate successful implementation of policy.

Animal management has long been a state function, but Susan Pearson and Kimberly Smith argue that animal management played a vital role in the development of the welfare state as a site where an ideology of protection facilitated regulatory innovation. Beginning in the 1860s, the American Society for the Prevention of Cruelty to Animals and animal welfare reformers pioneered creative public-private partnerships and institutional innovations that contributed to the state's capacity to protect the vulnerable—both animal and human. Private contributions and the efforts of organized women helped launch the movement, but there were distinctly gendered divisions of labor among the activists. The animal anticruelty movement that began to strengthen at this time spread rather rapidly through the states, with all states having some form of anticruelty legislation within about forty years. Yet even with this remarkable success, reformers were constrained by the frames that the state would recognize and adapt to their policy goals. Although animal welfare reformers increasingly spoke in terms of animal rights, courts did not readily embrace the rights framework, finding instead a commonweal in good morals. In New York, to which special attention is given, legislation allowed the SPCA to enter the home in their efforts to investigate, arrest, and prosecute offenders, wielding police powers. State officials viewed the organization as a "subordinate public agency"; in some states, humane societies eventually became state bureaus. However, the momentum did not easily spill over into federal government policy during this period. A corollary of enhanced state capacity to protect animals was the power of employing violence to manage the animal population, a legacy of the privileging of protection over rights.

In the late nineteenth century and into the 1920s, American citizens were heavily involved in enforcing regulatory policy. Creating voluntary associations or incorporating enforcement activities into existing organizations, they monitored their communities, conforming to common law expectations by public officials that private citizens would supplement public enforcement efforts. In the case of wildlife protection, as Anne Marie Szymanski's chapter demonstrates, beginning in the late nineteenth century sportsmen, naturalists, and progressive women targeted state governments with demands for laws to protect wildlife and were highly successful in rather short order; by 1920 reformers were also able to point to remarkable success at the national level. In this case, policy reform moved from the state to national level rather quickly, despite some tension in the courts over powers reserved to the states under the Tenth Amendment. Szymanski finds that during the Progressive Era, private policing (which was costly, controversial, and dangerous) yielded to public policing after a transitional period during which lines between public and private became especially blurry. In the early phases of the transition, public officials generally lacked resources (if they were willing) to enforce such legislation and private associations performed these functions, sometimes paying salaries and gathering evidence against offenders. Private associations were not merely lending capacity to the state—rather, Szymanski argues, associations could "borrow" regulatory power from the state until more favorable circumstances allowed them to engage in statebuilding. State wildlife organizations and sportsmen generally supported the transition of policing activities to the public sector, which, in many cases, was accomplished by 1909.

The Juvenile Court of Cook County (often referred to as the Chicago Juvenile Court) was an institution envisioned and built by Progressive Era reformers, and from it a juvenile court movement spread rapidly across the nation. With Julia Lathrop and Lucy Flower at the forefront, the Chicago Woman's Club and its allies—including both state and nonstate actors—created an effective network to generate legal and judicial change. The reformers were aided by a concomitant shift in Progressive Era legal culture away from formalism and toward administrative flexibility; reformers developed the argument that dependent and delinquent children were wards of the state, over whom the state could exercise paternal power to guide and reform. Carol Nackenoff and Kathleen Sullivan find that, in a pattern that would be repeated, reformers developed prototypes of the institutions and practices they wanted the state to recognize and embrace; they supplied personnel, equipment, and funding to launch the institution and to persuade policymakers that it worked until the state assumed responsibility for administration and funding. They expanded the new Juvenile Court, encouraging the state to add the offices of probation officers, medical personnel, and the Juvenile Psychopathic Institute. They placed their own activists into these public offices, from probation officer to judge and, beyond, to the federal Children's Bureau. Their own institutions in the private sphere developed alongside the development they encouraged in the public sphere. Judges for the Juvenile Court had to pass muster with the Juvenile Court Committee and, later, the Juvenile Protective Association. The institution that they built was a hybrid of public and private that did not necessarily have clearly delineated boundaries, yet was mutually beneficial for the state and the activists.

Mortgage redlining, which brought about disinvestment in center-city neighborhoods while suburban communities' housing markets expanded dramatically, is associated with policy initiatives of the New Deal. Its most important component was the creation of a national system of mortgage insurance backed by the finances of the federal government, a program then implemented by the Federal Housing Administration. As James Greer explains, however, few have recognized how rooted this dimension of U.S. housing policy is in the work of women in the aftermath of World War I. Better Homes for America, Inc., a private, civic organization founded in 1922 by Marie Meloney, editor of the *Delineator*, a million-reader circulation women's magazine, drew on the considerable administrative capacity of the General Federation of Women's Clubs throughout the country to define and popularize the minimal physical amenities of the affordable middle-class home. Widely popular and active throughout the 1920s with thousands of model home displays throughout the country, this movement culminated in the publication of a *Better Homes Manual*, a compendium of the building requirements of a standard American home. The FHA adopted in large part the detailed and comprehensive physical requirements of the American home described in the *Better Homes Manual*. The content of publicly sanctioned underwriting for the nation's mortgage insurance program—and the basis for redlining—was established by a private, civic organization. Thus again, a state institution's roots are readily traced to private entrepreneurs who initiated the work of building policy before state actors were convinced to embrace their agenda. And yet the civic organization's leadership included Secretary of

Commerce Herbert Hoover. In the case Greer describes, the FHA eventually assimilated and transformed the activists' agenda.

The Themes of the Book

The authors, each in a particular empirical context, have wrestled with a related set of questions about statebuilding and change in this critical period in American history. Taken together, the chapters demonstrate that, through pressure and direction from advocates, ideas about what constituted appropriate policy areas for state intervention changed. In the course of this change, state actors became increasingly invested in managing problems and concerns that had previously been addressed through voluntary collective action, or in some cases, not at all.

The chapters show, however, that the process involved more than the straightforward expansion of state policymaking authority and stretching of the perceived appropriate scope for public regulation. Statebuilding took place through a dynamic combination of strategies, including the borrowing of nonstate regulatory apparatuses assembled by concerned citizens, the implementation of formal legal change supplemented by the direct creation of state-based resources for investigation and enforcement, and the negotiation of collaborative, sometimes durable, arrangements between state and nonstate actors. This combination of approaches and actors meant that statebuilding was often not driven by a unified set of intentions, either those of private advocates or state actors. And, in most cases, statebuilding did not take place as a rational, linear developmental process, but rather, in Elisabeth Clemens's potent imagery, as the construction of a Rube Goldberg state, borrowing and transforming pieces that were assembled into state-based machinery through accident, nonstate advocacy, and competing political agendas. This conception of development adds complexity and contradiction even to William Novak's "exceedingly complex welter of institutions, jurisdictions, branches, offices, programs, rules, customs, laws, and regulations," and indeed helps to explain the sources of some of the multiple layers he describes.[42]

Agency

One significant question that cuts across the chapters is the role of agency. For a number of authors, individuals and groups play significant roles in driving the process and outcomes of institutionalization, especially when they seek to advance their agendas through multiple sites they perceive as policy windows. For Pearson and Smith, the story cannot be told without an account of the advocacy work of the Humane Society. Novkov's description of the shift in conceptions of citizenship gains flesh from the choices of individual government prosecutors to press claims and from the choice to invest significant resources in these endeavors. Nackenoff and Sullivan present a rich explanation of the significance of the relationship between the settlement house movement and women's clubs in developing and disseminating the juvenile court model. Steedman shows how the actions of influential newspaper editors framed politics and led to institutional development. For Greer, the well-placed editor of a wide-circulation women's magazine, working with the General Federation of Women's Clubs solidified a national movement that changed notions of the middle-class home.

Nonetheless, these accounts do not rely exclusively on agency to explain development. Rather, the authors untangle complex dynamics of agency and explain how the generation of institutions and the development of policy channeled and changed these agents' agendas. They also note how the structure of institutions provided or closed down different kinds of opportunities to achieve change. Agents sought institutional openings in which they could advance their visions of change and expand the state's capacity to promote their agendas. An excellent example is Szymanski's description of how sportsmen and advocates for the humane treatment of animals encouraged state actors to take an interest in animal-saving by in effect lending their regulatory frameworks and resources to the state. Many of the authors also attend carefully to the rhetorical framings these agents used to promote their desired outcomes, showing how the ideological underpinnings of their arguments influenced both how they approached the process of promoting institutionalization and which institutions they attempted to employ or build.

Sometimes, the work of advocates and agents, particularly those who were not formal state actors, was institutionalized in ways they most likely had not anticipated. At times, when state actors gained ownership of agendas and the mechanisms that nonstate actors had originally championed, they took these new institutions in different directions and tailored them to serve different purposes than their original advocates and crafters had intended. Greer's examination of the origins of redlining reveals that the work and the classificatory framework of housing quality developed by the Better Homes movement, spearheaded by the BHA, shaped government policy choices in the Depression, taking government further than the advocates had envisioned and doing so after the BHA had ceased to exist. In other cases, the relationships between institutions and agency limited nonstate actors' ability to exploit policy windows; as Sullivan and Strach illustrate, when the weaker New Orleans machine struggled to implement effective garbage collection in the face of more robust political struggle, the outcome was not as successful as it was in Pittsburgh, where the machine was more fully entrenched.

Taken together, these dynamics not only illuminate how change happens but also provide a broader conception of development. As Stephen Skowronek and Matthew Glassman have done in their edited volume, *Formative Acts*, this book seeks to move beyond systemic explanations, showing "how and to what extent [political actors'] actions change the American polity."[43] The chapters' analyses of the relationship between agency and institutions (those fully administered by the state, those that are partially integrated into the state, and those that exist alongside the state) explain change and also explain the limits of change.

Statebuilding

A second question concerns the nature of statebuilding. For the most part, narratives of statebuilding in American political development have addressed the actions of bureaucratic entrepreneurs or state actors; further, analysts have often primarily addressed what Novak terms "despotic power," or the "organizational capacity of state elites to rule unchecked by other centers of power or by civil society."[44] In this book, however, the chapters largely explore statebuilding from the margins, a theme that builds on Novak's recognition of the American state's long tradition of using the private sphere to achieve the public's interests. The authors in this volume show how agents outside the state or who have limited roles in it drive the creation of governing institutions and the development that flows from institutional change. This emphasis has three important implications. It calls into question where and how to identify development. It focuses attention directly on political entrepreneurship and the conditions under which it can be successful in agenda setting and in gaining legal authorization for new institutions. And it suggests that statebuilding may involve significant struggles over where a policy problem is most readily solved.

Orren and Skowronek define development as a durable shift in governing authority, "resulting in a new distribution of authority among persons or organizations within the polity at large or between them and their counterparts outside."[45] In this volume, chapter authors broaden this understanding of development by tracing transitions and shifts that are sometimes subtle, complex, and more complete in some states than in others, introducing interesting questions about periodization. Orren and Skowronek draw boundaries around change to make it manageable by focusing on governing authority as a function of state institutions and the acts that state actors take through these structures. This approach ensures that the identification of development will rest on an analysis of change that takes place in the structure and functioning of governing authority. The authors in this volume untether governance from direct association with state institutions and actors, thereby increasing the scope for identifying shifts. But they are clearly shifts, and the external actors and groups and institutional participants involved understand them as such. Institutions can be crafted by external actors and groups before state actors embrace these institutions as potential resources for the implementation of policy, as both Baker and Novak help us understand. For instance, as Nackenoff and Sullivan suggest, the "development" of juvenile courts as institutions becomes confirmed as development when state actors embrace or transform the institutions crafted outside or alongside the state. The chapters in this book also explore the ways nonstate actors who seek to change moral or cultural understandings in the broader society by working outside or alongside state institutions may turn to formal state apparatuses if their efforts to achieve cultural transformation have fallen short.[46]

Adam Sheingate admonishes scholars of American political development to attend more to "strategic, self-activated innovators who recast political institutions and governing relationships."[47] Many of the agents in the chapters can be classified as political entrepreneurs, and the authors of these chapters attend carefully not just to outsiders' individual acts of political creativity but also to the ways that politics and institutional structures provide both boundaries and opportunities for entrepreneurial behavior. For example, Steedman's Georgia newspaper editor saw an opportunity in the 1906 Atlanta race riot both for the enhancement of his own political prospects and for leveraging this event to generate support for a policy change implementing prohibition of alcohol. While his creativity generated the desired policy change, the racial framework needed to achieve it became embedded as part of the policy.

We consider when and why regulations are federalized, and which kinds are the most likely targets. In Novkov's analysis, federal governmental involvement comes through a more national understanding of citizenship and its meaning, and the Republican Party's commitment to strengthening its hold on political power. For Szymanski, the fact that the phenomenon to be regulated (wildlife) is mobile helps provide an opening for federal involvement. She also introduces the idea of geography of interests as a factor. For Nackenoff and Sullivan, the rapid national spread of the idea/institution of juvenile courts contributes to a climate in which national action may be seen as the next logical step, one facilitated by the consonance of ideas between the Chicago reformers and national administrative officials. Quite often in the cases discussed in the volume, a warrant for the exercise of new federal power requires articulation. In some cases, state power appears to be displaced under the commerce power, but in a number of cases the displacement is incomplete (again echoing Novak's point about the tiered distribution of power).[48] Several authors identify rapid spread throughout the states of particular institutionalized approaches to policy problems but no additional federal policy successes and no displacement of the states. Authors may offer explanations for rapid policy diffusion and, where appropriate, offer explanations for why diffusion cannot go beyond the state level. In most cases, the uneven spread of policy and its complex layerings reinforce Clemens's image of the Rube Goldberg state.

On "Public," "Private," and the Importance of Nonstate Actors for Development

A third significant question the chapters raise is how boundaries between public and private shifted or how public and private themselves changed over the course of the developmental trajectory that each author describes. Here too the volume follows through on Novak's insistence on the "recognition that American power has long been distributed among a series of individuals, groups, parties, associations, organizations, and institutions not readily designated as wholly *either* public *or* private."[49] Yet the authors identify something distinctive in the Progressive Era, particularly among activists who increasingly courted state interest and intervention, because they saw the state as the only entity with sufficient scope and resources to address the large-scale, and sometimes abstract, goals they had set.[50] As the analyses show, "public" and "private" as distinctive concepts do not effectively capture the complex, interpenetrated, and shifting boundaries between policies and actions managed and implemented directly by state actors and those administered by nonstate actors. It seems no accident that some participants in new initiatives themselves had trouble delineating such boundaries. As Strach and Sullivan, Nackenoff and Sullivan, Pearson and Smith, and Szymanski show, the institutions that were implementing policies in these years were often hybrids. In all of these chapters different elements of policy and implementation drew from formal legal and regulatory language, state-based and non-state-based investigators and enforcers, and dynamic interactions between advocates and state actors. Many of the authors in are trying to determine how to characterize these relationships, which are not necessarily stable across the time frames we have each chosen.

Several chapters grapple with the problem of how best to characterize the relationship between public and nonpublic work and workers. One significant developmental issue is the extent to which the boundaries between state and private institutions and actors are blurred or permeable, a blurring that Balogh finds common in the period we are addressing. A number of institutional innovators who attracted our attention are vested with considerable public power without having public jobs. In a number of cases examined here, activist initiators worked with networks of like-minded reformers and with sympathetic state actors. In the juvenile court case, Nackenoff and Sullivan find that the private funding, institutional modeling, and staffing began first, and that having a working experiment aided in the push for legislation to adopt the court as part of the state. It is interesting to consider whether blurred boundaries somehow help the state acquire new subjects and new topics of regulation. Likewise, it is a challenge to consider how the interaction of public and nonpublic workers affects regulation. Attending to these questions renders the state and its scope of authority much more visible, highlighting the areas in which policymaking takes place through collaboration and reading these areas into narratives of development (thereby helping to dismantle the myth of an underdeveloped or weak American state).[51] These questions also interrogate the relationship between agendas and capacity.

Several of the chapters show how state borrowings of capacity from advocacy groups or other nonstate actors led to development, even as defined strictly in Orren and Skowronek's terms. But more, they suggest that, in some cases, advocates who succeeded in convincing the state to act enabled the groups to advance their agendas with the backing and authority of the state. This particular pattern does not seem consistent with Baker's claim that the turn to the state diminished the vitality of voluntary groups.[52] Although in some circumstances the state ultimately absorbed these private forms of enforcement capacity and transformed them, in other cases nonstate actors remained intimately involved in shaping and enforcing agendas. Whereas for some authors capacity seems to be "borrowed" merely for a short time as state administrative capacities develop, for others the arrangement looks more chronic, systematic, or enduring. Clemens has suggested that both patterns occur, depending on the particular case being examined.

Chapters individually seek to understand what determines how and when advocates can "bring the state in" by convincing policymakers to take on and administer their agendas or provide an imprimatur of state-sponsored legitimacy for the work that they are doing. Taken as a whole, these chapters also say something about the scope of policy windows in the Progressive Era and the years preceding and immediately following it. As Baker notes, this period was distinctive because of the expansion of state agendas through the domestication of politics.[53] Accounting for how and why governments took on these specific tasks involves explaining how nongovernmental groups both took on these agendas and sought to define them as issues in which the state had a legitimate stake.

The chapters suggest that the enticement of state actors to engage in policy change and reform rested on reformers' culturally resonant arguments for change. Abolitionists decried slavery and demanded substantive citizens' rights for freedmen, and the antipolygamy activists condemned the destruction of womanly purity within the Mormon Church; later advocates employed heated racialized rhetoric promoting prohibition, sentimental claims for protection of animals, and child-saving frameworks to support juvenile courts. In almost all of these cases, the leverage for change came not from legal-rational expansion of the state's regulatory reach, but rather from advocates' "calculated enhancement of passion," a phrase Richard Bensel uses to describe William Jennings Bryan's rhetorical triumph in his 1896 "Cross of Gold" speech.[54] In each case, advocates employed passionate rhetorical frames to shift particular issues from private concerns to be dealt with by nonstate reforming organizations or advocates to issues lying directly within the state's purview as problems requiring formal regulatory oversight. Their appeals garnered broad attention to their causes and generated support from a number of legislators and other state actors. They also pressed for rapid solutions to the problems, increasing incentives for borrowing capacity rather than waiting for the construction of discrete state-driven solutions. Legal-rational expansion, then, often developed alongside, or subsequent to, the mobilization of passion.

It is remarkable to note that many authors have evidence that private organizations had the capacity/power to enforce legislation—investigating, prosecuting, arresting offenders, and even going into the home to do their work. These findings echo and supplement Baker's and Novak's more summary accounts, developing their analyses in inadequately explored substantive areas of policy. Private citizens' and organizations' use of the state's residual regulatory authority, police power (discussed independently below), is especially interesting. Szymanski and Nackenoff/Sullivan find evidence of private policing of public charges and expectations; even when armed with new statutory authority, public officials sometimes seemed less invested in enforcement and implementation than those private associations so passionately involved in bringing the new institutions into existence. Moreover, these authors show that organizations sometimes used their willingness to fund enforcement efforts to exert control or ownership over new public institutions or public authorities. The police powers exerted by humane societies (especially in New York) in the Pearson and Smith chapter are also especially noteworthy. We grapple with how to envision, describe, and understand these intertwined relationships.

Are volunteers from private organizations, often recognized by and somewhat incorporated within the state institution, really private at this point? Is it a parceling out of state power? Or is it better understood as the state's borrowing the capacity that it lacks, as Sullivan and Strach would have it? Szymanski thinks that the above-noted patterns, plus the fact that public officials lacked the resources for vigorous enforcement, may help explain the rapid achievement of wildlife conservation policies. But Smith and Pearson paint a different picture, with the ASPCA being seen as a "subordinate public agency" created to "perform a service [preventing cruelty to animals] which the Legislature might delegate to a citizen or public body." Understanding how public officials view the organizations that help them carry out the mandate of a new institution or new piece of legislation is fascinating work.

It has been common to view these mixed or complex institutional arrangements as just a transitional phase in institution-building. Is it more accurate to envision the public-private relationship as one in which the private funders and contributors of labor are like the parent who simply runs alongside the bike until the youngster can keep moving forward, or is it more reasonable to emphasize that the nonstate originators of a regulatory initiative seek to exert control over the public authorities nominally in charge? Or are the patterns case-specific? In considering these questions, we note that the trajectory of development is not necessarily linear, and institutions are not built through a fully rationalized process; they emerge at times as these public and private actors create friction. For Szymanski, the answer seems to be the former: the shift from private to public policing went through a transitional phase where the lines between public and private became especially blurry. For Nackenoff and Sullivan, reformers such as Jane Addams saw this blurry division themselves and sometimes struggled to clarify lines of responsibility. Does the institution remain a hybrid, dependent for certain purposes on volunteers and citizen groups, or does it ever become purely an organ of the state? For example, what explains why humane societies in some states become part of the state bureaucracy and why elsewhere they remain private charitable organizations? Under what circumstances do reformers lose—or willingly relinquish—control over organizations and projects they began? The chapters in this volume demonstrate that asking and answering these questions can greatly enhance our understanding of the mechanics of statebuilding.

Enforcing the Norms of Citizenship and Making Better Citizens

These observations about the relationship between public and private highlight another fascinating feature of these chapters: the particular concern the authors uncover for legislating or otherwise spreading and enforcing norms, a process driven, as noted above, by reformers' mobilization of passion to create new legal structures. As Novak notes, "law has long been an indispensable and creative source of expanding political and economic power, playing a uniquely positive rather than negative role in the creation of the modern American state."[55] This process, as he and other legal historians explain, takes place largely through the exercise of police power, the residual authority of American states to regulate in the interest of health, public safety, and morals. As Novak and Gillman have established, the late nineteenth and early twentieth centuries saw a great expansion of regulatory authority through police power.[56] Other scholars have shown how late nineteenth-century and Progressive Era reformers capitalized on growing anxieties about racial transformation, immigration, urban growth, and unstable gender and sex roles, but these chapters highlight how development addressed these anxieties through incorporation of specific norms into state policy by leveraging police power. These norms filled out conceptions of citizenship that were under intense negotiation in light of changes from the adoption of the Fourteenth Amendment to the establishment of large clusters of immigrants in American cities.

The chapters also show how complex legal enforcement of these norms could be. Some enforcement came directly from the top, as in Novkov's discussion of the federal effort to end polygamy through specifically focused prosecution. In other instances, enforcement combined public and private elements, as Pearson and Smith describe the use of private agents to investigate and provide evidence for the maltreatment of animals and children. In still other contexts, enforcement depended on private impetus, as Szymanski describes the structure for bringing complaints about killing wildlife to the state's attention. And some systems were genuinely hybrids, as Nackenoff and Sullivan describe the juvenile court system. These discussions enrich other work that outlines the importance of private litigation as a means of enforcing public norms, enabling the state to extend its regulatory power far beyond the reach of any public bureaucracy.[57]

The volume's chapters delineate how efforts to condition citizens to comply with norms and perform citizenship correctly influenced developmental trajectories. As Novkov shows, with the Fourteenth Amendment's extension of citizenship to freedmen, policymakers and agents of enforcement emphasized the protection of masculine rights of contract and political participation and pressed for the formalization of marriages among blacks. Likewise, only after polygamy was stamped out could Utah become a state. Steedman argues that the Atlanta newspaper campaign for temperance played on racialized and sexualized threats of civic disorder to motivate change. Nackenoff and Sullivan show how the juvenile court movement relied on sentimental concerns about the young, but also on the perceived dangers these girls and boys (not only working class but many of whom were Catholic) posed if not redirected into more acceptable performances of middle-class and appropriately gendered behavioral norms. This theme also plays through strongly in Greer's discussion of the BHA development of tightly bounded and class-related standards for what constituted an acceptable home for an American in the twentieth century.

In addition to concerns about norms, many of the reformers discussed here consciously relied on their own performance of these norms to enhance their authority and credibility. In this regard, the chapters call to mind Theda Skocpol's analysis of maternalist advocacy for pensions and protection of children in the early twentieth century; she shows how women's clubs and members of the National Consumers League leveraged their standpoints as women and mothers to press for reform.[58] Several chapters expand Skocpol's analysis of maternalism both temporally and to incorporate reformers' reliance on other performative identities in their advocacy. They also pick up on Baker's observations about the expansion of women's home- and maternally based responsibilities into the public sphere, and how this expansion augmented the efficacy of women and women's groups as political actors.[59] We found that some institutions and policies of the period allowed for new entry into or oversight of the home or over persons—that the boundary between public and private changed, and not necessarily without resistance from those who articulated older types of rights claims, such as the right of the family to be let alone. It seems that, in at least some of the cases discussed, women—often as volunteers—played a special role in governance extension into private spheres, and contributed to the redefinition of the public sphere. During an age of maternalist rhetoric, they often claimed special, home-based authority to enter the public sphere. Some of this work suggests that a precursor to statebuilding may be the extension of information-gathering, data collection, and surveillance by actors and organizations that traditionally were autonomous from the state.

Both female antislavery and antipolygamy reformers spoke in gendered voices about the particular evils of these systems. Although the gendered standpoint of prohibition activists has been addressed extensively, Steedman shifts the lens by focusing on how racialized standpoints gained leverage in the Atlanta campaign. Nackenoff and Sullivan describe the settlement house movement's own constructions and performances of gendered advocacy. As Greer shows, women's club members and the BHA conducted formal studies but also relied on their standpoints as primarily middle-class white women successfully performing maternalist roles to enhance both perceptions of their expertise and their engagement with the drive to develop models and standards for the American home. And as Pearson and Smith show, sportsmen and humane society advocates consciously positioned themselves in gendered terms, with an overlay of class, in arguing for regulation. Gendered, raced, and classed performances and enforcement of norms helped drive statebuilding.

The Role of Policy Failures

Policy failure can teach as much as policy success, as Richard Valelly observes in his analysis of partisan tensions that doomed the final congressional effort to enforce black rights in the 1890s.[60] Studying only successes leaves out an analysis of how and why developmental processes break down, and careful observation of the times momentum behind reform seems to stall can help delineate the limits of agency and institution-building. Several chapters develop this insight. Novkov's analysis of the failure to enforce black rights links this failure to the campaign against polygamy. Strach and Sullivan argue that the failure of the New Orleans machine to generate a stable system for garbage collection reveals the value of corruption; Pittsburgh had a more stable machine that exerted greater control over politics and maintained strong and predictable ties to business. For Pearson and Smith, policy successes turned into failure when the advocates for reform shifted their campaign from the state to the federal level (though Szymanski's account describes a rare regulatory success at the national level on the related issue of wildlife protection). In each case, failures to achieve regulation or implement policy successfully had important developmental consequences beyond the particular policy area. Failures delineated the boundaries of state power (at the local, state, and national level), but also determined how state resources were to be invested, establishing paths for further development and institutionalization.

Conclusion

These chapters trace the tangled processes of statebuilding in the late nineteenth and early twentieth centuries, offering several crucial insights into how and where it took place. We emphasize statebuilding as a dynamic engagement between reformers and policymakers, and see it as a complex and at times contradictory process, rather than as a smooth progression of rationalization, legalization, and bureaucratization. By focusing on the work of entrepreneurial agents (both inside and outside the state), the subnational level, and the generation of capacity wherever it can be found, we present pictures of statebuilding that emphasize its porous nature. We also suggest that the groundwork for many modern institutional arrangements lies in these acts of independent and entrepreneurial agency around disparate problems, not as part of a coordinated national effort to build capacity. With multiple agents within, alongside, and outside of the state, even those who participate in the early construction of institutions cannot anticipate the directions in which these institutions will develop, particularly if an institution's infrastructure develops privately and then is assimilated by state actors to serve public agendas.

Despite the pronounced emphasis in APD scholarship on the shift of power from states to the federal government during the late nineteenth and early twentieth centuries, our work underscores the point that the growth of state capacity is not simply a national level phenomenon, and many of the reforms we examine yield important evidence of statebuilding apart from the national government. Some of our case studies reveal shifting authority to the federal government and others demonstrate robust activity that remains largely subnational. We consider the reasons for some of these variations.

Instead of seeing statebuilding as driven by bureaucratic entrepreneurs or elected officials, we find that building state capacity frequently originates with activists outside the formal institutions of the state. Some of us see organized activists pushing the state to take on new jobs, developing allies within and outside state institutions, networking with intellectuals and conducting research, and pressing agendas on state officials who need to be persuaded to act. Statebuilding from the margins seems an apt characterization of most of the cases we examine. Organized women are often important to the dynamic in these cases. Race, gender, and class as norms are also central to processes of statebuilding in some of the cases. And yet, as outsiders' agendas become enmeshed within the state, these agendas are at times modified or transformed as state actors reshape the purposes the new capacity serves.

By offering various late nineteenth and early twentieth-century case studies in one volume, we invite comparisons across instances of institutional development. But in at least some cases in this volume, bringing two apparently different policies together reveals patterns in the extension of state power that would not be found by treating each separately. And bringing race and gender together in the examination of certain instances of the extension of national or state power offers a more complex, multidimensional analysis of prohibition, polygamy, or securing certain citizenship rights to freedmen.

Because evidence differs, these case studies do not ultimately settle the question of when, if at all, and under what conditions the state shifted from "borrowing" private resources and state capacity, to acquiring state capacity. Perhaps the American state, which in recent years has rediscovered public-private partnerships and the devolution of responsibilities, never was one that fully accepted or articulated the model of complete absorption of the problem-solving agenda of the programs it was charged with implementing. And by not recognizing the importance of these collaborations over the years, both scholars and political actors have perceived the state as less powerful and interventionist than it is, thereby attributing distributions of power and resources to "natural" or "private" competitive processes when, in reality, these distributions result in significant part from public law and institutions.[61] We hope that we have made a number of nonstate actors or policy entrepreneurs more visible in narratives of statebuilding. Not only in the decades we have interrogated but even more recently the relationship between state actors and nonstate actors in institution building and nurturing may be quite messy indeed.

Chapter 1

Making Citizens of Freedmen and Polygamists

Julie Novkov

The post-Civil War years were busy ones for activists, government agents, and federal government lawyers. As the war ended, the Constitution was amended and Congress passed legislation to facilitate the shift of African Americans from bondsmen (and women) to free citizens. Freedmen's Bureau agents operated in an uncertain legal environment initially, often in opposition to the actions of the reestablished southern states' legal systems. In part, they served as agents for individuals who were legal citizens but did not yet have the full capacity to exercise and defend their rights. Soon afterward, the Fourteenth Amendment underlined congressional authority to legislate, providing further legitimation for Reconstruction laws that empowered both aggrieved blacks and federal law enforcers to demand that the newly extended rights of citizenship be respected. The debate over when and how federal abandonment of emancipated blacks occurred can obscure the efforts and investment of collaborating activists and federal government agents to defend these rights, facilitate their exercise, and create meaning in the citizenship that emancipated blacks had earned. Regardless when and how abandonment occurred, governmental capacity to enforce citizens' rights increased tremendously in response to claims that black citizenship required governmental investment in enforcement. This shift was legal, but also cultural, as agents and advocates encouraged freedmen (and to a lesser extent, freedwomen) to act as rights bearers.

Between 1882 and 1896, after the settlement of 1876 that removed federal troops from most of the South, government lawyers, spurred on by dedicated activists, worked tirelessly to impose federal standards against extreme recalcitrance, evasion, and defiance on the part of local officials who argued strenuously that their authority to govern was being wrongfully superseded. More than nine hundred indictments were brought between 1886 and 1888 alone to stem what federal officials termed "barbarism," a term that had also been applied to slavery prior to the Civil War.[1] These prosecutions had two goals. First, prosecutors sought to crush the continuing resistance of local authorities who defied the national government's efforts to redefine civic membership. Second, the prosecutions constitutionally embedded early postbellum Republican theories about national supremacy, stripping local officials of their power even over issues that, prior to this struggle, had never been subject to any kind of federal oversight (much less direct regulation). This campaign, however, did not take place in South Carolina, Louisiana, or Alabama. It took place in the Utah Territory, and the prosecutions targeted polygamists.

The juxtaposition of the campaigns to protect blacks' civil rights and crush polygamy is worthy of consideration. Analyzed together, these efforts reveal how committed Republicans, with the backing of dedicated activists, sought to remake national government in the wake of the Civil War's disruption of long-standing understandings of the division between national and state authority. In doing so, the campaigns argued for broader scope and greater latitude for national action to resolve local issues. But to leverage such arguments, both activists and state actors articulated visions of citizenship that reconfigured the meaning of civic membership and its associated rights, and struggled to promote these visions in the public sphere, Congress, and the courts. This struggle highlights how statebuilding relied on shifting considerations of citizenship and its significance in an era when federal actors were entering the debate in a major way for the first time.

The fairly empty category of "citizen," which, with only a few exceptions the antebellum national government had left to the states to define, became the ground for the expansion of federalism, as private and federal suits brought under the new laws sought to enforce the rights of citizens and to leverage action through a public concern about citizens and their proper relationship to the nation. At the same time, national leaders envisioned a biracial polity, formally admitting blacks to citizenship and focusing anxieties on the scope and implications of this status while casting grave doubt upon the fitness of other racial and racialized groups for citizenship.[2] The struggle over the meaning of black citizenship first forged and then transformed the Republican Party, ultimately contributing to the national shift away from the often violent politics of Reconstruction toward the politics of legal and constitutional statebuilding, reconfigured the national state's posture toward the legal regulation of private individuals' lives, and established a national-state interest in families and their construction as civic institutions. This episode of statebuilding initiated a phase of intensive creativity and growth in capacity that foreshadowed a new political salience of public interest arguments for regulation of family, education, children, animals, and other aspects of what had previously been understood as private life.

The reconfiguration of intimate relationships as having a bearing on national interests provides another link between the two campaigns in the significance of gender for both. The citizenship rights that blacks gained—in part as compensation for their military service in the Civil War—were masculine rights.[3] These rights were configured specifically to enable black men to take their place in the polity as heads of household who could support and manage their own independent and individual private family domains through their exercise of contract and suffrage rights. At the same time, activists and federal agents attacked polygamy as an improper form of patriarchy for the American republic of free citizens. The logic of these claims ultimately led opponents of polygamy to oppose woman suffrage in Utah (after initially supporting it in the hopes that Utah women would eliminate the practice). In this chapter I analyze the political pressures and the ensuing campaigns to enforce civil rights for blacks and to suppress polygamy, showing how these campaigns, when considered together, underline the emergence of a more robust and normatively laden conception of federal citizenship, with implications for federalism and a new layer of state interest in the intimate lives of citizens. While initiatives to extend civil rights for blacks ultimately fizzled and the struggle to stamp out polygamy succeeded, both left interesting legacies in the form of compromises, partly crafted by the federal courts, that allowed local authorities to return to managing the day-to-day lives of their denizens without searching federal oversight. Unlike some chapters in this volume, these stories are not stories of borrowed private capacity or of the genesis of state institutions outside of the initiative of state actors. Nonetheless, they highlight this volume's attention to cultural concerns as strong motivation for increased institutionalization and growth in state capacity. They also highlight the extent to which state actors actively enhanced state capacity in the course of defining and extending citizenship.

Together, these campaigns produced much more federal governmental capacity to (1) address problematic citizens or potential citizens, (2) determine whether they were capable of transformation into fuller citizens, and (3) legally cede management of these problematic individuals to local and state authorities. They also left a legacy of increased capacity at the state level. The development of federal capacity would be crucial for the management of millions of new individuals placed under the sovereignty of the United States by the outcome of the Spanish American War and the defeat of the Philippine resistance to American rule during and after the turn of the century. Scholars generally see these territorial acquisitions as an important fracture in American expansionism with the introduction of the principle that the Constitution did not necessarily follow the flag.[4] The model that developed between 1866 and 1895, however, provided legal frameworks for dealing with individuals under U.S. authority who were not necessarily fit for citizenship by most elites' estimation. It also facilitated the development of new relationships between state or local authorities and national authorities in the management of troublesome citizens, allowing significant scope for freer dealings both with citizens and with those who were not yet ready for citizenship but could possibly be assimilated through cultural tutelage.

Making Black Citizens

From the Emancipation Proclamation through the late 1870s, the commitment of the national government's legal apparatuses to enforcing and sustaining black rights was more ambivalent than its commitment of resources to suppressing polygamy would be in in the 1880s and afterward. As the Civil War progressed and the Union increasingly relied on free and self-emancipated black soldiers and sailors, advocates for national emancipation and black citizenship pressed for reform both in popular avenues and through national policymaking. As Eric Foner concludes, "by and large . . . civil rights laws remained unenforced."[5] Nonetheless, even these ambivalent efforts illuminate how advocates and government agents understood the rights gained through emancipation and institutionalized in congressional legislation. Further, in the moments when the Republican Party rallied around the agenda of rights advancement, these efforts contributed to the development of new institutions and resources, both legal and cultural, that could contribute to the federally driven formulation of ideal citizenship and citizens.

The Republican postwar and Reconstruction efforts to achieve meaningful rights and citizenship have been discussed extensively, and this chapter does not reiterate this research. Instead, it looks specifically at the efforts of three groups of policymakers: military commanders, Freedmen's Bureau agents, and federal prosecutors. In considering these policymakers, the discussion sketches out how they promoted rights and ultimately a vision of citizenship, and how the shift to prosecution of those who violated new citizens' rights contributed to statebuilding on behalf of citizens understood to be incapable of enforcing rights on their own.

The proper construction of families provided an important focus for policymakers in several arenas, and intertwined with efforts to promote rights. Divisions among generals over how to manage the problem of the human contraband that had crossed Confederate lines to achieve freedom in part led to formal congressional study of the issue in 1863, and the establishment of the Bureau of Abandoned Lands, Refugees, and Freedmen in 1865 (rather than the Bureau of Emancipation recommended by the congressional commission).[6] Freedmen and their advocates now had a formal avenue through which they could press their top priorities, though moderate differences in emphasis among them quickly became evident.

As Foner, Garrett Epps, and others explain, emancipated blacks had clear ideas about what emancipation and citizenship should entail. Voting rights were critical for Frederick Douglass and his political allies; he demanded "immediate, unconditional and universal enfranchisement" for black men before the end of the Civil War.[7] Others, including Sojourner Truth, pressed for the expansion of fair wage labor, the enforcement of contracts, and the elimination of discrimination in public accommodations.[8] Most advocates agreed that education was likewise crucial for black advancement. These arguments encompassed gendered frameworks, as the advocates for these rights argued that they would enable the establishment of stable black families and the regularization of familial relations and responsibilities.

In addition to contract and voting rights and support for education, many pressed for land reform and hoped they would be permitted to own confiscated lands they had been cultivating.[9] Experiments like that of the Georgia Sea Islands, where blacks were given ownership of confiscated land and worked it for profit while the Civil War was still ongoing, raised hopes that the Freedmen's Bureau would facilitate the legal transfer and vesting of proper title in the freedmen in due course.[10] This model for emancipation envisioned bolstering individual rights and citizenship through property ownership, which would confer landholder status on freedmen as well as give them the economic and cultural wherewithal to exercise and defend other rights.

The Freedmen's Bureau in South Carolina, Georgia, and Florida initially supported this agenda under the leadership of General Rufus Saxton, and discussions were under way to begin allocating substantial portions of the 850,000 acres of land under the Bureau's control to blacks to bring them into the polity as landowning citizens.[11] But the Republican Party was not unified behind this conception of emancipation. President Andrew Johnson opposed the reallocation of land and acted vigorously throughout the summer of 1865 to restore land to former Confederates through special pardons. Freedmen's Bureau commissioner Oliver Howard issued a decree (Circular 13) that promised forty-acre tracts to freedmen, but he did so without securing presidential approval. Johnson ultimately removed Saxton and directed Howard to drop land reform and focus on restoring land to former Confederates; by early 1866, the Freedmen's Bureau's agenda had been redirected.[12] It now focused on promoting the negotiation and enforcement (on both sides) of labor contracts for emancipated blacks, which became a cornerstone of the federal government's investment in black citizenship. The abandonment of radical land reform in favor of support for contract rights by policymakers strengthened the connection to gendered rights that would establish black men as heads of stable households. This shift provided a more consensual ground around which most congressional Republicans could rally. As Angela Onwuachi-Willig and Priscilla Yamin note, it drew on continued interest and investment in regularizing marital relationships for black couples, alongside a wave of new state regulations prohibiting interracial marriage.[13]

Advocates and state actors nonetheless recognized that the rights could not be implemented immediately without a transitional period. Southern courts struggled with applying the ordinary rules of evidence in contract disputes in the postwar period, in part because Freedmen's Bureau agents became involved in the transactions. The involvement of these agents departed from the standard legal model of the arm's-length agreement between self interested and independent agents.[14] While the rights that emancipation granted were markers of the status of the independent citizen, agents at times acted on behalf of the inexperienced emancipated slaves, exercising these rights for them by proxy.

In Georgia, for instance, Freedmen's Bureau agents actively intervened in the negotiation of contracts between white landowners and black laborers, complicating questions of interpretation because the interventions called into question the usual practice of simply relying on the words of the contract to capture the interests of the contract's direct parties, who would ordinarily be understood as independent agents capable of reducing their intentions to writing. In *Williams v. Waters*, such a dispute reached the Georgia Supreme Court in 1867. James Williams, his wife (a subordinate party in the suit), and several other freedmen sued James Waters to compel compliance with a contract all had signed the previous year. The dispute was over whether or not Williams and his associates had agreed to pay for renting the land and hiring the mules and provisions necessary to make the crop, the proceeds of which were to be divided between Williams and Waters.[15] The freedmen who testified at the trial explained the unusual process of formalizing the contract: "they signed the contract in the presence of Judge Vason, at his office; all of them went with Waters, with the contract, to the Freedmen's Bureau, the agent approved the contract and said it was a good one, the agent handed Waters a paper, saying it was a copy of the contract."[16] Waters, too, assigned the agent a crucial role in the contract process, testifying "that the original was approved by F. A. Billingslea, Bureau-agent, who pronounced it a good contract for the freedmen." The freedmen and Waters tried to prove conflicting terms through controversial reliance on parole (spoken) evidence, but the court ruled that a written copy of the contract was valid and that the lower court should not have considered the parole evidence for this reason. The ruling held freedmen and Waters to the signed contract, situating the freedmen as fully capable civic members, in effect erasing the role of the Freedmen's Bureau in the contractual process.[17] Reading the Freedmen's Bureau out of contract formation in this case laid the groundwork for later (often disingenuous) arguments that the mere extension of rights to freedmen was sufficient, and that allowing state agents to intervene in or even facilitate the exercise of these rights was demeaning to the civic status of the right-bearer.

Yet courts at times framed such interventions as necessary aid for freedmen as a special class of citizens (a framing extended to animals and children as well, as discussed in this volume by Szymanski and Nackenoff and Sullivan). The Tennessee Supreme Court also adjudicated a case involving Freedmen's Bureau agents' intervention in the contract process. Like *Williams*, in *Hunt v. Wing* a group of freedmen attempted to extract payment for work they had performed under contract. In this case, the farm in question had gone bankrupt, leaving creditors with secured loans having claims exceeding the proceeds of the crop. The freedmen sought to intervene in the bankruptcy proceedings, arguing that their labor gave them a stronger claim to the proceeds than the mortgagees' claim.[18] The creditor parties in the case objected on the ground that the plea to intervene was brought not by the thirty-five or forty laborers aggrieved, but by a "next friend"—an agent of the Freedmen's Bureau. They argued that the use of a next friend was inappropriate for individuals who held full contract rights. The court disagreed, reasoning, "we know that the complainants . . . belong to a race which have but recently been emancipated from slavery; that as a race they are far below the white man in intelligence, but we also know that by law they are under no disability to sue, and have all the rights, before the courts of the country, possessed by any other class of citizens. Yet their want of intelligence, and their ignorance of the complicated relations of business life, appeal with great potency."[19] The court thus situated the freedmen as complex legal subjects—entitled to the rights of civic membership but without the full capacity to exercise them on their own behalf and in need of competent protection. The case proceeded, but the court concluded that unless the freedmen were able to establish that they had a lien on the crop (rather than simply a contract to benefit from the sale proceeds), they could not obtain relief. Thus, while the freedmen had the abstract satisfaction of legal recognition of their assisted autonomy, they lost on the merits.

As these examples suggest, agents of the federal government actively assisted freedmen to assert contractual rights, training them for the exercise of independent citizenship that they could aspire to practice on their own terms eventually. While the courts adjudicating these cases represented states undergoing and resisting reconstruction, they nonetheless acknowledged (albeit ambivalently) the federal government's increased capacity and exercise of direct authority on behalf of citizens in training. The end point of emancipation was assumed to be that the private citizen gained the capability to exercise and enforce his own rights without the help of a federally employed state proxy. In these early years, freedmen remained qualified citizens, culturally and legally situated as dependent and subject to public stewardship.

This frame of stewardship supported additional state interventions in the lives of freedmen and freedwomen. Freedmen's Bureau agents were significantly involved in promoting emancipated blacks' transition to formal marriage, and this involvement entailed both growth and a shift in capacity for the federal government. In this, they followed practices first established in the contraband camps, but used their broader capacity to advance the agenda.[20] As Peggy Pascoe, Yamin, and Onwuachi-Willig have argued, the federal program of finding and formalizing marital bonds was highly disciplinary in nature and incorporated multiply linked motivations. The contracts that the passage of the 1866 Civil Rights Act encouraged blacks to form (and which

Freedmen's Bureau agents at times negotiated on their behalf) were contracts for wage labor, for leasing or perhaps owning land, and for the purchase and control of other real and personal property. Another type of contract—the marriage contract—was more controversial and differently configured, as it was sometimes practically coerced (particularly between freedmen and freedwomen) and in other instances had long been legally forbidden (between blacks and whites).[21] Contractual rights regarding marriage had gendered dimensions that reinforced male rights, protecting women more as dependents than as independent contractually capable subjects.[22]

A few cases highlight the Freedmen's Bureau's role in reinforcing the importance of bringing freedmen and freedwomen into regularized family relations and in establishing the roles of black men as heads of households. The cases also underline the newly created authority of the federal government to impose its cultural standards in determining the legitimacy of intimate relationships. The Freedmen's Bureau had significant administrative authority not only to investigate but to order, in concrete terms, muddled relationships; the agents could effect marital or nonmarital statuses and enforce wills, even at times over the objections of the individuals involved. In a Georgia case, a black man appealed his murder conviction on the ground that the state had not adequately proven his motivations (the state argued that his wife's desire to separate from him in order to repartner with the father of one of her children established a motive and supported the conclusion that he had acted with malice in killing her). He objected to a charge regarding their separation, which would remove his inherent rights to approach his wife in her home. However, evidence entered at the trial included a divorce decree given to the dead woman by a Freedmen's Bureau agent; while the decree did not constitute a valid divorce, the jury accepted it as clear evidence of the couple's agreement to separate.[23] The jury, in doing so, signaled its trust in the Freedmen's Bureau as an appropriate arbiter of the state of familial relations and reinforced the capacity of the federal Bureau to intervene in and order private relationships. This theme dovetailed with the Bureau's framing of itself as steward in the development and cultural growth of the new black citizens' families, providing guidance toward their own internalization and enforcement of appropriate norms of ordering family life.

In another case, a black male defendant prosecuted for bigamy relied on a Kentucky statute requiring that all marriages be solemnized before "an authorized person," claiming that the black minister who had conducted his first marriage ceremony did not have proper state authorization to do so.[24] Unfortunately for the defendant, not only could the state demonstrate the marriage had been consummated but the prosecutor also produced a marriage license by the Freedmen's Bureau for his first marriage. His conviction was upheld.[25] The court commented on the wisdom of considering the license and marriage valid, stating, "we think that this statute so construed meets the evident design of its authors, comports with good order and the best interest of society, and rescues confiding females, both white and black, from deceptions often intended, and sometimes successfully practiced, for their disgrace and ruin."[26] The case underlined both the scope and legitimacy of the Freedmen's Bureau efforts to promote civic and domestic ordering, and again situated the Bureau as a steward, this time to protect the sexual integrity and morality of women, whose status as citizens was doubly conditioned by race and gender.

A third state case, this one in Tennessee, involved a widow's suit against her husband's estate administrator in which she attempted to claim a note the administrator had improperly executed on exempt property. The widow, a black woman, apparently turned to the Freedmen's Bureau for assistance: "by the interposition of the agent of the Freedmen's Bureau, [estate administrator] Perkins delivered the note to her. Perkins was told by the agent that if he did not surrender the note voluntarily, he would be forced to do."[27] Although the note itself was illegal under Tennessee law, the high court validated the widow's right to enforce its terms to her benefit. Again, the court recognized and legitimated the increase in federal capacity to enforce a private, domestic agenda and to facilitate the exercise of rights on behalf of a dependent citizen.

With the shift from military control and intervention back toward everyday law after the end of military reconstruction, the burden of enforcing and giving flesh to black rights also shifted, and the exercise of national capacity moved from the Freedmen's Bureau to another location. This shift occurred in the context of a rapid rise in Republican, and radical Republican, strength in Congress in the late 1860s and early 1870s, resulting in what Rick Valelly has described as a policy window for the passage of legislation intended to strengthen black rights and reinforce black attachment to—and voting for—the Republican Party.[28]

As legal historians have detailed, congressional legislation in the late 1860s and early 1870s provided two means for enforcing black rights: suits litigated by individual aggrieved African Americans and suits brought by the government. Barbara Welke has examined how black citizens sought to claim their rights through legal action, noting that they actively used federal civil rights laws to seek access to the privileges associated with middle-class purchasing power.[29] These suits contributed to the sense that such issues could legitimately be within the federal government's scope of concern, warranting direct intervention in the event of state failure to enforce rights. Yet private enforcement, while at times empowering for individual agents, was insufficient in the view of vocal Republican members of Congress, who grew increasingly frustrated with anemic enforcement at the state level. This frustration increased in light of white violence that was increasingly difficult to characterize as purely private, and Republican leaders in Congress ultimately investigated the activities of the Ku Klux Klan and other groups, producing a record of the outrages.[30]

As a result, Congress specifically provided tools to government attorneys to protect and enforce rights, which at least in abstract terms committed the federal government to a greatly enlarged scope for direct guarantee of civic membership. These tools included the statutory mechanisms that enabled attorneys to prosecute actions by the Klan. Congressional hearings also generated the political will to do so by exposing the outrages of white violence undertaken in the late 1860s to suppress black liberation. Probably the most assertive postbellum actions taken on behalf of blacks by legal representatives of the national government after the end of the war, the hearings generated support for proceeding against white perpetrators of racially motivated violence against blacks under congressional legislation targeting the Ku Klux Klan and related organizations. Federal prosecutors acted by directly pursuing wrongdoers under these new laws, but in some instances federal government lawyers also intervened to ensure that whites accused by the states of committing crimes against blacks would face legal consequences. These prosecutions supported the basic right to physical integrity for threatened blacks. However, they also sought to address the states' failure to protect blacks' vested private property interests against the threat of other private actors' insults, as the states often either initiated legal action and then dropped it, or never initiated it at all. These cases, as Pamela Brandwein argues, largely arose when state-based criminal processes were so weak or contrary to black interests as to constitute state neglect.[31]

Before the Klan hearings and the legislation they sparked, federal prosecutions chiefly sought to backstop weak state-enforcement efforts. One example comes from Kentucky, reported in a circuit court ruling in 1866; this case demonstrated how federal prosecution could guarantee protection where the ordinary recourse in a nonracialized case would have been to garden-variety state law. A group of whites allegedly broke into a black woman's dwelling and stole her property. The United States brought criminal charges against them for violating her civil rights. While the white defendants objected on various grounds, the circuit court allowed the convictions to stand, declaring that the Civil Rights Act of 1866 properly fell under the Thirteenth Amendment, which "trenches directly upon the power of the states and of the people of the states. . . . Those who insisted upon the adoption of this amendment . . . felt that much was due to the African race for the part it had borne during the war."[32] The opinion went on to ground both power and responsibility for enforcing the civil rights of blacks in the national government and its actors.[33] The validated congressional acts implied enforcement through the actions of government prosecutors, relying on increased state capacity for their effective implementation. Following clearly from the Freedmen's Bureau's framework, this prosecution enabled federal actors to stand in and assert rights on the behalf of subordinated citizens who could not effectively assert their own rights.

This kind of enforcement was spotty, however; in the late 1860s, federal prosecutions were relatively sporadic and geographically scattered. Legal and extralegal resistance and violence increased in the South, even as the federal government withdrew troops and allowed more direct governance at the state level. Still, some courts and prosecutors maintained the will to address the insurgency through legal means, and this will increased in the wake of revelations about the Klan's organized efforts to suppress blacks' civic and political autonomy. Another case that reached the U.S. Supreme Court in 1871 involved the appeal of two white men convicted in Kentucky for murdering a black woman in her nineties. (The men were prosecuted federally for the murder of Lucie Armstrong because of the particular brutality involved, though they had also murdered her daughter, son-in-law, and grandson.)[34] In defending the constitutionality of the federal prosecution, the U.S. attorney general and solicitor general argued jointly.[35] They explained that, while the Thirteenth Amendment had radically changed the nation, it "did not execute and was not meant to execute itself."[36] Nor, they implied, could it be executed by the independent actions of it subjects, who lacked the capacity to initiate legal proceedings themselves or demand them from the states. They had brought the case not only because of the outrageousness of the alleged crime but because Kentucky barred blacks from testifying in criminal trials against whites accused of committing crimes. The crux of the matter was not the dead grandmother, but the testimony of her grandson and granddaughter: "The son lingers long enough to tell the facts of this horrible transaction, and a little sister . . . survives the cruel wounds inflicted upon her at the same time. The dying declarations of the one and the parol testimony of the other in court . . . establish the guilt of the accused beyond all reasonable doubt. And yet under the law of the State the accused cannot be punished, because in Kentucky black men cannot give evidence of the crimes of white ones."[37] (They also cited Justice Noah Swayne's opinion in *Rhodes* to support their intervention in the workings of state criminal law.) The avenue of federal prosecution both gave these otherwise voiceless victims a voice and enhanced their capacity to seek justice. This solution, however, was inadequate on a large scale. Even though these men were held accountable for their crimes, such crimes were becoming increasingly widespread, and federal actors realized that a handful of convictions would not effectively deter the night riders. Republicans also understood that transforming blacks into independent citizens who could self-execute their own exercise of rights was an essential predicate to securing long-term political gains for the party. This provoked the development of a specific strategy.

The federal government, still in the hands of a Republican Party committed to black political empowerment, organized a legal campaign to rein in the Klan in its prime stronghold of South Carolina. The intensity and violence of the struggle in South Carolina significantly implicated the question of black manhood; as one analyst notes, "Black males in South Carolina demanded to be treated as men—not hired men, or colored men, or even freedmen—but men. Nothing less would satisfy their craving for justice and equality."[38] However, this demand provoked the rise of a violent insurgent movement: "whites inevitably jumped to the conclusion that granting the rights of manhood and citizenship to the freedmen would mean either black supremacy or a bloody war of extermination between the races."[39] As the paramilitary and insurgent intentions of the Klan became increasingly clear, Congress and the executive branch opted to respond through legal means: formal investigation of the violence through congressional hearings, and then a coordinated campaign of prosecutions designed to bring the Klan under control through the conscious exercise of the rule of law. The campaign was intended to serve multiple purposes: it would stem the tide of violence that alarmed and disgusted Republican lawmakers, it would facilitate greater access to the rights and privileges of citizenship for new black citizens, and it would enable these (male) citizens to support the Republican Party with their votes.

The Ku Klux Klan had formed in 1865 in Tennessee and reached South Carolina in 1868. Williams reports that the Klan interfered with voting in South Carolina's elections in 1868, preventing blacks from casting their votes and breaking up Union League meetings.[40] Republican governor Robert Scott, originally an Ohioan who had been the head of South Carolina's Freedmen's Bureau, responded by organizing black militia units in upcountry South Carolina to protect blacks and secure orderly voting procedures, resulting in Republican electoral victories (including the election of black state and federal legislators) in 1870.[41] Fearful upcountry whites largely supported countermobilization; leaders arose readily among former Confederate officers, and poor whites swelled the ranks. Investigations into Klan violence revealed a pattern in their attacks: Klansmen would forcibly enter black homes, question the male head of household about his political activities, demand that he foreswear political engagement, search the house for weapons and remove them, and administer severe whippings. For more politically prominent or vocal black men, death was a real risk. Black women, too, suffered whippings and attacks, including rapes, but these attacks appeared to be targeted explicitly to denigrate the masculine authority of the black men to whom they were connected as wives and daughters.[42]

Congress, observing the increasing violence across the South and recognizing the incapacity and unwillingness of Reconstruction-oriented southern state governments to address it effectively, took several steps to acquire and exercise the capacity to manage the situation. The reactions of Congress highlight both a desire to empower the independent exercise of rights by black citizens and to strengthen the Republican Party by backstopping black voting rights. First, it passed the Enforcement Act on May 31, 1870, which (unsurprisingly for an election year), sought to protect and reextend black voting rights.[43] This proved to be of little deterrent effect, and further legislation followed, culminating in the Ku Klux Klan Act on April 20, 1871, which empowered the president to suspend habeas corpus to combat the Klan. Congress also authorized the expansion of the mission of the Joint Select Committee to Inquire into the Condition of Affairs in the Late Insurrectionary States, which ultimately produced thirteen volumes of investigative reports that painstakingly detailed the scope of Klan-driven insurrectionary terror.[44]

In July 1870, Congress created the Department of Justice, apparently as a cost-saving measure eliminating the practice of hiring individual special counsels, but with the result of creating a new organizational structure that would facilitate the growth of national capacity.[45] Attorney General Amos Akerman, although a former Confederate, was committed to the Republican Party and its mission of expanding black rights as a means of party-building in the South. He worked with Solicitor General Benjamin Bristow to develop the legal infrastructure for this effort, engaging a process of jurisprudence building.[46] He identified South Carolina as the place to launch a massive enforcement effort, traveling there to assess the situation personally and then meeting with President Ulysses S. Grant, recommending stern action. Grant ordered the Klan to turn over their weapons and disguises to marshals within five days. When the Klansmen ignored his proclamation, the president suspended habeas corpus in several upcountry counties in November 1871. The legal battle was joined as the investigations and prosecutions began.[47]

Klansmen facing legal sanctions did not have to look far for support. Opponents of Reconstruction mustered an impressive array of legal talent, including prominent southern attorneys, former elected officials, and former Confederate cabinet level officers.[48] The Klan's supporters opposed the increased empowerment of black citizens on racial grounds, but their opposition was strongly partisan as well, and both sides recognized the political stakes in play. In South Carolina, Democratic elite Wade Hampton (who would succeed Scott as governor) launched a fund-raising drive to finance a sophisticated legal campaign to defend the Klan and challenge the Enforcement Acts' constitutionality.[49] Democrats hired former senator Reverdy Johnson, who had argued on John Sanford's behalf in *Dred Scott*, and Henry Stanbery, who had served as U.S. attorney general under Andrew Johnson and had defended Johnson in his impeachment trial. They coordinated the overall defense strategies together, though they had volunteer assistance from South Carolina attorneys.[50]

Attorney General Akerman, for his part, looked to the U.S. attorney for South Carolina, David Corbin, to manage these prosecutions. Corbin, who had practiced law in Vermont, had come to South Carolina as a Freedmen's Bureau agent and served as the solicitor for the state's constitutional convention in 1868. While Corbin kept Akerman informed about the progress of the mass prosecutions, the attorney general largely allowed Corbin free rein in preparing the indictments and trials and commanding the necessary resources. Corbin worked with South Carolina's attorney general, Daniel Chamberlain, and Major Lewis Merrill, who conducted the arrests.[51] By December 1871, he had apprehended approximately six hundred men, a stunning testimony to the national government's willingness to expend resources in this campaign.[52]

In the first round of Klan trials, the prosecution argued not only the straightforward applicability of the statutes but also the national government's constitutional theory that the Reconstruction Amendments had transformed the constitutional structure and reconfigured federalism. They also argued that the new amendments rendered the federal government the ultimate guarantor for core rights, which included contract rights, voting rights, and the right to bear arms for black citizens. This conception configured new black citizens as transitional figures, legally fit for citizenship but not fully capable of exercising and defending their rights without federal assistance. Although Corbin and his associates achieved convictions in many early, low-stakes cases, their constitutional arguments did not receive validation from the district court judges hearing the cases.[53]

Both the indictments and the prosecutions demonstrated the prosecutors' gendered conceptions of citizenship. Because indirect conspiracy convictions were difficult to ground, and the Klan Act focused narrowly on deprivation of a particular set of political rights, the Klan was allowed relatively free rein under federal law to cow black men by terrorizing their wives and children. In one case, Corbin sought to work within the narrow framework by charging Klansmen with assault and battery upon two women as the means through which they had hindered the voting rights of the black men to whom the women were attached, since he could not proceed directly through a simple theory of primary assault and battery.[54] This prosecutorial framing underlined the fundamental nature of political rights as the most accessible vehicle for justifying federal intervention while embedding more deeply the dependence of black women and children upon their connection to a familial relationship for protection.

By the beginning of 1872 Corbin had achieved convictions of all five of the men he had tried in four visible, lengthy, and highly expensive trials. While his ultimate goals were to convict Klansmen and ground his vision of a more extensive and expansive set of federally guaranteed constitutional protections for blacks, he also wanted the trials to document the atrocities of the Klan. He put dozens of black witnesses on the stand to swear to the whippings, threats, batteries, and terror they had endured themselves and witnessed Klansmen inflict on others. All eyes were on South Carolina, waiting to see how the convictions would fare in the Supreme Court. But Attorney General Akerman, beleaguered by strident opponents to his support for black rights and his refusal to allow the issuance of land grants and bonds to the Union Pacific Railroad, resigned at the end of 1871.[55] The loss of his advocacy was devastating for the agenda of strengthening black civic rights and foreshadowed the Republican Party's loss of commitment to transforming black men into citizens capable of enforcing their own rights claims. Grant replaced him with George Williams, who "deliberately blocked a thorough review of the case[s of convicted Klansmen] by the Supreme Court."[56] While Corbin continued to work diligently to secure convictions, Williams refused to support Corbin at the higher appellate level, entering a nolle prosequi to remove another major conviction from the Supreme Court's docket. Ultimately the Klan trials fizzled. While Corbin had won convictions at trial and convinced numerous other accused Klansmen to confess and accept plea bargains, "the attempt to punish the leading citizens who had spearheaded the Ku Klux Klan was, by and large, . . . a failure."[57] This failure led to a swift withdrawal of resources and loss of capacity to deal with the escalating violence.

Other regions saw similar trajectories. In northern Mississippi, U.S. Attorney G. Wiley Wells tried the first Enforcement Act case in the nation in Oxford in 1871, and continued to bring prosecutions at a rapid clip (325 in 1872, 268 in 1873, 120 in 1874, and 187 in 1875) until moving on to run for Congress as a moderate Republican in 1876.[58] Mississippi Republicans continued to bring Enforcement Act cases before successive grand juries, but divisions within the party and the federal government's refusal to use the military to back up enforcement efforts with force rendered the struggle increasingly difficult. In 1876, Attorney General Alphonso Taft refused to send troops or bolster the number of federal marshals in Mississippi, and the result was massive voting intimidation and repression, to the point that many blacks abandoned their homes and slept in the woods to escape violence.[59] After 1876, the rate of cases disposed of dropped dramatically, and although U.S. Attorney Greene Chandler attempted to revive the strategy of massive prosecution between 1881 and 1884 (avoiding the problem of reluctant grand juries by filing indictments by information for violation of the Enforcement Acts), his largely solitary efforts resulted only in his resounding defeat when he ran for Congress in 1884.[60]

The Klan trials' establishment of convictions remained a warning to purveyors of violence against black citizens, though the nature of the signal was rendered ambiguous by the depletion of resources and lack of political will at the federal level. Ultimately, the Supreme Court would have to weigh in to determine whether this route would be open should a new investment of federal resources become a realistic possibility. The case dealing most directly with this issue is *Ex parte Yarbrough*.[61] Jasper Yarbrough and seven others had been convicted for assaulting and beating a black man to intimidate him and prevent him from voting. He and the others convicted with him sought writs of habeas corpus on the ground that their detention was unconstitutional, as the congressional criminal statute under which they were convicted exceeded Congress's regulatory authority.[62]

The Court reasoned that Congress's authority extended beyond the plain language of the Constitution in logical terms to ensure the safe and non-fraudulent conduct of elections.[63] The Court distinguished its previous analysis in the *Civil Rights Cases*, declaring that "while it may be true that acts which are mere invasions of private rights, . . . are not within the scope of this amendment, it is quite a different matter when Congress undertakes to protect the citizen in the exercise of rights conferred by the Constitution . . . essential to the healthy organization of the government itself."[64] The Court denied relief to the white Klansmen, stating that "If the government of the United States has within its constitutional domain no authority to provide against these evils, if the very sources of power may be poisoned by corruption or controlled by violence and outrage, without legal restraint, then indeed is the country in danger . . . [and is] at the mercy of the combinations of those who respect no right but brute force, on the one hand, and unprincipled corruptionists on the other."[65] This reasoning, often neglected in accounts of Supreme Court decision making in the 1880s, underlined the new capacity of the federal government to serve as a backstop for citizens' rights, though, as Brandwein emphasizes, what constituted legally defensible rights was in contestation. Furthermore, the state of affairs established by the Court left blacks dependent on the federal government's willingness to continue to press the issue. Once federal agents were no longer promoting enforcement, black citizens were free—free to exercise a civic autonomy that was trammeled on all sides by the political and racial cage white southern resistors were rapidly constructing and legitimizing.

Tracing the trajectory of national efforts to enforce black rights demonstrates the national government's willingness to generate capacity through the creation of the Freedmen's Bureau and the reorganization and consolidation of resources in the new Justice Department. This capacity was readily mobilized by individual agents with the will to use it to bring form and meaning to the idea of black citizenship. Agents ranging from military commanders to Freedmen's Bureau officials and ultimately to federal prosecutors and the U.S. attorney general mounted a multipronged effort both to protect black freedmen and to advance black rights through backstopping their exercise until blacks were capable of exercising them independently. The campaign that had begun with military force and institutional presence during the war ended in the legal arena, as prosecutors both used criminal law and invoked the rule of law to advance their agendas.

This creative agency, however, was not enough. Although the legal framework remained available well into the 1880s, with the change of focus and direction in the attorney general's office after Akerman's departure, lower level prosecutors no longer had the support to pursue their mission of undergirding rights. National politics contributed strongly to this shift, as the Chester Alan Arthur administration moved away from efforts to bolster southern Republicans and sought new white allies in the South. As Democrats regained national electoral competitiveness in both presidential and congressional elections, the national Republican Party and its local functionaries increasingly isolated the Republicans who maintained a commitment to a biracial party.[66] Formal, abstracted access to narrowly construed basic rights that blacks themselves would largely have to assert and defend was what remained. Taken together, these activities on the part of the federal government's lawyers and agents present a particular picture of black citizenship and the national state's newly generated capacity to enforce it. This portrait intersected with struggles over federalism that would eventually be resolved largely in favor of local rule and state autonomy. Both the tripartite scheme of rights (civil, political, and social) and federalism were fluid during these years, but ultimately both resolved in favor of a narrowly conceived and weakly enforced set of rights that did not impinge significantly on state sovereignty.

Why did the campaign to transform blacks into citizens who both enjoyed the full protection of the laws and had the capacity to defend and exercise their own rights collapse? The simple answer is that, especially after 1875, the executive branch stepped back from vigorous enforcement to secure voting rights for blacks. This initiated a vicious circle in which the biracial wing of the Republican Party in the South and its white supporters in the North were increasingly disempowered in elections, providing successively less political incentive for strenuous investment on the part of ambivalent national Republican leaders.[67]

This answer, however, encompasses an additional question about the cultural and political factors that contributed to the incremental and then snowballing decisions to withdraw resources. Republicans were initially committed to helping dependent blacks and exercising federal power to assist them in framing claims for rights and access to the legal process. Ironically, the will to do so crumbled, however, as blacks began to exercise rights independently and to press aggressively both for political access through voting and holding office and for access to middle-class consumption and lifestyles.[68] This suggests that, like the troubled children discussed by Nackenoff and Sullivan and the animals discussed by Pearson and Smith and by Szymanski, blacks and black men in particular found it easier to attract the support and concern of national policymakers when they were structurally situated as conditional citizens, subordinates, and in need of protection. Disinvestment in blacks also corresponded with deeper investment in the more unifying cultural struggle against polygamy in the West, a struggle that also invoked the notion of protecting families and helpless exploited (and self-deluding) women.

Converting Deseret into Utah: Making Monogamous Citizens

At least some part of the federal Attorney General Office decision to limit its investments on the behalf of black citizens related to its decision to throw itself completely into a concerted campaign against polygamy among the Church of Jesus Christ of Latter-day Saints (LDS), commonly known as Mormons.[69] The state capacity built in the years immediately following the Civil War was put to good use in the antipolygamy campaign. The Republican Party platform of 1856 linked the issues by declaring black slavery and LDS polygamy to be "twin relics of barbarism." Between 1865 and the 1890s, both issues provoked significant congressional interest, triggering hearings and legislation. In each case, Congress specifically empowered government lawyers to bring prosecutions to suppress the perceived evils.

Sarah Barringer Gordon and Stephen Cresswell comprehensively analyze the legal and political campaign against LDS polygamy and its constitutional fallout in the last quarter of the nineteenth century. The campaign against polygamy began—as did that against slavery—largely as a popularly based movement driven by public lectures, popular fictionalizations, and dramatic exposés. In fact, from Gordon's description of the timing and conduct of the popular campaign against LDS polygamy, it appears that some of its leaders specifically patterned their strategy on the abolition movement and on Harriet Beecher Stowe in particular.[70]

The campaign, however, like the campaign against slavery and for the enhancement of blacks' civil rights, was ultimately driven by national-level state actors and thrived not on heated moral rhetoric but on the concrete augmentation of state capacity. Movement leaders continued to press for the suppression of polygamy, but the federal government saw the Mormon empire as a political threat to American sovereignty and responded in those terms. President James Buchanan launched a military campaign against Brigham Young in 1857 that resulted in Young's displacement as Utah's territorial governor, but during the Civil War the national government shifted to legal terms of engagement.[71] The initial legal step, taken in 1862, was the passage of the Morrill Act, making polygamy a federal crime.[72] By the end of the Civil War, national policymakers were questioning why the Morrill Act was not being vigorously enforced. In response, President Grant pressed his territorial agents to act.[73] Popular activists, too, continued to militate against polygamy. Ann Eliza Young, a plural wife of Brigham Young who fled the Latter-day Saints, conducted a popular campaign against polygamy and Mormonism in the 1870s, testifying before Congress in 1875 and publishing an account of her suffering entitled *Wife No. 19*, which she promoted through a national speaking campaign.[74]

Mormon polygamists resisted this pressure, relying primarily on a dual strategy of seeking statehood and cementing their control over territorial offices and institutions. They were opposed by federally appointed territorial judges, considered outsiders, who supported the national agenda against polygamy. Legal maneuvering across jurisdictional lines became increasingly intense and bitter.[75] The federal government refused to consider statehood as long as the polygamists maintained control over state and local institutions.

Through the 1860s, the conflict remained at a relative stalemate; although the Morrill Act banned polygamy, prosecutions were difficult due to local resistance by territorial officials. Stymied by lack of resources, U.S. attorney Charles Hempstead complained of his heavy workload and lack of adequate compensation; he resigned but reluctantly agreed to stay an additional seven months into 1871 while President Grant searched for a replacement. His interim replacement found himself in even worse circumstances: Congress had appropriated no funds to proceed with territorial prosecutions in Utah. Having to advance the money for his lawsuits out of pocket, he did not remain in the office long. The Grant administration finally located a candidate in Chicago lawyer Benjamin Bristow, who, having lost all he owned in the Great Chicago Fire, was desperate for work.[76] The lack of results under these circumstances led to an intentional increase in national-state capacity to address the problem directly (just as enforcement resources were being withdrawn from the South). The Poland Act, passed in 1874, provided for more direct federal intervention into Utah Territory, as it "reduced the powers of the territory's probate judges and provided for jury pools to be selected by the U.S. marshal as well as his territorial counterpart," a form of direct control never exercised in a territory before.[77] Mormon leaders, too, were no longer immune from the direct reach of the federal government. The federal government was ready to make the campaign against polygamy a priority, and only needed to bolster and compensate the necessary manpower.

Both sides—the federal government and the Saints—grew increasingly invested in winning a definitive victory. LDS leaders believed that they should have the authority to control the fundamentally local questions of marriage and family configuration, relying on the principle of religious liberty as protected under the First Amendment that hearkened back to antebellum formations of federalism. Federal officials, in contrast, insisted on their authority to regulate in the territories, continuing a struggle that had reached a flashpoint in *Dred Scott v. Sandford* (though the scope of direct interventionist power that the federal government claimed far outstripped that at issue in the struggle over slavery). In 1879, the conflict came to a head when the Supreme Court ruled in the critical case of *Reynolds v. United States*, looking to settle these assorted controversial topics and lay the groundwork both for federal regulation of the Latter-day Saints' land and for generating workable boundaries for religious freedom.

The *Reynolds* case was planned litigation, as both sides sought a definitive resolution through George Reynolds's appeal of his conviction for polygamy to the Supreme Court. The seriousness with which they took the case can be gauged by the status of their advocates. For the United States, the case was jointly argued by Attorney General Charles Devens and Solicitor General Samuel Phillips. The LDS leadership chose prominent attorney George Washington Biddle, a staunch Democrat and dean of the Philadelphia Bar, to present their arguments.[78] The formal issues on which Reynolds sought reversal of his conviction were fourfold. Biddle argued that jurors had been excluded improperly because they refused to say whether they were themselves polygamists; that the testimony of Amelia Reynolds from the first trial was improperly admitted in the second; that the court should have directed the jury to find for Reynolds if they were convinced that he acted from sincere religious belief; and that the judge's instruction to the jurors to "consider what are to be the consequences to the innocent victims of this delusion" was prejudicial.[79]

In his brief, Devens spoke briefly for national supremacy but focused most of his argumentation on the evils of polygamy. In effect, he used the extreme nature of the danger he portrayed to leverage a claim for federal intervention, despite the longstanding principle that marriage and family were subject to local regulation and control (Devens appeared not to notice the federal involvement in organizing marriages among freedmen and freedwomen that had occurred so recently). The particular dangers he discussed in his brief were the interrelated individual and social inequalities inherent in polygamous relationships and the risks this marriage structure posed to women. Women were subjugated both by their husbands and by priests in this system, which boded ill both for them and for the polity as a whole.[80] Even though Devens did not discuss slavery or the efforts to ensure formalized marriages among free blacks, his arguments against polygamy reinforced the conception of the monogamously married woman as a protected and supported citizen, with duties and rights that complemented those of the individual male heads of household responsible for her and their mutual children.

This argument seemed likely to garner some attention from a Court that had recently upheld an Illinois ban on women's serving as attorneys, which had triggered Justice Joseph Bradley's concurrence, discussing the state's inherent public interest in protecting the weaker sex due to women's crucial role in childbearing and childrearing.[81] Bradley's statements suggested that the protection of women could be the lever that would trigger investment of prosecutorial and financial resources based on the importance of the national-level state interests at stake. They also presaged the rise of the maternalist legal and cultural arguments that would shape Progressive Era statebuilding agendas, emphasizing the particular significance of mothers' work in the home as a public service.

Devens's oral argument focused even more specifically on polygamy, the moral and social risks it posed to women and families, and the potential damage it could do to the nation if permitted to persist in Utah.[82] He likewise picked up on increasingly common claims that Mormon polygamy was treasonous.[83] He drew a series of alarming parallels between polygamy and other repugnant religious/Oriental practices, or as news reports quoted him, "religious atrocities." To exonerate Reynolds, he argued, would be to give free rein to Hindu widows' suttee, "East Islanders'" exposure of newborn infants, and Indian Thugs' murderous practices.[84] This discussion underlined the emerging cultural and political framing of the United States as a biracial republic with little room for citizenship or civic membership for those who could not be identified as white or black. He also discussed the infamous 1857 Mountain Meadows massacre in lurid terms, claiming that this incident showed how Mormon abandonment of humanitarianism and insistence on local religious rule could lead to human sacrifice.[85]

Devens's claims about Mormon polygamy, while rhetorically striking, were not original—they followed along lines established through anti-Mormon advocacy over the previous several decades. These critiques of Mormonism intertwined Mormonism with polygamy to produce a racialized (ironically, since Latter-day Saints were descended from "native" white stock) conception of the dangers they posed. In these constructions, Mormons were framed as committing a form of racial treason, aligning them with the schematic critique of Oriental nations and peoples portrayed in sources ranging from popular pamphlets across several generations to the writings of Montesquieu and John Stuart Mill. A run of cartoons across several popular publications emphasized and reinforced these conceptions of Mormons, portraying them as "barbaric, lascivious, despotic, disorderly, foreign, Black, Asian, and/or childish."[86] And as Asian immigration and anxieties about it increased in this era, the Orientalization of Mormons rendered them as problematic citizens at best.

Devens's argument, however, also situated the national state as the appropriate overseer and enforcer of conventional performances of civic belonging among those who aspired to American citizenship. The national government was obligated to intervene, not only to protect women and to stamp out barbarism but to ensure that these behaviors would not contaminate the nation as a whole. In order to be eligible as citizens, individuals had to perform within the appropriate gendered limitations, and the national government was ready to enforce such performance, either by facilitating proper marriages (as in the case of freedmen and freedwomen) or by coercing them, as with polygamists. These policies set the stage for later uses of regulatory capacity to manage families both at the federal and state levels (as Nackenoff and Sullivan note).

Best known for its interpretation of the First Amendment as protecting belief rather than practice, *Reynolds* also presents pathbreaking analyses of federalism and the significance of marriage as a state institution. The majority's analysis rebutted the defense's claim that Reynolds had acted out of religious belief or duty, finding that the state could regulate practices that posed a threat to public health, morals, or safety.[87] It is this analysis that most constitutional law textbooks excerpt, identifying the case as a landmark First Amendment opinion. However, in order to reach this conclusion, the justices grappled with the meaning and significance of the practice in question.

The Court distinguished polygamy as an "odious" practice, previously only conducted by Asiatic and African people. It picked up Devens's oral argument, musing, "Suppose one believed that human sacrifices were a necessary part of religious worship, would it be seriously contended that the civil government under which he lived could not interfere to prevent a sacrifice? Or if a wife religiously believed it was her duty to burn herself upon the funeral pile of her dead husband, would it be beyond the power of the civil government to prevent her carrying her belief into practice?"[88] These hypothetical queries underlined the racialization of polygamy and its practitioners, generating a moral equivalence with stereotypical African savages and Indian wife-burners. No, the Court implied, the responsible civil government would have a duty to intervene, necessitating the enhancement of capacity if it were not present sufficiently at the outset.

Polygamy was not merely an odious religious practice, however. It was a direct attack on what the Court characterized as "this most important feature of social life": marriage.[89] While marriage, in the Court's view, had sacred elements, it was fundamentally a civil contract imbued with public interest.[90] The Court explained, "Upon [marriage] society may be said to be built, and out of its fruits spring social relations and social obligations and duties, with which government is necessarily required to deal."[91] In fact, for the Court, the organization and structure of marriage determined "the principles on which the government of the people . . . rests." In support of this proposition, the Court cited renowned political scientist Francis Lieber's description of the "stationary despotism" fostered by the patriarchal principles inherent in polygamous societies.[92]

These political observations, however, did not get the Court all the way to the answer, for similar reflections on marriage had led southern state courts to conclude that marriage was best managed and controlled by state authorities. This case, however, took place in a territory, not a state. The Court reasoned that the statute was within Congress's legislative authority: "It is constitutional and valid as prescribing a rule of action for all those residing in the Territories, and in places over which the United States have exclusive control."[93] The analysis here underlined not only congressional power but repudiated one of the pillars of *Dred Scott*, that of popular sovereignty. The reasoning in *Reynolds* simultaneously justified congressional authority to regulate in Utah and the previous decisions not to admit Utah as a state. Utah would not join the Union as the forty-fifth state until 1896, after the LDS leadership had definitively and publicly renounced the Mormon religious commitment to polygamy, a nonnegotiable condition that everyone understood as such.

Although polygamy had already been illegal under federal law for sixteen years by the time the Court ruled in *Reynolds*, the ruling opened the door to augment institutional capacity to act against polygamists. Gordon characterized the ruling as sparking a second Reconstruction, gathering together the creative energy and coercive authority of the national state to remake a recalcitrant region into a full participant in the American enterprise.[94] *Reynolds* marked the beginning of a concerted legal war to bring the Latter-day Saints into line, with a robust corps of government attorneys as the generals but also reliant upon crucial legal changes. The campaign was politically popular, as the public was increasingly engaged through the movement against polygamy, but it was also a useful means for rallying national interests around a common enemy in the wake of the Civil War and the struggles over Reconstruction.[95] With the political will in place and the first legal bridgehead established, the war against the Latter-day Saints could shift to a rule-of-law framework, in some regards mirroring the shift from military occupation to legal regulation in the South.

The first skirmish centered on the crime of bigamy. *Reynolds* had cleared up any ambiguity regarding the constitutional legitimacy of national laws rendering polygamy a crime, and prosecutors proceeded with charges. Yet between 1879 and 1890, only seventy-eight indictments were filed for polygamy. Polygamy was still difficult to prove because the Mormon community concealed marriage records and refused to testify honestly against each other about the existence of marriages; without conventional victims, prosecutors found investigations almost impossible to conduct.[96] *Miles v. United States* illustrates this difficulty. John Miles was indicted and convicted for the crime of bigamy. He objected to the empaneling of the jury on similar grounds to those dismissed in *Reynolds*, and in 1881 the Supreme Court cited *Reynolds* in repulsing this attack summarily.[97] Bigamy prosecutions, however, presented a difficult conundrum. The prosecutor attempted to prove the two marriages by putting Miles's alleged second wife on the stand. As the Court explained, "The marriage of [John Miles] with Caroline Owens was charged in the indictment and admitted by him upon the trial. The fact of his previous marriage with Emily Spencer was, therefore, the only issue in the case, and that was contested to the end of the trial. Until the fact of the marriage of Emily Spencer with [John Miles] was established, Caroline Owens was prima facie his wife, and she could not be used as a witness against him."[98] The Court conceded that this rule made the prosecution of polygamy quite difficult, but declared that only a legislative solution could ease the path for federal prosecutors.[99] This approach echoed its stance in some cases involving the Klan Acts, in which the Court's opinions laid out proper charging strategies for prosecutors; in this case, the direction was to Congress, which responded.

Partnering with Congress, federal prosecutors shifted their strategy to embrace new tools provided through a wave of antipolygamy legislation passed during the 1880s. In a tactic pioneered in the South during Reconstruction, polygamists were disenfranchised, and then offered reenfranchisement if they took an oath to renounce polygamy and act as loyal and compliant citizens.[100] The Edmunds Act in particular proved useful. Designed to target Mormon polygamy in the Utah Territory, it established cohabitation as a separate offense and formally excluded polygamists from eligibility for jury service.[101] The passage of the Edmunds Act marked the beginning of what Latter-day Saints would call the Raid, an overwhelming deployment of prosecutorial resources supported by legal changes to facilitate prosecution that was designed to force the Mormon Church to submit to federal authority under the pressure of legal war. Previous federal attorneys had wanted to move strongly against polygamy, but new U.S. attorney William Dickson and Utah chief justice Charles Zane had a different kind of legal and structural arsenal at their disposal.[102] The new laws provided for appeals from the supreme territorial court directly to the Supreme Court, coordinating the production and refinement of the legal mechanisms. And, unlike the situation in the South as interest in enforcing black rights waned, prosecutorial resources and state capacity were liberally provided to suppress polygamy. The new federal crime of cohabitation proved to be quite useful, and prosecutors exercised their discretion extensively along this track. While the Raid was unparalleled in scope and reach as a campaign of criminal legal regulation of sexuality in American history, for the Saints it was preferable to the final alternative of martial law, which they believed would have threatened not only the practice of polygamy but the continued existence of the Latter-day Saints.[103]

The Supreme Court calibrations of the legal mechanisms against polygamy were significant and contrasted sharply with their far more lukewarm and ambiguous collaboration with federal prosecutors in the South in the 1870s and 1880s. On the one hand, the Court allowed inmates to be held without bail while their appeals of convictions for polygamy or unlawful cohabitation were under way.[104] In a second appeal by Rudger Clawson, the Court also held that the jury-empaneling procedures that barred polygamists from serving as grand or petit jurors were constitutionally legitimate.[105] Likewise, the Court upheld a federal law disenfranchising polygamists, even in cases in which continuous cohabitation could not be proven.[106] The Court also endorsed the solicitor general's argument in favor of a legal definition of cohabitation that did not require concrete proof that sexual intercourse had occurred.[107]

Yet some elements of the prosecutors' campaign went too far even for the Court, which pulled back a bit from full-throated support in the late 1880s. In 1888, Hans Nielsen was convicted of cohabitation based on a guilty plea. After he had served his sentence, however, a second indictment was filed, charging him with adultery based on his relationship with the same two women whom he claimed as wives. He objected to the indictment, but was convicted and sentenced for adultery. He sought habeas relief on the ground that he had been subjected to double jeopardy.[108] The solicitor general argued vigorously in favor of allowing multiple indictments, claiming that in this case the two offenses (cohabitation and adultery) were different and that unlawful cohabitation was a continuous offense subject to indictment for any moment at which it could be credibly alleged.[109] The Court disagreed on both counts, citing several precedents to the contrary.[110]

The increased pressure was still not satisfactory for opponents of polygamy and Mormons. The final turn of the screw was the Edmunds-Tucker Act of 1887. This act was designed to deliver the death blow to LDS polygamy. It dissolved the LDS Church Corporation, a corporate charter first endorsed by Congress in the 1850s, and confiscated any assets amounting to more than $50,000. It also required the antipolygamy oath as a condition for exercising basic rights and responsibilities of citizenship, including voting, jury service, and serving as a public official. It disallowed inheritances by illegitimate children. It required civil marriage licenses and registration of marriages, to ensure that individual marriages could be tracked by the state and polygamists could not evade the law through solely ecclesiastical marriages. It consolidated and enhanced a public education system for children. And it disenfranchised women in the Utah Territory, who acquired the right to vote in 1870.[111] These provisions sought to incapacitate the Church and to force individual Latter-day Saints into compliance with national norms for civic familial behavior. The linkage between renouncing polygamy and gaining access to political and civil rights is striking in its direct insistence that proper performance of citizenship was a precondition of exercising the rights of citizenship. And the administration of both marriage and education were swept within the national-state's controls so that the families, "nurseries of the state," could be rendered compliant with these norms.

With the assistance of a marshal and an army of deputies, the U.S. attorney general marched forth to enforce the new law. LDS officials protested the removal of the Church's corporate status and the confiscation of its property, claiming that the law violated fundamental principles of corporate and constitutional law. The Supreme Court, however, upheld the confiscations in a decision announced on May 19, 1890.[112] This ruling was the end of the road. In September 1890, President Wilford Woodruff, the spiritual leader of the Saints, issued the Manifesto, a report of a revelation from God that he should no longer advise his flock to practice celestial (polygamous) marriage.[113] With the renunciation of polygamy, the Saints set themselves on a path that led quickly to statehood—and to the much more autonomous associated state-based governmental and institutional structures that *Plessy v. Ferguson* would legitimate a few months after Utah became a state in 1896.

The Expansion of National-State Capacity in the Making of Black and Mormon Citizens

On the surface, some elements of these two campaigns are strikingly similar. Polygamy, like slavery, sparked intense public and grassroots opposition in the years leading up to the Civil War. In both cases, the agenda for reform was gradually adopted first by Republican Party elites in an effort to help define the party and then by the federal government itself. In both cases as well, efforts to manage the problems through military force gave way to legal forms of management oriented around the use of national prosecutorial authority to enforce citizens' rights and citizens' appropriate behavior. In the postbellum years, Congress actively legislated to advance civil rights for blacks and to suppress polygamy. In doing so, Congress extended a veritable arsenal of legal weapons to government attorneys to push forward the agenda of reform. In both cases, the Supreme Court at times collaborated (particularly if we take seriously Pamela Brandwein's reconsideration of state neglect),[114] though the Court was more unambiguously supportive of the antipolygamy agenda. Both sets of changes brought about significant growth in the federal government's scope of regulatory authority, and depended upon major expansions of state capacity for their implementation. And both left lasting legacies in the form of greater state capacity for managing and controlling the configuration of families and the proper performance of familial roles.

In the South, this capacity took the form of widespread implementation and aggressive enforcement of bans on interracial marriage at the state level (among other things). In the West (and by extension nationally), the federal government maintained its interest in the direct management of families, which manifested in the age of immigration as Congress and the executive branch dealt with problems of wives, children, and concubines through measures such as the Chinese Exclusion Act of 1882 and efforts to limit the descendants of Chinese immigrants' access to citizenship; the Cable Act of 1922, which deprived female U.S. citizens of citizenship if they married Asian men, because Asians were ineligible for citizenship; and the Immigration Act of 1924, which closed the door to nearly all Asian immigrants.[115]

The cases of the Latter-day Saints and African American freedmen and women in some senses reached a similar resolution. The South abandoned its attempts to reinstitute slavery and accepted in superficial terms the federal imposition of equal civil rights for blacks. The Saints bent to federal supremacy and abandoned their dream of a Kingdom of Deseret, dedicated to the worship of God through the visible exercise of celestial marriage. The president of the Mormon Church publicly ended the Church's commitment to polygamy, though the practice continued in secret. In contrast, southern states bargained stringently for local control and authority to manage race relations; they quickly implemented this authority to subjugate African Americans and render them subject to a highly repressive legal regime. The Latter-day Saints' public reversal on the question of polygamy bought them statehood and all of the hard-fought elements of local sovereignty that statehood meant by the turn of the twentieth century. And the public reversal masked a silent, quiet maintenance of plural marriages among LDS leaders, ultimately resulting in the necessity for a second public manifesto repudiating the practice in 1904. And while the sanction of excommunication finally succeeded in purging the last polygamists from the ranks of the mainstream Saints, splinter polygamist groups persist to the present day.[116]

But the more interesting comparison is how the government's actions in both cases shaped the development of federalism and how they intertwined with efforts to breathe life into the category of citizenship in the postbellum era. The common thread in this process was the federal government's investment in configuring the cultural practices of citizenship, in terms of both proper ordering of families and facilitating the exercise of rights by subordinated or problematic citizens. In each case, the federal government actively intervened to produce appropriate family structures and to exercise rights by proxy for those who could not do so. But when the question in the South became more one of thwarting interference with blacks' independent exercise of the rights of manhood, the commitment both of prosecutorial resources and of the executive branch and Congress became increasingly uncertain.

Recent work in American political development has addressed the wartime dynamics that enabled blacks to claim rights through reference to their sacrifice and civic service.[117] New black citizens gained access to a set of rights that they could themselves enforce through recourse to the legal process, particularly in the area of contract rights. But the federal government also took on the formal agenda of supporting and enforcing access to rights, as well as facilitating their exercise by citizens who were ill equipped to assert them independently. These rights, as well as government actors' ambiguous commitment to them, underlined the shifting boundaries of citizenship in this era. Individual masculine rights designed to render black men heads of household and contracting wage laborers gained priority. As federal actors' commitments to black equality waned, the scope of enforcement efforts weakened, and black men were increasingly left to their own devices to assert and enforce these rights. Fundamentally, the strongest national commitments to investing legal resources on behalf of black citizens looked to support bodily integrity against assaults, and to enforce contract rights, at least for a brief while.

The process was different for the litigation over polygamy because the government was not seeking to support or advance rights, but rather to shape proper citizens. Strikingly, government officials were quite suspicious of one right usually associated with full citizenship—that of suffrage. Utah extended the vote to women early, a move initially applauded by advocates within the woman suffrage movement. However, as it became clear that female Saints were not going to exercise their rights to eliminate polygamy, even advocates for suffrage changed their minds, and Congress itself stripped Utah women of the right to vote.[118]

Another parallel to the broader legal struggle over the meaning of emancipation was the state's placement of marriage as a cornerstone. But whereas for blacks this led to state control of and advocacy for monogamous intraracial marriages, for the Mormons it led to the removal of marriage from local authority and its identification as an issue of concern for the national sphere.

In the heat of the campaign against polygamy, some members of Congress initiated discussions about developing a national marriage law to generate uniform standards and regulations for this vitally important state institution.[119] In addition, the experience of federal intervention in these two instances established new machinery and precedent for federal intervention in the family, particularly in ensuring that citizens would and could exercise appropriate gendered familial roles, and in actively shaping these performances in the case of individuals who were not yet full and unconditional citizens. This groundwork would smooth the path for government intervention on behalf of other subordinated individuals in the Progressive Era.

In the struggle over polygamy, rights and citizenship operated interdependently. Involvement in polygamy ultimately rendered its practitioners less citizen-like and justified the removal of citizens' rights. But at the same time, this separation intertwined with the increasingly resonant perception of Mormons as others, akin to Orientals and savage barbarians. One dynamic that is worthy of further investigation is the relationship between the culturally grounded Orientalization of Mormons alongside increasing anxieties about Chinese plural marriage and polygamy, which also led to national-level policy outcomes in the form of restrictive immigration laws passed at around the same time Congress was actively striking at the Mormon/polygamy threat. But the removal of citizens' rights increasingly associated Latter-day Saints not only with noncitizens but with racialized others, underlining the postwar configuration of the United States as a biracial republic. Once the Saints renounced polygamy publicly, they set themselves on a course toward absorption into the American polity, the regaining of the rights of citizens, and acknowledgment as whites, a process that Irish and, slightly later, Italian and Jewish immigrants were also undergoing.[120] It was basically a quid pro quo.[121]

The most notable effect of these campaigns taken together, however, was the expansion they wrought in national-state capacity and in the sense of what constituted a legitimate interest for the national government to address. The capacity and scope of interest built in the early days of Reconstruction did not evaporate as the national government lost its will to enforce black rights to manly citizenship. It shifted to the making of other citizens, and the national interventions addressed these citizens' proper performance of gendered civic membership. The campaign against polygamy among the Saints generated and used significant legal capacity in the form of new legislation and the commitment of federal investigators and prosecutorial resources, and this campaign provided a helpful rallying point that encompassed anxieties about problematic citizens, loyalty to the nation, and whiteness that could readily cross the North/South and East/West divides.[122]

Utah, as noted above, gained statehood in 1896, with the assurance of the Saints that they would perform their civic membership according to the monogamous script demanded by the national government. In 1898, after a brief war with Spain, the United States acquired several new territories with millions of new subjects (though some of these subjects in the Philippine Islands were not fully subdued until the 1910s). Management of the Utah Territory and its problematic citizens provided a helpful model for the newly acquired territories. Unlike the expansion across the North American continent, Congress did not presume that it was preparing the new lands for unconditional statehood with unconditional national citizens.

In both the processes described in this chapter, individuals exercised significant agency to promote their citizen-making agendas. David Corbin's tireless work against the Klan when supported by Attorney General Akerman vividly exemplified enhanced national capacity, just as the collaboration among U.S. Attorney Philip Van Zile, Attorney General Benjamin Brewster, and President Arthur generated the prosecutorial resources to conduct a massive legal campaign against polygamy. Yet the effective exercise of agency and capacity also depended on institutional will, as Corbin discovered when Akerman was replaced with an attorney general with a different set of concerns. After both legal campaigns, though, the national government had a new legal framework and a concrete set of resources to put to work in other spheres. Furthermore, this episode of statebuilding left a legacy of legitimized intervention that facilitated additional institution-building and growth of institutional capacity at the state level.

Through all this, the development of national governing capacity to manage and shape new citizens was critical. The commitment of national law enforcers and prosecutors, along with the development of newly available congressional tools, affected the development of citizenship. This expansion of capacity drew from culturally grounded beliefs about citizenship that were conditioned by race and gender, but it also influenced how these beliefs operated in the law by allowing the national government to invest the new resources to promote or withhold certain civic rights. This process contributed to an evolving federal compromise about the national government's role in defining, protecting, and delimiting core civic rights.

Chapter 2

Demagogues and the Demon Drink: Newspapers and the Revival of Prohibition in Georgia

Marek D. Steedman

> There is something in the whole [prohibition] movement that is hard to understand. It has come about, seemingly, with no special planning, without any special leadership, or the expenditure of any large sum of money, but it has taken thoroughly hold of the people.
>
> —Booker T. Washington, "Extracts from an Address in Brooklyn," 1907

> Modern demagoguery also makes use of oratory, even to a tremendous extent, if one considers the election speeches a modern candidate has to deliver. But the use of the printed word is more enduring. The political publicist, and above all the journalist, is nowadays the most important representative of the demagogic species.
>
> —Max Weber, "Politics as a Vocation," 1919

On July 30, 1907, the Georgia House of Representatives voted by an overwhelming margin to pass a bill mandating statewide prohibition. The bill had already successfully cleared the state Senate, and the signature of Governor Hoke Smith was assured. Statewide prohibition would take effect on January 1, 1908, as Georgia became the first state in the South ever to adopt the policy, and the first in the nation to do so since 1889. In the wake of the House vote, crowds of temperance advocates, white ribbons waving, chose two symbolic venues to stage their celebration: the offices of the Atlanta *Georgian*, the city newspaper that had given essential support to the cause, and a statue of the late Henry W. Grady, New South spokesman, city newspaper editor, and staunch prohibitionist.[1] State and city advocates of statewide prohibition, including members of the Woman's Christian Temperance Union (WCTU), the Anti-Saloon League (ASL), and local evangelical churches, had held rallies, given speeches, pressured politicians, organized local petitions and ballots, and hoped and prayed for this moment for almost twenty years. When it arrived, however, they paid tribute to the power of the printed word.

This chapter examines the ability of Progressive Era newspapers to shape public discourse, influence the policy agenda of state institutions, and expand conceptions of the appropriate scope of public powers held by the state. This ability, I suggest, is obscured by a focus on the media as a national political institution, and can only be properly identified once we turn our attention to political development emerging at the state and municipal level. The argument I make, is, however, strictly bounded in time by the precise interplay of press and state institutions in the Progressive Era itself. Newspapers were no longer the sponsored organs of partisan interests: their revenue was derived more from circulation and advertising than from political patronage. At the federal level, patronage was quickly replaced by a new form of state capture, as state agencies and political leaders established public relations offices to feed reporters the "news" they hoped to report.[2] At the state and local level, however, this symbiotic, but rationalized, relationship did not immediately take hold. Instead, local newspaper editors and publishers were able to parlay financial independence and influence over public opinion into direct political power in their own right. The power and influence of the "political editor" (or publisher) waned, however, as local newspapers were increasingly consolidated into national newspaper corporations and new methods of state capture developed.

The arc of the narrative, then, is not a straightforward development from patronage to rationalized administrative procedures. An intervening stage, highlighting a path not taken, emerges at the level of state and municipal political development in which newspaper editors and publishers could operate as policy entrepreneurs and power brokers, both within and outside established political parties. The argument depends on reading the press itself as a political institution: a set of organizations and practices through which public opinion is constituted, expressed, and brought to bear on governing structures, and thus policy outcomes.[3] But it illustrates a moment in which the fragmentation of this institution across local, state, and regional markets provided platforms for ambitious power-seekers not simply to influence, but to wield political power at multiple levels of government.

I illustrate these dynamics through a case study of the revival of statewide prohibition in Georgia between 1905 and 1908 and the subsequent spread of prohibition across the South by 1915. At one level I hope simply to illustrate the forms and extent of political power available to ambitious entrepreneurial newspaper editors and publishers in the period. Editors and publishers sought influence in local party apparatuses, ran for political office, and used their newspapers as campaign offices and platforms for political propaganda. They also rhetorically shaped public discourse, supplying facts and arguments in support of favored policies, marshaling or suppressing letters from the public on topics of the day, and seeking to influence the public reputation and voting behavior of elected officials.

At another level of analysis, however, I argue that attention to the power of the press during the Progressive Era in the South advances our understanding of the timing, character, and regional specificity of the movement for statewide prohibition in this period. No southern state had adopted prohibition before 1907, and even though temperance influence was strong, the shift from local option laws (under which individual counties could vote to go "dry") to statewide prohibition was relatively abrupt: all but Texas, Louisiana, and Florida had made the transition by 1915, only eight years after Georgia, and only Louisiana had failed to do so prior to ratification of the Eighteenth Amendment in 1919.[4] Explanations for this sudden adoption vary (the success of prior experience with local option, the triggering of racial panic following the 1906 Atlanta race riot, the regional strength of evangelical Christianity), but I argue below that none of them, alone or in combination, account simultaneously for the *timing* and *sectional character* of the shift. The missing ingredient is supplied by attention to the operation of city newspapers in Atlanta, which in large part provoked the Atlanta race riot in 1906, shaped its public meaning, and provided a rhetorical language capable of linking prohibition to the larger enterprise of establishing and securing Jim Crow. As Ann-Marie Szymanski finds for wildlife protection, the authority and capacity to enforce prohibition was rapidly (if incompletely) consolidated in the federal government, but its emergence, paradoxically, depended on the fragmentation of state-press relations at the state and local level.[5]

On the Demagogic Power of the Press

Between 1880 and 1920 shifts in the relation between state institutions and the press provided a brief window of opportunity for ambitious newspaper editors and publishers to translate their command of public opinion into direct political power.[6] An early indication of the potential can be seen in the failed 1872 presidential campaign of Horace Greeley, prominent editor of the *New York Tribune*, who sought to use his independence from party patronage as a platform for his own independent political movement.[7] Later editors pursued more traditional forms of political power within existing political party structures, building power bases at the state level, and sometimes attaining or seeking federal positions of power on the basis of their influence. Thus Henry Watterson in Kentucky, Josephus Daniels in North Carolina, and Henry Grady in Georgia each held important political positions in their state parties in the 1880s and 1890s, while Watterson and Daniels held federal political office (Watterson in Congress, Daniels in the Cleveland and Wilson administrations).[8] Nor is the phenomenon entirely southern: in 1920 Warren G. Harding of Ohio became the first (and last) newspaper publisher to be elected president. His opponent in that election, James M. Cox, had also made his career editing newspapers in Ohio, before serving two terms as governor of the state.[9]

Standard accounts of the rationalization of the newspaper industry in the late nineteenth and early twentieth centuries fail to capture this dynamic and its impact on political development, especially at the state and municipal level. Max Weber, for example, identified the printed word as a potential form of "demagogic" politics but doubted journalism could provide a steady source of party politicians: he believed that the day-to-day demands of production provided little time for active engagement in party politics.[10] By 1919, when Weber wrote "Politics as a Vocation," the newspaper business had reached a level of consolidation that stripped individual proprietors and editors of their autonomous role in determining the political "voice" of a particular paper.[11]

Consolidation of the newspaper industry, then, redirected the ambitions of successful editors toward editorships in larger markets, and gave publishers national rather than local interests. At the same time, as Timothy Cook has elaborated, journalism became more professionalized, lines of communication with government officials more standardized, and a national media institution began to take shape. Where newspapers had once been sponsored by political parties or factions, or sustained by political patronage, new forms of "subsidy" (access to political information, favorable regulation, and the like) allowed politicians and state actors to exert a more generalized influence over the industry as a whole. The result was an institution at once more national in scope, less overtly partisan in sympathy, and more devoted to professional norms of objectivity and impartiality.[12] Even the so-called yellow journalism of the turn of the century took on a more public spirited and reform cast.[13]

Beneath the surface, however, the variable pace of these developmental currents interacted to produce novel patterns of interaction between press and politics. In the progressive period in the United States newspaper consolidation had not yet gone very far. Many small towns sustained one or more independent newspapers, and large cities saw lively competition for readership and advertising revenue.[14] In 1906, Atlanta still had four locally and separately owned daily newspapers, along with a number of weekly and specialty publications.[15] Within a decade, northern newspaper companies would begin to move into this market, but in the period we are considering these local newspapers and their publishers and editors were freed from patronage, buoyed by circulation and advertising revenue, and unconstrained by corporate control. This puts a new, and more localized, twist on Richard Hofstadter's insight that "To an extraordinary degree the work of the Progressive movement rested upon its journalism."[16] Progressive editors, publishers, and journalists sought not only to attract readers and advertising revenue but also to mobilize public opinion and shape public discourse. At the state and local level, their ability to do so rested in part on their relative autonomy from other political and media institutions.

An examination of Georgia helps bring these developments into focus. By the 1880s a generation of newspaper editors had emerged in the South who were determined to bring southern newspapers up to modern standards in terms of production, revenue, content, and distribution.[17] Principal among these was Henry W. Grady, who joined the *Atlanta Constitution* in 1876. Grady is remembered now as the leading spokesman of the New South, giving voice to the movement's embrace of industrial development and reconciliation with the North. His political influence was built and sustained, however, through careful management of editorial policy at the *Constitution*. Grady came to Atlanta in 1872 as editor of the *Atlanta Herald*, a paper modeled in style and content on its New York namesake. Despite adopting salacious headlines and front-page stories, the *Herald* lacked the financial backing to survive a circulation battle with the more established *Constitution*. Grady himself was plucked from the wreckage by the *Constitution*'s new owner, Evan P. Howell, and offered the position of editor.[18] From that point Grady's influence in Atlanta and Georgia politics steadily grew. In part this was due to the impressive expansion in the paper's circulation figures, which grew from 5,200 in 1880 to 12,000 in 1890. The *Constitution* was published as a morning paper, and had very little competition until the arrival of the *Atlanta Journal* in 1883. But Grady also transformed the look and feel of the paper, blending national and international news with a liberal dose of southern boosterism, and just a dash of the sensationalism of his *Herald* days. Above all, Grady successfully "sought . . . the role of political-power broker within Georgia."[19]

Historians routinely describe Grady's *Constitution* as "the state's most powerful paper," or even "the leading organ of Southern opinion and sentiment."[20] And contemporary observers agreed. Of course the *Constitution* may simply have reflected the views of its readers, rather than shaping their voting behavior. But contemporaries clearly believed otherwise: newspaper editors were sought as allies and feared as foes. Grady, for example, did not content himself with periodic editorial endorsements. The *Constitution* functioned as a campaign headquarters for its favored candidates, with Grady orchestrating favorable news stories in the state's weeklies and printing and distributing campaign materials. Historians Louis Griffith and John Talmadge would later argue that "Not the number of supporting newspapers but the persistent and skillful use of promotional material usually decides a political battle," and Grady was among the best.[21] What mattered more than his purported influence over voters was the fact that candidates believed that support from Grady meant the difference between winning and losing. Grady traded that impression for direct counsel with the political leaders of the day (and was briefly promoted for a U.S. Senate seat, and even a vice presidential slot, himself).[22]

Numerous examples attest to this tight connection between politics and the press in Georgia. The *Constitution*'s owner and publisher, Evan Howell, began his career as a city councilman in 1868, was elected mayor in 1902, and became a central figure in the state's Democratic Party.[23] His son Clark Howell inherited the paper along with a political career, serving in the General Assembly for more than a decade, including stints as speaker of the House and president of the Senate.[24] Like his father, Howell moved back and forth between newsroom and open campaigning for political office, with connections, influence, and favors developed in one field paying off in the other. By 1906 he thought the governorship was within his grasp.

Howell's immediate competitor in 1906, Hoke Smith, had also developed his political power as a newspaper publisher. Smith had begun his career as a successful lawyer in Atlanta in the 1870s. Inspired by the success of his sometime friend Henry Grady, Smith actively sought a newspaper business through which he might challenge Grady's preeminent political position. In 1887 Smith purchased the *Journal*, the afternoon rival to the *Constitution*. Smith was at least as ambitious as Grady, and began to build an alternative political faction around the *Journal* in both city and state politics. One of the early flashpoints was prohibition: Grady favored statewide prohibition and actively campaigned for the "dry" vote when the issue came up in Fulton County (the county that contains Atlanta) in 1886, while Smith favored the local option and was associated with the "wets." The two newsmen came to a compromise slate of candidates for the 1888 city elections that carefully balanced wet and dry councilmen.[25] Smith finally threw the *Journal* behind Grover Cleveland in the race for the Democratic nomination in 1892 (the *Constitution* favored a rival candidate), organized a Cleveland Club in the city, and took credit for Cleveland's nomination by the state Democratic convention. Smith was rewarded with a cabinet position in Cleveland's administration. Like Grady, Smith combined advocacy through the printed word with hardnosed backroom dealing and skillful campaign promotion.[26] As the *Journal* circulation grew to meet and even exceed that of the *Constitution* (by 1900 it had briefly surpassed its rival), so did the political clout of its editor. The power of editors and publishers was not only rhetorical, then.[27] The capacity to mobilize public opinion made men such as Smith, Grady, and the Howells political leaders in their own right as formidable campaign managers, influential party power-brokers, and elected officials.

We should see newspaper editors and publishers in this period, then, as political actors in the full sense of the word. Certainly they were strategic actors, but their strategies played across two domains that were more entangled than they would later become, and in which the relation was less clearly one of dependence on political parties or the state. Circulation, for example, was not only a source of needed revenue and the basis of independence from political control. It was also, in a positive sense, a source of political power. The ease with which a competitive position in the newspaper market could be converted into political power attracted politically ambitious men to the newspaper business. Editorial strategies designed to boost circulation, therefore, were often simultaneously designed to augment political influence and provide a stepping-stone to political office.

Even editors and publishers less enmeshed in factional or party politics stood to gain from the perception that circulation meant political power and influence. In this context, we can see why two smaller papers, the *Atlanta Evening News* and the *Georgian*, competed so strongly for circulation, and wielded political influence despite lacking direct access to political power. A symbolic representation of that political power may be found in the following scene: William Jennings Bryan visited Atlanta following the Democratic primary in August 1906, just before the race riot occurred. A "Democratic Dollar Dinner" was held, partly in Bryan's honor, partly to congratulate Hoke Smith on winning the primary, and partly as a fund-raiser for the party. On the dais at the main table the guest of honor sat beside the political leadership of state and city, Governor Joseph M. Terrell and Mayor James G. Woodward. Seated with them were Charles Daniel of the *Evening News* and Fred Seely and John Graves of the *Georgian*.[28] Like the women of the WCTU the following year, the state political leadership recognized the power of those wielding the printed word in Georgia.

Prohibition: Revival at the Margins

Can a deeper appreciation of the political power of newspaper editors and publishers in the Progressive Era South give us additional purchase on the dynamics of political development at the state and municipal level? Attending to the fairly sudden emergence of statewide prohibition in the South suggests it can. As noted, Georgia abandoned its 1885 local option policy in favor of statutory prohibition, in 1907. The Georgia General Assembly had, however, considered a very similar piece of legislation in 1899. Known as the Willingham bill after its chief sponsor in the Georgia House, the legislation would have imposed statewide prohibition in much the same manner as the law passed in 1907. While it passed the House by a comfortable margin (93 to 65), the bill was defeated in the Senate (26 to 14).[29] Why did prohibition succeed in 1907 but fail in 1899? I will argue that existing explanations for the timing of prohibition in the South cannot account for this, and that the presence of a newspaper openly campaigning for prohibition in 1907 supplies the missing piece of the puzzle.

We must also account for the sectional character of the prohibition movement that emerged in the wake of the Georgia decision. As historian Daniel

Whitener put it in his study of prohibition in North Carolina (which adopted statewide prohibition in 1908 by referendum):

> Hitherto in North Carolina [prohibition] had been regarded almost exclusively as an internal issue, having no important connection with similar movements in other states. Now, because a trend for prohibition in all of the Southern states had followed the adoption of the suffrage amendments, many writers looked upon the agitation as part of a sectional movement and as a development distinctly southern.[30]

Although Whitener identifies the trend toward prohibition as following disfranchisement of African American voters (this wasn't the case in Georgia), he does not explain just why prohibition should have taken on this southern flavor: after all, the South had been relatively hostile territory for prohibition in the nineteenth century. Even if whites could now register political differences over nonracial issues "safely," without worrying about handing the balance of power to black voters, why did southern whites suddenly identify prohibition as part of a distinctively regional political agenda? I argue that this was the rhetorical achievement of prohibition's advocates in Georgia: to embed the politics of alcohol within the terms of a larger, progressive and reforming, white supremacist statebuilding project.[31] In this form, as an intrinsic element of the Jim Crow state, prohibition triumphed across the South.

Understanding why prohibition traveled so swiftly, and via a southern route, from the margins to the mainstream of American politics, meanwhile, is crucial to providing a full explanation for the emergence of prohibition at the national level. The context of World War I, the adoption of the income tax, and the organizational and strategic differences between the ASL and earlier temperance and prohibitionist organizations all shaped the outcome at the national level.[32] None, however, explain why prohibition emerged with such strength from the South. From 1914 the movement for statewide prohibition spread across the West and Midwest, but the ASL had decided as early as 1913 to push for a national amendment, largely on the strength of the southern revival (and the emergence of a prohibitionist bloc of southern Democrats in Congress following the 1912 election).[33] The factors explaining the final success of that national push cannot retroactively explain the southern revival itself. War was at best a distant prospect in 1907, federal income taxes would not solve state and municipal revenue shortfalls, and all observers appear united in the view that the ASL had very little presence in the South during this period. To fully understand passage of the Eighteenth Amendment, we need to explain why prohibition emerged when and where it did.[34]

The problem with prevailing explanations at the regional level, however, is that they mostly turn on factors that operated with at least as much force in 1899 as 1907. Consider, for example, the background strength of evangelical influence in the South, which might suggest the region was particularly ripe for a prohibition revival.[35] As many historians have shown, in the antebellum period temperance and prohibition was largely a northern movement, connected in part to the strain of evangelical reform politics from which abolitionist sentiment also emerged (as Richard Hamm notes, prohibitionists were "abolitionist" about alcohol).[36] These associations did not endear the movement to southern whites (a Georgia senator argued in 1899 that prohibitionists were motivated by the "same spirit of intollerance [*sic*]" as northern abolitionists), and though Methodist and Baptist influence in the region grew steadily, prohibition sentiment lagged well behind other regions of the country.[37] Thus while the United States experienced periodic waves of enthusiasm for statewide prohibition in the nineteenth century, no southern state was sufficiently caught up in the movement to join them.[38] This is not to say that temperance held no appeal. The region had the usual panoply of fraternal organizations. Local affiliates, or autonomous parallel units, of national temperance organizations sprang up across the South, especially after the Civil War. Temperance, as a duty to personal teetotalism and to the use of moral suasion to induce others to personal salvation, was increasingly popular and influential; prohibition, as a legal imposition of controls on the manufacture, distribution, and sale of alcohol, was not.[39] The background evangelical culture, in other words, did not lead to stronger attachment to prohibition and was, in any case, a relative constant over the years between 1885 and 1907.

Movement toward legal enforcement of temperance began with the emergence of the WCTU in the 1880s, but focused on local option laws allowing individual counties to go dry by popular vote. This strategy was more closely adapted to prevailing preferences in the South for local autonomy, and sat more comfortably with attachments to personal liberty.[40] Indeed, as Robert Wiebe suggested long ago, this combination of local control and laissez-faire principles animated much of nineteenth-century political culture and institutions throughout the United States.[41] By adopting a more moderate approach to pursuing prohibition (pressing for four-mile bans on saloons around schools and churches, local option laws, and other forms of local regulation short of full prohibition), southern activists, affiliated with the WCTU or with independent evangelical churches, increased the percentage of dry land across the region mile by mile, county by county, as the turn of the century approached. By 1907, on the eve of statewide prohibition, fully 125 of Georgia's 145 counties were dry by local option.[42]

This slow accretion of counties into the "dry" column might appear to have prepared the way for eventual adoption of prohibition in 1907. Szymanski, for example, argues that the emphasis on local option laws and local regulation was intended to build public sympathy for more expansive forms of prohibition; an approach Szymanski calls "local gradualism." The strategy was not to pursue local option for its own sake, but to develop the breadth of sympathy and support from which a groundswell for statewide prohibition might emerge.[43] Georgia, however, had operated under local option since 1885 and most counties (around 117 of the then 137 counties) had already gone dry well before 1899. Those that remained "wet" contained the larger cities: Augusta, Savannah, Columbus, Rome, Athens, Brunswick, Macon, and Atlanta itself, as well as a handful of counties in the southwest of the state. The roughly twenty-county gap each year suggests that prohibition forces had little additional success between 1899 and 1907. With fourteen years of local option experience behind them, at least eleven senators and thirty representatives representing dry counties in Georgia voted against statewide prohibition in 1899.[44] There is little reason to think, given the lack of momentum for prohibition at the county level in the intervening years, that further experience with local option was chiefly responsible for shifting their allegiances eight years later.

Once in place, local option could just as well provide a barrier to statewide prohibition as a stepping-stone. Local option imposed prohibition mainly on those who already wanted it while allowing dry counties to benefit from liquor taxes appropriated to, for example, public education (thus a principal argument against the Willingham bill was that it would gut funding for public schools across the state).[45] Statewide prohibition, meanwhile, would reduce revenue for all counties, while imposing the cost of enforcing the policy on counties that would rather be wet. "One of the strongest points" against statewide prohibition, the *Constitution* insisted in November 1899, was local option's success in calibrating policy to prevailing local sentiment.[46] Louisiana's hasty passage of the Gay-Shattuck law in 1908, strengthening the state's local option provisions, was an explicit attempt to divert the rising tide of prohibitionist sentiment.[47]

Although the WCTU and the ASL may have considered local option a gradual and moderate path toward eventual statewide prohibition, the available evidence does not suggest that the strategy was working prior to 1907. The state WCTU had almost completely collapsed over women's suffrage, though new leadership in 1905 sparked a revival of its fortunes.[48] The ASL, meanwhile, did not name a superintendent in Georgia or Atlanta until 1905, and even then there was very little organization below this. In Georgia, "by 1906," in any case, "most prohibitionists had become divided and dispirited," historian David Godshalk argues, largely because Democratic Party leaders tacitly agreed among themselves to maintain the status quo. In the 1906 primary election for governor, the issue simply didn't come up because both candidates were committed to local option.[49] This, according to historian Morton Keller, reflected the national mood. Prohibition appeared to be moving backward: after some bursts of enthusiasm in the nineteenth century, only three states retained it by 1906 (Maine, Kansas, and North Dakota) and the laws were honored more in the breach than in the observance.[50]

The shift toward statewide prohibition required a more sudden trigger than either the background commitment to temperance or more than twenty years of experience with local option. The Atlanta race riot, which occurred over four days in late September 1906, appears to fit the case nicely.[51] As James Morone argues, movements for moral reform are often accompanied by a drive to exclude or eliminate a strange "other" or prompted by fear of infiltration. Previous cycles of support for statewide prohibition tracked the politics of immigration in the United States, and alcohol had long been associated with immigrant ethnicities and minority religions.[52] Immigration to the South was more limited, but the region had (for whites) its own native "other" in the form of black southerners. White southerners often associated black men with alcohol and violence, and blacks generally with lack of sexual restraint. The fact that the riot was occasioned by panic over alleged sexual assaults of white women by drunk black men, and broke out in Atlanta's entertainment district (at the time unsegregated), makes the connection nearly inevitable.

The sense of inevitability, however, is largely a product of hindsight. Sexualized racial stereotypes had animated the white imagination at least since the colonial era; they were certainly not new in 1906–7.[53] Nor was Atlanta the first riot to weave together issues of race, alcohol, and sexuality. Race riots were not rare in the progressive South, and major riots (racial massacres might be a better term) had broken out in Wilmington, North Carolina, in November 1898 and New Orleans, Louisiana, in July 1900. The precise dynamics and causes were of course unique. But discernible patterns and significant parallels link them to events in Atlanta in 1906.

The Wilmington riot, for example, took place in the context of partisan electoral competition in which Democrats used a virulent politics and rhetoric of white supremacy to beat back a challenge from Republicans and Populists in the state. The underlying tension, as in Atlanta in 1906, linked black men with the rape of white women in rural settings. The case highlights the racial limits of the political resources I have been attributing to newspaper editors and publishers in the period. Whites responded with fury to the publication of an editorial by Alex Manly, editor of the region's only black daily newspaper, the *Daily Record* (who was also a local officeholder). The editorial, published in August 1898, responded to a speech by Rebecca Latimer Felton, a member of Georgia's WCTU and a leading voice for white women in Georgia's (and increasingly the region's) politics. That speech, delivered in the previous year, chastised white men for failing to adequately protect their women from black rapists, leaving lynching as the only response. Manly responded by suggesting that the morals of poor white women were none too pure, white women often chose black lovers, and white men had a history of both interracial sex and sexual violence. In the context of a heated election campaign focused on white purity, the reaction was immediate and intense. Every day leading up to election day, white newspapers ran Manly's editorial along with accounts of alleged assaults by black men. Calls for violence were frequent and two days after the election a mob of white men stormed Manly's offices, destroyed his printing press, and set about killing men, women, and children in the relatively prosperous black Wilmington neighborhood. The event led to the forcible removal of the Republican mayor, his replacement by the man who had led the violence, and the exodus of up to 1,400 African Americans from Wilmington.[54]

New Orleans presents an even closer analogue to the Atlanta riot. The immediate spark was an act of violent defiance by one black man, Robert Charles, who responded to police harassment with gunfire. The manhunt and riot lasted for days, at the end of which Charles had killed nine white police officers and vigilantes and been killed himself. But this was only part of the story. The city's three leading newspapers had been "stridently racist" in tone throughout the summer, and one, the *Daily States*, implicitly endorsed mob violence in response to Charles's actions.[55] The mobs who gathered had very specific targets in mind: Storyville and the French Quarter. Storyville, at the time, was an unsegregated entertainment district where black, white, and mixed-race prostitutes practiced legally for a mixed-race clientele.[56] It functioned in some respects like the area around Decatur and Marietta Streets in Atlanta prior to the riot, where cheap alcohol, lowbrow burlesque, and sexual proximity of races and genders provided the thrill of the risqué in the saloons, cabarets, and brothels.

Whatever their proximate cause, these race riots were fueled by the sexual anxieties of white men and women and the associations of black men and women with sexual danger. City newspapers bent on whipping up those racial fears and stimulating violence fomented each, and the events in New Orleans presented the opportunity to link this heady brew with the availability of alcohol in Storyville and the French Quarter. However, no such link was made, and so while white supremacy was reestablished in both cases, the politics of prohibition was unaffected.

The context in which the 1899 Willingham bill was considered differed little from that of 1907. The cast of characters (white women and evangelical ministers on one side, city politicians and liquor interests on the other) was much the same, the issue excited "keen interest" across the state, and the galleries were packed with representatives of both sides during the Assembly debates.[57] Local option, meanwhile, had functioned successfully in the state for a lengthy period, and the context of white supremacy was also similar: against a background of lynchings and race riots, the legislature was debating a bill to disenfranchise African American voters in 1899 as in 1907.[58] In the former year, however, only one member of the Assembly sought to tie race to prohibition (he contrasted "good white women" marching to defend "prohibition and their homes" in Macon with "vile negro women singing ribald songs that would bring the warm blush to the cheeks of innocence" who marched ahead of them), and none connected prohibition to the larger Jim Crow project.[59] That connection awaited the rhetorical innovation of a crusading newspaper publisher and his able editor, who in 1907 would campaign on behalf of prohibition in much the same way as their competitors campaigned on behalf of candidates for public office.

Jim Crow Goes Dry

Fred Seely and John Graves of the *Georgian* and their allies overcame attachments to local option by presenting it as inadequate to address the racial danger explicitly contained in the dominant narrative of the Atlanta race riot. Racializing alcohol in this way served two purposes. First, it greatly augmented the perceived danger to suburban and rural communities of the ease of transport of alcohol (and potential rapists) by rail. The odd shipment of whiskey into a dry county might be given a wink and a nod if the recipient was thought to be a local white business owner; the flow of liquor in Atlanta was a distant concern to farmers in most rural counties in Georgia. Connected to images of racial and sexual menace, however, the same phenomenon could constitute a threat to southern white manhood. Presenting prohibition as a solution to the race problem, meanwhile, bound the policy to the aims of the Jim Crow state. Segregation, like prohibition, entailed state encroachment on private liberty, but both could be defended as part of the means by which the Jim Crow state maintained social (and racial) order.

The success of Seely and Graves in July 1907, however, relied on both the rhetorical achievements and institutional position of their Atlanta rivals as those had manifested themselves in the previous year. As both policy entrepreneurs and newspapermen seeking to augment their circulation and political influence, Seely and Graves were opportunists. Theirs was the last act in a drama that would begin with the primary campaign for governor in late 1905 and 1906. That campaign would find both major rivals, Hoke Smith and Clark Howell, attempting to prove the other soft on race. An alleged incident of rape became the focal point of the racially charged rhetoric of the campaign, and unleashed a wave of reports of "assaults" and "outrages" that carried beyond the primary election itself in August 1906 and into September. Though none of the incidents occurred in or near the entertainment district, they were increasingly linked to the saloons. Riding the wave of fabricated rage, a crowd of white men gathered in the entertainment district on the night of September 22 and began targeting black men, women, and businesses. Alcohol (and not Atlanta newspapers) was quickly identified as the cause of both outrages and riot, but not until the next session of the General Assembly, in June and July 1907, could this official narrative be deployed in support of prohibition itself. When the time came, the publisher and editor of the *Georgian* were ready.

In what follows I develop the role of Atlanta's newspapers in producing this entirely contingent set of events. The point is not merely to list a series of chronological happenings, or demonstrate that they could have been otherwise. Rather, the discussion delineates the conditions of possibility for a particular outcome. Consistent with other chapters in this book, nonstate actors drive the development of state authority.[60] The actions of political entrepreneurs in one moment, further, create the conditions to be exploited in the next.[61] The argument is not that the institutional context of Georgia is unique. Rather the combination forged in Georgia was quickly transmitted across the South by newspaper editors in comparable positions to those in Atlanta, in a region grappling with similar ideological tensions. I conclude with evidence of the influence of the *Georgian*'s rhetoric on the rapid spread of prohibition across the Jim Crow South.

The Primary: June 1905–August 1906

It was hardly inevitable that race would play such a prominent role in the 1906 gubernatorial election. Clark Howell was known to oppose disfranchisement, and stuck to that position throughout the 1906 campaign. But even Hoke Smith had been opposed when the issue was first raised in Georgia in 1899. Both were thoroughly white supremacist, but they were also paternalists, and saw no reason to alter the status quo. A white primary prevented black Georgians from voting in Democratic primary elections, and relatively few blacks voted in the general election. Smith was even optimistic, historian Dewey Grantham suggests, that racial tensions were diminishing. Smith was also a canny politician, however (the product of lessons learned the hard way), and hoped to secure the backing of Tom Watson before announcing his candidacy. The old Populist continued to command a formidable following in Georgia, and had long ago concluded that, to succeed, populism required eliminating black voting rights. Smith sought his public endorsement, and Watson's price was support for full disfranchisement. Once Watson was on board, however, Smith focused on attacking corporate power and railroad rates and promoting his raft of reform proposals, rather than on disfranchisement.[62]

Clark Howell, who had been planning his run for governor for some time, was naturally worried by the alliance of Smith and Watson. Then the *Constitution* (now boasting circulation close to 39,000) uncovered what it hoped would prove Smith's Achilles' heel: his hiring practices while secretary of the interior under Cleveland.[63] Smith had gone out of his way, the paper asserted, to pass over white applicants in favor of blacks, and names and salaries were produced to give credibility to the claim. This frontal attack on Smith's credentials as a white supremacist provoked a blistering response. Now foregrounding his newly discovered support for disfranchisement, Smith, from the pages of the *Journal* (whose own circulation now topped 46,000), hammered Howell as an advocate for political equality.[64] From December 1905, white supremacy took center stage (Smith claimed the railroads orchestrated the shift to take the heat off themselves), and while Howell and his *Constitution* continued to oppose disfranchisement, the tone and content of their arguments matched Smith's for racial vitriol. Disfranchisement would undermine the voting rights of poor and working white Georgians, Howell claimed, while the proposed educational qualification would entice black laborers out of the fields and factories and into college, producing more black men dissatisfied with their "place."[65]

The contest reached fever pitch in summer 1906 when the *Journal* seized on reports of an assault by a black man on a young white woman, alleged to have occurred on July 31, to up the ante: black participation in politics led directly to rape, and Howell and the *Constitution* were responsible:

> Political equality being thus preached to the negro in the papers and on the stump, what wonder that he makes no distinction between political and social equality. He grows more bumptious on the street, more impudent in his dealing with white men; and then, when he cannot achieve social equality as he wishes with the instinct of a barbarian to destroy what he cannot attain to, he lies in wait, as that dastardly brute did yesterday near this city, and assaults the fair young girlhood of the south.[66]

It was heady stuff. I will return to the gendered structure of this rhetoric later, but for the present we can note that alcohol was not yet part of the equation. The *Journal* sought a political advantage, and to tie its rival's supposed endorsement of political equality to the "one crime more heinous than all others."[67] But the effect dramatically heightened the racial tensions already playing out through the campaign, linking the course and outcome of the election to white fears of black sexuality. A campaign that had already dispirited black Atlantans with its uniformly antiblack rhetoric and focus now risked veering into hysteria.[68]

The centrality of race and disfranchisement in the 1906 primary resulted from choices made by the campaigns themselves. But because those campaigns were conducted from the newsrooms and editorial offices of the city's papers, those choices were perpetuated in news stories, editorials, and letter campaigns conducted by both major dailies. Similarly, it was by no means inevitable that the heightened tensions surrounding the gubernatorial election on August 22 would result in a riot a month later. The *Journal* had seized on the potential political advantage of attempting to link an alleged assault to its competitor's opposition to disfranchisement, but it required a full-blown public campaign to produce the sense of emergency that preceded the riot itself. For this, the *Journal*'s afternoon rival, the *Evening News*, was largely, though not uniquely, responsible.[69]

The Riot: September 22–25, 1906

Of course it was hardly new for southern papers to feature allegations of assault by black men. But the Atlanta *Evening News* was in trouble by August 1906 (its circulation less than 25,000 and apparently falling), and it needed a campaign, not just a few dramatic stories.[70] Where the *Journal*, and Hoke Smith, sought political advantage from a story of black criminality, the *Evening News* hoped to gain in circulation and revenue, and circulation meant political power and influence, not just profit. In the end the strategy would lead to the demise of the paper, but in the short run, spurred by an apparent rise (indeed doubling, if briefly) in circulation for the *News*, the other city newspapers jumped on the campaign.

The resulting fear and panic triggered the riot in September. The details of the riot have been fully discussed elsewhere, and I will limit myself to a very brief synopsis.[71] The July 31 attack on a young woman named Annie Poole took place in the newly emerging Atlanta suburbs (the scene, in fact, of most of the alleged assaults). The allegations led to a manhunt and eventual lynching of a man named Frank Carmichael. All the city newspapers covered the events in great (and varying) detail, from Annie Poole's description of the attack through the shooting of Carmichael, but the *Evening News* began a campaign for greater police presence and protection in the suburbs. Over the next seven or so weeks, newspapers reported story after story of assault and rape, with the *Evening News* eventually calling for the establishment of a KKK-style vigilance committee (the *News* Protective League). Both the *News* and *Atlanta Georgian* (which had begun publication earlier that year, also as an afternoon paper) publicly defended lynching, though the *Georgian* stopped short of endorsing the vigilance committee itself. Reports of assaults reached a crescendo on September 22, with afternoon papers running "Extras" claiming additional attacks throughout the day. In the morning, police began a sweep of downtown saloons and restaurants, confiscating "nude" pictures and arresting several owners on charges of indecency. In the evening a group of white men gathered in the Decatur Street area, where many of the saloons were located, and within a short time a mob formed and began to attack black men and women on the streets. Black businesses were targeted for vandalism, people were pulled from passing streetcars, and a large number of black Atlantans were shot or beaten to death.

What matters for our purposes is the dateable, and debatable, connection drawn between saloons and the assaults. It is not necessary to claim that no black men raped or assaulted any white women in July and August 1906. W. E. B. Du Bois, Ray Stannard Baker, and J. Max Barber all narrowed down at least a couple of verifiable attacks, though perhaps only one instance of rape.[72] As Mark Bauerlein points out, however, "assault" was an extremely elastic category. Legally, an assault was "an attempt" to commit violent injury, and an "assault with intent to rape" might be deemed to have occurred even "without actually touching the female." Conviction hinged on clarifying "intent," usually by trying to judge the demeanor of the accused. In these circumstances, an "assault" might be charged, especially in the newspapers, under the most flimsy circumstances, and the distinction between assault and rape was not kept clearly before the eyes of newspaper readers. This was the "crime wave" that wasn't, a fact that even the *Georgian* felt compelled to admit after the riot itself. Meanwhile, cases of white men arraigned on charges of rape went unreported.[73]

It was not until after the primary election, beginning on August 24, that newspapers began to link this supposed crime wave to the saloons. Given the vagueness of the charges of assault, and their location in the suburbs rather than downtown, the connections look forced to contemporary eyes. Nevertheless, concern over criminal behavior and "dives" was widespread and shared by black and white observers. More conservative black leaders, such as Benjamin Davis and prominent Atlanta minister Rev. Hugh Proctor, inveighed against saloons with at least as much vigor as the white press, and radicals such as Du Bois and Barber also saw saloon culture as socially destructive.[74] But white-owned daily newspapers wove a narrative that connected these saloons to black vagrancy and black vagrancy to criminal assaults against white women in the suburbs. The saloons fostered idleness and through provocatively posed pictures of white women (termed "nude" though in fact clothed) on beer bottles and posters encouraged black men to fantasize about sex with white women. Frustrated and sexually charged, these "brutes" would then, the supposition went, track down white women in relatively unprotected suburbs. Are "Negro Clubs the Cause of Assaults?" speculated the *Georgian* on September 21. But the *Journal* and *Constitution* had already decided the question: "Drive out the Negro Dives" was the relatively calm headline in the *Journal*, while the *Constitution* opted for the more emphatic "Clean out the Dives! Drive the Loafers and Vagrants to the Chain-gangs!" The superintendent of the state ASL, Rev. J. C. Solomon, was aware that the perceived emergency represented an opportunity. "The wild, vile passions of the vagrant can have no stronger vent," he intoned in the *Journal*, "than through the open dram shop. From the wedlock of the negro vagrant and the liquor den come the unspeakable crime."[75] The result was a lengthy city council investigation of the saloons, ongoing at the time of the riot, with many licenses revoked for alleged indecency.

When the day of the riot came, for almost a full month white readers had been fed, across all four dailies, and from almost all quarters, a regular diet of accounts of purported attacks by black men, linked to vagrancy, saloons, and liquor. The campaign had resulted in an increased police presence in the city and a city council investigation into the saloons on Decatur and Peters Streets. But the papers suggested that neither of these developments had had much impact on the volume of alleged assaults. Instead, the *Evening News* and *Journal* ramped up their coverage of assaults, with publication of periodic "Extras" throughout September 22. These extras were highly successful: on the day of the primary election, the *Georgian* had printed ten extras, updating the election results, and sold 38,310 copies of the paper in a single day.[76] On the day of the riot, the *Evening News* ran through at least five extras, each blaring news of a fresh assault (the state militia would ban extras when they took control of the city four days later). With at least one newspaper advocating lynch mob tactics, a group of white men (apparently from a variety of occupational and class backgrounds) decided to take things into their own hands.

Were other narratives of the riot, ones that did not link its origins to saloons and black criminality, possible? We can see from the accounts of Barber and Du Bois that they were, though we can also see the costs of articulating them. Barber's and Du Bois's accounts are very similar, and so I'll focus on Barber, who is less well known. The editor of the *Voice of the Negro* (in an initially anonymous letter to the *New York World*) insisted on the political motivations behind the emphasis on black criminality. Smith himself, Barber claimed, had orchestrated the stories of black criminals, even going so far as to dress white men in black face to scare white women.[77] No evidence substantiates the charge of a specific conspiracy (though Barber claimed to have it from a "prominent banker"), but his larger statement of the cause of the riot ("sensational newspapers and unscrupulous politicians") was sound, as was his remedy ("an impartial enforcement of the laws of the land"). Indeed, one can piece together a fair approximation of this same account (though without the specific charges against Smith) from Mayor Woodward's remarks to the papers in the days following the riot. When the *Evening News* finally went out of business, in December 1906, and was bought by the *Georgian*, its failure was widely attributed to its role in the September riot.[78] In the mouth of a prominent black intellectual, however, the claims were beyond the pale, and when Barber was discovered to be the author of the anonymous letter, he was quickly drummed out of town.

Prohibition and the Georgian: July 1907

By the end of October, Atlanta elites had got their story straight. The riot was not caused by an irresponsibly racist campaign for governor waged by Clark Howell and Hoke Smith, nor by sensationalist newspapers seeking increased circulation with largely fabricated stories of black bestiality, nor by white Atlantans of all classes rioting and looting the city and terrorizing and assaulting their black neighbors for four days. The riot had been caused by a rash of black assaults on white women, fueled by liquor and sexually provocative pictures in dens of iniquity, and by lower-class white men, similarly loosened from restraint by alcohol consumed in downtown saloons. The response was swift: the complete closure of all saloons in the city, followed by a gradual reopening under a new regulatory and licensing system. The effect was to close almost all saloons catering to black customers, to enforce de facto segregation in saloons (which had not been the case before the riot), and to price alcohol sold in saloons and restaurants beyond the reach of lower-income whites and blacks. Taken together, the effort represented a coherent reordering of Atlanta's social space along white supremacist lines.[79]

Even so, the push for statewide prohibition was not foreordained, and considerable resistance to prohibition remained. The WCTU and ASL quickly coalesced around a common strategy to use the momentum of the riot to push for prohibition. But Atlanta mayor Woodward and the city council more generally opposed prohibition on the grounds of lost revenue to the city as well as local autonomy.[80] There was also a more general business (and especially tourist business) interest in maintaining legal access to alcohol under the newly imposed regime.[81] In addition, the *Constitution* and *Journal* opposed prohibition, along with Atlanta's representatives in the Assembly. Indeed, Hoke Smith, although he would cheerfully sign statewide prohibition when it reached his desk, took the opportunity of his inaugural speech to defend local option as preferable.[82] The situation was beginning to look a lot like 1899 all over again, suggesting the *Georgian* was not merely pushing an open door when it began its campaign: if politicians as calculating as Smith were prepared to stick with local option, public sentiment must have been mixed at least.

The inauguration of Governor Smith, and with it the start of the new legislative session, did not occur until the end of June 1907. The *Georgian* took the opportunity of the inauguration to reinforce its own support for Smith, and articulate its understanding of Jim Crow. The paper noted the "absence of ultra-radicalism" in Smith's address, but the governor was also "unflinching as to the call for the establishment of racial superiority and vigorous as to the demand for the purity of elections and the reform of politics." To the *Georgian*, the election of Smith not only ensured white supremacy but also signaled the end of corporate corruption of state politics, and the renewal of Georgia. The paper announced, "there is a quarter of a century of mistaken drift behind the current turned into a new and nobler channel today."[83]

Prohibitionists worried, however, that wavering Georgia senators would find sufficient cover behind Smith's inaugural address, as well as the delegations from Savannah, Augusta, and other cities, to vote to keep the local option status quo. Standing up for noble sentiment, once more, the *Georgian* came off the fence and announced its support for prohibition. Its intervention shifted the terms of the debate decisively, *substantively*, by linking prohibition to a state duty to protect whites from racial danger, and *performatively*, by presenting its stance as one of high principle, manly conduct, and moral purpose. On Saturday July 6, Fred Seely devoted the top half of the front page of the *Georgian* to a declaration of principles. The *Georgian* would commit itself to prohibition on three grounds. First, prohibition was best for the people as a whole. Second, the economy would benefit from money diverted from liquor to other activities. Third, "it would do more to regulate the negro who commits his greatest crime because of liquor, and whose most venal appetites are fired by it." "The *Georgian* believes," Seely declared, "that the acts that brought on the Atlanta riot were committed largely because of the aid of liquor. The *Georgian* and the people KNOW that the riot was started by men from the saloons on that Saturday night." The conclusion was clear, and Seely dismissed concerns that prohibition "did not prohibit" (as the phrase went) out of hand. The experience of northern states could not serve as an example to states with large black populations.[84]

From this beginning, the *Georgian* essentially devoted its remaining July issues to the promotion of prohibition. If the *Constitution* and *Journal* had formed the center of the respective campaigns of Howell and Smith, the *Georgian* now adopted the same techniques on behalf of prohibition. Mass meetings were announced, petitions printed, speeches transcribed and published, and the *Georgian* encouraged the ASL in its attempt to organize a slate of pro-prohibition candidates in the upcoming city primary elections. While the ASL was busy circulating old speeches by Henry Grady, the *Georgian* made sure its Saturday edition endorsing prohibition was on the desk of every member of the state Assembly when the session opened on July 9. The paper, the *Georgian* was pleased to note, "was read with keen interest."[85]

The development of particular arguments was often left to highlighted speeches. An especially powerful speech by Seaborn Wright, state senator from Floyd County, illustrates the technique. The speech was delivered to a reported crowd of 4,500 men and women at the Baptist Tabernacle on July 7. The meeting itself was preparatory to a day of meetings in which Methodist ministers and the Evangelical Minister's Association (the latter under the guiding hand of ASL superintendent Solomon) endorsed the public stand of the *Georgian*. The *Georgian* first reported the meeting at the Tabernacle on the front page, along with its resolution in favor of prohibition, and mentioned Wright's impassioned speech. On page 5, the paper offered its own summary of the speech, with dramatic commentary on its effect on the assembled crowd ("he told in vibrant intensity of voice of the nameless terror that lay on the humble country homes of the state since the riots in Atlanta," "faces grew tense and drawn with feeling," and so on). The speech itself was reproduced in full between pages 5 and 13 (the *Constitution* also reported on the speech, but without the scope of racial imagery reproduced in the *Georgian*).[86]

The effect was to pull the reader into a closer examination of the speech itself, and Seaborn Wright did not disappoint. The main arguments in favor of local option were financial and grounded in local autonomy. Wright made short work of the financial argument, noting the cost of the state militia sent in to control the riot; prohibition would not cost the state treasury as much as that. Local autonomy, on the other hand, assumed what another speaker called a "Chinese wall" between the counties, a wall easily breached by modern communications and roaming vagrants. It was not just, however, that roaming vagrants could drink in the downtown saloons of Atlanta and then make their way out to the suburbs. The problem had been extended across the entire state by the spread of telegraph wires and railroads. Now the vagrant in a rural dry county had access to the same liquor for sale in Atlanta. Of course, prohibitionists had argued in 1899 that orders by telegraph and mail order, delivered by railroads (and now further stimulated by the 1905 Supreme Court decision in *American Express Company v. Iowa*), made dead letters of local dry ordinances. But Wright's imagery connected this worry about the permeability of borders and loss of control to deeper fears of sexual violation and disruption of the home. The Atlanta riot had, Wright told the assembly, "put terror into the home of every white man in the country districts of this state": "There is not a moment when his wife and children are away from him that the shadow of a great fear does not rest upon him—and sometimes he comes back to find the dead body of his child, and his ruined wife before him. And do you know that your Atlanta liquor has done it?"[87]

The tension is palpable, intentionally heightened by the buildup the *Georgian* has given the speech, and by the interjections Wright delivered to the assembly in his apparent attempts to keep the attention of his emotional audience.

The argument of the *Georgian* pivoted around this central extension of racial threat across the state and into the homes of individual white men. Rural homes, far from the protection of city police, were contrasted to comfortable, protected, white businessmen who need not fear for their wives and children. The same city men were castigated for their lack of courage in defending white womanhood ("outside of the official life of this great city, white Anglo-Saxon men are going to defend their women. Do you hear it?" declared Wright), with perhaps a hint that their racial standing was also in question.[88] Indeed, the attack on moneyed liquor interests itself, while clearly in line with the *Georgian*'s generally anticorporation stance, here became caught up in innuendos of racial betrayal. Arguing for local autonomy began to look not merely unequal to the task of regulating liquor but craven, ignoble, and unmanly.

The *Georgian* highlighted this latter theme through the very performative stance adopted by the paper from the moment it declared itself for prohibition. The move, Seely claimed in his opening editorial, might prove to be financially ruinous for the paper, and he intimated that various advertisers had threatened to pull their advertisements should the *Georgian* not back local option. The *Georgian* was not to be moved by mere financial considerations, however (at least not if increased circulation was a possibility). Nor, Seely insisted, had the paper come under the sway of a "sentimental-religious point of view." The *Georgian*, rather, was "in the fight on a manly, free and business basis—not to be run by preachers and men, but to run with preachers—good men—and women, for God, home, and native land." Wright's references to the defense of women by white Anglo-Saxon men sounded a similar note, as did a guest editorial titled "An Appeal for Manhood with Backbone."[89]

The editorial stance of the *Georgian*, therefore, invited readers to the performance of whiteness as noble self-sacrifice, and as chivalrous defense of virtuous white womanhood. Merely buying the paper represented a stand against the (unnamed) nefarious interests seeking to use their wealth to ruin the paper and the state (the paper reported a 4,200 increase in circulation within a week). But letters and resolutions of support also flooded into the paper, as far-flung readers endorsed the mix of manly self-assertion, moral purpose, and white supremacy for which the paper stood: the *Georgian* went out of its way to print as many as possible.[90]

The performance suggests a deliberate displacement. John Temple Graves would later virtually airbrush the preachers, ASL, and the WCTU out of the story of Georgia prohibition.[91] But the Georgia WCTU was actively coordinating rallies and propaganda efforts with the ASL and local religious leaders, and its president, Mary Harris Armor, clearly hoped for the same arrangement with the *Georgian*. She wrote asking Seely to devote some portion of his paper, either daily or on Saturdays, to the WCTU for them to fill with prohibition propaganda. He printed the letter, but clearly had no intention of fulfilling the request.[92] When the bill passed the Senate, Armor simply thanked the paper for doing the next best thing (devoting itself to propaganda efforts of its own).[93] The interchange reveals both the limits of Armor's politics and the determination of Graves and Seely to mold prohibition to their own ideological vision. The Georgia WCTU was not above playing on the racial implications of its coding of wet and dry as black and white (the *Constitution*, unlike the *Georgian*, noted that a WCTU map of wet and dry counties had been left on the desk of each member of the Assembly with the caption "Shall the Blacks Rule the Whites?").[94] Armor's WCTU was substantially more conservative than its national counterpart in other ways as well, rejecting woman's suffrage in 1899, for example.[95] The greater attachment to gender norms in Southern politics thus mediated the "domestication" of politics described by historian Paula Baker.[96] Less threatening to the still masculine rituals of Southern politics, the WCTU was correspondingly less able to prevent the co-optation of social politics by those same rituals. Thus Graves and Seely presented prohibition as an assertion of masculinity, and a defense of the home. In their rhetorical space, women were sexually vulnerable wives contained within the home, or abstract emblems of "pure womanhood." As with animal welfare policy in the North, or municipal court reform in Chicago, women's groups were certainly active in pursuit of prohibition, but their capacity to shape the rhetorical meaning of the shift was constrained, at least in the South, by the degree to which the state itself was conceived, by white southern men, as an extension of male household authority.[97]

The *Georgian* then, along with its editor and publisher, performed what they sought to establish. Their own self-sacrifice and assertion of Anglo-Saxon manhood sustained the illusion of Jim Crow as the basis of a noble, principled reformation of state government, a seizing of power by men from craven interests, a righting of the natural order against assertive black men and against women of all races. Prohibition could be understood as coincident with and supportive of this white supremacist project insofar as it was seen to respond to an essentially racial threat to white masculinity. More than that, passing prohibition could be construed as itself an act of white manhood, in which white Anglo-Saxon men regained their capacity to defend their homes precisely by lodging that capacity in the white supremacist state itself. This rhetorical innovation gave license to white southern men across the region to identify their own masculinity, and their own racial identity, with the successful march of prohibition.

Across the South: 1907 and Beyond

Absent this identification with white supremacy it is difficult to explain why prohibition came to be seen as "distinctly southern," in Whitener's words. By 1909 six states had adopted statewide prohibition in rapid succession: Georgia, Alabama, Mississippi, Oklahoma, North Carolina, and Tennessee. Outside the South no new state other than West Virginia in 1912 adopted prohibition prior to 1914 when the ASL began to find success in the West and Midwest. Arkansas, Virginia, and South Carolina would all follow suit by 1915.[98] If Georgia was the spark, the resulting wildfire spread quickly. But it did not do so randomly. Initial policy adoption clustered primarily in those states coincidentally struggling to implement and secure a specific institutionalization of white supremacy. The rhetorical identification of prohibition as part of the solution to "the race problem" was new when the editor and publisher of the *Georgian* hit on it in 1907, but the conditions that facilitated the promulgation and reception of this rhetoric were shared with states across the South.

A search of southern newspapers in the Library of Congress Historic American Newspaper archive underscores the fact that such rhetorical connections were almost never made prior to the Atlanta race riot, and that the explicit connection of prohibition to Jim Crow developed out of the Georgia campaign.[99] In the period from November 9, 1897, to July 27, 1901 (from roughly a year before the Wilmington riot to around a year after the New Orleans riot), only one news story, in the *Sumter* (South Carolina) *Watchman and Southron*, linked saloons to black crime of any sort (here with a rise in youth crime).[100] Similarly, in the year leading up to the Atlanta riot (September 21, 1905–September 21, 1906), race was linked to defense of the state dispensary system in a gubernatorial debate printed in the *Keowee* (South Carolina) *Courier*, but only to suggest the dispensary allowed the state to "recoup" money spent on black education.[101]

The year after the Atlanta riot, by contrast, saw an explosion of stories connecting race and alcohol, often on front pages. A closer look at the stories reveals a temporal dimension to the coverage, as well as the influence of the Georgia debates. Between October 1906 and July 1907, newspapers across the South reported on the events in Atlanta, generally adopting the dominant white narrative of events, and thus beginning to connect alcohol with race relations. From July 1907 on, coverage shifted to the successful passage of statutory prohibition in Georgia, and the knock-on effects in other states: Alabama introduced a bill for prohibition in July of that year; by September Pensacola was in the midst of its own campaign for prohibition in the city.[102] A separate campaign in Jacksonville "comes as a result of the Georgia prohibition bill," the *Panama City* (Florida) *Pilot* noted in September 1907, and predicted that Florida, Alabama, Mississippi, Louisiana, and Texas would follow Georgia's lead "until we have a solid South for prohibition."[103] Seaborn Wright, John Graves, and Fred Seely, meanwhile, took an active part in all of these campaigns, giving speeches in Pensacola, visiting Birmingham, Alabama, and other cities. Newspapers across the region were crystal clear that Georgia had sparked a regionwide movement, and that Seely, Graves and Wright were driving it forward. They occasionally reprinted Seely's editorial in the *Georgian* from back in July to make the point.[104]

In the context of these fast-spreading prohibition drives, newspapers increasingly adopted the view that prohibition, if not defensible on its own terms, was now an integral part of managing the South's racial order. Many adopted the "manly" tone the *Georgian* had struck (one declared the "moral stamina and virility of the southern people" against the scourge of the open saloon), praising one another for their "courageous and patriotic manhood."[105] But the crucial shift was toward linking prohibition to white supremacy. Thus, a formerly antiprohibition Mississippi newspaper announced in September 1907, that "taking the saloon and its bearing on the race problem the [*Jackson Daily*] *News* has reached the point where it believes that prohibition is best for the South."[106] "Run the saloons out the South," the *Pensacola Journal* declared, "and the Race Problem will be practically solved."[107] Barely considered in relation to race before the Atlanta riot, prohibition had now become integral to the Jim Crow state.

We ought to see in this rhetorical achievement, then, not only a successful innovation on the part of proponents of prohibition but also a successful attempt to shape the meaning and purpose of Jim Crow. By attaching prohibition to the defense of white supremacy, advocates increased the popularity of a policy that had never commanded sufficient popular or elite support to become law. But folding prohibition (along with child labor laws, abolition of the convict lease system, opposition to railroads and other large corporations) in beside segregation and disfranchisement as part of a single political project formed an important part of the ideology of Jim Crow itself. The guiding impulse of Jim Crow was paternalist, and prohibition, as Alexander McKelway later explained in the pages of the *Outlook*, represented a voluntary renunciation of liberty on the part of white elites in the name of social order.[108] The capacity for self-denial, indeed, was just what distinguished these farsighted elites from black and lower-class white southerners, and grounded their right to rule.[109] Thus we should see the adoption of prohibition as part of the struggle to give ideological shape and legitimacy to the emerging Jim Crow order: a legitimacy that depended in part on its full-throated white supremacy, it is true, but also on its self-presentation as a moral response by powerful elites to corruption, violence and disorder on the part of the lower classes, and interference from northern busybodies. This process enabled the broader system of Jim Crow to generate the expectations of fairness and equal treatment that would later underpin efforts at its reform.[110]

Conclusion

Prohibition was propelled from the margins to the mainstream of southern, and then American, politics not merely by geographical proximity to race prejudice or temporal proximity to a race riot but by the cumulative effect of overlapping rhetorical, political, and market-driven strategies pursued by the four major newspapers in Atlanta between 1905 and 1907 (and then by similarly placed newspapers across the South). The account offered in this chapter illustrates the entanglement of press and politics in this era, and illustrates the direct role of newspapers in shaping electoral and policy outcomes, whether through influence over party platforms and policy agendas, by organizing and running electoral campaigns, or through mobilization of public opinion. All three processes influenced the tortured progress of prohibition through Georgia politics in the years prior to 1907, as local newspapers drove campaign agendas, framed narratives of race, crime, and alcohol, and rhetorically and performatively connected these narratives to prohibition. As in other cases in this book, actors positioned outside the formal institutions of the state were key to expanding its authority over private lives.[111]

In making this argument, I have described a series of interlocking events, distributed across a short window of time: if newspapers had not doubled as campaign offices, the story of the alleged assault on Annie Poole would not have become the centerpiece of a racially fraught electoral campaign; without this, the *Evening News* might have found a different cause to drive its quest for circulation; and had it done so, "outrages" might never have been connected with the "low dives" on Decatur. Prohibition would not, as a result, have received the boost of urgency it got from being discovered as "the solution" to the race problem.

But if we simply see a series of events that might have happened otherwise we miss the significance of the tale: a specific institutional arrangement (of newspapers and political power) structured the interactions and opportunities detailed above. Attending to this structure shows why newspaper editors and publishers, and not the ASL or WCTU, had the capacity to drive the campaign for prohibition and determine its terms. It provides an account of the resources available to newspaper editors and publishers as policy entrepreneurs, resources that offered them the power to shape and wield public opinion to their own ends, at times influencing the direction of public policy. True, white supremacist rage and anxiety, evangelical commitment, and experience with local option formed an essential backdrop to the particular framing of prohibition developed in the pages of the *Georgian*. But those ideas and assumptions had to be marshaled within institutions connected to political power, and shaped to the defense of accounts of state power and public policy that did not inevitably flow from popular or elite commitments alone.[112] Understanding the expansion of state capacity and state authority in the Progressive Era, even at the federal level, meanwhile, requires attending to the quite different constellations of political power at the state and municipal level that, for a time, structured these possibilities.

Chapter 3

Statebuilding Through Corruption: Graft and Trash in Pittsburgh and New Orleans

Kathleen S. Sullivan and Patricia Strach

Progressive Era cities faced garbage disposal problems. As mounting trash filled streets, dumps, and rivers, municipal officials in Pittsburgh and New Orleans considered a new and expensive solution, reduction, in which trash was converted into profitable byproducts such as grease and fertilizer.[1] In 1895, Pittsburgh awarded a reduction contract to the American Reduction Company while a year earlier New Orleans awarded one to the Southern Chemical and Fertilizer Company. Both cities followed a remarkably similar trajectory: garbage became a problem, reduction was a solution, the cities chose reduction, and controversy followed. However, while Pittsburgh built the plant and flourished, the New Orleans plant never got off the ground. Massive public resistance and accusations of corruption brought down reduction, the Southern Chemical and Fertilizer Company, and the New Orleans mayoral administration.[2] If the cities were similarly situated—large, important, commercial centers with corrupt political administrations—why was reduction successful in Pittsburgh but not in New Orleans?

In this chapter, we suggest that the answer lies in the nature of corruption in each city. Though historians describe both cities as having political machines, Pittsburgh's machine was both centralized and integrated (city, county, state, and business).[3] It was often legally (but unethically) able to accomplish its goals. The New Orleans machine, however, was not well established. Power in the city was diffuse (between city officials and between businessmen and city officials) and corruption took the form of boodle (or bribes) to city officials and bureaucrats. Stable and strong political machines, as in Pittsburgh, could better ensure that expensive long-term investments in public works, such as reduction plants, would be profitable. Machines that were not fully established, as in New Orleans, could not sustain this type of deep investment. We find that corruption—rather than always being a hindrance—is also a resource marshaled (more or less successfully) to solve municipal problems.[4] By comparing these two similarly situated governments (large commercial centers with corrupt administrations) we show that statebuilding does not just rely on reformers with good intentions but may also occur through the actions of unsavory actors who engage in illegal or unethical activities.

The Progressive Era is noted for those reformers who cleaned up government, society, and streets, often by establishing the necessary agencies and staffing them with qualified labor. City bosses and political machines have traditionally stood out as another urban problem that progressives sought to reform and do away with. Historians of cities, though, have pointed out that machines were equipped to engage in statebuilding projects of their own. Machine politicians built their voting base by reaching out to new immigrant populations, providing social services and order. The search for more opportunities for patronage and spoils invited them to launch new public works projects and open new agencies.[5]

Though reformers and machines seem to achieve results in radically different ways, Jon Teaford has suggested that the "boss-reformer synthesis" in the study of political corruption has diverted attention from "consideration of the vital services at the heart of urban rule."[6] Jessica Trounstine has likewise demonstrated that there are remarkable similarities between machines and reformers, referring to them as "political monopolies."[7] Building on Teaford and Trounstine we, too, assume that both reform and corrupt administrations can provide services, though how those services are provided may be very different. Our work differs, however, in the attention to variation within corrupt administrations. In short, not every form of corruption is equally able to meet municipal needs. Instead, we show under what circumstances corruption may ensure the provision of public services through public-private contracts. For developing municipal governments that lacked the capacity to provide services themselves, contracting to local businesses proved to be an attractive option. At the turn of the century, political corruption and collusion promised certainty: exclusive partnerships practically guaranteed favored individuals would receive contracts and these favored contractors, in turn, would invest in new technologies. According to Nathaniel Leff, "if entrepreneurs are to make investments, they must have some assurance that the future will not bring harmful intervention in their affairs."[8] Corrupt but stable administrations were able to withstand criticism and allow contractors to carry out the work. Weak ones could not. In short, political corruption paired with political stability allowed cities to provide new, expensive, and risky technology to municipalities in ways political corruption and political instability could not.

In this chapter we compare the role of corruption in Pittsburgh and New Orleans, as each city used public-private relations when they introduced garbage disposal by reduction. Taking a somewhat different tack from several of the other chapters in this volume, we put governance—how things are done—rather than government—the particular elected public actors (mayors, supervisors) or activists (progressive reformers)—at the center of our analysis.[9] Nonetheless, actors are important in our story for how they connect, and these connections link this chapter to others that explore public-private partnerships. By following the lines, or relations, between actors we construct a different picture of statebuilding, a statebuilding that does not just happen through the work of government officials, activists, or policy experts. Rather, capacity is built and authority seized through the work of what we typically think of as private or quasi-private agents using alternative means. In our narrative, political machines are agents of change and political corruption is a resource on which municipalities rely. In Pittsburgh, the machine successfully brought new technologies to meet local challenges while in New Orleans it failed and reverted to a primitive mode of trash disposal (dumping). In both cases, the machine-constructed architecture of trash disposal was appropriated by the following administration and continued on long after the machine was gone from power. Political machines and the corruption by which they accomplished their goals—however imperfect and marginalized in historical accounts—were important agents in political development, connecting a municipality with the actors and capacity it needed to provide new services.

The Rise of Garbage as a Problem

Where population concentrations were sparse, garbage was not usually a problem. Householders could bury their trash in the backyard, feed animal and vegetable waste to chickens, pigs, or hogs, and collect ashes from fires and use it as filler in low-lying lands and vacant lots.[10] In metropolitan areas, these individual methods were not viable on a large scale. For a while cities could accommodate the larger population by expanding on the usual, primitive ways waste was disposed of. In some cases, farmers set up routes in small cities and villages to collect garbage to feed to swine, while in others garbage was thrown onto fields or used as fill on streets.[11] However, as urban populations grew in the late nineteenth century, industrial changes in spatial patterns and schedules undermined individual capacity or piecemeal solutions to dispose of garbage. It was hard to ignore the resulting "Heaps of garbage, rubbish and manure" that "cluttered alleys and streets, putrefied in open dumps, and tainted the watercourses into which refuse was thrown."[12] Sanitarians from the engineering and public health professions were appalled by these mounting piles of decomposing waste. Businessmen lamented the impassibility of streets littered with trash. Social reformers sought to clean up the streets along with political corruption. Politicians, on the other hand, recognized garbage as a problem when it suited them; otherwise they were content to ignore it.

Sanitarians were some of the first and loudest advocates for addressing the garbage problem, especially in New Orleans, where the climate made the urban population susceptible to epidemic disease outbreaks. But the city did not heed their warnings. Despite the frequent and serious episodes of yellow fever in the antebellum era, the Board of Health was abandoned after each outbreak.[13] In 1852, for example, after erecting a swamp-draining program and successfully eliminating yellow fever for five years, its members were let go, with only a secretary remaining.[14] A Board of Health that existed in name only faced a yellow fever epidemic the next year. The New Orleans Sanitary Commission, established to study the outbreak of yellow fever and the city's sanitary conditions, condemned as sanitary threats the presence of kitchen offal, backyard filth, and reeking piles of filth along six miles of the riverbank.[15] Despite the concern, the city did not take measures to prevent another epidemic, leaving New Orleans "the filthiest hole in the land."[16]

The Board of Health lauded the contracting out of public works after the Civil War (even if due to financial constraints), citing resulting sanitary improvements.[17] After a ferocious bout of yellow fever in 1878, local, state, and national health agencies worked in coordination to combat the threat.[18] Sanitarians drew attention to dumping grounds described as a "festering, rotten mess" of garbage, containing dead dogs and cats, picked over by ragpickers and pigs alike.[19] New Orleans health experts were joined by the Auxiliary Sanitary Association (ASA). Formed in 1879 as a collection of merchants and concerned citizens, the ASA worked to diagnose the sanitary problems of New Orleans and lobbied for the creation of a board of public works. They were concerned less with sanitary standards than with clean, passable streets over which commerce could, literally, travel. The ASA believed that "political corporations cannot be depended upon for that prompt and sustained action which enables men trained in the severe school of business affairs to execute large undertakings with economy and dispatch." [20] The ASA initially identified problems with the city's privy systems, the drainage of lots, the water supply, and drainage canals.[21] The ASA went on to reform New Orleans' drainage system, extend its water supply, create public bath and wash-houses. It was prepared to finance garbage removal and disposal.[22]

The ASA was poised to work with the reform mayor, Joseph Shakspeare (who served in 1880–1882), and it looked as if sanitation in New Orleans, promoted by both sanitarians and businessmen, would finally make progress. But Shakspeare had to face John Fitzpatrick, an up-and-coming member of the New Orleans Ring, also known as the Regulars. Nicknamed "Captain John" for his service in the Louisiana National Guard, Fitzpatrick climbed the ranks of municipal politics in the 1880s, serving as the administrator of improvements and in the new position of commissioner of public works—the source of municipal patronage and corruption. He held this post for six years through reform and Ring mayors. Under his supervision, garbage collection was notoriously poor, but it employed many people. Records from June 1883 show that the Department of Public Works spent $7,614 on street "labor" (quotes in the original) and $3,422 on carts. The Department employed eighty carts (for various public projects, including garbage) to work an average of twenty-two days, at $2 per day. [23] But still, garbage was collected only sporadically.

By 1884, the Regulars were back in elected office. Any progress made by sanitarians and the ASA was rendered moot. The Fitzpatrick administration refused an ASA offer to provide resources for garbage collection and disposal.[24] A Citizens Committee formed to challenge the Ring, but it accomplished little.[25] The Board of Health reported in 1890 that householders and city employees were dumping garbage into the Mississippi River. Dumping was the preferred method of disposal, as the garbage would wash out to sea, but most of it lingered near shore, polluting the water supply and unleashing "another revolting odor to join those rising from the sewers and gutters."[26]

The New Orleans Ring was not much cleaner than its streets or its water. Historian Raymond Nussbaum explains: "Rarely had a machine administration been as corrupt as that headed by incumbent Mayor John Fitzpatrick. It had earned the dubious sobriquet 'boodle' administration and the city council had become known as the 'boodle' council."[27] The Ring was not merely corrupt, it was weak. In part, late nineteenth century New Orleans was characterized by instability—economic, political, and racial—and balance was elusive. Because neither reform nor Ring had enough votes to dominate electoral politics, both parties courted the black vote.[28] Reformers linked elite business interests and Creole support while the Ring relied on working-class and black residents.[29] Shifting elections back and forth reflected incomplete dominance by either party. But in part, the Ring's weakness reflected decentralized power. Unlike Pittsburgh, power was not in the hands of a single boss but held unevenly and collectively by city council members, city bureaucrats, and ward bosses. Thus, the Ring lacked the ability to enforce discipline on its affiliates and many of the city's businessmen were actively opposed to it.[30] To do business in New Orleans entailed boodling (bribing) a host of officials.

Like New Orleans, Pittsburgh's first foray into waste management was through its Board of Health. Though Pittsburgh's board was established later than New Orleans' board, it was authorized to do much more: "have all objects which may have a tendency to endanger the health of the citizens to be removed or corrected as they shall deem necessary for the health of the citizens."[31] The board took its job seriously, citing the "salvation of hundreds of human lives in this city, the health and happiness of thousands of this community" as dependent on clean streets and a pure atmosphere.[32] But the board lacked enforcement mechanisms, relying instead on individual compliance through privately initiated nuisance complaints with accompanying fines.[33] It also lacked administrative resources of its own, resorting to employing scavengers as needed to call on hotels, taverns, and dwelling houses.[34] Reliance on myriad scavengers and ragpickers for garbage collection was an imperfect solution in the eyes of health professionals.[35] Health officials attributed an 1880 typhoid epidemic and other disease outbreaks, especially in Pittsburgh's working-class South Side, to its topography, which was hilly and poorly drained, subjecting those in the low-lying lands to the refuse coming down the hillside.[36] Though the Board of Health suspected that the spread of disease was caused by the dirty reservoir, littered with the carcasses of cats and dogs, the filthy streets, alleys and sewers also came under suspicion.[37] One lot had garbage piled up to a depth of sixteen feet.[38] Health officials were skeptical that the city would be responsive.[39] Like New Orleans, the city's political officials did not heed the investigations and warnings of health officials.

Despite the skepticism, Pittsburgh's Ring was better disposed to develop public works than that of New Orleans. Run by City Treasurer Christopher Magee and street-paving contractor and Pittsburgh Republican Party Executive Committee Chairman William Flinn, the Magee-Flinn machine had a stable hold on Pittsburgh's politics from 1880 until the early twentieth century. Magee was a popular and well-liked politician who used his position to control utility and transportation franchises, the deposit of city funds, and the granting of construction contracts, as well as to funnel funds from the Pennsylvania Railroad and steer lucrative contracts to local magnates, including Flinn.[40] Magee consolidated power by pushing legislation through the state to reorganize the city charter in 1887 (electing heads of departments through city councils, which the Ring controlled). Together with the Upperman bill, which authorized second-class cities (of which Pittsburgh and Allegheny were the only ones in the state) to provide for municipal improvement, the reorganization "set the table for a veritable banquet of lucrative public works."[41] According to Lincoln Steffens, "The Magee-Flinn machine, perfect before, was made self-perpetuating. I know of nothing like it any other city. Tammany in comparison is a plaything, and in the management of a city [New York City's Richard] Croker was a child beside Chris Magee."[42]

Pittsburgh's director of public works, Edward Bigelow (who also happened to be Magee's nephew), kept the work flowing to Magee-Flinn leaders and loyalists. Page after page of Pittsburgh's annual report in 1897, for instance, lists Booth & Flinn as contractors hired for street paving and repairs.[43] In a report to the National Municipal League, reformer Oliver McClintock detailed the overt relationship between Pittsburgh's Public Works Department and Booth & Flinn in the nine years after the 1887 reorganization: "one firm [Flinn's] received practically all the asphalt-paving contracts at prices ranging from $1 to $1.80 per square yard higher than the average price paid in neighboring cities. Of the entire amount of asphalt pavements laid during these nine years, represented by 193 contracts, and costing $3,551,131, only nine street blocks paved in 1896, and costing $33,400 were not laid by this firm."[44] But Bigelow also required standards and improvements.[45]

After the Republican Party victory in the election of 1894, the newly elected regime got right to work when it took office in January 1895. It immediately raised revenue by introducing a new tax.[46] Flinn pursued his long-term plan of annexation of neighboring municipalities.[47] The state took initiative on sanitary measures, with state-associated health authorities meeting early in 1895 to discuss compulsory vaccinations, hygiene, typhoid control, rural public health, and the proper use of disinfectants. Pittsburgh's director of the Department of Public Safety was enlisted to draw up a general sanitary code for the state.[48]

Unlike Pittsburgh, where the Magee-Flinn machine was relatively stable for decades, in New Orleans the Ring was working hard to establish itself, using fraud, violence, and patronage to secure its position. Still, in the late nineteenth century New Orleans was incompletely dominated by machine politics as power shifted between Ring and reform governments. Joseph Shakspeare served as reform mayor for only two years (1880–82) before the reins were turned over to yet another administration. Mayor William Behan was elected as a Ring candidate in 1882, but failed to serve the Ring adequately during his administration. He joined the reform Citizens Party but was defeated by the Ring candidate, J. Valsin Guillotte, in 1884. Shakspeare was elected mayor once again in 1888 with hope for civic and political reform. By 1892, though, the Ring was back in power, this time with Fitzpatrick as mayor.

In his inaugural address, Fitzpatrick called attention to the contracts given out by the previous administration and promised to see that obligations were actually carried out.[49] A year later, however, complaints were mounting about trash. Though New Orleans' two major (and partisan) newspapers agreed on very little, they both ran critical stories about the trash problem. The City Council Committee on Public Health Reports and Actions noted an increasing number of proposed ordinances to solve the multiplying problems. Committee member William Garrelson proposed burning garbage under city contract while DesPorte recommended an ordinance for new garbage receptacles and penalties for failing to use them.[50] The Board of Health reported that "so many complaints come in from all directions . . . the garbage service of this city needs to be completely changed, since it is radically defective."[51] The city council planned to take up the problem with a fact-finding trip to determine how *other* cities dealt with removal and disposal. The *Daily Picayune* was critical: "Why is it that the refuse is not gathered up promptly and carried away to the garbage boats? Is it because there are too few carts, or because there is official neglect?"[52] And the *New Orleans Times Democrat* did not mince words: "The Department of Public Works, not only under its present Commissioner, but under the regime of previous commissioners as well, has made a complete and total failure of this municipal work. And, as after all these years of trial the result has been the same—failure, unmitigated failure—the hope may as well be abandoned at once that we are to have anything better with the continuation of the present unworkable system."[53]

While health experts, social reformers, and business interests had long been worried about garbage as a problem, they lacked the capacity to carry through on their own recommendations. Despite their vocal appeals to clean up cities, they did not bring about change and were largely shut out of the process. Unlike reformers in other policy areas discussed in this volume—Pearson and Smith's advocates for animals, Nackenoff and Sullivan's advocates for children, and Greer's private experts on American homes—the progressive sanitarians could neither organize their own intervention to address the problem nor convince state actors to partner with them. However, when the regime in each city was ready to dole out plum contracts and patronage, garbage was finally recognized as a problem. For the machine, garbage was a public problem now that it was a political opportunity.

The Solution: Reduction

New Orleans' and Pittsburgh's attention to garbage disposal were part of a national movement to address the problem of garbage collection and disposal. The National Municipal League met for the first time in 1894, and the League of American Municipalities in 1897. Such organizations allowed for shared research and cooperation across cities. Sanitarians and civic reformers spoke at annual meetings. Cities sent delegates on traveling tours to learn about methods of public works provision in other cities.[54]

As they made their decisions, cities had a variety of garbage disposal methods to choose from. "Primitive" methods were still in use and still considered adequate. Cities near large bodies of water could conveniently dump garbage into the ocean or lake. This worked until litter washed up on beaches, a problem as beaches began to attract visitors in the late nineteenth century.[55] To keep such disposal sanitary and acceptable, cities would need to invest in scows to dump the trash farther out at sea.[56] Cities might dump on land, which was not a problem if the city geography were laid out with adequate room. Developments in dumping included landfills, whereby organic and inorganic material were mixed, and plowing, in which garbage was tilled into soil. The latter was considered to be fully sanitary, yet the scope of trash made it difficult to plow it all.[57] Garbage could be fed to hogs. For years, cities allowed hogs to roam the streets, and when that became unwieldy some cities resorted to large-scale hog stations, which were sanitary if appropriate conditions were maintained.[58]

Some cities began to look beyond these primitive methods into the "artificial" methods of incineration and reduction. In 1887 the American Public Health Association established a committee on disposal of waste and garbage. The committee investigated garbage disposal technology in Europe, learning about the original reduction method developed in Vienna. By 1891, the majority of health officers, including renowned water and sanitary engineer Rudolph Hering recommended incineration (burning) or reduction (creating usable by-products).[59] For reduction to work properly, garbage (animal and vegetable waste) needed to be separated from ashes (which could be used as fill) and refuse (which could be scavenged and resold).[60] The reduction plant was designed to allow garbage carts to dump their contents into hoppers, "ingenious mechanical contrivances being used both to open the trap doors of the hopper and to dump the refuse."[61] Garbage continued its way along a series of chutes, conveyor belts, and specially appointed containers. Sorters picked out any remaining saleable refuse. A conveyor belt directed bottles and tin cans down their own chutes to their own bins. Worthless refuse was sent to an incinerator. Once sorted through, garbage that was to be reduced was heated and digested by using a solvent or by being squeezed in a hydraulic press. Either process removed the moisture and grease, which was then contained.[62] Dissolved and suspended organic matter were gathered as fertilizer.[63] Grease, fertilizer, and even excess steam could be sold.[64]

Though garbage *collection* did not require technical experts or equipment (it entailed coordination of horses, carts, drivers, and householders, and could be a decentralized operation), garbage *disposal* was increasingly the purview of specialists—technical experts in the mechanics of collection and disposal, not necessarily sanitation or municipal professionals. Garbage carts that collected trash arrived at a single disposal site, so garbage disposal required larger scale capacity than collection. The presence of animal and vegetable waste promised putrefaction and unsanitary conditions that had to be dealt with using methods of public health and engineering. Engineers had their own network, sharing information about innovative methods of garbage disposal in professional associations at the local, state, and national level, and circulating knowledge in professional journals. In contrast to other policy areas, this concentration of knowledge left reformers at a loss. Civic and social reformers and local business interests, who cared about clearing garbage off the streets and lots, lacked the expertise needed to develop and administer garbage disposal, especially when conducted through one of the more innovative artificial methods. Sanitarians, business interests, and social reformers were squeezed out of the decision-making process by political elites and technical experts who did not need to listen to their advocacy. By 1901 health officials lamented that

> in no branch of municipal service has so little progress been made in the United States as in the disposal of garbage. Why do such conditions exist? First, because the sanitary collection and disposal is appreciated neither by the general public nor the city officials, second because it is seldom recognized that the problems incident to final disposal are largely engineering in character and therefore should be entrusted to engineers.[65]

Because of the resources needed to run a reduction plant, plants were left to the technical authorities, namely, engineers, for their "very efficient technical administration," and to chemists and other highly skilled labor.[66] Experts were also needed to prevent the dangers created by the process—the use of a flammable solvent could ignite the reduction plant, as it did in Chicago, St. Paul, and Paterson, New Jersey.[67] Garbage disposal, then, by the end of the nineteenth century "already a most perplexing, municipal problem . . . [was] essentially engineering in character."[68] Once a city chose a reduction plant, it put those technical experts in charge. If their approach to garbage was in conflict with sanitarians or civic reformers, so be it.[69]

Reduction plants were also expensive. Although reduction promised an eventual profit from by-products, it required a large initial investment in construction of the plant, legal arrangements, sale of land, and engineering costs. Annual costs included the fixed charges of interest, depreciation, and sinking fund, and operation costs including supervision, labor, repairs, supplies, fuel and power, and miscellaneous costs.[70]

Table 1. Garbage Disposal Techniques (percent of cities)

Type of disposal	*Cities*	*Large cities*	*Northern cities*	*Southern cities*
Cremated	23	22	15	41
Fed to swine	23	20	38	0
Dumped	22	16	13	24
Reduced	**13**	**22**	**15**	**6**
Farmed/plowed/ fertilized	11	13	10	12
Buried	6	7	8	6
Burned	3	0	3	12

Data for 93 cities; 16 cities have two types of disposal; columns may not add due to rounding.
Authors' analysis of data from Charles V. Chapin, *Municipal Sanitation in the United States* (Providence, R.I.: Snow and Farnham, 1901), supplemented by C.-E. A. Winslow and P. Hansen, "Some Statistics of Garbage Disposal for the Larger American Cities in 1902," *Public Health Papers and Reports* 29 (1903): 141–65.

Table 2. Cities Using Reduction, 1900

City	*Region*	*Population*
New Bedford, Mass/	North	62,442
Buffalo, N.Y.	North	352,387
New York, N.Y.	North	3,437,202
Utica, N.Y.	North	56,383
Erie, Pa.	North	52,733
Philadelphia, Pa.	North	1,298,697
Pittsburgh, Pa.	North	321,616
Cincinnati, Oh.	Midwest	325,902
Cleveland, Oh.	Midwest	381,768
Columbus, Oh.	Midwest	125,560
Detroit, Mich.	Midwest	285,704
St. Louis, Mo.	Midwest	575,238
Washington, D.C.	South	278,718

Given the technical nature of the enterprise and its expense, few cities actually built reduction plants before 1900. At the turn of the century, thirteen cities (of the ninety-three for which we have data) used reduction (see Tables 1 and 2).[71] These cities were large (all had populations greater than 50,000, the vast majority more than 100,000) and had significant manufacturing or commercial industry, suggesting that adoption relied on recognizing gains from economies of scale.[72] However, by 1909, ninety-four reduction plants were operating in seventy-nine cities. Only two were owned by cities; the rest were run by private parties.[73] The proliferation of reduction plants accompanied a more general garbage reform movement in cities across the country in the late nineteenth and early twentieth centuries. The American Public Health Association continued to recommend new technologies, including reduction.[74] Some leading figures in the municipal sanitation movement, Col. W. F. Morse, Rudolph Hering, and Charles Chapin, touted reduction.[75] These findings were disseminated through such networks as the National Municipal League.[76] Because cities infrequently had funds on hand to invest in and operate reduction plants, they were likely to contract out reduction.[77] A business would take the risk in building a plant, be paid by the city for its services, and retain profits from sale of the by-products. Hence reduction plants were ripe for public-private contract arrangements. But who would choose to invest in such technology?

Choosing Reduction

Businesses that might not otherwise be willing to invest in this new, expensive, and risky technology did so when they were assured contracts with the city. Pittsburgh's garbage ordinance of 1895 provided, by contract and at the public expense, for the systematic collection, removal, and disposal of garbage, offal, dead animals, and condemned meat in the city.[78] The director of the Department of Public Safety was authorized to enter into a contract or contracts with private parties for the removal and disposal of refuse from private premises.[79] The contract for collection and disposal of garbage by reduction (at a cost of $93,890 per year for four years) was awarded to Charles Flinn, party boss William Flinn's brother.[80] Secure in knowing that the multiyear contract would go to him, Charles Flinn saw the investment as a risk worth taking. He constructed a reduction plant, serving as president of the American Reduction Company, with the sanction of city authorities.[81] Because reduction processes required sorting garbage so appropriate items could be processed by the plant, collection and disposal were efficiently placed in the same hands. The Flinns had the collection resources—in the form of horses, carts, and drivers–from the Booth & Flinn street paving company, which dominated Pittsburgh's street paving contracts.[82]

The Magee-Flinn machine was relatively effective at providing city services, and the reduction plant was no exception. The Pittsburgh reduction plant was known for being "up-to date." Its reinforced concrete building was located on a hillside so that wagons could dump their refuse on the top floor.

Materials were sent down chutes to be processed, unusable refuse was sent to a railway trestle to transport it away, and all the chutes, conveyor belts, and hoppers were used in the plant to sort and process materials.[83] Pittsburgh health officials marked 1895—the first year of the contract—as a new and important era in sanitary administration in many respects, "perhaps in none more so than in its influence upon public sanitation" not just in Pittsburgh but across the state.[84] Apart from a few complaints of offensive odors, Pittsburgh officials reported satisfactory improvement. They had reason to be optimistic. The reduction plant was an initial success. It produced high-quality grease and was able to net a profit of $921.[85]

New Orleans also chose contract, at least for a short while. The city council committees on health along with police and public buildings met in May 1892 at city hall with the president of the Louisiana State Board of Health (Dr. Olliphant), the chief sanitary inspector of the Board (Dr. Parham), and an inspector (Mr. Will), to talk about the best methods of collecting and disposing of trash. Chief Sanitary Inspector Parham believed garbage collection and disposal would be more thoroughly accomplished by contract, as in other major cities, "holding the contractor personally responsible for the faithful performance of work."[86] Health officials recommended that an ordinance could require watertight, covered, sanitary garbage carts.[87] They were eager to replace the existing system, with its "irregularity" in collection and "careless emptying" of garbage boxes.[88] A contract would be the occasion to employ "scientific and sanitary" methods under city supervision.[89]

The city comptroller advertised bids for collection and disposal of garbage, which, like Pittsburgh, would entail the construction of a new plant. The bids came in substantially higher than what the city had been paying for garbage disposal (and significantly more than Pittsburgh's $93,890 per year). The lowest bid proposed $120,000 per year for the first five years, $134,000 per year for the second five, and $150,000 per year for the third five. A councilman estimated the existing cost of (inadequate) garbage removal at only $70,000 a year.[90] Despite the overwhelming opposition of the *Daily Picayune*, on August 30, 1893 Mayor Fitzpatrick accepted the bid of E. G. Schleider (largely thought to be a front for politically connected—but corrupt—businessman Maurice Hart) of the Southern Chemical and Fertilizing Company to build a plant that would burn garbage and create fertilizer. In November, Schleider requested permission to build his plant and the site was agreed upon by city officials.

Controversy

Pittsburgh saw early indications that the reduction plant would not be the profitmaker it promised: the quality of its output (grease) was uneven,[91] the plant employed few workers,[92] and Charles Flinn's firm was irregular in garbage collection.[93] Furthermore, residents were displeased. In May 1896, fifty-two residents on the bluff above the reduction plant filed suit against the American Reduction Company, claiming that the odor from the plant constituted a public nuisance. In response, the company altered some of its practices, making sure the digesters were tight and the pipe dispensing waste into the river was secured. It stopped producing fertilizer, instead shipping that material to a plant in the countryside. The residents subsequently claimed it was still a nuisance. This time, the odor was found to have come from the garbage as it sat in a pit awaiting processing. The Supreme Court of Pennsylvania determined that the residents had to put up with the inconvenience. Recognizing that the reduction plant presented a nuisance, the court nonetheless determined that such nuisance was unavoidable. The bluff was once "probably the most delightful place about the city for residences," but the city had since grown and expanded and "the onward march of the business of the city cannot be arrested because it may be an annoyance to some of those living on the bluff."[94] At base, the court recognized that garbage was public business: "It is the duty of a large city like Pittsburg to make provision for gathering and disposing of the garbage of the city."[95]

The Civic Club of Allegheny County, which had little input into the disposal contract, kept its eye on Flinn's garbage collection and disposal practices. Formed in 1895 as a merger of the Ladies Protective Health Association (a women's municipal housekeeping group committed to cleaning up garbage, polluted water, and smoke) and the Twentieth Century Club (another women's organization), the Civic Club was committed to cleaning up Pittsburgh's city streets and its corrupt government.[96] The Club sought pure water and garbage disposal.[97] It advocated the removal of old bottles, waste paper, scrap metals, and all refuse not coming under the heading of garbage, pointing to New York's program of generating revenue from selling such items.[98] The Club listed complaints (of which there were many) about alleys and sanitary conditions, especially in the South Side working-class neighborhoods.[99]

Public health officials, too, took notice of the garbage disposal practices, reporting that the dump did not have enough watchmen, and those employed were not uniformed.[100] Carts were not covered with canvas as required.[101] The weighing of cart loads was not supervised by a weighmaster, allowing garbage collectors to overcharge the city.[102] The Department of Public Health reported that while individuals attempted to keep tenement yards clean, sanitation was impeded by broken pavement, infrequent collection of waste, and the impossibility of establishing responsibility among the many users of a yard. Many complaints addressed the uncertainty of garbage and rubbish collections. Ashes and dirt not coming under "rubbish" were stored in barrels, etc., and their removal depended on the owner or tenant. Uniformity was lacking, as was the supply of garbage pails. Filth notices, or orders to get garbage pails, were frequently given, but the department had unnecessarily and deplorably failed to prescribe standard receptacles for garbage. A report on the city program concluded that "The results are unfit and impossible to keep clean contrivances."[103]

Though the complaints may well have been valid, they were also reflective of city services at the time, which tended to serve the central business district first and move out into residential neighborhoods, prioritizing on a class basis.[104] Flinn withstood the criticism on all fronts and the American Reduction Company continued to receive the garbage contract, year after year.[105]

In New Orleans, by contrast, the reduction plant never got off the ground. Although the state Board of Health hailed the garbage plant plan as "the largest and most complete of its kind in the country," this was its only praise; overall, the garbage works sparked extreme controversy over corruption and the location of the plant.[106] Under Fitzpatrick's administration, "the Ring's friends and allies received the majority of the city's contracts," and the garbage plant became a casualty of popular dissatisfaction and a weak administration.[107]

The *New Orleans Daily Picayune* (a reform paper) printed a series of investigative articles suggesting that the elevated bid for collection and disposal indicated political corruption.[108] The newspaper charged: "To attempt any longer to justify the proposed act on any score of economy will require colossal cheek in the face of the official figures. Nor will the sanitary dodge avail. The only part of the old service which needs reform is in the character of the wagons in which the garbage is hauled, and in the certainty and promptitude of removal. The rest of it is all right. . . . The contract, if let, will in all probability be awarded to some specially favored person, who will no more be held to a strict construction of the contract than are other specially favored contractors."[109]

Shortly after the contractor began work, the streets were strewn with trash and city government was marred by scandals.[110] Southern Chemical and Fertilizer required that householders separate their own trash so materials would be available for the reduction process. When citizens refused, the mayor issued orders penalizing householders who did not properly sort their garbage and put it in the designated type of container.[111] The *Picayune* raised complaints about the mayor's proclamation requiring householders to use a special type of garbage box.[112]

Though Mayor Fitzpatrick insisted the process was more sanitary, he stood accused of corruption. A grand jury criticized the terms of the contract for being too generous to the contractor.[113] One-third of the city council (along with the city engineer and former tax collector) were indicted.[114] Indeed, the public outrage may have been a response to blatant political corruption in awarding the contract to Maurice Hart, a businessman "with an obscure and questionable background" who was rumored to be behind the formation of the fertilizer company.[115]

Hart was known to New Orleans residents and had a cozy relationship with the Ring—he was accused of being its real "Boss." [116] Hart was able to exert influence on reform and Ring politicians: he secured contracts for electricity, waterworks, ice, and street paving and used his privilege to try to keep competitors out. But Hart was controversial and a long-standing target of reform politicians, especially Shakspeare.[117] In 1891, the reform-minded Mayor Shakspeare stated:

> I am sick and tired of seeing the abject submission of the Council to Maurice Hart, and I propose to put an end to it if I can, and so long as I am mayor of New-Orleans I will do all I can to kill schemes which have a tendency to keep out honest competition and bestow the use of valuable property on one man for nothing. . . . I object to giving Maurice Hart or any other man the whole city of New-Orleans. He has a full power over the City Council which I do not understand. He is always asking for some privilege, and the Council gives him everything he asks for. I do not consider it right that any one man like Hart should wield the power which he does.[118]

The garbage contract offered an opportunity for the defeated Shakspeare and reformers to strike back at the Fitzpatrick administration. Hart had a checkered past. He was implicated in frauds perpetrated by the former state treasurer; the American Loan and Trust Company of Boston filed suit in federal court against Hart and a business partner for sale of worthless stock of the Louisiana Light Company.[119] In New Orleans, Hart was included in a sweeping indictment against city officials for perjury and fraudulent representation and "corrupt practices."[120] The "boodle Council" was an easy target. After a few months of unsuccessful efforts the reduction contract was abandoned at great loss to the investors. Southern Chemical and Fertilizer went into receivership in 1897. More than just a temporary setback, the failure of the reduction plant set the path for New Orleans to revert to and continue dumping for another twenty-five years.[121]

Granted, reduction might not have been ideal for any southern city. Heating trash, whether by incineration or reduction, was challenging in the South, where natural gas had difficulties reaching the temperatures needed to process the material, and garbage that sat around waiting to be processed decomposed more quickly in the wet, hot conditions of New Orleans.[122] It was more palatable to get rid of garbage quickly by dumping it into the river. As the New Orleans city engineer pointed out, reduction was most profitable when it extracted high amounts of grease from garbage; northern cities tended to consume more meat than southern cities and, hence, their garbage produced more grease in reduction.[123] Yet those particularities do not explain why such a high proportion of southern cities used incineration or why Southern Chemical and Fertilizer invested in the plant in the first place.

Though there are many differences between Pittsburgh and New Orleans, we did not find that the weather, the processes by which reduction was chosen and played out, or even the behavior of elected officials explained why reduction was successful in one city and not the other. Instead, our analysis highlights the strength and organization of each city's political machine. Pittsburgh's Magee-Flinn Ring dated back to 1880 and increased its power after revision of the city charter in 1887. It maintained influence over state government as well, so it could ensure policies favorable to the city. But the New Orleans machine operated under political and economic uncertainty. It was in the process of establishing itself and had not yet gained the more secure footing (as it would after 1904) that would keep it in power for fifty years. Instead, the machine was in ongoing electoral conflict with its reformer opposition. Elections swung back and forth in the 1880s and 1890s, and losers, such as Shakspeare, were never far off as an ongoing threat.

In contrast, Pittsburgh's machine worked with local businesses and used patronage and graft to promote public works projects. The Magee-Flinn machine owned and controlled local government and dealt with business directly. As Steffens explained: "In [other corrupt cities like] St. Louis the business man boodled for his street. In Pittsburg he went to Magee, and I have heard such a man praise Chris, 'because when I called on him his outer office was filled with waiting politicians, but he knew I was a business man and in a hurry; he called me in first, and he gave me the street without any fuss.'"[124] However, New Orleans' Ring was in tension with local business elites and largely ignored public works. Business elites in New Orleans were not given a privileged position in the city and they had to boodle for what they wanted. They were also in conflict with local small-business owners, often the friends of the Ring and recipients of contracts. Notably, Martin Manion, a plumber and John Fitizpatrick's brother-in-law, profited handsomely from local contracts.[125]

Pittsburgh's Flinns won the garbage contract, as they won nearly every street paving contract, but William Flinn was a boss in the machine, and his capture of contracts was no secret. His shell lay in his brother, which distanced him enough to relieve him of legal liability for the garbage contract, but the relationship was transparent enough to make it, politically, an open secret. New Orleans' Hart, on the other hand, was a businessman who captured contracts in a number of different industries, used fronts to hide his involvement, and used his privilege to shut out competitors. He had less political clout and was, in turn, involved with a less secure political regime than the Pittsburgh Ring. Although Magee-Flinn were susceptible to criticism and challenge (as both reduction plants were), they could fend it off but Fitzpatrick and Hart could not.

Statebuilding at the Margins

Garbage practices in both Pittsburgh and New Orleans were established on a bed of corrupt contracts and faulty collection, which continued long afterward. As inadequate as the machines may have been for achieving efficient disposal, they did shape development in both cities. When reform governments came to power in Pittsburgh and New Orleans, they cleaned up practices but did not alter these foundations. Pittsburgh continued with the American Reduction Company and New Orleans continued dumping in the Mississippi River.

Pittsburgh's machine disbanded after Magee's death in 1901.[126] But the end of the Ring did not mean the end of contract collection, the Flinns, or the

American Reduction Company. Reform mayor George Guthrie and the reform-minded Voters League merely sought to make the dirty politics of garbage collection cleaner, not change how it was done altogether. Garbage contracts continued to be awarded to the American Reduction Company.[127] The new reform movement still relied on Flinn's infrastructure, both Booth & Flinn and the American Reduction Company, the latter until 1931. If disposal was impeded, it was by householders who failed to comply with the separation of garbage from rubbish required for the reduction process.[128]

In contrast, New Orleans struggled with its garbage disposal. Together with the Screwman's Riots, which drove a wedge between formerly cooperative black and white unions and broke the Ring's working-class coalition, Fitzpatrick's vulnerability in the garbage contract scandal was a blow to his power.[129] In a stunning election in April 1896, the New Orleans Ring was removed from power. Walter Flower was elected mayor at the head of a reform ticket with solid support from black residents.[130] A new city charter went into effect in July, making important changes once again to the way New Orleans government would work. The city consolidated power in one chamber and vested executive power in the mayor, treasurer, and comptroller. The mayor, in turn, selected the commissioner of public works, commissioner of police and public buildings, and city engineer. Aside from these elected and appointed officials, the charter also established civil service provisions.[131]

Control reverted back to the machine in 1904, when Martin Behrman was elected mayor. Behrman headed the reconstituted Ring, now known as the Choctaw Club (self-consciously modeled after Chicago's Iroquois Club). Although the 1898 election destroyed Fitzpatrick's reign, Louisiana's formal disenfranchisement of blacks that same year (which Fitzpatrick supported) provided new political opportunities for Democrats to seize and maintain power.[132] When Behrman won the mayoral election in 1904, the Choctaw Club was "seemingly invincible."[133] Behrman reigned until 1920, and after a brief respite with a reform mayor, was reelected in 1925. He was a boss who knew how to compromise with opposing interests to mollify them.[134] Businessmen were finally able to forge a relationship with the administration, and the Behrman administration was known for its civic advances.[135]

It was a new era for New Orleans governing, but not for garbage disposal. The city attempted to get a handle on its garbage. It tried burying the garbage in outlying areas of the city, but tidal overflows immediately brought the garbage back up. It tried incineration, but the odors wafted through the city. It tried a dump, but the site became overrun with rats, mice, flies, mosquitoes, and buzzards.[136] George S. Smith, Department of Public Works bookkeeper and later commissioner, reported collecting up to 12,000 loads of garbage a month. His monthly reports, however, indicate the lack of capacity in the method of disposal, regardless of the zeal for reform. When Smith came into office in 1904, garbage was removed by loading it onto a boat and towing it downriver, where it was dumped. Smith was frustrated by the city's lack of attention to the deteriorating state of the garbage boats, leading him to appeal to the mayor's office month after month, urging the administration to direct resources to a new boat.[137] Boats sank and were in constant need of repair. Disposal by dumping meant the department had to deal with problems both when the river rose and when it reached its low stage because boats were in danger of being grounded and the bottom of the river had to be dredged.[138]

By 1908, garbage collection in New Orleans finally saw some progress. The state required New Orleans to reserve $400,000 a year for permanent public improvements. The city appealed to the state for aid and used ten years of funds between 1908 and 1910.[139] Smith reported,

> the garbage ordinance has been strictly enforced by this department and I am pleased to report the department is meeting with some success, and as it is a point of education it will be some time before the public will conform to the provision of said ordinance, but this Department will use every means at its command to enforce the provision of the ordinance, and I trust that the citizens of New Orleans will realize that it will be necessary for them to cooperate and comply with said ordinance in order to carry it out the same in its entirety.[140]

In 1909, the city finally decided to abandon the Mississippi as a dumping ground and chose, instead, land in the "rear section of the city, "consisting of "old unused drainage canals and swamp lands." Smith lauded such practices, by which the fill leveled the surfaces, transforming those spaces into "beautiful parks, healthful playgrounds for children and good streets, all of which is a big asset to a city."[141] An epidemic of bubonic plague in 1914 made residents more cooperative in their household role in garbage collection.[142] Another epidemic in 1921 invited a reconsideration of garbage disposal.[143] In 1922, New Orleans implemented more professional standards, erecting an incinerator in each of the five districts.[144] Incineration was a likely improvement over dumping in the river or on the land, but it fell short of the productive technology of reduction Pittsburgh had adopted three decades earlier.

Conclusion

Even though reformers were the first parties to recognize garbage as a public problem, it was not a problem that they were equipped to solve. Disposal through reduction required skilled personnel, such as engineers, and resources to build large plants. Corruption provided the solution, fulfilling the collaborative role that fell to reformers in the contexts described in several other chapters in this volume. Both Pittsburgh and New Orleans had a garbage problem, both cities contracted with industry to build a reduction plant, and both cities suffered controversy and legal action over it. Whereas Magee-Flinn and the American Reduction Company in Pittsburgh were easily able to weather the storm, Fitzpatrick-Hart and Southern Chemical and Fertilizer were not. Disgruntled citizens (who did not wish to buy receptacles or separate their trash) closed the New Orleans plant and brought down the administration.

Pittsburgh's machine was strong and its ties to government stable. Steffens explains: "Magee and Flinn were the government and the law. How could they commit a crime? If they wanted something from the city they passed an ordinance granting it, and if some other ordinance was in conflict it was repealed or amended. If the laws of the State stood in the way, so much the worse for the laws of the State; they were amended. If the constitution of the State proved a barrier . . . the Legislature enacted a law for cities of the second class (which was Pittsburg alone) and the courts upheld the Legislature."[145] Flinn not only had contracts but the evidence shows that he had the capacity to carry out the obligations of those contracts. Garbage collection and disposal was imperfect in Pittsburgh (to say the least), but trash was collected and disposed of using modern innovations.

In New Orleans, the unstable political economy and incomplete dominance of either reform or Ring in the late nineteenth century meant that contractors and their ties to government were more easily severed and could not sustain the development of an institutional solution. Power in New Orleans was diffuse. The Ring was unable to secure compliance from city officials, let alone from citizens. Garbage collection and disposal in the Crescent City was inadequate. City collectors refused to pick up trash that was not properly sorted and Mayor Fitzpatrick proposed a stick (rather than a carrot) to get citizens to comply. He overestimated his hand.

The narratives of these cities show that the garbage disposal practices that developed (or that failed to develop) had a certain amount of path dependence. Future governments that came to power relied on these methods, even if they altered them somewhat. Thus, Pittsburgh's trash disposal practices are inextricably intertwined with the machine that created them. New Orleans' practices (through failure of the reduction plant and dumping waste in the river) would also continue for decades. Corruption and political (in)stability translated directly into the strength of each city's municipal development.

Regardless of our normative views of corruption and collusion, cities depended on it as a resource, and though we may dislike machines, they were no doubt agents of political change. At the same time, Rings and their corruption are not equal everywhere or equally effective. The counterfactual to machine politics is not necessarily reform, but stronger/weaker regimes that are more/less able to address municipal concerns. A comparison of Pittsburgh (a strong regime) and New Orleans (a weak one) shows variation in the role that corruption played to accomplish municipal goals. In Pittsburgh the regime created new processes, invested in new technologies, and was effectively deployed even after the Ring was "smashed." But in New Orleans the regime had far less power, less capacity, and was accordingly able to accomplish less in terms of municipal governance. Administrations after the Fitzpatrick-Hart arrangement continued to rely on a rather provincial form of collection (carts) and disposal (dumping).

Though reformers and machines may have different motivations, our research suggests that both worked to secure their power through public works and both relied on structures built on collusion between government officials and particular business interests. Like Jon Teaford, who calls for a reevaluation of the "duel" between machines and reformers in studies of cities, and Jessica Trounstine, who collapses the distinction between machines and reformers and shifts the focus to political monopolies, we think there is much to be gained in treating political machines as agents that provide the resources a growing city needs to develop its capacity.[146] Trounstine's focus on political regimes shows the importance of power and centralization for achieving regime goals. When we, likewise, attend to the stability and centralization of different machines we illuminate the facets of corruption that were employed for statebuilding. But whether or not we like the collusion between government officials and businessmen, it was a source of both government authority and capacity in the Progressive Era, a time when cities required creative responses to intractable problems.

Chapter 4

Developing the Animal Welfare State

Susan J. Pearson and Kimberly K. Smith

No subject has been more marginal to scholarship on American political development than animals. Indeed, Stephen Skowronek's seminal study of state-building is perfectly silent on the topic in spite of the fact that one of his major case studies is the army, an organization centrally concerned throughout the nineteenth century with managing horses, draft animals, and other livestock.[1] Yet animals are and long have been critical to human social and economic organization and their management has always been a critical function of American governments. It could hardly be otherwise in a society so heavily dependent on animal power. Recent research on the history of human-animal relations in the United States, however, has begun to document the role of animals in American development. As we shall demonstrate, the "animal welfare state" is highly contradictory. It seeks to balance different—sometimes competing—conceptions of animals as property, laborers, nuisances, threats to public health, objects of sentiment, and bearers of rights. Because the animal welfare state that developed during the second half of the nineteenth century built on, but did not challenge, the state's traditional view of animals as property and subjects of police regulation, it sought to protect both animals from humans and humans from animals. Indeed, managing animal welfare often involved the state's capacity to kill animals—a fact that underscores the complexity of the state's animal welfare regime.

Its contradictory origins and purposes notwithstanding, the development of the animal welfare state illustrates several important themes in American political development. Many developments in the state's capacity to protect animal welfare preceded and even constituted the model for later welfare regimes. Specifically, the state's traditional authority over animals helped to create warrants for state intervention into the private domestic sphere, as well as fostering institutional innovations that extended the state's capacity to protect children. Animal protection and regulation not only extended the role and reach of the state but it did so in ways that demonstrate a common pattern of American statebuilding: the extension of public power through "private" means.[2] The animal protection functions of the state were created and enforced by nongovernmental organizations that articulated and then carried out new functions for government's management of human-animal relations. And though the gender politics of the animal welfare movement was complicated by these organizations' law enforcement responsibilities, women's groups, working mostly at the local level, played a significant role in these developments—a pattern consistent with the findings of other chapters in this book.

Development of Animal Administrative Apparatuses

As sources of wealth and labor power, and as constituents of the public peace, domestic animals were subject to extensive communal control during the colonial and early republic periods. Wild animals, by contrast, were treated primarily as an unregulated resource or a threat to be eliminated. American colonists enjoyed considerable freedom from the restrictive hunting laws common to European polities.[3] But domestic animals were well integrated into colonial social communities and a major concern of colonial governments. New Englanders exercised the greatest degree of communal control over animals; town governments were well organized and the settlers practiced mixed husbandry. Raising livestock and crops together in close proximity to human habitation required close control of animals, and local governments exercised considerable authority to manage animal/human relationships. In addition to requiring farmers to pay for damages caused by wandering livestock, town governments typically took responsibility for providing pasture, paying herders' fees, and ensuring that cropland was adequately fenced. The New England colonies developed a complex set of land use practices designed to keep livestock separate from croplands and under strict control.[4] Some towns even regulated livestock breeding, appointing officials to determine which bull calves would be allowed to breed.[5]

Additionally, the Massachusetts Bay Colony Body of Liberties, the code of laws passed by the colony in 1641, made it a crime to "exercise any Tirranny or Crueltie towards any bruite Creature which are usuallie kept for man's use."[6] Like regulations governing movement and breeding of livestock, the prohibition on "crueltie" stemmed from colonists' understanding that animals comprised part of the social order, not from any recognition of rights held by animals. Allowing humans to treat animals cruelly would accordingly disrupt the moral and social order, breach the public peace, and damage property. All these functions—regulating the movement, breeding, and even treatment of livestock—were examples of what English legal commentator William Blackstone called "police power," state regulation to protect public health and welfare.

Communal control of livestock was less developed in the southern colonies, where the settlers adopted free range husbandry, letting their pigs and cattle roam in the woods most of the year. This style of husbandry made it difficult for the colonial governors even to enforce property rights in livestock; despite draconian penalties, theft was common.[7] Nevertheless, the free range system also depended on a suitable legal structure. In contrast to New England, South Carolina made farmers responsible for fencing their crops to protect them from roaming livestock. It also provided for registration of brands and earmarks so that wandering animals could be identified.[8]

Though the nineteenth-century American state developed more extensive regulatory power over animals (primarily at the local and state level) and began to articulate a concern with animals' welfare, the direction of change was not from anarchy to authority. Rather, as Karen Orren and Stephen Skowronek contend, American political development is best understood not as filling in gaps in governmental authority but rather as changing the prior set of rules by which a collectivity has been governed.[9] That principle applies here as well. Colonial governments regulated domestic animals because they were, as species of property, central to social and economic order. In addition, their unregulated movements had the potential to—and often did—disturb the public peace. The development of the American state's authority over animals during the nineteenth century represents a change in how, but not whether, the community exercised concern and control over animals. While colonial communities typically relied on social pressure and nonstate institutions (the family, the church), the early American republic increasingly relied on statutes, courts, and new institutions such as police forces and administrative agencies.[10] Over the course of the nineteenth century a modern administrative state apparatus devoted to the welfare and management of animals was developed through public-private partnerships. Following the Civil War, numerous private organizations devoted to animal welfare and management were formed and responsibility for animal management moved from the local to the state and (eventually) the federal level.

Such developments grew from familiar sources; as property and labor, animals required management. As animals congregated in the nation's rapidly growing cities, providing one of the chief motive forces for its rapidly expanding capitalist economy, their effect on human health and welfare multiplied. Historian Clay McShane notes that the concentration of horses in Boston rose from one for every 40 persons in 1840 to one for every 26.3 in 1880.[11] As cities grew larger and more crowded, the local state (that is, city government) extended its traditional concern with livestock control, using nuisance law to regulate the locations of liveries and slaughterhouses. If, as William Novak has argued, the nineteenth-century American state was devoted to a "vision of a well-regulated society," animals were clearly part of that vision. An 1837 enumeration of the powers of the city of Chicago, for example, regulated the "running at large of cattle, horses, swine, sheep, goats and geese." The city had the power to impound and sell errant livestock, and it could also impound and destroy stray dogs and regulate or prohibit animal slaughter in certain areas of the city.[12] Boston enacted in 1856 an extensive set of regulations to govern horse-drawn traffic, including licensing requirements, regulation of harnessing, and a prohibition on galloping.[13] The need to control growing numbers of urban livestock was in fact a major impetus for the development of the administrative state. By the 1860s and 1870s, cities had begun creating boards of health with regulatory power over animal-related businesses. In 1866, for example, the New York state legislature created an agency, the Metropolitan Board of Health, to manage public health issues in New York City and Brooklyn. According to Novak, the board was a prototypical administrative agency, with broad powers to investigate, hold hearings, pass ordinances, and close establishments it deemed health hazards in the city—thus displacing local officials' traditional authority in this area.[14] Such boards were principally concerned not with animal welfare but with protecting property owners from noise and odors. Still, they represented a new institutional approach to state regulation of livestock. They were "progenitors of a new administrative state" and their concern with the connection between animals and public health added a new dimension to traditional property- and police-based governance of animals.[15]

But an even more significant development in animal-state relations during this period was the growth of the animal welfare movement, beginning in the 1860s. Modeled on the London Society for the Prevention of Cruelty to Animals (established in 1824), the American Society for the Prevention of Cruelty to Animals (ASPCA) played a critical role in creating and legitimating new forms of state regulation of animal welfare.[16] In doing so, it paved the way for much greater state involvement in regulation of the domestic sphere in general, an involvement that it, like the Better Homes for America activists described by Greer, did not necessarily fully foresee in its initial efforts.

The Animal Welfare Movement and Expansion of State Authority

During the colonial era, the public's interest in the welfare of domesticated animals was perhaps too obvious to require much explicit justification. Small, somewhat isolated farming communities understood well enough that their survival depended on healthy, well-managed livestock. But if justification was needed, it could be found in the Christian belief that, although domestic animals were created by God to serve humans, humans had a stewardship relationship toward them.[17] By the mid-nineteenth century, however, new and more intensive uses of animals and new forms of public protection for their welfare (as well as the growing secularization of American political culture) meant that different grounds were needed for traditional communal protections for domestic animals. Animal welfare advocates helped to articulate those grounds.

At the center of this effort was Henry Bergh, founder of the ASPCA and the principal force behind what is usually considered the nation's first modern anticruelty statute. The law, passed by the New York legislature in 1867, defined as misdemeanors several offenses, including cockfighting, bearbaiting, impounding an animal without food and water, and mistreating draft animals. The first section runs, "If any person shall over-drive, over-load, torture, torment, deprive of necessary sustenance, or unnecessarily or cruelly beat, or needlessly mutilate or kill . . . any living creature, every such offender shall . . . be guilty of a misdemeanor."[18] Violators could be arrested, held in custody, and fined. The New York anticruelty statute included several important departures from both common law and existing statutory prohibitions on mistreatment of animals, expanding the scope for intervention. First, the law was not limited by its terms to *public* acts of cruelty; cruelty was criminal whether it was performed in public or in private. This departed from existing prohibitions on cruelty that treated public mistreatment of animals as a species of nuisance or morals corruption. Second, owners of animals could be prosecuted for cruelty toward their *own* property, a construction that departed from common law protection of property in animals under the heading of malicious mischief. Subsequent anticruelty statutes adopted by other states in the latter half of the nineteenth century also criminalized cruelty itself, not merely cruelty that could be characterized as a breach of the peace, and made cruelty a crime irrespective of ownership. Under such laws, as nineteenth-century legal commentator Joel Prentiss Bishop explained, cruelty was "a crime against the animal itself." By 1900, all forty-seven states had adopted such anticruelty legislation.[19] Just as important, the law also empowered officers of the ASPCA to enforce it. The new law thus mingled public with private authority—it declared the state's commitment to animal protection while delegating enforcement powers to a private, though publicly chartered, organization. In this regard, it created a hybrid system that bore a family relationship to the development of the juvenile court system described by Nackenoff and Sullivan in this volume.

New York's anticruelty legislation was a critical step in the creation of a liberal welfare state not only because it created new powers but also because it shifted the grounds for state protection of animals from preventing public acts of violence to prohibiting private acts of cruelty or neglect. Specifically, animal welfare advocates helped to create a new role for the liberal state by insisting that animals had rights that could be legally enforced. The language of rights pervaded the animal welfare movement from the beginning: Bergh began his crusade for animal protection by issuing a "Declaration of the Rights of Animals" in 1865; he was followed in 1869 by Harriet Beecher Stowe's article "Rights of Dumb Animals." Other animal welfare reformers adopted rights language, developing a sentimental rights discourse aimed at ensuring protection of welfare rather than liberty. By 1888, the concept of animal rights was so common that lawyer Charles Barnard, representing the Massachusetts SPCA, could insist that the new animal welfare laws "differ from earlier enactments, and from the common law regarding this class of offences, in proceeding more clearly upon the principle that animals have rights."[20]

The concept of animal rights posed a profound challenge to the liberal concept of rights. Traditional liberal theory held that only rational, independent beings could hold rights; dependents (such as women, the poor, children, and slaves) must rely on their masters for protection. Accordingly, freed slaves, women, and workers typically sought rights during the late nineteenth century by asserting their *independence* from patriarchal institutions. That strategy could not work for animals, the quintessential dependent creature. Thus animal welfare advocates argued that vulnerable, dependent beings could also have rights, based on their ability to suffer and our ability to feel compassion for them. Under this view, empathy—sympathetic identification with another being's suffering—constituted the grounds for recognizing rights. Animal welfare advocates were not the first to put forward this idea; a similar argument had been developed by the abolitionists on behalf of slaves—including, notably, by Harriet Beecher Stowe in *Uncle Tom's Cabin*. By the late nineteenth century, this sentimental rights discourse had become a standard argument in the arsenal of many reformers.[21] But it was particularly central to the campaign for animals, since domestic animals could not be liberated from their positions of dependence. Bergh and others in the postbellum anticruelty movement had to reconcile a liberal language of rights with the persistent hierarchies and forms of dependence that characterized human-animal and household relations. That is, they used the language of rights not to pursue independence for animals but to protect and correct the human-animal relationship—a relationship inescapably characterized by dependence.[22] This notion of the rights of dependent beings would eventually be used to justify state protection not only of animals but also of children, which in turn would authorize state intrusion into the private sphere. By articulating a new ground—that of rights protection—for state regulation of human-animal relationships, SPCAs extended the reach and role of both state and civil society. And like the juvenile court reformers described by Nackenoff and Sullivan in the volume, anticruelty activists believed that protecting the rights of the dependent required regulation rather than liberty.

Though Bergh and others claimed that SPCAs—and the laws they enforced—acted to recognize and protect animal rights, both the activities and the governing logic of the animal welfare movement faced considerable resistance. Indeed, the resistance faced by SPCAs underscores the novelty of their approach. The exercise of public power by ASPCA officials—the statutory grant of law enforcement powers—raised questions about the legitimacy of state regulation of animal welfare. Although Bergh's law had public support, particularly among New York's elite, it ran into fierce resistance from the stagecoach drivers of New York City. To them, Bergh was the very embodiment of intrusive governmental meddling. He would walk the streets of New York, stopping drivers in order to inspect their horses and pointing out their poor condition and overloaded carts. Dennis Christie, for example, was driving his coach along his usual route when Bergh called a policeman over to arrest him. Bergh insisted that the horse was lame and Christie was overdriving him. Christie was taken away from his coach and committed to the local police court, where he was eventually acquitted, but not compensated for his loss of time and income.

The stage companies weren't accustomed to this sort of interference. In 1873 they brought several lawsuits against Bergh (including an action by Christie for false arrest). They lost all of them. Dubbed the *Stage Horse Cases*, these decisions offer the first judicial interpretations of the 1867 anticruelty law, and reveal how jurists viewed the government's coercive power to protect animals from their owners. In considering the stagecoach companies' complaints, the court (in the person of Judge Daly) first established, without argument, that the statute did authorize officers of the ASPCA to arrest people for violating the law. But Daly went on to consider why the government had the power to pass such a law in the first place. Citing several precedents, he noted that cruelty to animals was a common law offense long before the legislature enacted the criminal statute. He explained that such legislation was not merely governmental meddling in private property rights in animals but had a clear public purpose:

> It truly has its origins in the intent to save a just standard of humane feeling from being debased by pernicious effects of bad example, the human heart being hardened by public and frequent exhibitions of cruelty to dumb creatures, committed to the care and which were created for the beneficial use of man.[23]

In other words, the court classified anticruelty laws as a species of morals legislation akin to laws against "lewd prints," public drunkenness, and prize fighting. Daly's construction of the law's purpose was commonplace among jurists in the late nineteenth and early twentieth centuries. Like Daly, most commentators construed animal welfare laws as aimed at protecting the moral character of humans rather than protecting the animals themselves. Ernst Freund's 1904 work on the police power, for example, classed animal welfare laws under public morals regulation, along with prostitution and habitual intemperance, and Christopher Tiedeman's 1900 *Treatise on State and*

Federal Control of Persons and Property classified them as state regulation of personal property.[24] But such legal constructions were somewhat awkward attempts to limit the reach of statutes that appeared, on their face, to protect the rights of animals themselves. They attest to how the burgeoning animal welfare state built upon rather than eclipsed earlier common law and statutory regulation of human-animal relations. Nevertheless, these new animal welfare laws represented an important challenge to the traditional limits of state power.

The rationale cited by Daly and others—that protecting animals from harm upheld the human moral order—did indeed have a long pedigree. The judge cited approvingly William Hogarth, the eighteenth-century British artist whose series *The Four Stages of Cruelty* shows its protagonist Tom Nero progressing through several stages of moral decline, from treating animals cruelly to murder. For Daly, this moral corruption rationale served to justify a broad sphere for state regulation of animal welfare: the state could protect animals from cruelty because it had the power to protect public morals and prevent violence. He did, however, think that the liberal state had limits: "private vices . . . are not, cannot be, the object of any municipal law." But "when by their evil example or other pernicious effects they may prejudice the community, they thereby become a species of public crimes." These acts constitute a breach of duties owed to the "whole community, considered as a community, in its social aggregate capacity."[25]

Judge Daly's argument rested on drawing a bright line between public and private displays of immoral conduct. The state, under his reasoning, had authority only over public acts that might be considered a breach of the peace—beating one's horse in a public street, for example, as opposed to neglecting one's horse at home; indeed, it had long had such powers under both common law and by specific statutes in several states. But the animal welfare movement—and the post-1867 animal protection laws passed in New York and other states—challenged that line. Animal protection advocates argued in their speeches, books, and editorials that even private acts of cruelty to animals constituted a serious social problem. People who were cruel to animals, according to this argument, were likely to disregard the rights of humans, and their victims would likely become cruel and violent as well.[26] Henry Bergh, addressing the fourth annual meeting of the ASPCA, gave voice to this argument. "The man who gives unrestrained license to his violent passions must inevitably make a miserable end," he warned. Invoking the Hogarthian teleology of cruelty, Bergh predicted that "He that ill-treats his horse is insensibly led to ill-treat his wife and children." Having torn apart his home, the "cruelist" would then seek refuge and comfort in the local saloon, where he finds further stimulus for his violence among "companions as riotous and unprincipled as himself."[27] Bergh and others believed that stemming cruelty was effectively nipping other forms of violence and unlicensed behavior in the bud. Thus, while protectionists such as Bergh used a "slippery slope theory of violence" to connect both private to public acts of violence and violence against animals to violence against humans, such arguments positioned the state's animal welfare work on fairly traditional grounds: as a species of police legislation undertaken to protect human moral order and social welfare.[28] Policing private acts of cruelty was supposed to serve a kind of preventative or prophylactic function, identifying dangerous elements who were undermining the social fabric behind closed doors.

The animal welfare movement's arguments for protecting animals from abuse not only challenged the exclusion of the state from the domestic sphere, they also helped to create a new policy domain, that of "animal welfare," rather than subsuming animal welfare in various other domains, such as public health or morals regulation. But even while SPCAs attempted to articulate new grounds for state governance of animals—and though the laws passed at their behest did criminalize private as well as public acts of cruelty and neglect—animal welfare regulations could also be understood in familiar ways. Not only, as we have seen, did jurists tend to interpret these new statutes according to the law's traditional role as protector of public peace and public morals, but so too could animal welfare be understood in terms of another traditional role for state regulation: the protection and preservation of property in animals. Stagecoach owners, for example, eventually realized that supporting animal welfare laws and the SPCAs was good business. As historian Clay McShane has noted, stagecoach companies actually benefitted from the work of SPCAs. These organizations helped monitor drivers to make sure the companies' horses were well treated, and they also served as disinterested parties that could determine whether a sick or lame horse should be destroyed. "In order to collect insurance for their destroyed property," McShane writes, "owners [had] to cooperate with SPCAs and acknowledge their authority."[29] In fact, many directors of SPCAs had substantial investments in transportation firms with large herds of horses.[30]

Nor should this surprise us. In a community heavily dependent on animals, there was a good economic case for protecting their welfare, as Henry Bergh himself insisted. In an 1881 article in the *North American Review*, he estimated that the mistreatment of cattle in rail transit caused losses of 10 to 15 percent, resulting in millions of dollars wasted. "That lesson of humanity to the lower animals," he notes, "should be enforced in the counting-house, as well as in the nursery."[31] These economic incentives helped support the expansion of state regulatory power over livestock; protecting the welfare of livestock could always be justified as an extension of the power to protect property and regulate commerce. The harder task was extending government protection to animals with little or no market value—namely, pet animals. Achieving protection for pets depended in part on the anticruelty argument, but also on the gradual recognition that pets could be considered a special kind of property with a distinctive kind of legally cognizable value.

Consider, for example, how dogs came to enjoy their current favored status under animal welfare statutes. Dogs were not always considered proper subjects for government protection. The practice of keeping dogs as pets was well established by the eighteenth century; Native Americans, European colonists, and even slaves kept dogs for hunting, guarding, and companionship.[32] Despite their ubiquity and usefulness, however, dogs during the nineteenth century were often viewed (by the non-dog-loving public) in the same way as wolves—as pests that could be destroyed if they became a problem.[33] Because they were a nuisance to livestock owners, they increasingly absorbed the attention of lawmakers. Complaints about dogs harassing livestock led to the widespread adoption of "dog laws" in the 1850s and 1860s.[34] By the 1860s, seventeen states had such laws.

The dog laws were aimed at controlling stray dogs and reducing their numbers, but ironically they also ended up giving greater legal protection to dog owners' property rights. The common law rule, still being followed by many judges in the late nineteenth century, was that dogs were not domestic animals; they were essentially wild animals and could be killed with impunity. But the dog laws overrode that rule. To be sure, these laws defined dogs as nuisances and therefore liable to be killed when they were not on their master's land. But they also protected dogs that were under their master's control, and created procedures that recognized the owners' property rights. Maryland, for example, set up a summary judicial procedure for putting down marauding dogs, which included providing notice to the owner and allowing the owner to pay a fine in lieu of the state's killing the dog. Similarly, some states imposed taxes on dogs, with the aim of making it more expensive to keep dogs (and thereby reduce their numbers). But taxing dogs also implied that they were property. Even the U.S. Department of Agriculture, in an

1863 report, insisted in defiance of the common law that "dogs are property, and therefore taxable."[35] Moreover, dog taxes required local officials to take a census of dogs and determine who owned them, which further enhanced dogs' legal status. Historian Katherine Kete recounts how this process worked in France, which had a similar experience with the dog tax. Imposed in order to reduce the numbers of dogs, the tax had the unexpected effect of conferring on dogs a kind of civic personality that justified government attention to their welfare.[36]

In addition, the debates over dog laws and dog taxes provided dog lovers a forum to assert the value of dogs to their owners and to the community. For example, one member of the Maine Board of Agriculture argued to his colleagues that the dog "was of great benefit in Aroostock county, in protecting the sheep from bears . . . [and the] property saved was greater than the value of all the sheep killed" by marauding dogs.[37] In addition to this economic argument, defenders of dogs could draw on the sentimental language of the anticruelty advocates and insist on the value of the dog's famed loyalty and companionship. Historian Katherine Grier notes that stories featuring virtuous and loving dogs were the most common narratives highlighting the moral qualities of animals during the nineteenth century. By midcentury, the dog had become the chief exemplar of fidelity in popular culture.[38] Thus one sheep farmer defended the sheepdog by citing their loyalty: "their attachment to their own flock, and devotion to their master, would . . . make them an acquisition of infinite value." Advocates of dog taxes also recognized the value of the "noble, generous dog"; they sought only to reduce the numbers of "yelping, nameless, homeless curs."[39] Such defenses, combining economic and sentimental appeals, contributed to the growing belief that dogs were a special kind of property deserving of legal protection. Like other elements of the animal welfare state, the dog laws mingled several constructions of animals: as nuisance, property, and objects of sentiment. In the case of dogs, at least, these constructions worked to create a legally protected relationship between pet and owner that would eventually become firmly entrenched in American law and help to authorize state action on its behalf (most recently, for example, in the Pet Evacuation and Transportation Act of 2006, which requires rescue organizations to make accommodations for pets in the event of natural and other disasters).

Building the Animal Welfare State

Even as animal welfare organizations were articulating new warrants for state regulation of animal welfare, they were also expanding the state's and civil society's capacity to do so. From the mid-nineteenth century on, the ASPCA and local SPCAs engaged in a wide range of institution-building projects. For example, the Women's Branch of the Pennsylvania SPCA prompted Philadelphia to open an animal shelter in 1869, and then lobbied the mayor for control of the local dog pound. They not only developed new, more humane methods for capturing and euthanizing strays, but also regularized the accounting process for dog fines. Bergh's organization was similarly creative, inventing the first ambulance service for injured horses.[40] But perhaps the most significant contribution of the animal welfare movement to the development of state capacity was the creation of humane societies.

This story properly begins with the most novel element of New York's 1867 anticruelty act: it authorized members of the ASPCA to arrest violators and bring them to court. This melding of public and private functions by animal protection societies was not entirely unprecedented. As Elisabeth Clemens has noted, the delegation of public authority to private associations was common during this era. State governments often "borrowed" administrative capacity, funding private charities to perform a variety of welfare functions, such as caring for orphans and for the elderly.[41] Nor was the idea of delegating enforcement power entirely novel. The British Royal Society for the Prevention of Cruelty to Animals (RSPCA) had been granted similar authority,[42] and we see a similar dynamic in the area of wildlife protection, as discussed by Ann-Marie Szymanski in her chapter in this volume. Szymanski notes that state and local wildlife protection associations often supplemented the efforts of public officials to enforce game laws, by encouraging private actions against trespassers, offering rewards for information leading to the conviction of offenders, employing detectives, and even paying for prosecutions. But these associations did not actually succeed in winning authority to arrest and prosecute offenders, as did the ASPCA.

To put this issue in context, it's helpful to understand the status of urban police forces in the late nineteenth century.[43] The creation of professional police forces was of course fairly recent. The first American police force was established in New York in 1845, and other cities quickly followed suit. But at the same time, private law enforcement flourished, often in dramatic and disturbing forms. Vigilantism—organized, extralegal movements, the members of which take the law into their own hands—was widespread in the South and West. Private law enforcement in the East and the Midwest generally took the form of policing for hire. Private police agencies offered patrol and detection services; often run by former police officers, they began to operate in major American cities in the 1840s. But the line between public and private policing was often hard to draw; private detectives and privately employed patrol personnel often were publicly appointed as "special policemen." Eventually, however, the idea of policing as an inherently public function took hold, especially in cities with uniformed, publicly funded police forces. By midcentury, we begin to find judicial opinions refusing to enforce contracts providing for private compensation to public law enforcement officers, on the ground that a police officer is a public official, not the agent or employee of a private prosecutor. The line grew more distinct between police officers and detectives, on the one hand, and private guards and investigators, on the other. But the prosecutorial power requested by SPCAs tended to muddy this emerging distinction between public and private law enforcement.

Thus courts occasionally questioned whether the legislature could legitimately vest this sort of regulatory power in private organizations. An 1878 case heard by the Court of Appeals in New York affirmed that the state could and did delegate its police powers to private organizations such as the ASPCA. Under the terms of the state's anticruelty law, Bergh and other officers of the ASPCA were "clothed with authority to execute the law, by the arrest of all offenders found violating it."[44] The court characterized this delegation as an unexceptional example of the power of a sheriff to appoint a special deputy to enforce the law. But this case did not settle the issue; defendants in prosecutions for cruelty and other cases involving violation of animal welfare laws enforced by SPCAs often found it hard to believe that a "private" organization could govern their relationships with their own property, their domestic animals. In a 1904 challenge to the ASPCA's power to enforce New York's dog-registration law, for example, the court concluded that the society is "a subordinate public agency" created to "perform a service which the Legislature might delegate to a citizen or public body."[45] This delegation of public powers to a private organization meant that the ASPCA could not only administer dog-licensing laws and run animal shelters, but could also create a quasi-official police force—composed in large part of former police officers, sporting badges and uniforms—who were trained to investigate cruelty to animals.[46] Indeed, criminal prosecutions constituted a significant part of the work of the SPCAs. Historian Diane Beers reports that by 1879 the ASPCA had prosecuted 6,000 cases. The Philadelphia SPCA alone investigated 1,192,203 cases between 1867 and 1921, and won 17,826 convictions.[47] Of course, these numbers represent only a small percentage of animal cruelty cases, most of which never reached a courtroom. But the ability of SPCAs to bring charges probably facilitated their ability to negotiate behavioral changes in the vast majority of cases that did not go to court. In an urban landscape increasingly characterized by public police forces on one hand and private investigators on the other, SPCAs were anomalous—a kind of quasi-public police force dedicated to the protection of animals.

This quasi-police force came to the rescue of Mary Ellen Wilson in one of the more celebrated cases of 1874. The Connolly family held Mary Ellen, a ten-year-old girl, as a prisoner in a dark, cramped tenement and subjected her to severe beatings. Eventually, rumors of the girl's situation came to the attention of mission worker Etta Wheeler, who tried to get help from her church, local charities, and the police. But the charities explained they had no authority to enter a private residence. The police insisted they needed evidence of abuse, not hearsay, in order to intervene. In desperation, she turned to the ASPCA, which was happy to help. Mrs. Wheeler found several neighbors who could testify to the girl's abuse, and that was enough for Henry Bergh. On April 9, 1874, an ASPCA agent entered the Connolly home and carried Mary Ellen to the chambers of a New York Supreme Court judge. The subsequent prosecution of Mary Connolly for assault and battery earned her a year in prison. But the other notable result of the case was the creation, by Henry Bergh and Elbridge Gerry, of the New York Society for the Prevention of Cruelty to Children (NYSPCC). This organization prompted the creation of the first humane societies, devoted to the welfare of both animals and children.[48]

The combination of animal and child welfare functions in the same organization was facilitated by the ASPCA talk of animal rights—rights based in humane sentiments and held by dependent, nonrational beings, such as children. Thus the concept of animal rights helped to lay the foundation for the concept of children's rights. But it also supported the view that the state is justified in intruding into the domestic sphere in order to protect the welfare of children.[49] Indeed, this was a major impetus linking child to animal welfare: as discussed above, animal protection societies were unique among the reform and charity groups of the day in having not only investigative but prosecutorial powers. Although there was a state law against child abuse, the police were often reluctant to get involved in domestic conflicts. Police authority was traditionally exercised in public spaces; their job was to keep the public peace, not to enter into the home and try to regulate private relationships. But animal welfare activists routinely interfered with "private" relationships. Their agents were trained to enter homes, investigate, and prosecute violations of the animal welfare laws. Their power to penetrate the curtain of domestic privacy made them well positioned to address other kinds of domestic abuse. Thus child protection groups adopted the organizational model, as well as some of the statutory precedents, of animal protection. Along with the animal welfare societies, the humane societies were "private charities with public powers." They not only lobbied legislatures but also investigated cases of child abuse, neglect, and abandonment, and even pursued delinquent fathers for desertion and nonsupport, acting very much like regular police officers.[50]

Indeed, some humane societies—in Colorado, Wyoming, Minnesota, and Texas—eventually became state bureaus.[51] In Colorado, the state's twenty-year-old Humane Society became a state bureau in 1901, a change that had little effect on its daily operations but did provide it with a more consistent source of funding. Similarly, in Minnesota, the transformation of the existing humane society into a state agency came decades after its initial incorporation. In Wyoming and Texas, the transition from private organization to state bureau was much more rapid, perhaps owing to the fact that in these states humane societies were not incorporated until the early twentieth century. Though we know little about why these states opted to make their humane societies into state bureaus, officials of the Colorado Humane Society (CHS) spoke openly about their desire for this change and their language suggests the close relationship among animal and child protection, law enforcement, and statebuilding. In 1900, the year before it would become a state bureau, the leaders of the CHS outlined the reasons their organization should become a state agency. The CHS, its leaders claimed, was not "a charitable or benevolent organization but an arm of the law." As law enforcers, agents of the CHS helped the state of Colorado—and its citizens—live up to the standards they set for themselves. In other words, they performed a public function on behalf of the entire state and thus "should be supported by general taxation, as the other official agencies of law and order are." CHS officials also argued that their services formed "an indispensable feature in the social machinery of the State," and they identified the adoption and enforcement of humane legislation with the progressive transformation in the functions of governance to include state protection of the weak.[52]

In recent decades, the late nineteenth- and early twentieth-century efflorescence of statebuilding has often been identified ideologically with maternalism and organizationally with the agency of women's groups acting on behalf of mothers and children.[53] The combination of anticruelty advocacy with law enforcement, however, created some rather interesting problems of gender politics for the animal (and child) welfare organizers. Animal welfare organizations, like other such reform organizations of the time, were usually led by men, although the majority of the members were women. But the men who organized and led anticruelty societies struggled to make sympathy with animals consistent with the gendered ideal of vigorous manhood. Many of the male leaders adopted militant language, talking of "waging war" on lawbreakers, and even advocating the return of corporal punishment for offenders.[54] Some anticruelty warriors drew on the language of chivalry: "What is the oath of gentle blood and knighthood?" asked Illinois Humane Society president John Shortall. "It is to protect the weak and lowly against the strong oppressor."[55] But such language frequently shaded into outright militarism. Elbridge Gerry, for example, frequently portrayed his organization as confronting a state of war. Calling those the NYSPCC prosecuted the "enemies of children," Gerry enumerated the available "weapons of war": "legal enactments and the support of the Press, with the cooperation of the Judiciary and the supplies for maintaining the fight through the liberality of the Public."[56] Apparently neither mere relief nor moral suasion could adequately meet the demands of true sympathy. In a state of war, it was not talk but action that was needed. As a later NYSPCC president put it, "our work is not a missionary or charitable nature. We are . . . 'engaged in the stern task of making war upon crime and vice in peculiar forms.'"[57] As part of their effort to identify animal and child protection with vigorous masculinity, anticruelty leaders also drew a firm line between "charity" and law enforcement, identifying themselves with the latter. As Elbridge Gerry put it, the humane society served as "the hand of the Law, attached to the arm of the Law, created for the enforcement of the Law."[58]

Emphasizing the militant aspects of anticruelty work—and forging an image of the organizations as primarily dedicated to law enforcement—helped their (male) leaders to justify their practice of excluding women from leadership positions. Even Caroline Earle White, one of the chief founders of the Pennsylvania SPCA, was excluded from its board of directors. She went on to form the Women's Branch, which followed the pattern of women's auxiliaries in focusing on education and institution-building, rather than law enforcement.[59] Thus it was often the women's branch or a separate female-only animal welfare organization that ran the local animal shelter, administered dog laws, organized the youth clubs, and promoted humane education.

As historian Diane Beers documents, women were in fact responsible for many institutional innovations of the animal welfare movement. The majority of SPCAs created women's auxiliaries, which gradually took control of what were dubbed "feminine" issues, such as humane education, animal refuges, and water fountains and other services for workhorses. In other words, women were often the service providers in the animal welfare field. The ASPCA auxiliary in New York was particularly active, organizing workhorse parades, spearheading construction of two animal shelters, and building and administering the city's first low-cost animal clinic. Beers notes that these auxiliaries served as stepping stones to greater power for women in the movement. Indeed, many of them eventually sought financial and administrative independence by breaking away from the men's groups. The ASPCA auxiliary, for example, severed its ties to the APSCA only four years after its creation, renaming itself the New York Women's League for Animals. The Women's Branch of the Philadelphia SPCA—which was responsible for creating the country's first animal shelter in 1874—followed suit, becoming an independent organization in 1897. Philadelphia was in fact a hub for women's independent anticruelty activity. It was Philadelphia's Lydia Ryerss, for example, who funded the nation's first retirement farm and infirmary for workhorses. Her example may have inspired other female activists, such as New York's Flora Kibbe, who designed, funded, and administered the country's first "no-kill" shelter in 1903.[60] Despite this trend toward a gendered differentiation in function, however, both the women's and the men's societies combined many different kinds of activities. They operated as charities and law enforcement agencies, pursued prosecution, advocacy, and education, and generally defied any simple distinction between civil society and public power.

Federalizing Animal Welfare

We might expect that during the Progressive Era efforts to develop state capacity for animal welfare would shift from the local to the federal level, following the standard pattern of centralization and consolidation of administrative functions that usually characterizes state development. As Ann-Marie Szymanski's chapter shows, the protection of wildlife followed that pattern, moving rather smoothly from the state to the federal level during this era. It would not be unreasonable to expect animal welfare policy to develop similarly. The federal government had after all already taken some responsibility for animal welfare. The federal Department of Agriculture, along with the land-grant universities, was established in the 1860s to promote scientific knowledge to increase agricultural productivity. In 1887, the Hatch Act provided federal funds for agricultural experiment stations, helping to institutionalize agricultural science in the nation's universities. Both the Department of Agriculture and universities focused their research on increasing agricultural productivity and fighting diseases, which gave them an important role to play in the protection of livestock.[61] Moreover, the animal welfare movement won at least one federal victory in 1877 with the passage of the 28-hour law, which regulated the treatment of animals being transported by rail. And of course, the mass production of livestock in the early twentieth century famously led to the expansion of the federal role in livestock management. *The Jungle*, Upton Sinclair's exposé of the meatpacking industry, prompted passage of the federal Pure Food and Drugs Act and the Meat Inspection Act in 1906 (both administered, initially, by the Department of Agriculture). These acts did not directly regulate the treatment of livestock, but they provided for inspection of meat and other food products, and the inspectors appointed to administer this act would eventually be given responsibility for enforcing humane slaughter regulations.[62]

Despite this promising beginning, however, efforts to develop federal animal welfare protections faltered during the early twentieth century. As Diane Beers notes, the movement became more conservative after 1915, and many anticruelty advocates turned their attention to child welfare and other reform efforts. This is not to suggest that animal welfare organizations became less active, however; a number of their core activities, like administering shelters and licensing dogs, simply became routine. But these responsibilities undoubtedly absorbed some of the resources that might otherwise have been used for legislative campaigns.[63] Thus it took several decades before the federal government would pursue additional animal welfare regulations. The next federal animal welfare statute, the Humane Slaughter Act, would not be passed until 1958.[64]

The movement instead focused most of its energies on the local and state level. In fact, many anticruelty advocates actively resisted greater federal action in this field. True, some Progressive Era humane societies thought federal protection of livestock not only appropriate but a model for the protection of children. In an odd inversion of nineteenth-century rhetoric, child welfare advocates increasingly compared children to livestock. (For example, following the lead of livestock breeders, they promoted "better baby" contests at state fairs, encouraging women to produce a better "crop" of babies.) This comparison was also used by child welfare advocates lobbying Congress to create a Children's Bureau, who argued that children were an even more valuable "resource" than the cows and pigs that the USDA was so concerned about.[65] But several leaders of the anticruelty movement, including Elbridge Gerry (president of the NYSPCC) and William O. Stillman (president of the American Humane Association) opposed centralization at the federal level, believing that federal involvement might weaken protections that had been won at the state level (and possibly encroach on state organizations' hard-won authority).[66] Indeed, the SPCCs and SPCAs had been highly successful at the local and state level, carving out a territory for themselves outside of the patronage and cronyism of state government, wielding state power without being associated with partisan interests. Their successful entrenchment seems to be an example of the dynamic described by Orren and Skowronek: interests that are able to thrive in niches and channels provided by the existing institutional environment serve to bolster the governing arrangements that sustain them over time.[67]

Of course, there are also critical differences between animals and children. Livestock are property as well as sentient creatures with welfare interests. Regulating their welfare at the federal level risked opposition from powerful economic interests; even the federal 28-hour law was seldom enforced. Moreover, animal populations have to be managed and, at times, forcibly reduced. During the late nineteenth and early twentieth centuries, local governments, in pursuit of public health goals, often organized campaigns to eradicate nuisance animals. Concern about rabies supported very active government intervention in controlling the dog population. Early efforts at control involved organizing hunts in which stray dogs were brutally beaten to death (despite protests from animal lovers). The control of dogs and, later, cats has been a persistent area of state violence. Ironically, SPCAs have taken the lead in developing the state's capacity for killing animals. In addition to less brutal means of dealing with unwanted animals, such as spaying and neutering, adoption, and shelters, they have invented several new and more efficient forms of euthanasia.[68] These functions are consistent with states' management of animals under the aegis of protection of public health and peace, but accord less well with the sentimental, rights-based approach of the later nineteenth-century animal welfare movement.

State-sanctioned and state-sponsored violence against animals should not be seen as anomalous or inconsistent; it's simply the other side of state responsibility for animal welfare. The populations of domestic animals, both pets and livestock, have to be managed by humans. And with the elimination or reduction of many predators, game animal populations also require human management. To take responsibility for the welfare of animals is also to take responsibility for determining when and how they will die. Thus, developing the capacity for protecting animal welfare includes developing the capacity for state-regulated and state-perpetrated violence. Animals, like humans, occupy multiple subject positions both serially and simultaneously. The rules structuring their relations with humans reflect both these multiple subject positions and the layered development of different state capacities and functions over time.

Conclusion

This brief overview is, we hope, sufficient to suggest that animals deserve greater attention from scholars of American political development. Far from being at the margins of the welfare state, animals have been central to American state development. As natural resource, private property, and sentient being, animals are subject to a bewildering variety of regulatory regimes, from the protection of endangered species to the management of military working animals. There is much here for scholars of American political development to investigate. How has the state's capacity to exploit animal power and animal minds evolved? To what extent have animal management strategies served as a model for the management of the human population? Who are the key players in shaping the state's relationship to animals? How has animals' dual status as property and social beings complicated the state's authority to regulate them?

Such explorations have the potential to give us fresh insights into the process of American political development. For example, a focus on animal management might produce a new narrative of state development, centered perhaps on such activities as cattle ranching and game management. Similarly, some historians of animals have suggested that we view animals not merely as objects of state regulation but as actors themselves. What if we treated some state actors as human-animal teams (postal worker + horse, DEA agent + dog)? How would that approach affect our concept of agency and our models of political behavior? Attending to the creation of an animal welfare state reminds us, moreover, of the important nexus between public authority and private organizations in American political development. Likewise, while many historians and political scientists have been apt to focus on federal politics and the statebuilding efflorescence of the Progressive Era and the New Deal, regulation of animals in its many guises reorients our gaze not only across many policy domains but also down to local and state regulation as important arenas of governance. These are only a few of the many promising lines of inquiry that open up once we shift our attention from humans to our larger community of fellow creatures.

Chapter 5

Wildlife Protection and the Development of Centralized Governance in the Progressive Era

Ann-Marie Szymanski

As scholars such as Elisabeth Clemens have demonstrated, statebuilding in the United States has never been a purely linear process. Over time, there has been no wholesale, systematic progression, culminating in the centralization of power in autonomous national agencies. Instead, political entrepreneurs and public officials have ultimately fashioned a muddled, fragmented government that mixes national efforts with those of state, local, and private actors to create a bewildering array of governing structures—in short, Clemens's "Rube Goldberg state."[1]

However, wildlife protection is one policy area where the march from provincial to centralized governance proceeded in a relatively linear fashion. Beginning in the late nineteenth century, sportsmen, naturalists, and progressive women increasingly lobbied state governments for laws that reduced the length of fishing and hunting seasons; they also sought to regulate the sale and transportation of wildlife out of state, to restrict the use of hunting and fishing techniques that often produced mass slaughter, and to set limits on the number of animals an individual was allowed to take. Though they initially targeted state governments, these reformers could claim remarkable success at the national level during the Progressive Era. Indeed, by 1920 they could point to the congressional enactment of the Lacey Act (1900), the Weeks-McLean Act (1913), and, most significantly, the Migratory Bird Treaty Act (1918)—upheld by *Missouri v. Holland* (1920). Under this federal regime, the

Department of the Agriculture (and later the Department of Interior) gained new regulatory authority and the power to impose uniformity on the states in the area of wildlife protection. In the process, reformers helped expand federal police power and established a lasting pattern of federal-state cooperation in administration.

In fact, to this day the Migratory Bird Treaty Act (MBTA) is considered a "model and pacesetter in federal wildlife law." Designed to protect migratory birds from unrestrained killing, the act implemented a bilateral treaty with Great Britain (on Canada's behalf) that led to the adoption of stringent bans on the take, capture, and killing of protected birds. In subsequent years, the MBTA was amended to incorporate similar agreements with Mexico (1936), Japan (1972), and the USSR (1976). Though overshadowed in recent years by newer laws such as the Endangered Species Act, the MBTA affects more species than any other federal wildlife statute, it applies regardless of the population levels of protected birds, and it is not riddled with a myriad of exceptions. Hence, this regulatory regime continues to serve as one of the cornerstones of national wildlife protection in the United States.[2]

The federal government's adoption of the MBTA was particularly impressive because it occurred during the Progressive Era, a period in which many campaigns for national regulation faltered. Why were wildlife protection reformers so successful at scaling the walls of federalism? Many students of their efforts suggest that the shift from local-to-state-to-federal action was the inevitable by-product of the mobility of wildlife and the inconsistent protection offered by state policies. As Marge Davis notes, state laws did not generally "apply to migratory wildfowl, since ducks, geese and many insect-eating songbirds regularly crossed state boundaries in their annual migrations." Moreover, the uneven quality of state laws allowed market hunters to tailor their operations to take advantage of more lenient regulatory regimes. In short, Davis contends that most conservationists concluded that "some sort of uniform control was needed that would override the differences of individual states. Such regulation would have to be federally mandated, they said, for voluntary compliance would probably not work."[3]

While Davis is correct to note that wildlife (and especially birds) recognized no jurisdictional boundaries and that the states had widely varying policies, she fails to acknowledge that wildlife defenders were in an unusually strong position to make claims on the federal government during the Progressive Era. Other reformers also grappled with regulating mobile phenomena and encountered a range of local policies but were not as fortunate during these years. For example, neither opponents of air pollution nor advocates of a comprehensive national waterways policy secured the degree of policy centralization achieved by wildlife conservationists during the Progressive Era.[4] While recognizing that advocates of federal wildlife management could make some convincing arguments for the necessity of federal action, this chapter argues that their statebuilding success also reflected the geography of interests involved in this policy area (most notably the urban-rural divide), the creation of a broad coalition of support for federal action in both government and society, and the development of new legal ideas that allowed wildlife protection advocates to overcome claims that national regulation of wildlife was an unconstitutional interference with states' rights under the Tenth Amendment, which stipulates that powers not delegated to the federal government are reserved for the states.

Geographically speaking, students of the Progressive Era have long underscored the significance of urban elites in organizing the reform networks that initiated legislative proposals and campaigns that contributed to the various reforms adopted during this period. Not surprisingly, progressive academics, professionals, and reformers were often notable participants in city politics, and could often parlay their influence at the local level into broader political eminence.[5] Despite their renown in city and sometimes higher circles, progressives could not automatically command the loyalty of Americans who resided in the hinterlands. In some instances (e.g., prohibition and the good roads movement), rural Americans embraced their aims; in others (e.g., the anti-child labor movement and the country life movement's campaign for agricultural efficiency), progressives encountered rural resistance to their goals.[6] In the case of wildlife protection, reformers ultimately discovered that many rural Americans defied hunting and fishing limits and local authorities tolerated such unlawful behavior. Stymied at the local level, wildlife protection advocates grew to appreciate the advantages of centralized regulation as a means of overcoming pockets of resistance to limits on acquisition and sale of wildlife. Moreover, they were able to forge a broad-based reform network to support their efforts, and to provide a legal defense of the MBTA against those who preferred the traditional decentralized approach.

Their successful endeavor touches on the question of whether statebuilding in the United States should be viewed as a process where society-based associations and reformers influenced state formation, or where public officials "borrowed" state capacity and authority from social actors. With respect to the U.S. Department of Agriculture (the original site of the MBTA's implementation), Daniel Carpenter maintains that autonomous bureaucrats and elected officials "nursed and maintained" multifaceted coalitions of associations and reformers which then helped provide the USDA with the social basis of reputation. However, the autonomous bureaucrats were responsible for policy innovations such as national food and drug regulation and the transfer of the nation's forest preserves from the jurisdiction of the Department of the Interior to that of the USDA (through its agency, the Forest Service). Their leverage in the political system was bolstered by reform coalitions, and yet they remained relatively autonomous from them.[7] Whereas Carpenter's approach has much to recommend it, this chapter maintains that for many reform efforts the lines between private and public action remained blurry during the Progressive Era. Public agencies were gaining new responsibilities and discretion as voluntary associations increasingly deferred to them as a source of more systematic efforts than they themselves could mobilize. During this transitional period, however, reformers could (and often did) wear two hats (bureaucrat and association leader), and one can find evidence of this practice in even the most autonomous agencies such as the USDA.

From Sportsmen to Game Wardens: Wildlife Protection as a Public Endeavor

While the creation of a national wildlife protection regime was perhaps the most dramatic achievement of wildlife defenders during the Progressive Era, this period was also important because public officials (most notably, game wardens) increasingly replaced sportsmen as the political actors most responsible for imposing restrictions on hunting and fishing, thus following a general trend that saw private policing replaced by public regulation. Significantly, from 1800 to 1925, American citizens were heavily involved in regulatory policy, particularly its enforcement. They often either created voluntary associations to accomplish this purpose or incorporated enforcement activities into existing organizations, thus providing institutional support for their vision of a cooperative polity comprised of alert citizens. Citizens were central to regulation because public officials were more reactive than proactive, and the common-law regulatory regime depended heavily on citizens to monitor their communities and prod officials to act, or to use private lawsuits as a means of enforcing public standards. Indeed, this regime was no accident: when enacting new regulatory policies, state and local lawmakers often assumed that private citizens would supplement public enforcement efforts. For instance, when the Michigan legislature enacted the state's first limits on hunting in 1859, the law in question did not appoint game wardens to enforce it, but instead assumed citizens would make complaints about illicit hunting, and offered them half the penalties assessed for birds and deer killed during the closed season.[8]

In the case of wildlife protection, private citizens had taken action to help sustain American wildlife from the earliest years of the Republic. For example, the first wildlife preserves in the United States had private origins. Beginning in colonial times, owners of country estates in Virginia and Maryland maintained "deer parks," enclosed spaces designed for deer to live and be hunted. Later, after the Civil War, sportsmen's clubs typically leased or owned substantial acreage that was maintained in its natural condition and governed by rules that supplemented existing public game laws. Of course, the clubs maintained these preserves to ensure that sportsmen had access to sufficient game and fish. Still, in the process of keeping such land free of development, they also sustained nongame species and existing ecosystems. Indeed, as John F. Reiger notes, "In many areas the only substantial acreage remaining in an undeveloped state was the land controlled by sportsmen's clubs."[9]

Private citizens and associations also played significant roles in the enactment and enforcement of laws designed to preserve fish, game, and other wildlife. Initially, the citizens who were most concerned about the depletion of wildlife in the United States were commercial fishermen, sportsmen, and naturalists, though drawing a firm line between the latter two categories is difficult, since so many naturalists hunted and fished at some point in their lives. In any case, they advanced arguments for fish and animal protection that focused on the intrinsic value of animal species as well as on preserving them for use by future generations. Their alarm over the disappearance of wildlife was not misplaced; by the middle of the nineteenth century, large-scale hunting and trawling operations were rapidly depleting the nation's once-plentiful supply of fish, game, and birds. During the 1870s, sportsmen and naturalists lobbied state governments for laws that regulated fishing and hunting seasons, the sale and transportation of game out of state, the use of particular hunting and fishing techniques, and the number of animals an individual was allowed to take.[10]

After 1890, sportsmen and naturalists were joined by progressive women in their quest for stronger wildlife protection. Women participated in outdoor sports and even belonged to sportsmen's clubs at the turn of the century, but progressive women had their greatest impact on national wildlife policy through various Audubon Societies and affiliates of the General Federation of Women's Clubs. Women in these groups proved to be particularly instrumental in drawing the country's attention to the declining numbers of Florida's wading birds, such as herons, flamingos, and egrets. After the Civil War, the millinery industry increasingly incorporated birds and feathers into their hat designs. While milliners used a variety of bird species in their designs, the hat industry exacted a particularly heavy toll on wading birds. Not only were their plumes especially favored for women's hats, but those plumes were only available during mating and nesting season. Hunters easily shot the birds while they nested and then left their unprotected young to starve or be eaten by predators. In response to the massive loss of these birds, the American Ornithologists' Union (AOU) drew up a "model law" in 1886 for state legislatures that outlined provisions that it believed would protect nongame birds, their eggs, and their nests. As proponents for these "model laws," women joined their male colleagues in seeking to secure state measures to preserve wildlife.[11]

State governments were the natural targets for such lobbying because the power to regulate wildlife was presumably one of the powers reserved to them by the Tenth Amendment of the U.S. Constitution. Some states adopted constitutional provisions that explicitly authorized wildlife protection; in others, state courts recognized that states held the police power to protect and preserve wildlife, and upheld reasonable regulations on hunting, fishing, and prohibitions on the traffic in illegally acquired animals.[12] Likewise, the U.S. Supreme Court issued a strong affirmation of the states' power to control their own wildlife in *Geer v. Connecticut* (1896), when it held that states had the common-law right to control and regulate the taking of animals because they were the common property of the state in which they resided.[13] So empowered, nineteenth-century state legislatures endorsed a wide range of limits on fishing and hunting and increasingly extended legal protections to nongame birds as the twentieth century approached. Naturally, the long-established, heavily populated states in the Northeast and upper Midwest tended to produce more comprehensive regulatory regimes than their more rural counterparts. Moreover, many rural states (especially in the South) reduced the effectiveness of general wildlife laws through special legislation, which allowed some counties and localities to opt out of their operation. Still, T. S. Palmer of the U.S. Biological Survey could write in 1912 that "In no other country in the world have laws for the protection of game been passed in such numbers or amended so frequently."[14]

Though often successful at securing state wildlife laws, wildlife protection associations quickly discovered that many public officials lacked the resources or the will to vigorously enforce such legislation. States in the Northeast began establishing state fish commissions as early as the 1860s, but these agencies focused more on artificial fish culture to restock depleted fisheries than on imposing fishing restrictions on the powerful commercial fishing industry.[15] Instead of relying on state-level regulatory agencies, then, most state governments delegated the public enforcement of wildlife protection laws to local officials who were associated with still-rudimentary rural governments.[16] While city governments took the lead in administrative innovation after the Civil War, rural governments typically lacked the cities' administrative complexity, although generalizing about them is difficult since the powers of counties and towns varied by region. In New England, where counties were little more than judicial units, town-meeting governments were the primary source of local control; elsewhere in the North, where counties were often endowed with significant powers, town-meeting governments or townships collaborated with counties in addressing local concerns.[17] During this period in the rural South and West, county governments served as the principal instruments of rural governance, completely eclipsing townships and their limited powers.[18] Whether town or county, rural governments were simple structures that relied heavily on a small number of general officers, such as selectmen and commissioners, and lesser officers, such as constables and sheriffs, who were compensated by fee systems or special appropriations rather than regular salaries. Not surprisingly, rural areas were often woefully underpoliced, as they relied on a handful of part-time, unsalaried officials who often rotated in and out of office on an annual basis.

Even if rural governments had been more professionalized and fully staffed, there was no guarantee that they would have been reliable allies for sportsmen's associations in wildlife protection. These associations were the province of elite, urban sportsmen who wielded more political influence in urban, state, and national affairs than they ever would in the countryside. The prominent Boone and Crockett Club could count Theodore Roosevelt and Gifford Pinchot as members, while Tennessee's first conservationists included a U.S. senator, lawyers, doctors, bankers, professors, engineers, and journalists.[19] As outsiders, organized sportsmen frequently complained that rural governments and legal systems resisted their attempts to impose regulations on their communities. For instance, sportsmen's associations grumbled that too many poachers and "pot" hunters escaped conviction because game laws were typically administered by the nearest district attorneys or justices of the peace, a situation that often led to their vindication by sympathetic area juries. In Clare County, Michigan, the East Saginaw Game Protection Club lodged a complaint about illicit deer hunting, only to see the prosecution of the suspects undermined by the county attorney who "boasted of killing deer out of season himself," witnesses who "conveniently forgot what they had seen," and a jury that exonerated the two defendants by claiming that the prosecution failed to prove that the slain deer used as evidence had been a wild animal.[20]

To compensate for defects in enforcement, sportsmen and naturalists turned to their local and state associations for wildlife protection, many of which had lobbied for the protective laws in question. Their techniques varied, depending on the legal remedies available in their locale. In some states, sportsmen's clubs advocated the use of trespassing laws to prevent shooting and fishing out of season. The Virginia Fish and Game Protective Association reasoned in 1879 that since "No man can shoot, trap, or fish on the land of another man without the latter's consent," Virginia landowners could take action against those who violated game laws on private property.[21] Indeed, many sportsmen believed that their focus on trespass laws would allow them to form alliances with farmers, many of whom either violated game laws or showed indifference to illicit hunting and fishing. As the editors of *Forest and Stream* opined,

> We know of no better method of reaching poachers and violators of closed seasons than through the *trespass laws.* If we can inculcate in the minds of our farmers that these sumptuary game laws are very proper and based upon true principles of economy, and induce them to respect and obey these laws themselves, then each farmer becomes a special constable, and each farm a police district directly under his own surveillance. Sportsmen found shooting on his land out of season or with the *prima facie* evidence of a gun in their hands, would be prosecuted without any trouble whatever, and brought to summary punishment.[22]

Such an approach was adopted in San Patricio County, Texas, where Captain Charles E. H. Glazbook prosecuted several market hunters for trespassing on the property of the Coleman-Fulton Pasture Company.[23]

Another tactic used to enforce wildlife restrictions involved funding the detection and prosecution of illicit hunting and fishing. Some associations offered rewards for information leading to the conviction of offenders, and then sponsored prosecutions. Others were more proactive. In 1878, for example, the Virginia Fish and Game Protective Association sponsored "Twelve prosecutions of offenders," employed detectives "to break up unlawful fishing," and kept the markets, especially in Richmond and Norfolk, "under constant observation" to ensure that "no game now appears there out of season." Likewise, the Connecticut Association of Farmers and Sportsmen for the Protection of Game and Fish (CAFSPGF) employed W. C. Fielding and others as detectives, who gathered evidence against likely offenders and either arrested them themselves (probably acting as local game wardens or deputy sheriffs) or turned their findings over to local law enforcement authorities, who would proceed with the arrests. Then, the CAFSPGF paid for the prosecution of suspects before local justices of the peace. Using such methods, the group boasted of several victories, securing 50 arrests and 48 convictions during the 1888–1890 period.[24]

In fact, wildlife protection societies sometimes used their willingness to fund enforcement efforts to exert control over public authorities. In the Florida Everglades, for instance, the Monroe County Commission and the Florida Audubon Society appointed Guy Bradley deputy sheriff and game warden, respectively, to enforce the state ban on "plume hunting" (a practice that supplied plumes to adorn women's hats from large wading birds like the egret). When personal pique led a suspected plume hunter, Captain Walter Smith, to challenge Bradley for the deputy sheriff position, the Monroe County Commission turned Smith down. Since the Audubon Society was paying Bradley's entire salary and wanted nothing to do with Smith, the board agreed to retain Bradley, just as the Society wished.[25]

Though they often exercised some control over game-law enforcement, sportsmen and naturalists periodically expressed frustration with the limits of their power. One New York sportsman argued that state game protection associations "should be delegated all matters pertaining to the enforcement of the game laws in the same manner as is given to the 'Society for the Prevention of Cruelty to Animals' for the enforcement of its laws." At best, however, only a few state legislatures converted private wildlife protection societies into state wildlife commissions. In 1879, the Delaware state legislature empowered the Delaware Game Protective Association to assume this function and granted every member of the Association the powers of game warden in the process. Meanwhile, in North Carolina (1903) and South Carolina (1907), the state Audubon Societies assumed responsibility for enforcing wildlife laws. In both of these cases, the groups relied on the monies received from the sale of hunting licenses to out-of-state residents to finance the activities of their game wardens. By becoming de facto public agencies and accepting government funds, however, these two societies were subject to more scrutiny than other wildlife protection groups. Just as many humane societies lacked complete freedom in employing agents for enforcement purposes, the Audubon Societies could recommend the appointment of game wardens, but the state governor ultimately had the power to appoint (and presumably to reject) their proposed wardens.[26]

Aside from the handful of private wildlife protection associations that evolved into public agencies, most of these groups remained independent of government control. Indeed, their capacity to enforce laws drew admiring remarks from one antiliquor reformer, who hoped to encourage his fellow drys to assume some responsibility for enforcing prohibition measures:

> For a half century or more there have been laws to protect game and fish, and they are so in harmony with public opinion that no attempt to repeal them has ever been made, . . . yet those who are interested in fish and game do not leave the enforcement of the law to the automatic workings of our criminal courts; but in every county there are "leagues" whose business it is to see the laws enforced and to see that they are amended as experience demands, and there have not been a dozen convictions under these laws in all these years, or an amendment to them but has come through these leagues.[27]

Despite such sanguine reports, however, private policing was often a controversial, costly, and dangerous endeavor. In 1905, Guy Bradley, Audubon game warden for Monroe County, Florida, was fatally shot while on duty; three years later, two other Audubon employees were killed in Florida and South Carolina.[28] In a way, then, the puzzle isn't why private policing declined, but why it endured as long as it did.

One possible explanation is that political reformers initially had no choice but to "borrow" organizational capacity from private associations, only to discontinue such practices once they had the opportunity to "build" bureaucracies. Stymied by a political system characterized by patronage politics and limited by public fears of centralized authority, reformers were free to undertake the project of constructing professional agencies only after they had overcome these obstacles to bureaucratic development. Originally presented by Elisabeth Clemens as a "top-down" process, led by politicians and political entrepreneurs, this process could also be driven by associations that "borrowed" regulatory power from the state until more propitious circumstances allowed them to become state "builders."[29] Thus modified, this theory appears to account for some of the decrease in private policing by sportsmen.

After they organized in the 1870s, sportsmen witnessed the ineffectiveness of public officials in implementing game laws, and thus promoted private enforcement efforts. While some state governments authorized the appointment of local game wardens to enforce these measures, most made it the responsibility of existing local officers, such as constables and sheriffs. Game protection associations found both methods to be lacking. Regardless whether they were specialists or generalists, local public officials were "entirely indifferent to the violation of the law"; above all, the sportsmen contended that these officials were frequently subject to parochial considerations that interfered with the discharge of their duties.[30]

As they gained more experience with private policing, however, many sportsmen began to question its efficacy as well. For one thing, this technique was both indirect and costly, as game protection associations typically lacked the power to arrest and were self-financed. Secondly, sportsmen found it difficult to sustain their efforts, year in and year out. Though capable of securing game protection in the short run, "they fail in the end," opined *Forest and Stream* in 1888. "It is not to be expected of average human nature that private citizens shall keep on forever doing the work which properly belongs to the State or town administration. Game law enforcement, like all other law enforcement, is a public concern; provision should be made for it by the community at large."[31]

Given this quandary, some sportsmen's clubs proposed collaborative arrangements in which game protection societies would appoint agents who were empowered to enforce wildlife protection legislation by the state governments. In some schemes, the agents' pay was to come from the fines collected from violators; in others, the association was responsible for any compensation.[32] Ultimately, as mentioned previously, three game protection groups did share power with state governments: those in Delaware, North Carolina, and South Carolina. In most states, though, sportsmen focused on establishing state fish and game warden departments that were to be staffed by public employees appointed by the governor and financed by public funds. Most game protection societies recognized that these departments were not panaceas; indeed, their effectiveness depended on the quality of the personnel and the size of their operating budgets. Moreover, because conservationists typically played no official role in appointing department staff, they were aware of the dangers posed to the agency by patronage politics. In Michigan, for example, the first state game warden was William Alden Smith, a lawyer and a member of the state Republican Party's central committee. At the time of his appointment in 1887, Michigan sportsmen regarded his appointment as purely political, and some wondered whether Smith could tell a "ruffled grouse from a blue jay."[33]

Despite such apprehensions, forty-one states entrusted the enforcement of game laws to state game commissioners, wardens, or other state officers by 1909 and sportsmen's associations supported these developments. The sportsmen's growing appreciation for state agencies can be seen in Connecticut. Connecticut had maintained a fish commission since 1866, but it primarily focused on replenishing the dwindling stocks of fish in the state's rivers, lakes, and coastal waters.[34] Hence, after its founding in 1888, the Connecticut Association of Farmers and Sportsmen for the Protection of Game and Fish was the statewide organization which took the most vigorous action to enforce state wildlife protection laws for several years. During the years 1888–1885, Abbott C. Collins simultaneously served as the CAFSPGF's president and as a game warden for the city of Hartford; in these dual capacities, Collins became a leading expert on state wildlife laws as well as a critic of local enforcement efforts and the state fish commission. In Collins's view, local game wardens struggled to police areas in which they were well known, and the state fish commission typically failed to pursue violators of the state's fish laws despite the fact that the state legislature had granted enforcement powers to the commission. By the mid-1890s, opinion leaders and politicians had joined Collins in questioning the efficacy of the fish commission as the number of shad continued to decline in state waters. Furthermore, one of the state fish commissioners embroiled his agency in scandal (1894–1895) when he eloped with a fifteen-year-old girl and was arrested and convicted of violating the fish laws of Massachusetts. Shortly thereafter, the Connecticut state legislature abolished the fish commission and replaced it with a newly constituted state Commission of Fisheries and Game, which had the power and the financial support to appoint paid "special protectors to assist in the protection of fish and game who may serve in any County during the pleasure of the Commission." As one might expect, Collins was one of the three individuals appointed to head this new body in 1895.[35]

Indeed, the shift from private policing to centralized, state-level agencies proceeded far more smoothly in the case of wildlife protection than in other policy areas. First of all, as was the case in Connecticut, many states had already experimented with state fish commissions during the 1860s and 1870s in response to concerns raised by commercial fishermen, sportsmen, and those who fished for personal consumption. While often poorly funded and focused on restocking depleted lakes and rivers, fish commissions served as forums for public debate about fish policies and as points of access for sportsmen, naturalists, and other interested parties. Unsurprisingly, they sometimes provided an institutional base for state protection of wildlife, and about fifteen states expanded the jurisdiction of their fish commissions to address game protection.[36]

Furthermore, sportsmen and naturalists viewed state game officials as far less likely to succumb to parochialism than local officers entrusted with game protection. Most local constables and sheriffs were elected officials who had to live among the people they regulated. State game wardens did not, and they could appoint subordinates who were free from local pressures. Of course, diligent state employees were just as likely to spark resentment and opposition from rural populations as their private counterparts, and several were assaulted with gunshots, sometimes in warning and sometimes with the intent to kill. In Lawrence County, Pennsylvania, for instance, Deputy Game Commissioner Seely Houk was murdered while on patrol in 1906; he was particularly zealous in pursuing Italian violators of the state game laws, and an Italian American, Rocco Racca, was convicted and hanged for his murder. Significantly, the Houk case illustrates how the shift from private to public policing often went through a transitional phase where the lines between public and private became especially blurry. After the local police investigation into Houk's death stalled, Game Commission secretary Joseph Kalfbus secured the governor's permission to hire the infamous Pinkerton Detective Agency to investigate the crime. (Pennsylvania lacked a state police force at the time.) However, since the Game Commission initially lacked the requisite funds to pursue the inquiry, its members turned to private sources of funding to pay the Pinkertons, who eventually provided key evidence against Racca.[37]

While wildlife associations remained available after the turn of the century to sponsor wildlife protection and some continued to do so, their leaders generally recognized that the development of state game commissions meant they would play a reduced role in enforcement. In 1913, Philip S. Farman of the American Game Protective and Propagation Association told sportsmen in West Virginia that employing their own wardens to enforce state laws was inadvisable, "as it is liable to lead to antagonism with the regular wardens." Instead, he encouraged the West Virginia Forest, Fish and Game Protective Association to "devote the energy of the organization to securing the appointment of a good man for the state work and then give him all the support possible." Such support could include informing public officials about state wildlife laws and notifying them of violations encountered while hunting and fishing, but members would leave the systematic surveillance and the arrests to duly appointed authorities.[38]

As wildlife protection groups increasingly deferred to the authority of state game commissions, the efforts of the latter received a significant boost from two developments after 1900: the adoption of state licensing laws and the creation of state police forces. Licensing laws required state residents and out-of-state sportsmen wishing to hunt to pay fees for various licenses; the cumulative fees were then typically available to state game commissions to support their activities. By 1912, thirty-six states had laws requiring residents to buy hunting licenses and forty-six required the same of nonresidents, thus providing many state agencies with their first steady source of income and an opportunity to expand their activities. In Pennsylvania, for instance, the game commission increased its salaried game protectors from thirteen to twenty-three after the enactment of its 1913 license law, and quickly accumulated $275,000 in a fund for the stocking and feeding of game.[39] Likewise, state wildlife protection agencies welcomed the creation of state police forces. After 1900, business interests and administrative reformers lobbied in favor of state police forces, so as to provide for more effective control of traffic, rural crime, and labor unrest. Ultimately, the state police movement won several victories prior to 1920, including the formation of centralized, paramilitary units in Pennsylvania (1905) and New York (1917). For state game commissions like the one in Pennsylvania, the state police greatly enhanced the enforcement of wildlife protection laws. As Game Commission secretary Kalfbus gushed in 1908, "This force appears to be to a man constantly keeping its eyes open for violations of the law protecting game and wild birds. Every request from this office for help has been promptly honored. Men have been detailed to investigate charges made and to police territories that I found . . . impossible to cover."[40]

Finally, state game agencies were blessed with powerful allies in the press and other boosters who saw tourism as an important growth industry. As increasing numbers of urban Americans headed to extant wilderness areas to hunt and fish for pleasure, rural entrepreneurs began to realize the value of abundant game and fish. In fact, some market hunters abandoned their mass shooting in order to provide services to visiting sportsmen. For example, Abe Nelson, a noted pothunter from Heron Lake, Minnesota, "hired out as a guide for gun clubs, building duck blinds, leading members through the marsh, and at the end of a day's hunt, using his own skill as a shooter to ensure that his clients reached their limit."[41]

Associations, Experts, and the Creation of National Wildlife Policy

Wildlife protection undoubtedly benefited in the long run from the creation of state game commissions, the ascendancy of public game wardens, and the development of steady revenue streams to support their work. That is not to say that state-level regulation was always wise or beneficial to the environment in the short run; even the best-funded, well-staffed game commissions often miscalculated when designing their policies. For example, when the Pennsylvania Game Commission combined the enforcement of hunting restrictions with the importation of deer from Michigan, Kentucky, Maine, and elsewhere beginning in 1905, the result was an explosion in the deer population that vexed local farmers, who increasingly sought compensation from the commission for "deer damage" to their crops. Still, the states' maintenance of public agencies devoted to wildlife protection committed institutional space to this policy area that could later be occupied by better informed and sometimes better intentioned public officials. Furthermore, as members of the National Association of Game Wardens and Commissioners, founded in 1902, state game commissioners and wardens became vocal proponents of congressional measures like the Migratory Bird Treaty Act.[42]

While the development of state-level wildlife protection agencies was a step forward in many respects, the commissions produced a wide range of approaches to regulating hunting and fishing. State governments had already produced a bewildering array of restrictions on fishing and hunting by the late nineteenth century, and their commissions likewise adopted enforcement and stocking policies, which varied according to local interests and public sentiment. From the perspective of wildlife advocates, one of the biggest problems with this variation is that it allowed market hunters and commercial fishermen to take advantage of the weaknesses in state regulatory regimes to evade the intent of many state regulations. In an era of improved transportation, the trade in wildlife was easier than ever before, and laxly regulated areas became notable commercial hunting and fishing sites. For example, fishermen from Missouri and Arkansas "laundered their crappy through the Reelfoot [Lake, Tennessee] market, since Tennessee was the only state still allowing trade in game fish." Moreover, because migratory birds crossed state boundaries on a regular basis, one state's effort to ban the hunting of such birds could easily be negated by another state's toleration of such hunting. States in the "Mississippi Flyway," the leading migratory route, permitted residents to hunt ducks, geese, and other waterfowl during the spring, thus diminishing their flocks before they arrived at their nesting areas in the northern Great Plains, where state governments provided considerably more protection for these species.[43]

Still, the demand for national—as opposed to state—protection for wildlife reflected more than just the mobility of wildlife or the unevenness of state wildlife laws. Indeed, though Congress generally strengthened federal protection for animal wildlife through the Lacey Act (1900) and sought to create national standards for preserving migratory birds through the Weeks-McLean Act (1913) and the Migratory Bird Treaty Act (1918), federal lawmakers remained relatively indifferent to the plight of fish despite their plummeting numbers in many areas, their mobility and migratory behavior in some species, and the inconsistency of state and international fish regulation. Kurkpatrick Dorsey partly accounts for the federal neglect of fish by pointing to their lack of intrinsic appeal: "For the preservationists, fish simply did not have the appeal of other wild animals. Aesthetically, fish had three shortcomings: they were hard to find, they had neither fur nor feathers, and they did not sing. In short, they were not beautiful. Preservationists who already stretched to protect mammals, birds, and parks had little energy left for mere fish." That said, the federal government also struggled to assert national control over fish because the coalition that favored relevant policies was narrowly based in conservation experts and leaders. For example, the International Fisheries Treaty (IFT) garnered the support of the prominent conservationists associated with the American Fisheries Society and the New York Fish, Game, and Forest League, as well as that of prominent ichthyologists such as David Starr Jordan. However, the treaty simultaneously raised the ire of many commercial fishermen, state officials, and senators from the affected states, and Congress failed to pass the enabling legislation.[44]

In contrast to the narrow base of support for the IFT, public support for the Lacey Act, the Weeks-McClean Act, and the Migratory Bird Treaty Act was much broader. While elite, urban sportsmen and naturalists formed the core of the movement for state game commissions, they were somewhat less prominent participants in the national debate about federal wildlife protection. In the national political arena, sportsmen's groups were joined by progressive women, enterprising bureaucrats, and even shotgun and ammunition manufacturers, who helped finance the American Game Protective and Propagation Association. Why were wildlife protection advocates so successful at creating a broad base of support for protecting animals, and particularly birds? One explanation could be that enterprising bureaucrats in the Department of Agriculture had utilized their relative autonomy to expand federal authority in this area.

As was the case with the states, the federal government's first foray into developing a bureaucracy devoted to wildlife protection involved the creation of a fish commission, namely the U.S. Commission of Fish and Fisheries (1871), at the behest of naturalists and conservationists. Though this commission recognized that fish raised many questions about the states' capacity to regulate fishing, it failed to assert the federal government's control over migratory species, even when confronted with a dispute over declining coastal fish stocks off southern New England. Situated within the Department of Commerce, this agency instead established federal fisheries around the country that used artificial propagation to make young or newly hatched fish available to state officials, sportsmen's clubs, and private individuals who wished to stock local ponds, lakes, rivers, or bays. Indeed, anyone could apply to the fisheries for fry through his congressman, and members of Congress vied with one another for funds to establish fisheries in their states and districts. In short, the U.S. Fish Commission never assumed regulatory functions during the nineteenth century but instead became an integral participant in the distributive politics of this period.[45]

Ultimately, the Fish Commission would not provide an institutional base for the growth of administrative capacity in federal wildlife management. In a way, it was an agency typical of what Daniel Carpenter calls the "clerical state." The commission had the capacity "to distribute federal largesse to electorally favored constituencies," but lacked the ability to plan and the ambition to expand its mission beyond fisheries management. In contrast, the U.S. Biological Survey played a more important role in the development of national wildlife protection policy, which might be expected, given its home department. Whereas the Fish Commission was part of the Commerce Department, the Survey was situated in the U.S. Department of Agriculture, an executive department that Carpenter depicts as having secured a relatively high degree of bureaucratic autonomy by the Progressive Era. As the leading scientific agency of the national government, the Department of Agriculture employed network-based recruiting to create "small but forceful organizations of scientists within their divisions" which could forge "crucial ties outside of them to professional associations, Mugwumps, politicians, women's associations and moral reformers" to help maintain their agencies' autonomy. In some ways, though, the Survey does not entirely conform to Carpenter's broader characterization of the Department of Agriculture. Although the Survey certainly developed its own preferences and interests separate from those of Congress, this autonomy came at a cost: small budgets and increased congressional scrutiny. Furthermore, the overlap between the Survey and the private conservation community highlights one of the weaknesses in Carpenter's analysis: his failure to clearly distinguish between social reformers and bureaucrats in his discussion of the networks that help to sustain agency autonomy. If reformers were at the forefront of spearheading government innovation, then the story is again more about social forces harnessing state authority and less about bureaucrats borrowing the power of those forces.[46]

In fact, a professional association, the American Ornithologists' Union, was crucial to the establishment of the U.S. Biological Survey. The AOU had been collecting bird migration data from hundreds of volunteer observers in the United States and Canada, and C. Hart Merriam, the chairman of the Committee on the Migration of Birds, came to the conclusion that these amateur efforts needed to be managed by a professional government agency. With the aid of an old family friend, Senator Warner Miller (R-N.Y.), Merriam secured congressional approval in 1885 for the creation of an office within the Department of Agriculture's Division of Entomology called the Office of Economic Ornithology and Mammalogy. Though this agency was originally created to study the relationship of birds and mammals to agriculture and forestry, Merriam, its first chief, was not really interested in pursuing research with practical value for farmers and foresters. While the office's early publications informed the nation's farmers about the economic importance of birds and mammals and their various habits, Merriam eventually used the agency's resources to pursue a research agenda that focused on achieving a more comprehensive understanding of North American fauna and its relationship to the environment, as well as on explaining the distribution of birds and mammals in North America. In 1896, the agency's true purpose was finally reflected in its new name, Division of Biological Survey.[47]

While Merriam was able to use the office to pursue his preferences as a naturalist, his partiality for basic research exacerbated his already tenuous relations with Capitol Hill. He did not relish politics, and so disliked participating in the annual budget hearings in Congress that he often sent his subordinates to appear in his place. In turn, Congress was not generous to the Survey; between 1885 and 1910 its budget never rose above $62,000, and its total allocation for salaries never went beyond $17,500. By 1905, congressional demands for economically relevant research rose to such a pitch that Merriam reassigned some of his men from biological surveys to conduct economic studies. Moreover, in 1907, the agricultural appropriation bill included no appropriation for the Survey when it was reported out of committee. Though interpreted by some to be an attack on Merriam's close friend, President Theodore Roosevelt, who supported his work, rumors also swirled "to the effect that it was because of [Merriam's] disproportionate interest in research rather than directly practical work." In fact, the appropriation bill requested that the Survey "explain its practical value to the agricultural interests of the country." Roosevelt intervened to restore the Survey's funding, but Merriam grew so weary of trying to placate Congress and other political actors who interfered with his conception of the Survey's mission that he resigned in 1910.[48]

Even though the U.S. Biological Survey seems to have suffered some costs for pursuing an autonomous path, it nevertheless played a noteworthy role in the development of national wildlife protection policy. C. Hart Merriam might have been somewhat inept as a state builder,[49] but his principal administrative assistant, T. S. Palmer, was not. It was Palmer who founded an office in the Survey called Game and Bird Conservation, which kept track of state hunting and wildlife protection laws. He also participated in drafting a preliminary version of the Migratory Bird Treaty and its regulations, which would govern the protection of Canadian and American migratory birds. Furthermore, no agency leader was more involved with the enforcement of federal and state wildlife protection laws than Palmer. Still, one cannot classify Palmer clearly as merely an entrepreneurial bureaucrat whose actions were either distinctive or contrary to organized interests. After all, Palmer had been a member of the AOU prior to joining the Survey, helped establish the Audubon Society of the District of Columbia in 1898, and, in 1905, he was a founding member of the National Audubon Society, a group he would variously serve as director, vice-president, and member of its board of directors for thirty years.[50]

In any case, the Biological Survey's most important contributions to the development of national wildlife protection policy may have been its voluminous studies, which advanced conservationists' arguments about the necessity, desirability, and feasibility of national wildlife protection. Its surveys revealed the declining numbers of animal and bird species, and its studies supported the claim that migratory birds played a significant role in sustaining agriculture by consuming pests. Although its investigations could not determine the precise impact of birds on the insect population, the Biological Survey had undertaken research that revealed that a variety of bird species consumed crop-destroying insects and weeds. By linking birds to agricultural prosperity, wildlife protection advocates could hope to obtain the support of senators and congressmen who represented farm constituencies. Moreover, because of Merriam's studies of the distribution of bird species in North America, scientists had a fuller grasp of the migration paths taken by various bird species. This, in turn, enabled the Survey to devise regulations for different parts of the country and even the continent.[51]

Still, the Survey's expertise would have been for naught if wildlife protection advocates had proven unable to mobilize the citizenry beyond the small community of national conservationists and naturalists who believed that federal policies were vital to the welfare of the bird and animal populations. The Survey could marshal the power of science and statistics on behalf of its cause, but progressive women, as prominent consumers of the products of the millinery industry, could directly shape the buying patterns of other women. Like the sportsmen who fought for wildlife protection, the women who led the charge against plume hunting came from privileged backgrounds and embodied the sensibilities of northern urban elites. As such, they were well positioned to encourage other fashionable women to boycott the plume industry through their extensive writings and educational efforts. Though their impact on the industry is difficult to assess, the demand for feathers did diminish by 1917 and plume wearing came to be associated with prostitutes in some parts of the country. Moreover, their crusade against plume hunting drew women into the campaign for federal legislation. As their interests broadened to include songbirds, waterfowl, and other animals, women became well acquainted with the weaknesses of state-level game commissions and the particular challenges of protecting migratory birds. Hence, as members of various Audubon groups and women's clubs, they provided staunch support for the Lacey Act, the Weeks-McLean Act, and the Migratory Bird Treaty Act.[52]

A more unusual source of support was provided by the shotgun and ammunition makers, who decided to bankroll a new hunters' organization, the American Game Protective and Propagation Association (AGPPA) in 1911. These companies, which included the Winchester Repeating Arms Company, the Remington Repeating Arms Company, and E. I. du Pont de Nemours Powder Company, had decided that their economic viability depended on the continued existence of wild birds and animals. Hence, they invested $25,000 annually in the AGPPA, providing the resources to engage in political advocacy and send agents into the field to encourage wildlife protection efforts. From the outset, the AGPPA announced its support for federal legislation to protect migratory wildfowl, and its leader, John Burnham, was a fixture on Capitol Hill, lobbying for the Weeks-McLean Act and the Migratory Bird Treaty Act. In fact, Burnham personally assisted in the negotiations with Canadian officials regarding the treaty, and he circulated form letters to AGPPA members, which they were supposed to mail to Congress, demanding the enactment of the treaty's enabling act.[53]

Meanwhile, the U.S. Biological Survey's research illustrating the role of birds in pest management trickled down to farm journals and secured the approval of some of their editors for the national protection of migratory birds. After Congress passed the Weeks-McLean Bill, *Colman's Rural World* approvingly noted that "Birds are of immense value to the farmer in the destruction of insects, and steps are being taken for the preservation of migrating birds by the present Congress."[54] Whether or not farmers supported national wildlife protection in large numbers is unclear. When Kurkpatrick Dorsey sifted through the extant letters sent to Congress and President Wilson in support of the Migratory Bird Treaty Act during the years 1917–1918, he found letters from game commissioners and wardens, sportsmen, conservationists, members of local bird clubs (many of whom were women), business and civic leaders, scientists, and various others, including a few farmers. Regardless of whether farmers were active supporters, the "birds eat farm pests" argument gave the wildlife protection cause the appearance of serving a substantial rural constituency beyond its urban core. Indeed, this line of argument helped conservationists thwart opponents who sometimes portrayed them as "bird cranks and resort-visiting fellows" rather than average citizens, a depiction that wasn't too far from the truth. (For example, many of the members of the Florida Audubon Society were wealthy northerners who vacationed in the state during the winter.)[55] In the end, advocates for congressional measures to protect wildlife would need all the rhetorical ammunition they could muster, for they faced serious questions about the legitimacy of national efforts to regulate wildlife, namely whether or not such policies encroached on the states' capacity to exercise their police power.

Wildlife Protection and the Expansion of Federal Police Power

For the first hundred years of U.S. history, jurists, public officials, and other political actors viewed the federal government as limited by its enumerated powers under the U.S. Constitution. The federal government could exercise police power—the power to legislate concerning the safety, health, morals and general welfare of the people—in those small territories (e.g., the District of Columbia) where the Constitution granted it direct control. For the most part, however, it was primarily the state governments, bolstered by the Tenth Amendment, that possessed this broad expanse of unlimited authority that could serve as the basis of regulatory power within state boundaries. Moreover, the federal courts enhanced the states' claim to such power after the Civil War when they issued a series of rulings that held that the federal government could not impose its will on intrastate commerce, for that remained the dominion of state governments.[56]

Not surprisingly, then, one of the most important obstacles to the development of national wildlife protection policies involved the state governments and their prerogatives to regulate wildlife. When confronted with federal measures that seemingly limited these prerogatives, several state governments insisted that they had the sole power to control the animals within their borders, a position seemingly upheld by the aforementioned *Geer v. Connecticut*.[57] At first, though, it looked as though Congress was going to work within the parameters of the *Geer* decision. With the adoption of the Lacey Act (1900), Congress made it a federal crime to poach game in one state with the purpose of selling the illicitly acquired goods in another. The law also prohibited the transportation of illegally captured or prohibited animals across state lines, and banned the importation of animal species (such as mongooses, fruit bats, and English sparrows) that could harm U.S. crop production and horticulture.[58]

To state game commissions seeking the unquestioned authority to confiscate imported game, the Lacey Act provided welcome support for their efforts. In fact, the law "infused new life into State laws and made possible the enforcement of provisions which previously had been of little effect." For example, the U.S. Biological Survey reported in 1902 that the law contributed to "the seizure and confiscation of 2,600 plume birds, offered for sale in violation of the State law of Maryland," a prosecution that persuaded some wholesale millinery firms to "withdraw from sale and discourage the use of these and other birds protected by local laws." Moreover, the adoption of this statute in 1900 encouraged state governments to enact more comprehensive wildlife protection measures, especially laws that banned the possession and sale of illicitly obtained wildlife. Prior to the Lacey Act, only five states had adopted laws that met the standards of the "model law" recommended by the AOU in 1885 for the protection of wild nongame birds; during the five years after this measure's enactment, twenty-eight additional states and the District of Columbia had adopted versions of the "model law," including its ban on the possession and sale of all wild birds and their plumage.[59]

Ultimately, the national efforts to enforce the Lacey Act reveal that its administrators took pains to respect the states' claims to their authority over wildlife. As the U.S. Biological Survey noted in 1902,

> The aid of the Department has been sought in connection with the enforcement of the provisions against illegal shipment of game to a greater extent than was anticipated. Such aid has been freely rendered, though it has been the aim to confine action merely to supplementing the efforts of local authorities, and to refer cases to State authorities whenever possible. The provisions of the law are such that violation of the Federal statute necessarily involves a previous violation of a local law, and it is possible, therefore, to prosecute cases either in local or Federal courts. Whenever conditions have been favorable to success in State courts, or the evidence in the hands of the Department has been such as can be used in a prosecution in such courts, the case has been promptly turned over to local authorities; otherwise it has been referred to the Department of Justice.[60]

This federal deference to state laws and courts seemed to end, however, with the adoption of the Weeks-McLean Act (1913). By adopting this law, Congress took unprecedented action to assert federal power over wildlife. This law gave the federal government jurisdiction over migratory birds by granting the secretary of agriculture (through the U.S. Biological Survey) the power to establish hunting seasons for migratory game birds nationwide, and it imposed a national ban on shooting almost all nongame birds.[61]

From the beginning, its supporters recognized that the Weeks-McLean Act stood on shaky constitutional ground, given the *Geer* decision. Indeed, when Representative George Shiras (R-Pa.) first proposed an early version of this bill, he acknowledged that he introduced the measure just to provoke discussion. Two years later, Shiras wrote at length about the constitutional challenges facing legislation that gave the federal government the power to regulate migratory birds. To detractors of such legislation, he asserted that "we have a Federal police power as complete and far-reaching under the sphere of the general government as is that within the boundaries of a State." As evidence for his claim, Shiras pointed to the protective tariff, immigration laws, quarantine laws, the ban on using the mail to conduct lotteries, and other federal policies that were presumably adopted to promote the safety, health, morals, and general welfare of the nation. With respect to federal wildlife control, Shiras noted that migratory animals were similar to epidemic diseases that traveled across state boundaries and thus lacked a local character. "Local or non-contagious diseases are properly under the exclusive jurisdiction of the State, while diseases of an epidemic character, so destructive to human life, are properly within the jurisdiction of the Federal government," Shiras wrote. In a similar fashion, he argued, his proposed measure retained state control over local animals while granting the federal government jurisdiction over transient ones.[62]

Unfortunately for Shiras and others who found his argument persuasive, many national and state politicians did not agree with his line of reasoning, and federal migratory bird legislation stalled until the 62nd Congress (1912–1913). During this session, advocates of a measure to regulate the hunting of migratory birds secured the support of Congress by framing the Weeks-McLean bill as a boon to agriculture. However, wildlife protection advocates fully expected President William Howard Taft to veto the measure, for he had criticized it as an unconstitutional usurpation of state police power. This veto did not come to pass, though, because the Senate had included the bill as a rider to the Agriculture Department appropriations bill, and Taft—busy with moving out of the White House—signed the measure in 1913 without reading it first. The Weeks-McLean Bill thus became law, but the constitutional issue created such doubt about its legitimacy that its supporters began to consider different approaches to regulating migratory birds almost immediately after it was signed.[63]

After the Weeks-McLean Act was signed into law, the Wilson administration dutifully drew up regulations designed to impose federally mandated hunting seasons for migratory game birds. These rules divided the country up into several zones, each with its own open and closed hunting seasons, based on the breeding habits and migratory patterns of game birds. Congress appropriated a mere $10,000 for the law's enforcement in 1913, however, and state and local opponents to the law mobilized quickly against it. In particular, midwestern hunters contended that the law's ban on the spring shooting of ducks deprived them of the right to hunt ducks, for waterfowl stopped in their part of the country only during the spring. Led by Senator James A. Reed (D-Mo.) in Congress, the opposition soon transcended the Midwest, as hunters elsewhere complained about the unfairness of their hunting opportunities compared to those of hunters in other zones. Ultimately, a number of hunters challenged the operation of the Weeks-McLean Act in federal and state courts on the grounds that it encroached on the states' power to regulate game within their borders. In 1913 alone, there were seventeen legal challenges to the act; by 1916, twenty cases were pending in state and federal courts, with thirty-three more wending their way through the legal process. When a federal court declared the law unconstitutional in May 1914 in *United States v. Shauver* on the grounds that Congress had exceeded its authority to regulate state property, its supporters estimated they had approximately a year to eighteen months to devise a strategy before the *Shauver* case reached the Supreme Court.[64]

Even before *Shauver* and similar cases were decided, wildlife protection advocates had considered two alternatives to the Weeks-McLean Act in light of its dubious legality: amending the Constitution and pursuing a treaty with Mexico, Canada, or both of these countries.[65] While a constitutional amendment was not out of the question,[66] recent developments in conservation diplomacy encouraged the pursuit of a treaty, though, of course, any treaty might also be subject to constitutional scrutiny by the courts. Both the Roosevelt and Taft administrations had actively engaged in conservation diplomacy in recent years, and had worked on the Inland Fisheries Treaty (1908) and the North Pacific Fur Seal Convention (1911), though the former was never implemented. As Roosevelt's secretary of state, Elihu Root had participated in negotiations about the fisheries treaty and the fur seal issue; as a senator from New York during the 62nd Congress, he preferred diplomacy to the Weeks-McLean Bill and had recommended that the Senate instead pass a resolution urging the president to negotiate a treaty with other North American countries to protect migratory birds. Root's preference for a treaty was not merely a by-product of his own experience as a statesman; rather, he believed that the

U.S. Supreme Court would be less likely to find a treaty unconstitutional than a statute. Root's posture on this issue reflected a legal perspective which held that the treaty-making power was "one of the powers delegated to the Federal Government and therefore was not affected by the Tenth Amendment to the Constitution reserving to the States or to the people the powers not delegated to the United States by the Constitution." In other words, he saw treaty-making as a constitutional power granted to the national government in Article VI that could be exercised without any deference to the states' jurisdictional claims.[67]

Although other wildlife advocates supported the Weeks-McLean measure rather than diplomatic efforts during the 1912–1913 congressional session, they circled back to Root's position that a treaty might give migratory bird regulations more constitutional legitimacy after the opposition mobilized against the 1913 statute. For instance, Henry Chase, a conservationist and sometime game warden from Vermont, conceded that the Weeks-McLean Act "is of doubtful validity, to say the least, while on the other hand, few legal authorities will dispute the constitutionality of an enactment to the same effect by Congress carrying out the provisions of an international treaty." In a similar fashion, William Hornaday, director of the New York Zoological Society, optimistically announced that "As a constitutional instrument a treaty is unassailable by the courts; for by virtue of international law, and the terms of the ratification, a treaty becomes the supreme law of the land. Congress never negotiates a treaty which is in conflict with the Constitution of the United States or even open to a charge of being so." Given this understanding of treaties, it is not surprising that the wildlife protection community rallied around the Migratory Bird Treaty and its enabling legislation.[68]

In contrast to the Weeks-McLean Act, which was brief, vague, and delegated the formulation of regulations to the U.S. Biological Survey, the Migratory Bird Treaty provided a more detailed set of restrictions on hunting and harvesting, and had much stronger enforcement provisions. Its goal was to provide an effective framework for a uniform hunting season for both the United States and Canada. When representatives of the United States and Great Britain (acting for Canada) settled on the final language and provisions of the Migratory Bird Treaty, they agreed that the measure would not go into effect until the two countries enacted enabling legislation. Canada adopted the Migratory Birds Convention Act in 1917, and the U.S. Congress passed the Migratory Bird Treaty Act in 1918. Once in place, the Migratory Bird Treaty Act nullified all state and local laws that were inconsistent with its provisions but authorized the states to make and enforce statutes that provided greater protection than the treaty for migratory birds and their nests.[69]

When the Supreme Court upheld the enabling act's constitutionality, wildlife protection advocates discovered that their faith in the treaty-making approach had been warranted. In *Missouri v. Holland,* Oliver Wendell Holmes, writing for the 7-2 majority, maintained that the Migratory Bird Treaty Act was constitutional because it involved "a national interest of very nearly the first magnitude" that could "be protected only by national action in concert with that of another Power." In doing so, Holmes rejected the argument that the states could own migratory animals, for the "whole foundation of the State's rights is the presence within their jurisdiction of birds that yesterday had not arrived, tomorrow may be in another state and in a week a thousand miles away." Moreover, he echoed the conservationists' own rhetoric about the utility of birds for agriculture when he wrote that "We see nothing in the Constitution that compels the Government to sit by while a food supply is cut off and the protectors of our forests and our crops are destroyed." In a gesture to those who viewed treaties as unassailable, Holmes also held that Congress can constitutionally enact a statute to enforce a treaty even if the law itself would otherwise have been unconstitutional. He explained, "If the treaty is valid there can be no dispute about the validity of the statute under Article I, Section 8, as a necessary and proper means to execute the powers of the Government." Still, Holmes did not fully embrace the conservationists' posture that treaty-making could never be limited by the Tenth Amendment because it was an explicitly national power granted by Article VI. At most, he stated that "qualifications to treaty-making power" must be "ascertained in a different way" than statutes. Furthermore, the Court did not positively affirm the existence of a federal police power, as proposed by Shiras. Still, Holmes's opinion undermined the enumerated/reserved powers framework, an important step for the eventual development of such a power.[70]

According to the enumerated/reserved powers framework, the federal government derived its authority from specific constitutional provisions while the states enjoyed the residuum of power not granted to the national state. In *Missouri v. Holland*, however, Holmes never bothered to associate the enabling act with any particular provision of the U.S. Constitution, though he noted that the treaty-making power itself was "delegated expressly." Instead, he wrote, "The treaty in question does not contravene any prohibitory words to be found in the Constitution. The only question is whether it is forbidden by some invisible radiation from the general terms of the Tenth Amendment."

In other words, Holmes suggested that federal power need not be specifically authorized by the Constitution; rather, a congressional act is legitimate unless otherwise forbidden by a constitutional provision or the "general terms of the Tenth Amendment." Furthermore, his rejection of the enumerated/reserved powers approach framed the Constitution as a document that has evolved over time:

> we may add that when we are dealing with words that are also a constituent act, like the Constitution of the United States, we must realize that they have called into life a being the development of which could not have been foreseen completely by the most gifted of its begetters. It was enough for them to realize or to hope that they have created an organism; it has taken a century and cost their successors much sweat and blood to prove that they created a nation. The case before us must be considered in the light of our whole experience and not merely in what was said a hundred years ago.

By adopting this looser approach to constitutional interpretation, Holmes helped set the stage for a national police power that would allow the federal government to act on behalf of the safety, health, morals, and general welfare of the people.[71]

Conclusion

With the Supreme Court stamp of approval, the Migratory Bird Treaty Act joined a growing number of federal policies that suggested that the national government possessed some kind of police power, including the Indian Intermarriage Act (1888), the Anti-Lottery Act (1895), the Oleomargarine Acts (1896), the Mann Act (1910), and the White Phosphorus Match Act (1912).[72] However, the Supreme Court had recently rebuffed child labor reformers in their attempts to expand federal authority into the states' dominion in *Hammer v. Dagenhart* (1918), which struck down the Keating-Owen Act (1916). As was the case with the conservationists, opponents of child labor had first sought state bans on employing young children, and only later sought national limits on this labor practice when they recognized the inadequacy of state measures. When they secured the Keating-Owen Act, child labor reformers hoped that the Supreme Court would affirm the measure as a legitimate exercise of congressional power to regulate interstate commerce. However, the Court ruled that only states had the power to regulate the production of goods, and that Congress had violated the Constitution by seeking to create uniform labor conditions in the states. Undeterred, child labor opponents obtained congressional support for the Child Labor Tax Law (1919), only to watch the Court nullify that statute in *Bailey v. Drexel Furniture Co.* (1922) because it deemed the tax on companies that employed children to be an improper use of regulatory authority by Congress. In both of these cases, then, the states' prerogatives were upheld, and national claims to regulatory power were thwarted.[73]

So, why did conservationists succeed while child labor reformers failed? The conservationists were not legal geniuses; indeed, it truly was the case that "they had not been able to develop a strong legal reasoning to support the treaty." Their claims about the federal monopoly of the treaty power weren't without precedent, but Holmes did not find them convincing enough to use them as the sole foundation for his decision. Holmes may have assimilated the wildlife protectors' argument that the nation's migratory birds were threatened with elimination, an event that would have dire consequences for the nation's food supply, crops, and forests.[74]

Another possible explanation is that, by 1920, Holmes's "current of commerce" theory had gained stronger support from his colleagues on the Supreme Court. Through this theory, Holmes had sought to provide the Court with a means of determining which kinds of intrastate commercial activities could be legitimately regulated by the national government in a system of dual federalism. According to this theory, a local business activity could be subject to national regulation if it was "affected with a public interest" and disrupted the flow of commerce. Migrating birds did not constitute commercial activities, of course, but the claim that states had a monopoly on wildlife policies was premised on an assertion of local control that Holmes had found wanting in other cases where police power was presumed to govern. In *Swift and Co. v. United States* (1905), for example, Holmes had rejected the claim that Congress could not regulate the Chicago slaughterhouse industry because the sale of cattle was a local event. Instead, he wrote that "When cattle are sent for sale from a place in one state, with the expectation that they will end their transit, after purchase, in another, and when in effect they do so, with only the interruption necessary to find a purchaser at the stock yards, and when this is a typical, constantly recurring course, the current thus existing is a current of commerce among the states, and the purchase of the cattle is a part and incident of such commerce."[75] Likewise, in *Missouri v. Holland*, Holmes wrote that the "whole foundation of the State's rights is the presence within their jurisdiction of birds that yesterday had not arrived, tomorrow may be in another state and in a week a thousand miles away."[76] In both cases, entities that necessarily moved from state to state could not be construed as solely a state responsibility, thus opening up the possibility of national regulation.

Finally, it could be argued that his colleagues on the Supreme Court tended to defer to Holmes's views about sovereignty when they involved international rather than domestic concerns, and that *Missouri v. Holland* reflected this general trend.[77] In domestic affairs, Holmes recognized Congress as the sovereign authority, and was willing to uphold congressional authority even when it encroached on the states' claims to exclusive jurisdiction. Although this understanding of sovereignty was not the predominant approach adopted by the Supreme Court during the Progressive Era, his colleagues apparently found Holmes's views on the United States as a sovereign nation in the international arena to be more palatable. In the wake of the Spanish-American War and the acquisition of the Panama Canal Zone, the Supreme Court was called on, time and time again, to sort out the extent of the federal government's jurisdiction over the Philippines, Puerto Rico, the Canal Zone, and other territorial possessions. In several of these cases, the Court entrusted Holmes with the responsibility of defining the scope of the federal government's sovereignty, and his opinions typically secured unanimous support.[78] His colleagues' support in these cases may have reflected the fact that Holmes often carefully laid out jurisdictional boundaries in his decisions, and he did not always interpret questions of sovereignty in ways that increased the federal government's power.[79] In *Missouri v. Holland*, of course, Holmes's decision essentially expanded the power of Congress to legislate on matters that had traditionally been the states' responsibility. However, he portrayed the fate of migrating birds as a situation that "can be protected only by national action in concert with that of another power," and his decision found support from six of his colleagues and several prominent legal commentators, including George Sutherland, the future author of *U.S. v. Curtiss-Wright Export Corp.* and a champion of the perspective that foreign and domestic policymaking were different and ought to be treated as such.[80]

With the emergence of thinkers such as Sutherland and a legal community that increasingly shared his views, wildlife advocates were probably wise to frame the protection of wildlife as an international issue. Significantly, it is unlikely that conservationists would have taken this approach if they didn't already conceive of wildlife in international terms. By 1910, the U. S. Biological Survey had already conducted extensive fieldwork in Canada and Mexico, and its officials could speak knowledgeably about the threats posed to migratory birds in other parts of the Western Hemisphere. Moreover, conservationists were already enmeshed in international diplomacy to address wildlife protection, and they saw the migratory bird treaty as a continuation of their earlier efforts in this regard. In fact, it was no accident that the United States initially negotiated the treaty with Canada and not Mexico; the United States and Canada (with British involvement) had just concluded the North Pacific Fur Seal Convention and their citizens had a shared interest in conservation, as demonstrated by several Canadians who joined the Audubon Association and the American Game Protective Association.[81]

In the end, the network for wildlife protection policy became international in scope and fell into the hands of experts who were state actors. Bolstered by the arguments of policy experts, conservationists were able to mobilize thousands of Americans and Canadians to secure a uniform framework for regulating the hunting of game birds and to ban the killing of nongame birds. However, before this became possible, reformers first had to accept the necessity for professionalization and public bureaucracies. To achieve comprehensive regulation, naturalists and sportsmen had to support state actors who might later act contrary to their aims. Indeed, while the distinction between "reformer" and "bureaucrat" often remained blurry during the Progressive Era, agency leaders would eventually achieve some degree of autonomy from reform coalitions. Unlike the situation of juvenile courts (Nackenoff and Sullivan) or animal protection (Pearson and Smith), once reformers had engaged the attention of the state, the state absorbed the entire agenda and moved it into the field of public regulation, leaving little political room for external collaboration and direction. Yet unlike the BHA development of standards for proper American homes (Greer), these reformers and nonstate policy experts had hoped all along to engage the attention of state actors, and to convince them to embrace the tasks of study and regulation. Hence, this period of history is best understood as a transitional phase in which amateurs assented to the guidance of experts, and assumed a secondary role in securing the nation's regulation.

Chapter 6

The House That Julia (and Friends) Built: Networking Chicago's Juvenile Court

Carol Nackenoff and Kathleen S. Sullivan

At the turn of the twentieth century, reformers in Chicago, deeply concerned about social conditions and moral influences on children, created a juvenile court system. This innovation led to the extension of the juvenile court idea and other institutional efforts in child saving across the nation and gave rise to social programs at the city, state, and federal level. The origin and early development of the juvenile court system provides an important case study in Progressive Era statebuilding and the public-private collaborations that initiated and sustained it. Nonstate actors and organizations played a vital and dynamic role in pressing the idea of the Juvenile Court on policymakers.[1] The networks they built included allies on the court, in elective office, in academia, and in newly professionalizing fields. As in the children's rhyme, "The House That Jack Built," Julia Lathrop (and friends) built an institution by building a network that generated, sustained, and expanded the juvenile court system.

Our investigation leads us to be skeptical about some of the Weberian and linear assumptions in the literature on statebuilding in the Progressive Era. In the case of the Juvenile Court, statebuilding did not simply move from the state to the national level, nor were courts left out of the pattern of growth in bureaucratic organization and state capacity. Much of the American statebuilding literature focuses on the role of legislators, executives, and bureaucrats in the transition from a "state of courts and parties" to a new administrative state, and the bulk of that literature addresses development at the federal level. Dan Carpenter's work emphasizes the role of bureaucratic entrepreneurs, who, in the process of building bureaucratic legitimacy, engage in small, experimental programs that precede the building of coalitions and forging of public support. Carpenter's administrative leaders create these "pockets of limited discretion" and "By nurturing local constituencies and by using their multiple network affiliations to build broad support coalitions among professionals, agrarians, women's groups, moral crusaders, and congressional and partisan elites, they won for their young programs both political currency and administrative legitimacy."[2] Those networks had to develop somehow. In Chicago, we find that reformers actively generated and fostered those networks, which then provided financial resources, trained personnel, and experienced recordkeeping. The development of networks themselves was a precondition for formal institutional development. And the network of reformers pressured legislative and administrative elites into channels of reform that do not appear to have been on their agendas previously.

The end of the nineteenth century ushered in a new era for the "intermingling of state and private means of extending public authority."[3] In this era, Brian Balogh finds the federal government parceling out state authority to a number of voluntary associations and professional societies to do state work. We discover here that these nonstate actors are not merely doing work already envisioned by the state or bureaucratic actors. Rather, they are often moving the state into new work, forging the warrants for, and helping to create, public authority. Drawing on firsthand experiences and experiments, Lathrop and her largely female reformer allies in Chicago pressed the idea of the Juvenile Court on the state of Illinois, and subsequently, pressed child-saving ideas upon the nation.

Julia Lathrop, with many of her friends and associates, built an institution to deal with a newly defined public problem. Organized women activists loom large in the history of the juvenile court movement in the United States, and nowhere is this more evident than in Chicago, home of the first Juvenile Court.[4] Hull House, founded in 1889, and the Chicago Woman's Club (CWC), founded in 1876, provided many of the activists who would lead the battle for the Juvenile Court Bill in the Illinois legislature in 1899. Advancing their vision for coping with newly defined—or redefined—social problems, these reformers made use of opportunities and resources, both material and social, to make a "private" contribution to statebuilding. These reformers were not self-interested beneficiaries of the policies they advanced in the conventional sense; however, some parlayed the expertise they developed into new positions in the growing administrative state. The origins and early operation of the Juvenile Court places female reformers at the center of this statebuilding story.

There have been a number of fine studies of the Juvenile Court and of municipal court reform in Chicago. From works produced by participants and by some of their students to later works on Progressive Era female reformers and newly professionalizing social sciences, to the recent past, we have gained insights into particular dimensions of these activities. Among the most recent, David Tanenhaus has wonderfully demonstrated how the Juvenile Court was a work in progress, not a single act of creation, and how action also bred reaction. Michael Willrich has made a major contribution to understanding how the transformation of American law, so that law and courts became more responsive to felt social needs, played out in the transformation of the municipal court in Chicago. Elizabeth Clapp has offered a rich historical exploration of the role of the Chicago Woman's Club and the Hull House community in establishing the Juvenile Court of Cook County (sometimes simply referred to as the Chicago Juvenile Court). Victoria Getis has examined the ways the court combined legal and social welfare functions, combining uneasily a number of tensions and contradictions.[5] We build on their contributions, bringing the court and its allies and helpers into narratives of statebuilding.

When we place the Chicago Juvenile Court and the spread of the juvenile court idea in a statebuilding narrative, it highlights, in instance after instance, the difficulty of sharply delineating public-private boundaries in turn-of-the-century reform efforts. While the state seemed to "borrow" capacity from private organizations during early phases in the construction of the Juvenile Court, building the court proved to be hardly a matter of passing all innovation and responsibility from nonstate initiators to bureaucrats. In the instance of the Juvenile Court, while some activities spearheaded by philanthropic organizations were absorbed into the public sector, the operation of the institution continued to depend in part on the involvement of the philanthropic and voluntary organizations that had helped bring them into existence.

The state retained complex relationships with these organizations, including these organizations in various ways in processes of governance at different stages of institutional development. This may be in part because organizations are powerful stakeholders and in part because, as Elisabeth Clemens suggests, "Within a political culture suspicious of governmental power, action through collaboration might well be less costly than the construction of explicitly public state capacity."[6]

Because of perceived advantages on both sides, activists did not simply hand off their hard-won projects to the state. Our evidence places us partially at odds with historian Paula Baker, who argued that women's charitable work was passed along to the state in this period.[7] Legislatures sometimes used the prototypical institutions developed by voluntary effort as templates for new institutions sanctioned at law—institutions that would function with some public infusion of resources but that also depended on continued voluntary and private activities. And activists often turned their attention from winning a legislative victory to volunteering their expertise, developed from having worked on the problem—along with their time and financial investment—to supporting and helping shape the practices of a fledgling institution such as the Juvenile Court. Public-private imbrication is evident in the case of the Juvenile Court, which is best understood as a hybrid institution that relied on both public and private initiatives as it developed. We doubt this was unusual; as Elisabeth Clemens notes, one can find many "complex and hybridized arrangements" between organizations and public agencies.[8] Other examples can be found in this volume. Hull House cofounder Jane Addams, who was herself a participant in the new court initiatives, was well aware of the boundary crossing and blurring, writing of a "wavering line between the public and private activities, so that you can scarcely tell what is philanthropy and what is public service."[9] Reformers secured a place for themselves in new state functions. These reformers, many of them women, drew on a network of academics, lawyers, businessmen, and progressive fellow travelers to push for their vision of needed institutional generation to cope with newly defined—or redefined—social problems. They found allies in the field who had invested in earlier charitable institutions to deal with the problems of abused and neglected children and who were now overwhelmed with the burdens they had been expected to take on. Once this coalition had succeeded in getting a Juvenile Court law passed, central reformers and their networks continued to be indispensable in implementing the law and building the institution.

Government relied on private actors to carry out the directives in the new juvenile court legislation, and reformers had the greatest enthusiasm for doing so.[10] The reformers, who had studied the issue, visited experiments elsewhere, and invested in passage of the Juvenile Court Bill, saw themselves as stakeholders in the new institution, and the roles they envisioned for themselves allowed them to further develop their own capacities alongside it. In this period, it continued to develop and morph as a vision and an institution in response to the developing thought and activities of reformers. What the reformers contributed shifted over time; when they were able to withdraw monetary support and personnel, they turned their attention to expanding the role and mission of the institution, to ancillary organizations, and to exerting greater control over adults who helped endanger or corrupt minors.

How Child Work Became State Work

The juvenile court movement spoke to felt needs at the turn of the century, although little institutional capacity existed to meet those increasingly perceived needs. Late nineteenth-century reformers began to forge a new narrative involving children, in which a problem and its roots were identified, and solutions involving organized human intervention envisioned.[11] Identifying environmental contributions, rather than innate character or genetics, as the cause of criminality and depravity led reformers to be optimistic that they could devise approaches to the prevention and cure of delinquency. Reformers' desire to rescue young people from harmful environments and their belief that healthy environments could help reform bad habits led them to advocate removing children from jails and from the influence of hardened criminals. In this period adolescence was invented as a category, and child development experts argued that adolescents were more like children than adults and should be treated accordingly.[12] Rootless adolescent males and females—especially girls who might be lured by wily men—moving to the city of Chicago in search of work or excitement greatly concerned moral reformers. It did not matter whether they were arriving from farms or from foreign nations. Not even the presence of the family was a satisfactory bulwark against the temptations and improper moral influences the young could encounter in urban neighborhoods. Inadequate parental supervision, dysfunctional families suffering from alcoholism, neglect, sending children out as vendors or to labor, school truancy, improper amusements, gangs, and association with criminal elements all threatened the young. No public or private institution effectively dealt with these emerging problems.

A growing urban population and economic hardships for families provided a steady supply of children in need. With children deemed a vulnerable class, organizations increasingly stepped in on behalf of those whose families were unable to protect them or whose families harmed them through neglect or abuse. Police who encountered children in need, lacking resources to provide for them, brought them to the attention of the Illinois Humane Society, which worked on "behalf of those forms of life that are themselves helpless," aiding children and animals alike. [13] The two institutions continued to work together, the Society enjoying the "cordial support" of the mayor and the chief of police, who gave them information and aid.[14] The Humane Society also rescued children in labor, particularly concerned with those who worked at night, such as lamplighters or acrobats.[15] It investigated children's conditions at home, routinely finding intemperate, drunk, or vagrant parents or abandoned mothers.[16] Its resources lay in coordinating with other city agencies and with other chapters of the Humane Society across the country, placing children with agencies in Chicago, or, for those who had migrated to the city, with humane societies in their hometowns to track down absent fathers and try to get the children placed at home.[17] The chapter by Susan Pearson and Kimberly Smith in this volume explores some of the complex partnerships that developed between animal and child welfare societies and police in some of the states.[18] The Illinois Humane Society worked case-by-case as children were brought to them. The Society was gratified to serve ill-used children and animals,[19] but lacked a comprehensive plan to aid children and recognized its limitations. It lacked the resources to adequately respond to any one of its cases, much less to address the scope of the problem. In the year ending April 30, 1884, the Society aided 1,467 children, against 955 the previous year, on a total budget of $7,518, reporting that it could do much more if it had the means.[20]

Young people who had run afoul of the law, even for offenses such as disorderly conduct, raised additional challenges for reformers, who saw many abused, neglected, and needy children among those classed as criminals. Children faced legal proceedings and possible incarceration alongside adults if they were as old as ten. Rather than class delinquents as criminals, reformers redefined the young offenders "as misdirected and misguided and needing aid, encouragement, help and assistance."[21] The delinquent would become a ward of the state, under the doctrine of *parens patriae*—that is, the state owned that it was the parent of those who were not being cared for and who could not care for themselves, in the name of the commonweal. When the children in question had not come to the attention of the legal system because of violations of criminal laws, they nonetheless might be considered dependent on the state because of the failure of parents or guardians to guard them from risky behavior and habits. Parents and guardians who demonstrated unfitness to raise moral citizens—even due to poverty and unemployment—might find the state asserting its prerogatives under *parens patriae*, substituting itself for the family.

The doctrine of *parens patriae*, while not new, was deployed in the attempt to broaden the power of the state in the case of juveniles. The doctrine dated to English chancery courts, given authority over the estates of orphaned minors, and made its appearance in the United States as early as 1838 in Pennsylvania, when the state sought to commit a troublesome child to a house of refuge.[22] However, when the State Board of Charities in Illinois tried to exercise such authority, it was rebuffed. Shortly after its formation in 1869 to oversee charitable institutions in the state, it attempted to open a state reform school, but a decision by the Supreme Court of Illinois in 1870 held that no child could be sent to reform school for their well-being or for the "good of society" "without charge or conviction of crime."[23] Going against a trend in state court decisions elsewhere, Illinois held that the state could not simply step in as *parens patriae*; the court held that children could not be deprived of their liberty for the good of society. Parental rights were not to be lightly abrogated and parental unfitness had to be clearly proved. In 1872, the superintendent's application to add more buildings to house the 165 students was denied.[24] The decision did much to destroy the Reform School and the Great Chicago Fire did the rest.[25] The court, which then posed a formidable stumbling block, would later support a modified claim by juvenile court advocates for *parens patriae*.[26]

Implementing Reform Through Networks

It was no simple task to muster the capacity and authority to save children. In the late 1880s and early 1890s, organizations at the margins of the state began to combine their resources, creating a reform network. The network included female reformers and male allies who began to mobilize from Hull House. Women's clubs, where a number of Chicago's elite could draw on their social networks and tap financial resources, joined in. Many reform leaders were members of multiple organizations involved in the cause of saving children. They talked with reformers in other states and shared ideas.

Religious organizations had long been interested in the well-being of children. Presbyterian minister Martin Van Buren Van Arsdale preached the duty to rescue neglected children and in 1883 founded the Children's Home and Aid Society of Illinois. He took young children into his own home until suitable placements could be found. He broadened the cause by traveling around the state, explaining his work and organizing local advisory boards in communities where any children were placed.[27] The organization had spread to other states by 1889; by 1891 the national organization began publishing the *Children's Home Finder*, with copies sold by local advisory board members, and by 1893 there were 1,500 local advisory boards in the United States. The organization gained support from other Protestant denominations.[28]

Timothy Hurley drew on his professional status as a lawyer and his religious commitment to found the Visitation and Aid Society, a progressive lay Catholic organization, in 1888. The Visitation and Aid Society was highly active in prison reform, and in other child-saving and social welfare causes in Cook County, Illinois. Hurley drafted an 1891 bill that would have authorized county courts to commit neglected, abandoned, destitute, or morally untutored children to approved placement corporations, calling this the first Juvenile Court Bill.[29]

In the run-up to planning the Chicago Exposition of 1893, more religious organizations concerning themselves with reform efforts were founded. This included the National Council of Jewish Women (NCJW), organized in the World's Fair Parliament of Religions. Hannah Greenbaum Solomon, active in the Chicago Woman's Club and the Reform Sinai Temple in Chicago, called upon Jewish women to join in philanthropic activities and middle-class women's reform efforts.[30] Solomon urged Jewish women to consider their proper sphere the entire world, and not simply the home. One of the early NCJW activists, Minnie Low, became director of the NCJW Bureau of Personal Service, where she would play an important role in court reform.[31] The progressive Sinai Congregation connection would yield up leadership in Rabbi Emil G. Hirsch and Julian Mack. Rabbi Hirsch, who led Sinai Temple for a number of years, was a leader in support of a number of child-saving efforts. As secretary of the United Jewish Charities of Chicago (later renamed Associated Jewish Charities), Mack was a strong fund-raiser in Chicago's Jewish community, and among those he could often tap for progressive causes was fellow congregant Julius Rosenwald, founder of Sears and Roebuck. Beginning in 1893 with the meetings to found the Maxwell Street Settlement, Mack established a lasting connection to Jane Addams and Hull House.[32]

Hull House was a very important part of this reform network. Addams and Ellen Gates Starr founded the Hull House settlement in 1889 in a working-class neighborhood populated by many recent immigrants, who turned to Hull House for assistance in times of emergency. Residents saw at close hand many of the problems besetting the poor. Hull House was an incubator for leadership. Among the earliest residents were Julia Lathrop, who would play a central role in juvenile court reform; Florence Kelley, labor reformer, factory inspector, and a founder of the National Consumers' League; Mary McDowell, union supporter who would later head the University of Chicago Settlement and help found the Woman's Trade Union League; and Mary Kenney, who had been hired briefly by Samuel Gompers as the first woman labor union organizer.[33]

Hull House hosted a number of clubs for self-improvement, culture, and discussion and became the place where many budding reform organizations held their meetings. It was a place of intellectual ferment, attracting a number of important scholars and writers as visitors, including John Dewey, who stayed for a week on his first visit.[34] The Working People's Social Science Club began and met at Hull House for the discussion of social and economic issues. The Hull House Woman's Club, begun by McDowell and presided over during a number of its early years by wealthy supporter Louise de Koven Bowen, drew many neighborhood women as participants. Bowen contributed to the construction of a larger meeting hall at Hull House for the weekly meetings, which had outgrown their original space. The number of well-connected and wealthy women (and men) who passed through Hull House and participated in activities sponsored by Hull House, combined with the large audiences Addams reached through her writing and speaking, meant that the settlement on Halsted Street had the capacity to tap resources in the Chicago area and broader reform circles.

Some residents of Hull House, including Julia Lathrop and Jane Addams, were concomitantly members of the Chicago Woman's Club, which spearheaded the reform of policies regarding children in criminal detention. Prior to 1899, children arrested in Chicago appeared before police court justices in the Cook County criminal court, awaited trial in the county jail and police station lockups, and did time with adult criminals. Settlement house workers and Women's Club members found it unconscionable for young boys to be locked up with hardened criminals—they needed to be surrounded by good, not harmful, moral influences.[35] Even when criminal courts were lenient on children, the alternative to imprisonment was discharge. Children were sent back to the environments that, reformers determined, were responsible for their delinquency. Children were not receiving the treatment they needed. Juvenile delinquency, reformers insisted, resulted from poverty, home life, associates, the school system, and other social influences.[36]

As early as 1883, the CWC had established a school for boys awaiting trial or serving sentences and had secured women matrons for police stations and the county jail. Starting in 1892, the CWC Reform Department funded the salary of a teacher, who taught for two morning hours in the corridor of the jail. Pupils ranged in age from ten to sixteen. The Cook County Board of Commissioners approved of the work accomplished and eventually paid the teacher's salary.[37] The CWC agitated for the building of the John Worthy School, which trained boys in prison, operating as part of the Bridewell in the House of Corrections, with control of the school by the Board of Education.[38] The CWC turned over this work to the Board of Education once the school was up and running.

The CWC used its committee structure and membership to network with other organizations, and it actively pressed forward on children's issues. In 1896–1897, the CWC sent twenty delegates to the School Children Aid Society and donated $500 and clothed 4,994 schoolchildren.[39] Thirty members of the Woman's Club were on the board of the Protective Agency for Women and Children. The Agency provided funds for women and children who, "through poverty or friendlessness," were in need of legal aid.[40] In January 1896, the CWC Reform Department announced new monthly meetings for the study of laws regarding women and children, on which they declared Illinois to be behind other states. The following week, CWC reported on a proposal from Mrs. Ellen Henrotin, who was also then serving as president of the rapidly expanding General Federation of Women's Clubs, for a meeting of a congress of city clubs to consider the condition of childhood; issues of concern included truancy and delinquency. This meeting was held at the end of January at the CWC meeting rooms, drawing representatives from women's organizations in and around Chicago. From this grew a proposal for a larger conference from a federation of women's clubs in May, with Lucy Flower as delegate; Flower became a major figure in the establishment of the Juvenile Court. Also circulated was an appeal signed by Flower, Henrotin, and others to "The Women and Women's Clubs of Illinois" to draw attention to the plight of poor children, a number of whom are "growing up to constitute an ignorant and criminal class, dangerous to the welfare of the country." The CWC paid for the rental of the hall for the May conference.[41]

In spring 1898, the CWC Reform and Philanthropy Departments organized a probation committee chaired by Julia Lathrop.[42] Lathrop was particularly well suited to lead this effort. Following the Columbian Exposition, Lathrop had been a "county visitor" to hospitals and other county institutions, serving in a volunteer position of what would later become United Charities. Importantly, she held a state position as member of the State Board of Charities in 1893, appointed by Governor John Peter Altgeld.[43] In 1895, Lathrop had written a little book entitled *Suggestions for Institution Visitors*, published by the Public Charities Committee of the Illinois Federation of Women's Clubs. She was distressed that dependent children were rather haphazardly handled by Illinois judges and often not provided with schooling until they were committed to the state home for delinquents.[44] Lathrop was unique among CWC activists in having a state-appointed position; it gave her access to some public officials, although many wealthy or upper-middle-class women in CWC likewise had access. And while Lathrop's position gave her independent opportunities to advance the cause of reform, much of her work was through CWC and its network partners.

The CWC probation committee placed women in quasi-public if unofficial roles as probation officers. Florence Haythorn, the CWC prison school teacher, worked as probation officer, in police stations, in court with the boys, and visited homes.[45] At the same time, Hull House resident Alzina Stevens held a semiofficial position in the nearest police station. "The sergeant agreed to give her provisional charge of every boy and girl under arrest for a trivial offense."[46] Stevens visited the Maxwell Street Station, Mrs. Mary Sly of the Northwestern Settlement served as a probation officer at West Chicago Avenue Station, and Mr. Carl Kelsey worked (apparently with salary) at the East Chicago Avenue Station. The Children's Home and Aid Society, with Hastings Hart as superintendent, worked with the CWC Philanthropy and Reform Departments to pay the salary of a probation officer.[47]

Certain a separate court was needed for the young, CWC activists began implementing a set of practices in Chicago that served as a kind of template for what they would soon seek to establish at law. In late 1894, the CWC sought (and ultimately received) approval from the office of the State's Attorney to expedite boys' trials. The judge who agreed to expedite these trials, separate them from adult trials, and hold court for this purpose one morning per week, was Circuit Court Judge R. S. Tuthill. The CWC and Hull House introduced the probation officer into this court. Haythorn "brought her records to the court, she having investigated every phase of each case, members of the committee accompanying her." Judge Tuthill claimed the records of these boys were especially important in building a case for the legal establishment of the Juvenile Court of Cook County.[48]

These relationships would then be deployed in collaborative efforts to pass a Juvenile Court Bill. Lathrop made use of her position in the State Board of Charities. She and Flower co-organized the Third Annual Illinois Conference of Charities with the theme "The Children of the State." They brought together interested reformers, including Mary Bartelme, Northwestern Law School graduate and member of the Illinois bar, to speak at the conference.[49] The enthusiasm from the conference carried over to a newly formed Chicago Bar Association committee, chaired by Judge Harvey Hurd and including Ephraim Banning (another of Lathrop's colleagues from the Board of Charities) and Hurley, author of the earlier bill.[50] Lathrop and Flower would work with this committee to draft and promote the Juvenile Court Bill.

Lathrop and Flower recognized that, while a Juvenile Court would serve a number of social purposes, the Illinois Legislature would have to authorize it. They decided that the bill should be introduced to the legislature by lawyers rather than have it appear as a women's measure, so the Bar Association connection was just the one they needed.[51] Judge Hurd, chair of the Chicago Bar Association committee that proposed the Juvenile Court Bill, took pains to make the committee representative, making a place for the organizations that had been hard at work at child-saving, such as the Chicago Woman's Club, the Illinois State Conference of Charities and Correction, the Catholic Visitation and Aid Society, and the Children's Home and Aid Society.[52] The network of social service organizations, religious organizations, and lawyers and judges converged to support passage of the bill.

"An Act To Regulate the Treatment and Control of Dependent, Neglected and Delinquent Children" became known as the "Bar Association Bill" and, later, the Juvenile Court Law. In counties having population of 500,000 or more, the judges of the Circuit Court of Cook County were to designate one or more of their number to hear juvenile cases.[53] The new law had three significant features: separate hearing of children's cases, detention of children apart from adult offenders, and a probation system.[54]

Public-Private Institution Building

Simply passing legislation neither implemented policy nor built institutions. Far from signaling the end of reformers' work and influence, passage of the Juvenile Court Law would mean their continued, deep involvement in the implementation and maintenance of the new court, and in helping deploy its powers. Reformers worked with and through both existing public institutions and private organizations. While Lathrop had initially launched this effort through her work on the State Board of Charities, the board did not join the juvenile court network, and Lathrop did not continue to focus her efforts there. Lathrop was frustrated by the corruption of the board. She tried to make the best of it, conducting the survey of charitable institutions and organizing the crucial conference, but the board was not so attractive to her, especially now that the Juvenile Court provided new opportunities for her work in child saving. She tendered her resignation in 1901, citing habitual, unchecked spoils.[55] She was persuaded to return under a new administration before resigning for good in 1909.[56] She turned her energies toward making connections with other juvenile court reformers. Not all of the originally interested private organizations remained in the coalition, either. The Illinois Humane Society enthusiastically welcomed the Juvenile Court, indicating it "inaugurated a new era in the child-life of Chicago," but it was ready to relinquish its own role of rescuing children and their mothers. Between 1895 and 1898, the IHS had investigated over 4,000 complaints each year. After the founding of the Juvenile Court, those numbers declined. By 1907 it received 2,764 complaints of cruelty to animals and only 539 complaints of cruelty to children.[57]

The new court provided a number of new public and private opportunities for reformers. The first Juvenile Court judge, R. S. Tuthill, had already worked closely with the CWC in expediting and separating boys' cases and had spread his enthusiasm for the idea of the court.[58] The new Juvenile Court judge position was not a popular one for judges, but Tuthill took it on, bringing with him the network he had worked with in the preceding years.[59] Judge Tuthill considered the probation officer to be "the keystone which supports the arch of this law, an arch which shall be as a rainbow of hope to all who love children and who desire that *all* children shall be properly cared for and who would provide such care for those without it, and who else would almost inevitably come to lead vicious and criminal lives, so that they may be saved and develop into good citizens, honest and useful men and women."[60]

Hurley, founder of the Visitation and Aid Society and participant in drafting the earliest juvenile court bill, was appointed the first chief probation officer. The law provided for probation officers, but did not fund their salaries.[61] Hurley needed a slate of assistants to carry out the specialized casework. Reformers had already demonstrated their capacity to provide probation officers, both in the form of funding and personnel. At the first session of the Juvenile Court, Flower and Stevens came forward, Flower offering to "accumulate a fund on which a staff of probation officers might be maintained" and

Stevens her services as first probation officer.[62] By the time of her death at Hull House in 1900, "she was the senior officer of a corps of six."[63] In its first year, six probation officers were paid by private sources and others worked as volunteers. Probation officers reported to the police during the first year, and the Mayor's Office also assigned a police officer from each district to dress in civilian clothing and patrol the street in the conduct of probation work; however, by 1900, those doing probation work reported to the Juvenile Court's chief of probation.[64]

Beginning with staffing and funding, the women who had been most instrumental in spearheading the reform threw themselves into the work of the Juvenile Court they had helped create. Several Hull House residents joined the early ranks of probation officers maintained by private contributions; Addams recounts that they "brought to the house for many years a sad little procession of children struggling against all sorts of handicaps." She recalled that at least once, a member of the Hull House Woman's Club, took in a ward of the Juvenile Court and kept the child for at least six months. Sophonisba Breckinridge, who sometimes resided at Hull House, served for a time as a probation officer.[65]

The women of the CWC were also responsible for the creation of new organizations that participated in and supported the work of the court. Through providing these services the Juvenile Court Committee (JCC) was born.[66] An association that emerged out of the CWC, it served as an auxiliary to the Juvenile Court, co-operating with the court as well as other child helping agencies.[67] Flower served as chair, and women delegates from the various clubs provided additional leadership. Some members had been leaders in the origins of the court, and wives of some of the leading male advocates of the court.[68]

Every year when a new judge was to be appointed to the Juvenile Court by the Circuit Court judges, members of the JCC saw all the judges and indicated the preference of the committee for some particular judge. And judges deferred to the choice of probation officers proffered by the JCC. Bowen recalled that "During this time the probation officers were most carefully selected by the Juvenile Court Committee; they met frequently with the members of the committee at Hull-House and we talked over their duties with them."[69] The JCC joined other organizations in funding the salaries of probation officers, the court stenographer, and clerks.

Whether paid or unpaid, probation officers served as case workers, collecting information about children to present to the judge. They would investigate, interview, provide the court with information about the child's environment, help make decisions about the disposition of particular cases, and provide "guidance and friendly interest."[70] Their investigations provided them glimpses into the homes and lives of children in order to discern the children's environment, and in the course of collecting information they might instruct families on how to improve their circumstances, or provide services or goods, essentially serving as proto-social workers. The probation officer operated, therefore, as a "jack-of-all-trades" in what was, essentially, a kind of "department of children."[71]

The prevailing sensibility was that probation officers, who would likely be visiting the home, should be of the same religion and race as the child if they were to have an influence. African American women were also enlisted as probation officers, recruited from the Illinois Federation of Colored Women's Clubs. The first was Elizabeth McDonald, described in the first annual report of the CCJC as "one colored woman who devote[d] her entire time to the work, free of charge, and whose services [we]re invaluable to the court as she takes charge of all colored children." No club offered her a salary, but the CWC provided donations of food and clothing for her to distribute to needy families.[72] Others who followed included Irene McCoy Gaines and Ida B. Wells-Barnett, and Gaines also served as a secretary to the Juvenile Court.[73]

For similar reasons, religious organizations were included in probation work. The Visitation and Aid Society, the Children's Home and Aid Society, and the Bureau of Personal Service of the National Council of Jewish Women were among those who sent representatives to become probation officers.[74] Objections to the proposed court legislation had included concern that private, sectarian associations would be imposing their morality upon the working classes of Chicago, and that private institutions and individuals would be placed in a position to proselytize and attempt to convert children of Catholics and Jews. While reformers emphasized the use of probation rather than institutionalization whenever possible, critics presumably saw problems in the power the friends of the court might exert. The reformers wanted to retain the idea of denominational placement agencies in which the religious background of the child would, "as far as practicable," determine the child's nurture and care.[75] The final version of the bill read: "The court in committing children shall place them as far as practicable in the care and custody of some individual holding the same religious belief as the parents of said child, or with some association which is controlled by persons of like religious faith."[76] From the institutions in which children and youth were placed, to probation officers, chosen from religious and racial backgrounds to reflect the constituencies served by the court, religion mattered.

Since the Juvenile Court had charge of the Illinois compulsory school attendance law, twenty-one truant officers from the Board of Education were commissioned as probation officers in cases of truancy. Fourteen officers and agents of organizations that assisted the court were commissioned as probation officers in cases of dependent children. Sixteen police officers from the City of Chicago were commissioned as probation officers, as well as accompanying the probation officers in their visiting work. The court appointed thirty-six other persons to take charge of individual cases.[77] By 1902, fifteen probation officers were funded by private agencies: The Visitation and Aid Society funded six, the Chicago Woman's Club, three; and one probation officer each was funded by the South Side Woman's Club, Hull House, Jewish Charities, the Illinois Industrial Association, the Women's Protective Agency, and Lucy Flower respectively.[78] They were joined by twenty police probation officers.[79] The lengthy list of institutions and organizations supplying and funding probation officers, plus consideration of the nature of their mission, illustrates the complexity of both public-private relations and the lines of responsibility in juvenile court work.

The Juvenile Court Law failed to provide for a detention home to house children while awaiting their hearing. The detention home issue was a longstanding concern for the women reformers, but they lacked the capacity to house children. So they relied on resources available in their networks. The Illinois Industrial Association had traditionally provided a home for discharged criminals, out of Christian charity for the friendless and homeless.[80] Rev. A. C. Dodds, a Presbyterian minister with the IIA arranged for donation of a house by philanthropists Mrs. and Mr. Potter Palmer.[81] In 1903, the Juvenile Court Committee was ready to take over the detention home, and it moved the home into a new building at 202 Ewing Street in 1907, with Sara Hart as director.[82]

At this time, the detention home relied on both public and private sources for its funding, but it hardly looked like a public operation. The arrangement left lines of responsibility confusing and sometimes frustrating for the JCC. The city and county assisted in funding the home, the county contributing approximately $3,600 of the $8,500 operating costs in 1903.[83] The city board of education assigned a teacher to the detention home for boys in 1906.[84] However, the Juvenile Court Committee was left to do quite a bit of the early work. Bowen recalled that it was difficult to get city or county authorities to provide funds or equipment. When an old omnibus supplied by the county broke down and efforts to obtain a new one from the county were futile, the JCC purchased an omnibus for $500 and a double harness for $60, to transport children from the Home to the court. The new omnibus was too heavy for the pony they had been using, so an old, retired Fire Department horse was obtained, but it could not pair with the pony. The JCC had to purchase a pair of horses and also paid for horseshoes. The barn given by the city was four miles from the Home and had stalls so small the horses could not lie down. The JCC rented a stable and tried to get the city to provide food for the horses, even letting the horses go for three days without food, hoping to force the city to provide. Ultimately, the JCC had to provide its own horse feed.[85] Club women involved with the JCC visited the juvenile home frequently, nearly every day. They pulled down bedcovers to see if beds were clean, tasted the food, and were considered responsible in court for what was served.[86] The Hull House Woman's Club also made pillowcases for the detention home.[87] The JCC not only paid the lease on the detention home but nudged the county toward the adoption of standards, arranging with the president of the Cook County Board of Commissioners and the mayor to have the home inspected.[88]

To support its evolving mission, the JCC continued seeking the assistance of the CWC and other organizations for resources in the form of personnel and finances. When the Committee determined that cocaine usage among boys contributed to its failure to secure jobs for them, the JCC partnered with the Legal Aid Society to conduct a study. When it became clear that the caseload of probation officers was too high, the JCC added half-time probation officers and established a force of volunteers and friendly visitors. The JCC sent circulars to all area women's clubs, soliciting volunteers, and Bowen wrote letters to local clergy.[89]

The JCC also knew how to train workers and sustain institutions. A volunteer coordinator provided court workers with copies of the national publication *Charities*, and a leaflet, "Suggestions to Juvenile Court Workers of Cook County, Illinois," as well as registration cards and postal notices, all generated and funded by the JCC.[90] With Bowen at the helm, the JCC put on high-visibility cultural events to raise money for their court activities, helping link the court with Chicago's society leaders in the public mind.[91] By 1907, the JCC had raised and expended about $100,000 for the salaries of probation officers and maintenance of the detention home, from a budget that was drawn primarily from private contributions.[92]

In 1907, the county took over the funding of probation officers. While this shift followed a familiar path whereby certain functions handled at the outset by private organizations are taken over as the state gains capacity, this public funding may not have necessarily meant a more smoothly functioning or adequately funded probation system. County support increased from thirty-one probation officers in 1906 to eighty-one in 1916. Although the county increased the number of positions, it did not go so far as to increase the pay, and Cook County probation officers' pay lagged behind their peers across the country.[93] Field expenses came out of probation officers' salaries. Helen Jeter noted in the 1920s that, under county funding, the court was dependent on "a separate and, at times, hostile department of the government for the provision of funds to establish a competent and sufficient force of probation officers," and that women's positions were "notoriously underpaid."[94]

Public responsibility for the Juvenile Court increased in other ways. The county board of commissioners increased its detention home contribution from $3,600 to $4,200 in 1905 and allocated $5,686 for the Juvenile Court. Funding for the Juvenile Court leaped to $20,260 in 1906 and $29,440 in 1907, while funding for the detention home increased to $6,800. At the same time, the volume of children and demands on facilities escalated. Increasing county funding coincided with building the Juvenile Court building and the Detention Home, for which the county expended $150,000.[95] A committee, which included Julia Lathrop, Timothy Hurley, Judge Orrin Carter, and three county commissioners, was formed to negotiate with representatives for costs and placement of these buildings.[96] In 1906, an entire city block was dedicated to "the interests of children," with the Juvenile Court next to a detention home, playground, and school building, just down the street from Hull House.[97] It was erected quickly—two hundred days after groundbreaking. It was the first building in the country "planned and equipped solely for the use and benefit of unfortunate children."[98] In taking responsibility for the infrastructure, the Board of Commissioners acknowledged the myriad private organizations that aided the county.[99] This building served its mission until 1913, when the number of cases outgrew its capacity. Judge Merritt W. Pinckney of the Juvenile Court lobbied the Board of Commissioners to fund a new and larger detention home, so that children were not improperly kept with repeat delinquents or in police stations or subjected to unhealthful conditions.[100] The Juvenile Court moved into the tenth floor of the county building, and the entire facility was given over to purposes of detention.[101]

With Juvenile Court operations now more directly publicly funded, reformers envisioned additional offices for the court, and frequently paid for the start-up efforts. Initially, the Children's Hospital Society paid for a trained nurse to be present in court and secure necessary medical care. The county assumed financial responsibility in 1909 and expanded services, adding a dentist, more nurses, and a woman physician in the girls' detention home.[102] But perhaps the most innovative addition to the Juvenile Court was the Juvenile Psychopathic Institute. Charged in 1909 by Judge Pinckney to study the problem of recidivism, a committee composed of Ethel Dummer, Julia Lathrop, and local physician and neurologist William Healy established the institute. Dummer provided funding for its first five years.[103] Lathrop became its president and Healy its director.[104] Mack, still an elected judge in the Circuit Court of Cook County, helped facilitate this collaboration.[105] The JPI served as a clinic, examining children brought into the court and providing or directing them to medical services. It also performed research, taking advantage of the sheer number of cases to conduct systematic studies of children, collecting data to determine the root causes of crime and recidivism, and other criminal explanations. In 1914, the county took over the funding of the JPI, as Judge Pinckney had urged.[106] The county paid for one psychologist and one stenographer.[107] If the medical personnel in the JPI wanted to engage in research, they needed to seek private funding.[108] In 1917 the JPI became a state agency—part of the state Department of Public Welfare—but it continued to be administered through county-state cooperation.[109]

The shift toward public funding did not deal the reformers out as much as it shifted the direction of their involvement and readjusted the public-private relationship. Reformers were pleased to turn over a number of these functions to government, since they could not sustain the funding or energy indefinitely. Furthermore, they believed that these reforms should be recognized as legitimate government purposes and, as a duty of the state, institutionalized. After the county took over court funding in 1907, the fund-raising and administrative burdens shouldered by the Juvenile Court Committee declined significantly. But even with the county taking over the budget, reformers had plenty of roles to play, and dealt themselves in by generating new court-related work. They retained connections with the public institutions they had helped create. The Advisory Council to the public Juvenile Psychopathic Institute, for instance, included the key Juvenile Court members—Mack, Henry Thurston, Judge Pinckney, and Judge Harry Olson. The executive committee included Addams and Lathrop.[110]

The path of development, then, was not simply the transition from women's charitable work to state absorption.[111]

The work of private organizations not only fostered and supplemented state development but their court work tended to promote further development of the missions of these organizations. The JCC worked for a short while in tandem with Judge Mack's Juvenile Protective League, which had been organized by such Juvenile Court personnel as Mack, Hurley, Low, and Thurston. Directors included Hastings Hart (of the Children's Home and Aid Society) and Sara Hart (of the Detention Home).[112] The JCC and JPL joined together for a short time in a Juvenile Welfare League, beginning in March 1906, with Mack providing his courtroom for meetings. The League resolved to take concerted action to "remove those conditions and foster those institutions, conditions and agencies that tend to build up child-life." To accomplish this, it would provide an "atmosphere of purity and moral cleanliness," suppress vice, prosecute agencies that contribute to the delinquency of children, create "permanent wholesome attractions," establish a personal service corps, and start an educational campaign.[113]

The Juvenile Protective League and the Juvenile Court Committee combined their efforts for "unity of appeal to the public and for efficiency of administration."[114] With assurance that the JPL would have delegates in the JCC, the JPL was willing to be incorporated into the JCC and phase out of existence. The merged association became known as the Juvenile Protective Association in 1909. From its origins as a committee inside a CWC department in 1899, the JPA now became a stand-alone organization, independent of the CWC. It had a steady supply of donors, was firmly situated in the network of reformers, and had access to the Juvenile Court.

The JCC, and subsequently the JPA, took on another court project. Lathrop, a long-standing foe of corruption and patronage, had been advocating that probation officers for the Juvenile Court be selected by civil service examination. In this early period of civil service reform, written exams for specialized positions were just beginning to be designed, and while improving the quality of public service was an object of federal and state civil service reformers, the chief object was still to remove positions from patronage and the spoils system.[115] Illinois had passed civil service reform legislation in 1895, allowing cities to adopt civil service exams if they chose. Chicago adopted the plan by popular vote, but Illinois did not make the civil service system applicable to appointees in state institutions until 1905.[116] Subsequently, the JCC and its heir, the JPA, took on the task of implementing a civil service exam for probation officers. Addams and Bowen were both members of the five-person committee administering the first civil service exams for these officers. Each member of the committee wrote questions and several questions were selected from each list.[117] In the exams designed by this committee, probation officers needed to be able to provide the intent and purpose of the Juvenile Court Law and to list other state laws regarding children. They needed to know how the law dealt with parents. They were asked to answer hypotheticals and demonstrate their penmanship, spelling, arithmetic, and letter writing skills. The candidate for chief probation officer was asked to write a letter setting forth details about his or her life, and to write an account of the conditions that led to the establishment of the Juvenile Court.[118] Bowen claims that diversity was maintained and Addams remembered that everyone currently serving passed the exam, but in fact racial and religious representation was not readily maintained. McDonald, the single African American woman who was serving, failed to pass (though she continued to serve as she had),[119] and "not one Catholic probation officer had qualified to work with the dependent and delinquent children of Cook County, a very considerable percentage of whom were immigrant and Catholic."[120] The replacement of Hurley with Thurston as chief probation officer at this time added to the imbalance.[121]

Even though probation officers came to office via the civil service commission, their legal status as officers of the court was ambiguous from 1905 until 1912. In 1912 a chief probation officer, after being dismissed, filed suit, claiming a separation of powers violation in the hiring and firing of probation officers. The case determined that the court had the right to be free from interference in the selection of its own personnel. Probation officers were classed as assistants to the court, and the judge devised a civil service test of his own design. Nevertheless, he continued to rely on private resources, with the test administered by a "committee of citizens chosen by the judge," such committee, naturally, being drawn from the JPA.[122]

With its ongoing relationship with the Juvenile Court, the JPA remained a resource to be called upon by the court when needed. One such instance occurred in 1917 when the probation officer position was placed in jeopardy by a bill that enjoined the county treasurer from paying probation officer salaries. The attack on paying probation officers was the salvo in a larger assault that the court ultimately weathered (with the caveat that it would have to be more careful in determining that parents were unfit).[123] The suspension of salaries for probation officers was appealed, but the proceedings were held up for a year. In the interim, thirty-five Chicago citizens and court personnel pledged amounts of $100–5,000 to secure an indemnifying bond of $200,000, providing a cushion until the affair could be sorted out.[124]

Once primary responsibility for probation officers was assumed by the county, the JPA turned its attention and efforts toward homes and streets. In early 1906 Chief Probation Officer Thurston enlisted "the co-operation of 2,500 housewives, settlement and charity workers in extirpating dance halls, ice cream parlors, moving picture shows, etc., which lead boys and girls astray."[125] Thurston's idea was to have a group of fifty volunteers work with each of the fifty regular probation officers employed by the court, working to improve conditions surrounding the city's children and reforming delinquents. The *Tribune* reported that 150 representative women enrolled as friendly visitors, with the number set to expand, and that it would not be long before "the authorities will know the location of every den of vice frequented by juveniles. Every cheap hotel will be watched, accurate information will be secured regarding the character of every play produced at the cheap theaters; every ice cream parlor and every dance hall, large or small, public or private, will be kept under constant surveillance."[126]

The JPA also lobbied successfully for the creation of several more specialized courts in Chicago. A Court of Domestic Relations to enforce new legislation concerning contribution to the delinquency and dependency of a minor, and for desertion and nonsupport was formed in 1911. On opening day, Addams and the superintendent of the JPA were photographed with the judge. This success was followed by a Morals Court for prostitution in 1913 and a Boys' Court in 1914 to hear cases of boys aged seventeen to twenty-one. Bowen spoke at the opening of the Boys' Court. Again, the JPA assisted in the support of officers to this court during its start-up years.[127]

Some of the juvenile court reformers secured places for themselves in the new courts. Mary Bartelme, a graduate of Northwestern University School of Law, had become the first female public guardian in 1897.[128] She worked alongside Lathrop and Flower to secure the Juvenile Court Law.[129] In 1913 she was appointed as assistant to the Juvenile Court judge.[130] Bartelme was elected to the Circuit Court of Cook County in 1923, becoming the first woman judge in Illinois.[131] Bartelme retained her relationship with Women's Clubs and a number of other clubs and organizations, making full use of the public-private partnership to provide services in the Juvenile Court. The Women's Clubs, working with Judge Bartelme, established a service council in order to obtain funds for suitcases and supplies, and a group of ten women met weekly in Evanston to sew about 150 dresses a year. The suitcase practice was sufficiently well known that Judge Bartelme was dubbed "suitcase Mary" by Chicago journalists.[132] Judge Bartelme developed a number of alternative placements for delinquent girls. She created a few halfway homes—popularly known as Mary Clubs—where girls could learn to be better behaved and develop better demeanor before being placed with families. Sara Hart was asked to form and head a committee of volunteers to manage the first Mary Club and raise the money for its operation.[133] A subsequent one of these homes was created for African American girls in collaboration with African American women reformers.[134]

Courts specialized, and as the workload of the Juvenile Court expanded, it did too. By 1924, the Juvenile Court alone had over 115 employees. Chief Justice Victor Arnold and Judge Mary Bartelme presided, with chief and deputy chief probation officers. They oversaw eight divisions—the Investigation Division, Family Supervision, Delinquent Boys Division, Child Placing Division, Mothers' Pension Division, Probation Officers and Special Works, Clerical Assistants, and Police Probation Officers (this latter division funded by the city).[135]

An Institution Becomes a Movement

When they had launched the institution for which they had fought in Illinois, the reformers who led in juvenile court reform did not stop. They took their work in various directions—to expand the Juvenile Court as an institution, to develop their own local organizations, to disseminate information and resources across the country into a juvenile court movement, and to advocate reforms to the federal government. Institution-building moved laterally, spreading throughout the states. Although some reforms and initiatives were pressed at the national level, the states remained crucial to reformers' child-saving efforts.

Building this reform movement included cross-metropolitan network building. The annual report of the Juvenile Court Committee for the year 1906 reveals some of this work, most notably with Denver, the other path-breaking city in establishing juvenile courts. In February 1906, the JCC hosted Denver's Judge Ben Lindsey, the pioneer of Denver's Juvenile Court, with a luncheon in his honor. All the staff of the Juvenile Court were present—including JCC members, probation officers, volunteer probation officers, friendly visitors, police probation officers, and others interested in the work of the Juvenile Court—215 guests in all. The event was hosted by the Chicago Woman's Club, which had space to accommodate the hundreds of guests. When Mack and Thurston were the guest speakers at another JCC meeting hosted by the Chicago Woman's Club, the entire probation force was invited.[136] Judge Mack and Henry Thurston, in turn, visited Denver. The JCC also held a conference at Hull House that led to the formation of the National Juvenile Improvement Association.

Chicago's success, along with Denver's, initiated a juvenile court movement across the nation, with Chicago reformers mobilizing to assist juvenile court reformers elsewhere. Whether writing or publishing about the Juvenile Court, speaking before the legislatures of other states considering such bills, or to groups of lawyers, women's clubs, and national women's associations such as the National Congress of Mothers, they watched with pride as the movement caught fire. The large and well-organized Industrial Committee of the General Federation of Women's Clubs mailed a circular to its clubs and federations in May 1903 suggesting that these clubs work for a juvenile court bill in each state.[137] Hurley, Mack, Lathrop, and Lindsey visited other state charities conferences in Minnesota, Washington, Oregon, and California. Hurley, addressing the Minnesota State Conference of Charities and Correction meeting in 1904, insisted that each state needed juvenile court legislation and each county needed a court. "It was a speech calculated to lead people to undertake the work," the recorder of the event noted.[138] By the time he attended the National Conference of Charities and Correction in Detroit in May 1902, Lindsey was becoming an exceedingly important publicist for the juvenile court idea, writing and speaking around the country and perhaps becoming its most tireless advocate. The juvenile court subcommittee of the National Conference of Charities and Correction embarked on a national campaign for state juvenile court laws in 1904. Lindsey chaired the subcommittee.[139]

Some reformers who had participated in the Chicago-based effort continued to lead when they moved elsewhere. For example, Dorothea Moore, a resident of Hull House in the late 1890s who had participated in the juvenile court campaign in Illinois, relocated to San Francisco and led the California Federation of Women's Clubs' campaign as chair of its Civic Committee in 1902. She helped spread the word at the WCTU Congress of Reform that year, spoke at individual clubs, and spoke to suffragists.[140] Rev. A. C. Dodds, who had provided for the first Chicago detention home building, became chief probation officer in the Los Angeles Juvenile Court.[141]

For the 1904 World's Fair in St. Louis, Lindsey organized a juvenile court exhibit that included contributions from the Juvenile Court of Cook County and the National Congress of Mothers.[142] In St. Louis, Roger N. Baldwin, who would later found the American Civil Liberties Union, crusaded for the juvenile court when he was a settlement worker in the slums of the city; he would become chief probation officer for the St. Louis Juvenile Court. Baldwin, personally acquainted with Mack, considered him one of his earliest ideals.[143]

Juvenile courts were quickly established in Washington, D.C., Richmond, Brooklyn, Newark, Elizabeth, Pittsburgh, Cleveland, Columbus, Toledo, Cincinnati, Louisville, Indianapolis, Kansas City, Denver, Salt Lake City, Los Angeles, San Francisco, Portland, Seattle, Vancouver, Winnipeg, Toronto, Minneapolis, St. Paul, and Des Moines.[144] The organization of these courts varied, and some were not separate from criminal courts, but all sought to cure rather than punish, using probation rather than incarceration where possible. Hull House resident Grace Abbott—who had studied law with Roscoe Pound at both the University of Nebraska and University of Chicago and received a Master of Philosophy degree from the University of Chicago in 1909 before beginning to teach at the Chicago School of Civics and Philanthropy—compiled a topical abstract of laws governing trial and disposition of juvenile offenders and noted that, once Illinois initiated a new epoch of lawmaking in 1899, twenty-two additional states and the District of Columbia had passed laws modeled on the Illinois Juvenile Court Law through 1909.[145]

Just as they built organizations alongside the development of the Juvenile Court of Cook County, reformers built national associations alongside this national movement. The National Probation Officers' Association was established in 1906 to "study, establish, extend and standardize adult and juvenile probation, juvenile courts and other specialized courts using probation," as well as to coordinate probation systems and increase public knowledge.[146] A Committee on the Development of Standards in Juvenile Court Work included Lathrop and Pinckney. Baldwin, chair of the committee, pointed out that they had hoped for some windfall from some philanthropist to conduct a comprehensive study. Lacking that, the committee networked with the Children's Bureau, which circulated the questionnaire to probation officers across the country.[147]

Chicago's juvenile court reformers were well represented at the White House Conference on the Care of Dependent Children, summoned by outgoing President Theodore Roosevelt in January 1909, a conference that gave rise to the Children's Bureau. Mack, Addams, and Lindsey were co-vice chairmen.

The conference attracted notable reformers and philanthropists from across the country. The Chicago contingent included Bowen, Hastings Hart, Rabbi Hirsch, Hurley, Minnie Low, Judge Pinckney, Julius Rosenwald, and Henry Thurston. Julia Lathrop and Sara L. Hart were also on the invitation list.[148] (Figure 1 displays ways four key individuals in the creation of Chicago's juvenile courts connected to the network and to the national agenda.) The conference would result in the establishment of the Children's Bureau in 1912, with

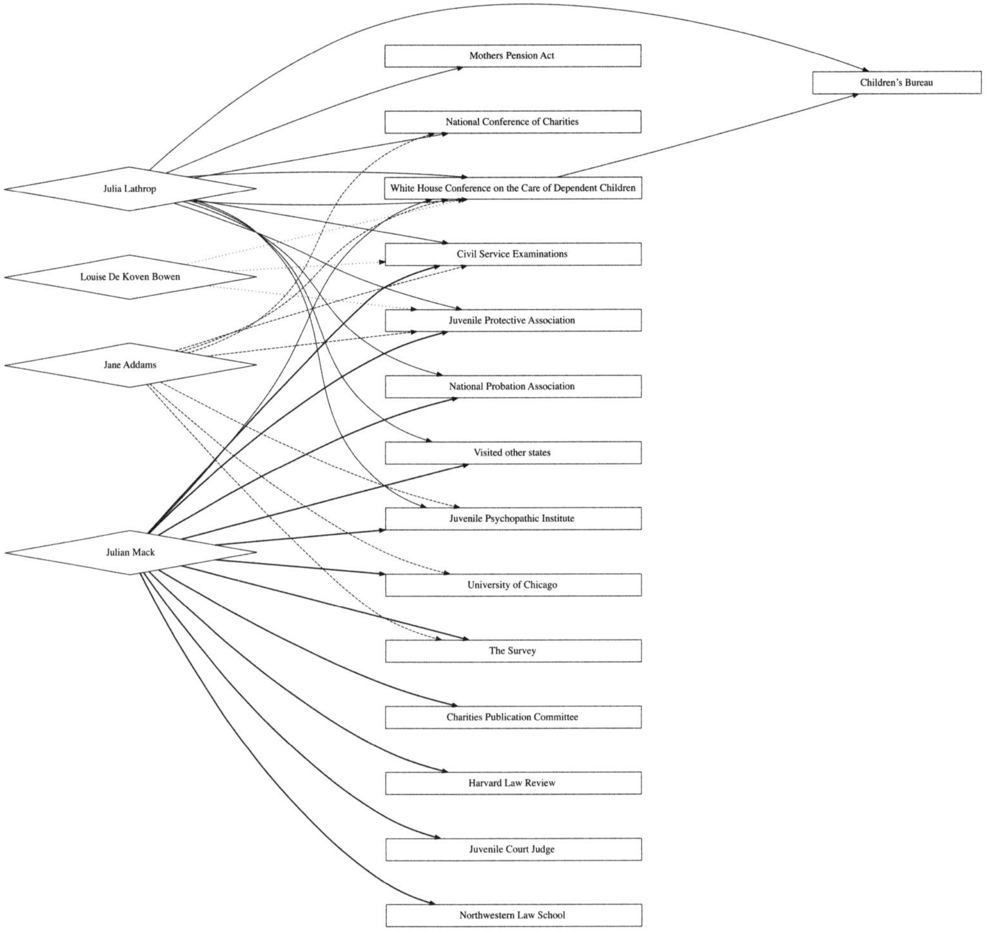

Figure 1. Juvenile Court Movement activities of selected leaders.

Lathrop as the first chief, succeeded by her handpicked successor Grace Abbott in 1921. The Children's Bureau continued to pursue causes close to Lathrop's heart, including work with delinquent and dependent juveniles. The Children's Bureau invited the National Probation and Parole Association, along with other interested parties, to meet in 1921 to formulate juvenile court standards, which were eventually adopted by the Children's Bureau and published in 1923.[149]

Reformers' vigorous efforts to publicize the juvenile court as the centerpiece of a solution to problems of dependency and delinquency were also vital to the national networking that helped spread the juvenile court and produce the Children's Bureau. Timothy Hurley began publishing the *Juvenile Record* in late 1899. Advertising the work of the Juvenile Court of Cook County and disseminating information about amendments to the law, this paper was soon urging reformers in every state to adopt the same legislation. The banner on the front page of each issue of the *Juvenile Record* proclaimed, "We advocate the establishment of a juvenile court in every state in the Union." Judge Lindsey contributed to the *Juvenile Record* in pushing for legislation in other states.[150] In *McClure's* magazine, muckraking journalist Lincoln Steffens ran a three-part series on Lindsey in 1906. Steffens helped popularize Lindsey's work, calling him the "just judge" and his court the "kids' court."[151] Lindsey also circulated a report he wrote in part to secure legislation in Colorado to reformers, charitable workers, and educators around the country.[152]

Publications reaching charity workers and newly professionalizing social workers also featured juvenile court work. The New York Charity Organization Society published an influential journal, *Charities*, which absorbed *Charities Review* in 1901 and became *Charities and the Commons* (November 1905). *Charities* devoted virtually an entire issue in January 1905 to the work of the juvenile court. Among the contributors were Judge Hurd, who wrote of the "minimum principles which should be stood for" in a juvenile court law, attempting to standardize such legislation as far as possible, as Hurley also advocated. Lindsey contributed one of a number of pieces he would contribute to *Charities* and its successors. Another contributor was Lathrop, who authored a piece on "The Development of the Probation System in a Large City."[153] Helen Page Bates, working with the sociology section of the New York State Library, contributed her digest of existing statutes relating to juvenile courts and probation systems of the juvenile court.[154]

By 1909, this journal had become *The Survey*, a name chosen to better reflect its transition toward a journal of best practices of social analysis and research and the increasing professionalization of social work. Editor Paul U. Kellogg proclaimed the *Survey* "an investigator and interpreter of the objective conditions of life and labor and as a chronicler of undertakings to improve them."[155] The *Survey* continued to be a vehicle for publication and dissemination of work by Lindsey and other juvenile court reformers while also alerting readers to new research and writing projects such as the compilation of papers given at the commemoration of the twenty-fifth anniversary of the establishment of the Juvenile Court of Cook County, published as *The Child, the Clinic, and the Court* (1925) and introduced by Jane Addams.[156] Addams and Mack were members of the Board of Directors for publisher Survey Associates, Inc., and in 1914 the National Council of Survey Associates, an advisory group to the publishers, included Addams, Mack, Julian Rosenwald, and Lillian Wald from New York's Henry Street Settlement, with Addams also serving as an associate editor and probation officer Henry W. Thurston listed as a contributing editor.[157]

An important network of legal scholars also helped disseminate and popularize the work of the juvenile court. Mack, like Lindsey, had a heavy speaking schedule around the nation, hammering away at constitutional objections that had been raised and reminding audiences that saving the child was very different from punishing it.[158] Mack wrote an influential 1909 *Harvard Law Review* article, a follow-up to a similar address to the American Bar Association, that was frequently cited as the authoritative statement on the legal status of the juvenile court.[159] Mack, a founder of the *Harvard Law Review* and part-time professor at the University of Chicago Law School, maintained connections to Roscoe Pound, Louis Brandeis, Ernst Freund, and other prominent jurists and legal scholars. He spoke to a new movement of progressive legal scholars who sought to make law less formalistic and more responsive to demonstrable changes in the culture. Pound, one of the most influential legal scholars in America by the time he moved from Chicago to Harvard in 1910, had been introduced to the Hull House reform circle by former student Edith Abbott and had served on the Juvenile Court Committee. He maintained his interest in the work of the juvenile court, writing of the Chicago model as a good example of new thinking with regard to the administration of law.[160] Along with Judge Harry Olson of the Municipal Court, Pound helped found the Chicago-based American Judicature Society, an organization that "spread the gospel of court organization to cities and states across the nation."[161] Near the end of his career as dean of the Harvard Law

School, Pound claimed juvenile courts were "the greatest forward step in Anglo-American jurisprudence since Magna Charta."[162]

The nearby University of Chicago was an important institution through which many of the juvenile court reformers helped to establish, or subsequently extend, their influence. A number of the reformers taught as adjuncts at the university: Mack, and, briefly, Pound in the law school; Rabbi Emil G. Hirsch teaching ancient languages; Addams as an extension faculty member for several years between 1900 and 1912; Mary McDowell as a special instructor in sociology beginning in 1894; Lathrop taught sociology beginning in 1907; and Breckinridge, who received a Ph.D. and a law degree from the university, taught sociology beginning in 1899.[163]

When the University of Chicago opened in fall 1892, it included the nation's first Department of Sociology. In 1895, the head of the department, Albion Small, founded the *American Journal of Sociology*, which would publish a number of articles by those involved in reforms undertaken in the name of delinquent and dependent children of Illinois. That journal published Hirsch's University of Chicago convocation address of 1895 on "The American University." Addams penned a number of articles, and Florence Kelley, Hastings Hart, Dorothea Moore, and Lathrop were also represented in the journal, as were a number of scholars who influenced these reformers. And Pound used the *American Journal of Sociology* to applaud the excellent work in Chicago to provide for flexible judicial organization and data gathering by judicial bodies.[164]

The boundary between academic research and outside research conducted by reformers was not sharply defined during this time; this was a period of reciprocal influence. The issue of what research and activity conducted by reformers should be linked to the university was being negotiated in this era. An example was the tension over the proper location for the Chicago School of Civics and Philanthropy (originally, Institute of Social Science and Arts), associated with the settlement house movement and of which Lathrop had been a founding member and research director.[165] Opening as an independent school in 1908, the Chicago School of Civics and Philanthropy had Julia Lathrop as its vice president; board members included Addams, Rosenwald, and Mack.[166] Academics thought it should be incorporated into a university, and with an increasing sense that social workers needed to be formally trained, that their training should be at a university. When, in 1916, the school faced the possibility of closure for lack of funds, Mack and other board members helped the school acquire the money to survive, and also helped incorporate the school into the University of Chicago,[167] where it became the School of Social Service Administration in 1920.[168]

The newly created federal Children's Bureau became an important institution through which juvenile court studies and projects could be advanced. When Lathrop became its first bureau chief in 1912, she relied heavily on her networks and she made it possible for the School of Social Service Administration at the University of Chicago "to carry on some other juvenile court studies which appeared later as Children's Bureau publications."[169] The Children's Bureau employed studies as a means for continued advocacy for policies and programs supported by Lathrop and networked reformers.[170] The year Lathrop joined the Children's Bureau, she wrote the introduction to *The Delinquent Child and the Home*, written by network allies Sophonisba Breckinridge and Edith Abbott, then directors of the Department of Social Investigation for the Chicago School of Civics and Philanthropy. [171] Lathrop would preside over the National Conference of Charities and Correction in 1919, having been preceded in the prior decade by network members Addams and Mack.[172]

Conclusion: Network Legacies

As varied as the work in the juvenile court movement was in Chicago and across the country, the original reformers sustained their network and used it to successfully press some of their concerns at the level of national policy. Although many of the initial reformers had scattered far from the Juvenile Court of Cook County, they remained connected by the networks they had created. They were found working together in other policy arenas, including child labor, mothers' pensions, protection of women and children, and immigrant protection.

Many of them returned for the 25th anniversary celebration of the founding of the Juvenile Court of Cook County in Chicago, January 2–4, 1925.[173] While reformers at the celebration saw better than they had at the outset the enormity of the problems the Juvenile Court faced relative to its resources, recognized that it had a number of shortfalls, and worked in a more conservative and punitive climate of opinion, they were proud of what they had accomplished.[174] The celebration began with a gathering of some of the leaders of the movement. In the opening session, the mayor and the president of the Board of Commissioners of Cook County illustrated the ongoing city-county collaboration in administration of the Juvenile Court. That the session was presided over by Addams, chair of the Citizen Advisory Committee, hints at who was really running the show. Lathrop, Bowen, Hurley, Judge Lindsey, and Grace Abbott spoke on the origins of the court and the juvenile court movement. Other sessions featured members of Chicago's juvenile court and other courts across the country, faculty members from universities and law schools, presidents of the National Probation Association and Chicago Bar Association, health care practitioners and members of social service agencies. In short, the 25th anniversary celebration both marked their achievements and illustrated how they had gotten there—by staying connected, reaching out to experts, and creating spaces for new voices and new professions.

Political scientists often think of policies in terms of punctuated equilibria; stasis and incremental drift are the rule and change requires windows of opportunity that include policy entrepreneurs and a perceived breakdown of old policies.[175] In a period when state capacity was weak in this area, where child saving was largely the domain of charitable institutions, and in the aftermath of an Illinois Supreme Court rebuff to existing institutions in 1870, reformers such as Lathrop and Flower, with their allies and the organizations with which they were affiliated or had connections, became policy entrepreneurs; Lathrop's position on the Illinois State Board of Charities gave her an institutional base from which to act at an important moment, but the State Board of Charities itself did not remain an important player in the development of the Juvenile Court. Getting new laws through the state legislature was important to the reformers' goals, but this was hardly enough to tell the story of the house that Julia (and friends) built.

In our case study, institutional experiments and prototypes indeed allowed for incremental innovation, building support for the ideas of reformers. The experimental program that preceded legislation in Illinois was initiated by reformers; the repetition of this pattern at additional points in the development of the court as an institution suggests this was no accident. However, bureaucratic entrepreneurs inside the state were not at the forefront of the juvenile court movement. Building the institution of the Juvenile Court of Cook County meant that civic-minded reform groups helped grow state capacity. Time and again, when they were successful in lobbying for new departures, organizations provided financial support, temporary facilities, equipment, and staffing to help launch their projects. They used their networks, which included friends inside the court system, to build prototypes of the organizations they wanted to see created at law, demonstrated their experiment could work with the investment of their own money and labor, and used their success to convince allies and legislators to recognize and extend their reforms through additional legislation.

At some point, the private provision of resources necessary to the institution's mission yielded to public provision as the administrative state and the warrant for the exercise of its expanded powers grew. And yet, even when government took on commitments, public institutions often depended on the capacities of civic-minded reform organizations to carry out parts of the mandate. In the institution-building we have examined, the line between public and private responsibility was circumstantial and contingent. For participants, the rules of the game during times of flux were sometimes unclear, as they were for the JCC and the Detention Home. There was no simple, linear progression from private initiative to public ownership of the Juvenile Court, and reformers played ongoing and important roles in its transformation.

These female reformers and their allies were surely leaders, but they led in a context in which the direction of changes they sought was consonant with the budding social scientific and reform sensibilities of the period. They looked about them, saw what innovations were afoot elsewhere, and rode on a wave of thinking that was being produced not only by settlement workers and child savers but by researchers, scholars, and legal reformers. The "policy window" that opened for Chicago reformers opened in state after state in a rapid wave of reform, and spread to the creation of the Children's Bureau at the national level. These reformers worked in a period of statebuilding that was generating new public roles and institutions more broadly. By their activities, female reformers made themselves potential authorities on all sorts of issues relating to children and the family, and through their investment in such policy issues they became authorities to be reckoned with. Reformers in the network reinforced each other, celebrated victories together, and helped each other spread enthusiasm for reforms that they believed would cure many urban ills and help preserve many middle-class ideals. They used their networks, vehicles for disseminating their ideas, and their skills honed in previous campaigns to wage new ones.

Although caution must be exercised when generalizing from a case study, in the case of the Juvenile Court, organized interests outside the state clearly must be placed at the center of the institution-building narrative. Judging from other evidence presented in this volume, there is every reason to cast serious doubt on the idea that this pattern is exceptional.

Chapter 7

The Better Homes Movement and the Origins of Mortgage Redlining in the United States

James L. Greer

In the second year of the New Deal, the federal government continued to grapple with the daunting economic problems of the Great Depression, especially with the ongoing problems of the nation's financial system and the continuing plague of extensive unemployment. One of the most important pieces of legislation of the "First New Deal" formulated in the second session of the 73rd Congress and explicitly designed to deal with the overwhelming problems of unemployment and the nation's housing market was the National Housing Act of 1934. The intent of the Act was to address the ongoing stagnant state of the nation's housing market and in so doing to spur employment in the critical housing construction sector.[1] The Act, drafted by a small group of high-level bureaucratic officials in the Treasury Department, the Reconstruction Finance Corporation, the Federal Reserve Board, and the Federal Home Loan Bank, had several important objectives, not the least of which was to foster lending by banks, savings and loan associations (SLAs), thrifts, and insurance companies in order to stimulate the housing sector.[2] This mundane objective nonetheless led to a stark revolution in the way in which home mortgage financing occurred in the United States. The Act was passed against the strident objections of the national trade organization of the SLAs, which at that time dominated home mortgage financing. It created a new standard mortgage, a mortgage insurance program to entice all financial institutions to participate in this new mortgage financing system, and last, a new institution, the Federal Housing Administration (FHA) to administer this mortgage loan guarantee program.

Congress created the FHA as an independent public corporation requiring the agency to finance its operations (and the reserves of the mortgage insurance fund) from fees charged to mortagees.[3] Thus removed from congressional appropriation, the FHA held considerable autonomy as well as a mandate to implement the sweeping provisions of the Housing Act. The agency transformed mortgage financing, upgraded and regularized building standards for housing construction, and restructured the geography of mortgage financing across American metropolitan areas. Writing in 1984, historian Kenneth Jackson argued that "No agency of the United States government has had a more pervasive and powerful impact on the American people over the past half century than the Federal Housing Administration."[4]

The FHA played such an important role because, in implementing mortgage insurance, the agency both refused to offer mortgage insurance (redlined) on a very high proportion of the extant housing and, at the same time, created a powerful set of incentives for the construction of new housing on the edges of already built-up cities.

The FHA adopted a set of underwriting standards that implemented in elaborate detail an extensive array of requirements concerning the physical plant of the home, and the public and private amenities of the neighborhood including transportation access and public facilities. These standards also required assurance about the likely economic future of the metropolitan area, and appropriate neighborhood characteristics, including the social class, ethnicity, and race of the community's residents. The FHA used many reasons to deny mortgage insurance, often premised on the construction, structure, amenities, and infrastructural features of the home. Additionally, of course, the FHA adopted the belief, which was nearly universally held by real estate appraisal experts, lenders, and the realty industry at the time, that the entry of nonwhite residents into a previously all-white neighborhood inevitably initiated a process whereby property values would necessarily decline, probably precipitously.[5] As such, the FHA refused to offer mortgage insurance, even on newly constructed housing, if African Americans, Latinos, and occasionally people of other ethnicities were potential purchasers.[6] Also, the agency, from the earliest incarnations of its *Underwriting Manual*, sanctioned the adoption of racially restrictive covenants, already widespread throughout American cities at that time,[7] as a condition of mortgage insurance.[8] Redlining affected large swaths of American cities and probably two-thirds or more of the nation's standing housing stock. Both white and nonwhite neighborhoods were denied mortgage insurance, that is, redlined.[9]

That the FHA from its very origins was thoroughly imbued with racist (and nativist as well as antisemitic) sentiments and implemented its programs in concert with these beliefs is clear and uniformly recognized in the historical and sociological literature.[10] However, race was neither the sole nor perhaps the most important factor shaping the FHA's decisions implementing mortgage insurance. An array of requirements were necessary for a home to be covered by FHA mortgage insurance guarantees, and each of these numerous prerequisites had to be met in full before the FHA would insure the mortgage. Most of these involved the physical structure of the home, the number of rooms, a minimal size for the lot and a minimum setback from the street, as well as the essential requirements that the home have full plumbing, central heating, and a modernized electrical system. Bluntly, if the home did not have a central heating system, full indoor and private toilet and water, and an up-to-date electrical system—and a shocking proportion of American housing at this time did not meet these requirements—then mortgage insurance, independent of the race or ethnicity of the occupants and the adjacent neighborhood, would not be available.

Following in the footsteps of an earlier New Deal housing agency—the Home Owners' Loan Corporation (HOLC)—the FHA created uniform property appraisal standards that guided the agency's willingness to extend mortgage guarantees on specific homes in particular communities. These appraisal standards were elaborated in extraordinary detail in the FHA's *Underwriting Manuals* published and revised several times in the 1930s.[11] Impressively, the agency was able to write and publish the first *Underwriting Manual* in 1935, just a year after the agency was created.

This immediately poses a puzzle: how did a newly created (albeit quite autonomous) agency develop such an elaborate and authoritative document in such short order? That a public bureaucracy could so rapidly and independently produce such comprehensive and exceedingly detailed standards seems unlikely. This is especially so because these standards covered all feasible facets of the physical construction of a house, all plumbing, heating, and electrical systems, and dictated minimal construction materials and techniques for the home's substructures, setbacks from the street, and neighborhood standards, including public infrastructure, public facilities, transportation networks, schools, parks, and public facilities, and the social makeup of the community. Rather, the agency relied on a wealth of analytical work that had been previously formulated by a private, nationally prominent organization (Better Homes in America, BHA) (1922–1934), and adopted and sanctioned these standards as those of the national state. BHA was founded in 1922 and headed by Herbert Hoover, then secretary of commerce, who was president of its board of directors. BHA was spearheaded by an extraordinary woman journalist, Marie Meloney, editor of a prominent women's publication, the *Delineator*, who secured the participation of the General Federation of Women's Clubs, a national association with substantial organizational capacities, in BHA's activities. With these resources, it formulated and popularized an ideological vision of the basic home for the typical American middle-class family that itself was but the culmination of over half a century of advocacy by proponents of housing reform.

The origins of property appraisal standards adopted and sanctioned by the FHA—the basis of home mortgage redlining—reside in the extensive work by housing reformers largely carried out by private advocacy organizations over the previous half century. During the Progressive Era, the nation was rife with organizations, some overtly political, some civic, as well as umbrella associations of private corporations, active in formulating their solutions to a host of national or local problems. As other chapters in this volume have also described, clear defining lines between what was public and what was private were frequently anything but obvious. This rich and ever changing fabric of organizations created capacities and administrative protocols that could and would be adopted by public agencies and absorbed quickly to respond to a range of issues; in this regard, the experience of housing regulation resembles the private creation and later public absorption of mechanisms for animal protection and rescue that Pearson and Smith describe. These organizations had a diverse range of expressed objectives that not infrequently led to unintended results.[12]

This is a notable part of the unique story of housing in America, especially the revolution in the financing of residential real estate that led to the extensive disinvestment of large swaths of central city neighborhoods. Three sources, all lodged in Progressive Era politics and organizational activities, led to this system of mortgage redlining across American cities. First, the creation of a national system of deposit insurance created the system of banking regulation that largely dictated to regulated financial institutions what loans and investments they could and could not make. Deposit insurance was not, however, an invention of the federal government. Many states, primarily in the Midwest and South during the Populist Era, had created similar systems—all of which ended in failure.[13] Second, beginning in the 1890s but flourishing during the 1920s, America's corporations, especially those producing automobiles and household equipment and furniture, developed and perfected a system of installment purchasing. Private corporations developed, in other words, the financial analytics that, with relatively low fixed monthly costs, permitted consumers to purchase expensive durable goods over a period of time.[14] It was but a small step to extend this model to the financing of homes.

The last source is the detailed elaboration of a widely disseminated and accepted set of standards for a well-built home acceptable to the American family. This was the unique contribution of a now largely forgotten private, civic movement active throughout the 1920s—Better Homes in America, Inc. Over a decade, BHA annually sponsored thousands of model home demonstrations that they used to create and popularize a clear, coherent, and uncontested model of the basic adequate home. Through BHA, women defined the prerequisites of the American home. These were elaborated in great detail in BHA's 1931 publication of the *Better Homes Manual* by the University of Chicago Press. The standards formulated in the *Manual* by this private civic women's organization were adopted by the newly created FHA as the basis of the underwriting standards of the mortgage insurance program the FHA was to administer.

Housing reform has a long history in the United States. As America became an urban society, civic activists and journalists discovered that the nation was awash in bad housing. Throughout the Progressive Era, civic organizations conducted innumerable surveys of housing conditions and found a shocking concentration of poor quality housing: units were badly maintained and overcrowded, with an alarming absence of privacy; lacked basic sanitation as well as natural light and fresh air; and were located in neighborhoods teeming with disease and crime.[15] A common theme adopted by reformers was that the slums, where illnesses and all manner of social dysfunction abounded, undermined the ability of the republic to nurture children and mold immigrants into citizens.[16]

During the Progressive Era, but especially after 1890, reformers developed a common set of practices to respond to the housing problems they confronted. Extensive and detailed empirical research was a prerequisite. Reformers organized to publicize housing issues, propose solutions, and create programs that led to, or formed the basis of, later publicly assumed responsibilities of the state. These organizations, some short-lived and others permanent fixtures on the civic and political landscape for a generation, advanced their agenda along several fronts. Wide-scale publicity utilizing all elements of the media and exhibits to provide visual and palpable examples to the public soon followed. Frequently, contests and demonstration projects were used to identify a range of acceptable solutions to these clear housing problems. Housing reformers marshaled the considered opinion and recommendations of experts, forged public opinion, and created on an ostensibly private basis a focused and, they believed, a comprehensive solution to cities' tenement housing problems. Based on the research they conducted, reformers of the 1890s drafted and lobbied for proposed legislation.[17]

Later, at the very end of the Progressive Era, housing reform took a much different form. In the early 1920s housing reformers formed an extensive national organization, Better Homes in America Inc., to popularize a comprehensive and detailed model of the basic components of the American home. They did so, following the lead of their predecessors, through annual demonstration housing contests conducted among thousands of communities large and small across the country. These contests and demonstrations, in turn, depended on the efforts of local clubs, most of them local chapters of the General Federation of Women's Clubs (GFWC), a private civic organization that already had over thirty years' experience and considerable success in pressing claims against the states for widows' and soldiers' pensions.[18] BHA's activities culminated in the publication of a compendium that provided in detail the requirements of the American home. These, in turn, became the basis of the underwriting standards adopted by the new Federal Housing Administration (FHA) from the mid-1930s onward.

BHA's model of a single-family home equipped with a full array of structural amenities played a role in the wide-scale disinvestment in existing homes across the country. Because BHA's standards required that all homes have a full and adequate array of plumbing, heating, and electrical systems (and the majority of American homes in the early 1930s did not), these standards rendered a large proportion of the housing stock obsolete. As adopted by the FHA, these standards determined whether or not a property would qualify for mortgage insurance. They became, in other words, the basis of home mortgage redlining that adversely affected a huge share of already standing housing, especially in older cities.

BHA's contribution to the housing policy of the federal government was the creation of a single, unified, and unchallenged definition of not simply the ideological (and gendered) construct of a standard home but also of the necessary and mundane components of a home for the American family. BHA's lasting achievement was the publication of its *Better Homes Manual*, a book that BHA envisioned as a textbook and a resource for housing developers, architects, builders, planners, local officials, and, most important, private home owners. In the *Manual*, written by over seventy experts in this field, all feasible elements pertaining to the American home were covered. While its hopes for the manual were ambitious, the BHA did not anticipate one use to which it was put: the standards were so completely elaborated in the *Better Homes Manual* that they were one and the same as the underwriting standards adopted by the FHA.

BHA becomes important, then, because the work of this private, civic initiative, albeit substantively supported by selective administrative arms of the national state, formulated the empirical basis for the underwriting standards administered by the FHA.[19] These underwriting standards, in turn, determined where and for what homes this mortgage insurance would be available, and importantly, where and for which homes they would not. BHA, like reformers in other contexts discussed in this volume, created and popularized what became the content of public policy in the nation's future.

Post-World War I Housing Crisis

At the conclusion of World War I, politicians and reformers from across the political spectrum concluded that the country was in the midst of a severe housing crisis. This had several dimensions. First and foremost, housing shortages affected cities large and small across the country but were especially severe in metropolitan areas along the Eastern Seaboard. The dearth of acceptable housing units, notably, affected nearly all spectra of the American social structure: housing deficiencies now affected middle-class families as well the poor and working classes. Indeed, one contemporary estimated that there were 121 families for every 100 housing units in American cities.[20]

The cause of the housing shortage was twofold. The second decade of the twentieth century saw a dramatic increase in the urban population as urban economic development created hundreds of thousands of jobs that provided on ongoing basis of rural to urban in-migration. Yet, while American cities increasingly became home to innumerable new residents (even when immigration declined precipitously at the onset of the war), the nation's war effort diverted nearly all economic efforts and financing to construction of weapons and military materiel.[21] Housing production plummeted severely, leaving large numbers of new residents to fend for shelter in cities where there were nearly no vacancies. In short order, several problems ensued. Rent gouging and housing price inflation occurred, seriously undercutting the increased wages offered to wartime workers.[22] Overcrowding followed, with many families finding it necessary to double up in quarters appropriate for individual families. To absorb exploitative rents, families also found it necessary to take on boarders. An additional component of the rural to city in-migration in the United States that squeezed the housing market was the first Great Migration of African Americans from southern states to manufacturing employment centers in northern cities, which began in the mid-1910s. Over the coming decade, while nonwhites rarely exceeded 8 to 10 percent of northern metropolises, the number of blacks entering industrial cities was substantial, visible, and immediately evoked the unease and displeasure of the cities' white residents.[23] Indeed, in many cities the intermittent violence against black residents that all too frequently troubled non-whites when they purchased (and attempted to occupy) housing in all-white neighborhoods escalated into full-scale race riots, most prominently in Chicago, Detroit, and East St. Louis.[24]

The crisis brought about the first intervention (albeit timid) of the federal government in the direct provision of housing. With the production of housing plummeting, in some contemporary estimates, to just 10 percent of prewar levels, numerous and widely publicized accounts reported that war production was severely compromised by high worker turnover directly caused by the lack of adequate and affordable housing. The problem was seen as so pressing to national policymakers that Congress appropriated nearly $175 million to fund two separate initiatives to provide housing to war workers. Both acts were passed late in the war effort, and brought only modest relief in alleviating housing shortages in a few locations along the Eastern Seaboard.[25]

To all observers, the extent of the nation's housing shortage was dramatic. Homer Hoyt, who would become among the most prominent real estate analysts in the 1930s with the publication of *100 Years of Land Value in Chicago*,[26] provided the most optimistic estimates of America's housing shortage at between 450,000 to 1 million in 1921. Other contemporaries were much less sanguine: Herbert Hoover, as secretary of commerce, publicly held that at least one million new homes needed to be built in the immediate future while other informed contemporaries guessed the figure to be triple that. Clearly, reformers and the real estate industry agreed that a severe housing shortage existed.[27]

America's housing crisis, however, was seen as much more than a quantitative shortage of adequate housing units. The nation's home ownership rate, after growing continuously over the previous forty years, had stagnated. In fact, levels of private home ownership had declined in the nation's cities.[28] Elites, Hoover prominently among them, openly worried about the diminishing level of home ownership, particularly in cities. Added to this were demographic changes that were transforming American society. Cities had nearly doubled in size since the turn of the century and, with more and more Americans residing in cities, the average size of the family had decreased. In cities, teens and young adults availed themselves of the expanding variety of entertainment—movies, cars, dancing, and access to alcohol—all with diminished direct parental supervision. To many at the time, including leaders of women's organizations and editors of women's publications, the American family was under threat as well.

The American response to this newly perceived housing crisis took many forms. First, there was a strident withdrawal from the nation's first and very limited experience with "public housing." With anticommunism sweeping the country, these ventures were easily condemned as "socialistic" and un-American. They were quickly abandoned, leaving the private market to supply the hundreds of thousands of housing units needed in American cities.[29] The federal government's first foray into the direct provision of housing ended, was generally considered a failure, and as such precluded public housing as a viable policy alternative for nearly two decades.

Second, housing reformers, while they generally agreed on a set of common, intersecting findings about poor housing, overcrowding, slums, crime, and the breakdown of social mores, divided in their programmatic responses to the country's housing problems, no more so than in the post-World War I era. During the New Era (1920–1929), when Herbert Hoover so dramatically restructured and reoriented the U.S. Department of Commerce to focus on housing and community development issues, the American housing reform movement split into two camps. Housing reformers debated whether the housing needs of all social classes—including the poor and working class as well as the middle class—could be adequately met by the private marketplace. One group, in alliance with, but nonetheless clearly separate and independent from Hoover's Commerce Department, believed that the private real estate market could adequately resolve the nation's housing crisis. These advocates included not only the nation's real estate industry and its powerful National Association of Real Estate Boards (NAREB) but also national women's organizations and clubs. On the other hand, housing movement activists more directly tied to Progressive Era housing reform organizations and their leaders held that the need for adequate, sound, and safe housing for all Americans, including most importantly the poor, could not be met solely through the operations of the private marketplace. Based in part on their knowledge of, and research about the housing policies of European nations, these reformers argued that government, whether local, state, or federal, must provide some (perhaps small) portion of housing needs directly. The state must, in their eyes, directly develop, construct, maintain, and rent housing directly to the poorer strata of the nation's citizenry.[30]

These diverging approaches on the part of progressives to America's housing needs and problems have received widely different treatments by historians and social scientists. Namely, the story of advocacy and research that finds its roots in Progressive Era housing investigations and legislation is directly tied to the writing, active participation in innumerable civic organizations, and lobbying for public housing of such prominent figures as Carol Aronovici, Edith Elmer Wood, and Catherine Bauer, all prolific authors on housing issues throughout the 1920s and 1930s. Each was knowledgeable about European policy solutions to housing problems that included state-provided public housing, and all were strong advocates for public housing in the United States.[31] These housing reformers developed the analytic framework that only came to fruition when the federal government finally adopted the development of a public housing together with an urban slum clearance program in the Housing Act of 1937.[32] The nation's public housing program led the way to the development of hundreds of thousands of units of public housing, typically in high-density compact housing projects, as well as extensive and nearly ubiquitous urban renewal programs in nearly all cities in the country.

This is a well-known and frequently retold story of American housing policy. In contrast, scholars, historians and social scientists alike, have largely been silent on the contribution of the other wing of housing reform in the United States that flourished throughout the 1920s. Generally, their contributions have largely been lost, with the exception of Herbert Hoover's very active Department of Commerce throughout both the Harding and Coolidge administrations. The contribution of civic organizations—especially women's organizations—has generally been ignored. The puzzle in these varying treatments can be put bluntly: these accounts highlight the advocacy from the left, from more progressive housing reformers who ultimately successfully forged public housing and urban renewal programs. Yet these are also programs that, through the critical 1950s and 1960s, came to be seen as abject failures—particularly public housing—and, now, are largely removed from the urban landscape. Urban renewal has received slightly more generous evaluations but, again, in large part, these programs were largely unsuccessful in restraining the tide of central business district economic deterioration. Regardless of their treatment in the scholarly literature, most concede that neither public housing nor urban renewal have had a lasting or positive and significant impact on the landscape of American metropolitan centers.[33]

In contrast, the story that has only quietly been told before—the involvement of women's organizations in articulating and widely publicizing the basic requirements of a standard American home—was critical in providing the substance of the property underwriting criteria of the FHA. Ancillary research, again conducted by a women's organization during the mid1920s on home equipment, formed the basis of the (albeit methodologically much different) Real Property Inventories that the Works Progress Administration (WPA) conducted in 1934. These Real Property Inventories, in turn, became the basis of the FHA's assignment of mortgage risk grades to individual city blocks and consequently the basis for granting or refusing mortgage insurance. There is an irony, then, in these alternative treatments of the progressive and more conservative branches of housing reform that split in response to the nationally perceived housing crisis in the 1920s; the arm that has received most academic attention—that which led to public housing and urban renewal—left few lasting achievements on the American urban landscape. In contrast, the activities of BHA and the GFWC, which defined the basic standards of an American home, provided the underlying analytics to FHA underwriting standards. We have lived with the overwhelming impact of these standards for over seven decades. Considering this story, like the other stories in this volume of institution-building that began outside the boundaries of the state, provides a better sense of how a powerful and influential state institution was able to emerge without the kind of initially visible and public commitment of intellectual, political, structural, economic, and ideological resources that usually triggers scholarly attention.

Policies and Programs at the National Level

In the immediate aftermath of World War I, private real estate interests (especially the newly renamed National Association of Real Estate Boards) and their allies in Congress quickly moved on two initiatives. First, NAREB, riding a wave of anticommunism in the aftermath of the Russian Revolution, moved to immediately dismantle both of the federal government's wartime public housing ventures. These federally funded public housing programs had provided at best only modest benefits to workers, businessmen, or the war effort, and furthermore the more visible of the two, the U.S. Housing Corporation, had lost money for the government. Congress quickly obliged.

Second, and positively, NAREB launched a nationwide Own Your Own Home (OYOH) campaign beginning in 1917. NAREB undertook this program primarily for the material benefits that would accrue to its members as homes were built and sold by NAREB members. Additionally, however, this ideological program supported a complex of ideas already present in American political discourse that associated home ownership with nurturing citizens. Indeed, home ownership was framed as critical for the American family and its children. Children brought up in clean, well-lit, sanitary, and, importantly, single-family homes owned by the family were sure to become the valuable American citizens of the future. NAREB sought to associate in the public mind a clear distinction between the American ideal, where families owned their home and as such were rooted in their communities, and the socialist ideal of multifamily collectively owned residences.[34]

OYOH was almost immediately adopted as a program to be administered by the Department of Labor in the waning years of the Wilson administration. The Labor Department's efforts to promote this home ownership campaign were substantial and reached all regions of the country. Millions of OYOH pamphlets were published and distributed. In them, the department elaborated the elements of the local campaigns that would hopefully increase the desire for home ownership among the citizens. According to the pamphlet, local campaigns were to include newspaper articles and editorials, essay contests in local high schools (the winner to be published) on the benefits of private home ownership, OYOH buttons and banners for local schools and civil buildings, and, perhaps most oddly, efforts to encourage chefs in local restaurants to create OYOH dishes. The Labor Department also offered assistance in providing speakers for lecture series for civic organizations or local colleges.[35]

When Herbert Hoover became secretary of commerce in 1921 with the new Harding administration, the Commerce Department inherited the OYOH program and in the same year published a small book entitled *How to Own Your Own Home*, a work that largely dealt with the financing of homes. Hoover later revealed in his memoirs that he had little faith in the OYOH campaign, believing that it had run its course and public sympathy and interest had diminished.[36] Additionally, he thought that the OYOH campaign was unlikely to increase home ownership and did not address what Hoover believed to be the critical issues undermining enhanced home ownership in the United States: high construction costs and poor design.[37] As he reorganized the Commerce Department, especially the new Division of Building and Housing that he hoped would assist in expanding and standardizing zoning ordinances and building codes in municipalities, Hoover remained interested in governmental, private, or, best from his mind-set, an alliance in which the private association took the lead.[38]

Events conspired to respond to Hoover's ongoing concerns about home construction. Marie Meloney, editor of the *Delineator*, a women's magazine with over one million readers, originated the idea of a Better Homes for America campaign and asked for Hoover's assistance. By this time, Marie Meloney had already been a journalist for over two decades. Hired by the *Washington Post* to cover the 1900 national party conventions, she then took a position with the Washington bureau of the *Denver Post*. She was the first woman journalist to be accredited to the U.S. Senate press gallery. She moved to New York City, where she married William Brown Meloney, IV, editor of the *New York Sun*, and continued to work as a journalist. She was active in New York social circles and maintained correspondence with such journalistic and literary luminaries as Ida Tarbell, Walter Lippmann, Robert Frost, and Bertrand Russell. Later in life she became close friends with Eleanor Roosevelt.

Hoover immediately agreed to back the BHA effort, believing that, as originally outlined by Meloney, it conformed to the type of public-private collaboration that he termed "cooperative associationalism." Furthermore, Hoover sought a largely private answer to the housing crisis that persisted after the end of the war. "The cooperative associationalism" he advocated entailed that government should act as a national information center, collecting and distributing information to the public (and the private sector) through the coordinating efforts of voluntary groups and associations.[39]

Better Homes in America Inc.

Meloney and Hoover had worked closely together previously on the Food Conservation Campaign that Hoover had administered in Europe in the aftermath of World War I. The management of the food relief effort, as Hoover designed it, depended upon extensive and widespread voluntary efforts and contributions from American civic organizations. He quickly found that among the most successful means to achieve the wide-ranging participation needed to initiate and sustain this campaign was publicizing and coordinating the efforts through women's magazines, of which Meloney's *Delineator* was especially important. Not only did Hoover and Marie Meloney foster a friendship, Hoover was impressed with the enthusiasm and effectiveness of women's magazines to generate quick national attention to this cause, and with women's organizations in providing the volunteers to carry out the program.[40] Thus, unlike some other policy areas discussed in this volume, the impetus for reform came simultaneously from within and outside of the state; outside reformers did not first have to engage state actors in their agenda. A partnership was formed.

In Meloney's eyes, this new housing campaign was clearly distinct from OYOH, which was an initiative of the national state whose execution was top-down. Furthermore, OYOH was solely focused on encouraging home ownership. BHA, in her view, was to be a cooperative effort among women's clubs, chambers of commerce, churches, and schools to build a model home in every community in the country. She was expressly worried about the state of the American family: using this largely community-based movement, she wished to restore traditional family values and to promote the image of the wife as an "efficient technocrat" within the home. BHA would advocate home ownership, of course, but Meloney's vision was to promote the model home in its entirety—its architecture but also the array of home equipment that would allow women in their domain to be both nurturing and efficient.[41]

The principals who created and developed BHA had different, if overlapping, objectives. To Meloney, BHA sought to construct an overtly ideological vision of the American home. Americans needed more and better privately owned homes, but BHA's goals, as successor to earlier housing reform movements, were much more. Meloney, in a poetic moment, provided a succinct summary:

> Better Homes mean better communities—a finer nation.
> Better Homes mean better babies.

Better Homes mean boys and girls staying at home.
Better Homes mean healthier families.
Better Homes mean happier people.
Better Homes mean better times.[42]

Despite her own background and work history she strongly advocated through BHA for the proper place of a woman in a domestic setting. In contrast to other feminists of the age, she rejected calls for housewives to receive appropriate compensation for their considerable labor in the home. Rather, Meloney wanted to create a modern women's identity that was inextricably tied to the family and home. Indeed, one of Meloney's central aims with BHA was to restore traditional family values in a modern setting. The ideal home would emphatically be a single-family unit residing on a small plot that enhanced the privacy of the family. This home was critical to the development of children as future responsible members of the democratic community—citizens. The modern home and the modern woman would assure that the children and the family would be healthy, productive, and patriotic, and the modern women could best fulfill the multiple roles she was routinely called on to perform if she was appropriately equipped with a modern home. For the housewife to carry out the myriad tasks required to maintain a nurturing and supportive environment for children, she must be provided with a home invariably equipped with an array of standard infrastructural features—the water, plumbing, and electrical systems—along with modern efficient appliances. Only then could the modern housewife be a successful technocrat in her own home.[43]

To Hoover, BHA represented a nearly ideal relationship between the national state and the private economy. The function of the agencies in the national state (such as Commerce) was to collect, summarize, and convey "scientific" knowledge to the private sector, hopefully through civic intermediaries like BHA. Hoover thought of himself as a progressive and a technocrat who was above the political fray. He had high esteem for "scientific" knowledge, especially if this knowledge was conveyed to the public and the corporate sector through carefully coordinated public relations and popularization efforts.[44] Just as Frederick Taylor had "scientifically" analyzed the work process in the factory, so too could all factors contributing to the development, planning, construction, financing, and functioning of the home be more comprehensively understood through the prudent use of experts, and it could be done more efficiently, at lower prices, and for the benefit of American citizens. To Hoover, BHA, with its thousands of chapters organized and active at the local level, was one of many ways to convey widely an increasingly common set of housing standards, along with extensive publicity and with the widespread participation of the public. BHA was effective, like the Division of Housing and Construction, because the standards promulgated by this civic organization were premised on the considered opinion of innumerable experts. Furthermore, and in concert with the voluntarism implicit in Hoover's view, these standards were noncoercive. Housing was also a special commodity for the future president. The commerce secretary considered the increased number of single-family dwellings as a direct spur to the purchase of an array of American products—automobiles, washing machines, plumbing equipment, and the like. Finally, Hoover wished to promote home ownership for its "spiritual" impact on American society. In his mind, homeowners were rooted in and committed to their communities in a way that renters never could be. Hoover, Meloney, most leaders of civic organizations at the time, and indeed, the entire sweep of the progressive housing reform movement, believed that good quality housing, privately owned, was a key to developing and sustaining good citizens. Renters, these reformers believed, held no real stake in their community. Renters were but temporary residents in any one community and had no interest in establishing the permanent ties to a neighborhood or town that would establish the prerequisites of civic engagement.[45]

Finally, private industry, especially at the national level, strongly supported BHA because of its message of consumption. The BHA movement advocated the building and ownership of detached single-family homes that of necessity had to be constructed with all structural features of a home (plumbing, electrical, and waste disposal) as well as filled with the entire complement of modern appliances (washing machines, electric sweepers, kitchen stoves, and cars) to permit the sustenance of the modern American family. BHA, in other words, helped to create a housing culture premised on extensive and continuous consumption of the wide variety of consumer goods that were being produced in American factories in the postwar era. Furthermore, BHA explicitly endorsed the increasingly popular practice of installment purchasing, arguing, like its corporate sponsors (especially automobile companies), that this new system of relatively modest monthly payments was a legitimate way for the American family in the New Era to finance a modern, and higher, standard of living.[46]

Using the *Delineator* as her springboard for national publicity, Meloney began to advocate for the national yet decentralized housing program that became BHA. Using her extensive professional network of friends and acquaintances, she contacted governors, high-ranking officials in the Harding administration, as well as the U.S. Chamber of Commerce, the GFWC, and the American Red Cross. From each of these national organizations she secured lists of state and local leaders, of which those from the GFWC were especially important. Over the course of its history (1922–1934), more than half of local BHA leaders who organized model home demonstrations in localities throughout the country were members of women's clubs and arms of the GFWC. The organizational capacities and political effectiveness of the GFWC was already well established. Women's organizations in the first decade of the twentieth century had been successful in setting the agenda on the public debate over social welfare spending, and had also successfully lobbied state legislatures to enact mothers' pension laws, particularly in the West and Midwest.[47] Meloney, from the very beginning of BHA, was able to use and build upon the existing organizational channels, capacity, leadership, and membership of women's associations to launch and sustain this program. She was, in other words, successful in exploiting these preexisting capacities of women's organizations that had persisted for decades.[48]

BHA commenced its efforts with the construction of a model home on the Mall in Washington D.C. Entitled "Home Sweet Home" in honor of the hundredth anniversary of the song by John Howard Payne, this first home was a replica of Payne's home in Easthampton, Massachusetts. The downstairs contained a living room, kitchen, breakfast room, dining room, and hall. The upstairs had a nursery, bedroom, children's bedroom, two baths and a linen closet. The project, dedicated by President Harding on June 4, 1922, attracted some 40,000 visitors during the exhibition. The GFWC newsletter reported that officials from the U.S. army, Department of Agriculture, and manufacturers' representatives made requests for special, private tours.[49]

From this anything but humble initial demonstration of the "Home, Sweet, Home," BHA developed and expanded quickly. From an impressive array of federal officials, governors, and prominent individuals, Meloney formed the board and advisory committee of BHA. Then, building upon the organizational structure of the GFWC, BHA quickly expanded into numerous local chapters. Aggressively publicized by the *Delineator*, along with the newsletters, pamphlets, and publications of the GFWC, BHA became well known throughout the country and gained a nationwide following. The number of chapters increased from 500 in 1922, doubled to over 1,000 the following year, and increased steadily to over 3,000 in 1926 and to 5,657 in 1929.

Even the onset of the Depression did not diminish its growth—in 1932, the last year the national organization provided these data, BHA boasted some 7,040 chapters across the country.[50]

The major activity of the local chapters was to organize an annual Better Home demonstration week. The rules and standards for these local demonstration projects were established by the national office of BHA and conveyed to the local branches of BHA.[51] As per this detailed directive, ideally, the local BHA chapter was to locate, renovate, or build a demonstration home that they then furnished. Local businesses donated money, materials, and labor to renovate or build, as well as to decorate and furnish, these homes. If, as happened frequently, the chapter was unable to locate a home to renovate or could not build a demonstration home, they could either temporarily adopt a home and augment the décor or secure use of a public space such as a library or government building and assemble a BHA exhibit composed of models, pictures, and blueprints along with BHA literature. Local chapters were encouraged to submit their homes in the annual national demonstration competition, and one such home was selected annually as an exemplar of the objectives of BHA—private ownership, modern design, provision of all the basic necessities of the home, and supportive of child rearing.[52]

Although BHA is little remembered today, it was a highly visible, active movement that spread through all areas of the nation, annually engaged the activities of thousands of volunteers (30,000 at its apex), and attracted millions of visitors to the demonstration homes. The annual BHA demonstration weeks received ample publicity planned carefully by the local chapters; this almost invariably intersected with efforts by a women's club associated with the GFWC and included generous press coverage from local newspapers as well as numerous stories in Meloney's *Delineator* and the GFWC newsletters. Both the public and the real estate industry were cognizant of BHA activities and its advocacy for extensive ownership of well-built and equipped homes.[53]

The General Federation and the Home Equipment Surveys

However cooperative the relationship between Meloney and BHA and her acquaintances at the GFWC was at the beginning of their collaboration, and the benefits that accrued to the fledgling BHA in exploiting the considerable administrative capacities of the GFWC, tensions soon arose between the two organizations. While continuing to provide publicity and support for BHA activities, the GFWC, especially in the national office, chafed at what they saw as the BHA monopolizing the credit for the demonstration homes and the national competition that GFWC believed, not without good reason, to be dependent upon their considerable resources.[54] Perhaps as an effort to assert some autonomy from BHA as well as to provide an independent contribution to this effort, the GFWC in 1925 and 1926 conducted a "Home Equipment Survey" through its individual women's clubs. As with BHA, the GFWC conducted these research efforts with the knowledge of, and contributions from, the Division of Building and Housing in the Commerce Department.[55] With this project, GFWC complemented BHA's activities. BHA was interested in identifying and highlighting houses that were exemplars of the American home: well designed, protective of health and privacy, fully equipped and architecturally sound, and capable of nurturing well-developed children, families, and citizens. GFWC's two-year survey, in contrast, aimed at empirically measuring the number of homes that not only met the somewhat idealized standards of the BHA demonstration home but also sought to assess the number of urban and rural homes that were deficient in terms of physical structure, amenities, or household equipment.[56]

The GFWC was intent on using the survey as a lobbying tool, a practice they had honed with success in the previous decades.[57] Stressing the importance of the home and noting that numerically homemaking was the largest industry in the country, the Federation urged the widespread participation of its members in conducting this survey. Noting that the federal government was collecting data on the nation's farms and factories and developing its policies and laws regarding those sectors of the economy, the GFWC leadership argued that this Household Equipment Survey was necessary so that federal programs and policies pertinent to the home could be comparably informed by empirical research.[58] Indeed, the explicit objective of the Federation leadership was to use this initiative as the basis for a battery of questions to be included in the next decennial census so that, from the 1930 census onwards, the federal government would have consistent information on the home and homemaking that would, as the GFWC leadership argued, tabulate what the "American standard of living is."[59]

In the end, the Federation was partially successful. Early in Hoover's administration, the new Secretary of Commerce, Robert P. Lamont, recognized that the nearly 14,500 women's clubs in the GFWC were active in nearly two-thirds of the counties of the United States and pledged cooperation with the Federation on programs of "community improvement." These involved many

The Home Equipment Survey

By MARY SHERMAN

President General Federation of Women's Clubs

(Nov., 1926, Woman's Home Companion)

The Questionnaire

That disclosed the amazing facts given in this article

What it asked about home equipment:

1. First of all, it asked if there were a *Public Water Supply;* and if not, what substitute was available. On this hung all the subsequent questions as to sinks, washbasins, laundry tubs, bathtubs and flush toilets that gave us knowledge as to what percentage of our surveyed homes were equipped with these conveniences. In this section the methods of sewage disposal and protection of drinking water also were inquired into.
2. Next: *Garbage Disposal,* public or private, with some details as to methods, was the subject of a section and finished the inquiry into fundamental conveniences.
3. The third section dealt with *Heating Systems* and its answers recorded the various types in use in each given community, whether coal, gas or oil furnaces, coal or wood stoves, gas stoves or electric heaters, or oil stoves.
4. The fourth section was devoted to the use of *gas* as an aid to comfortable living and tabulated returns from these questions show where natural gas and manufactured gas are used, how many dwellings in each community are connected with gas mains, and in how many it is used for lighting, cooking and hot-water heating. A supplementary question reported the yearly gas bill per family.
5. *Electrical Equipment* came next with inquiry made as to its source (public or private plant) and then specific questions to show the number of each item in use—electric washing machines, sadirons, flatwork ironers, dishwashers, ranges, vacuum cleaners, sewing machines and refrigeration. A note was also made on the amount of the yearly bill for electric light and power.
6. The concluding section was built around the more *Recreational Equipment* of the home and included listings of telephones, automobiles, radios, phonographs and pianos, with a final question about the library facilities of the place surveyed.

Figure 2. Front page of Mary Sherman, "The Questionnaire That Discloses the Amazing Facts Given in This Article," *Woman's Home Companion*, November 1926.

of the topics covered in the home surveys.[60] In the 1930 Census, "Homemaker" was included for the first time as an occupation counted by the census; this came about as a result of Federation lobbying.

This modest, if significant, achievement, however, is dwarfed by the material contribution of the survey to the critically important Real Property Inventories that the New Deal's Works Progress Administration conducted. The GFWC survey formulated the set of topics that, much as BHA had, determined the quality and value of homes. First and foremost, the survey identified in any community the proportion of homes connected to public utility systems—the water, sewer, electrical, and natural gas utilities. This determined the proportion of homes that had internal plumbing, sewer disposal, and access to the electricity needed to run the array of modern appliances. Overall, the 1934 Real Property Inventories revealed that 16.8 percent of urban homes were overcrowded, 13.5 percent had no indoor private toilet, 20.6 percent had no private bath or shower, and 8.1 percent were connected to neither natural gas nor electricity. The findings for rural homes were even more shocking. A 1934 rural home survey found that 69.6 percent had no indoor running water, 88.8 percent no bathtub, 82.2 percent no electricity, and 91.5 percent no indoor flush toilet.[61] Many homes in the United States were clearly deficient in one or many of these structural amenities. The presence or absence of one or many of these basic structural requirements of the home determined the quality and value of homes and whole communities. The age of housing and neighborhoods were clearly important factors in the adequacy of housing, its appropriateness for child rearing, and the type of occupants living in these residences.[62]

The numerous local chapters of the Federation were instructed to collect their data in the aggregate from city officials as well as public utilities, real estate brokers, and local department stores. From the city utility engineers, for instance, women volunteers established the total number of homes connected to the public water and sewer systems; from the real estate board, they collected information on the character of the community's housing stock; and from local department stores, they would establish the sales of washing machines, sweepers, and other appliances.[63] Although professionally trained analysts distrusted these methods of information gathering, the GFWC survey helped inform many of the questions posed in the 1934 Real Property Inventories executed by the WPA.[64] Furthermore, when data from the Real Property Inventories (in which data was collected on a building-by-building canvass by thousands of WPA employees) was finally tabulated, direct comparisons of these results and those generated by the GFWC largely agreed. Perhaps not surprisingly, local utility company data proved to provide reasonable estimates of homes that did or did not have an indoor water supply or bathroom facilities.[65]

From 1934 (the year the first inventories were conducted and the FHA was created by an act of Congress) and in subsequent years, the FHA used these data collected in the Real Property Inventories to assign mortgage risks by individual city blocks. Using the information collected by these inventories, the FHA established a matrix to determine the likely safety or risk of mortgage lending across the neighborhoods of America's cities. Many of these factors were the kinds of data originally collected in the GFWC surveys in 1925 and 1926, particularly the basic structural features of each housing unit (water, sewer, electrical systems), plumbing, housing quality, as well as the percentage of owner-occupied homes and extant vacancies. Additionally, the WPA collected information on home pricing (rents and housing values) as well as on the residents of properties (where race was of prominent interest). This information was scored so that each city block had a score conceivably from 1 to 100 and all blocks, based on early analytic work at the FHA, were sorted into one of three kinds of neighborhoods: reject, intermediate, and best.[66] Apparently, the FHA used these scores to develop their own set of mortgage risk maps, of which only one for the city of Chicago still exists. The FHA maps identified neighborhoods where the agency would not insure home mortgages under Title II of the National Housing Act (and where homes would be redlined), the reject category; communities where the agency would insure mortgages, but only for relatively short terms (under twenty, and under ten years); and finally those areas where long-term mortgages were eligible for FHA insurance (over twenty years).[67]

The GFWC, in other words, used its considerable administrative capacity along with support for BHA annual demonstration projects in a very large number of localities (over 7,000), but also played a role in developing the information infrastructure that the FHA ultimately used to assign mortgage risks. The early efforts of the Federation as it conducted its surveys relate directly to those later surveys (albeit conducted using a very different method) that were crucial for the FHA to do its initial work in administering the nation's first mortgage insurance program. GFWC thus had several achievements with its home surveys. In concert with its Progressive Era roots, the Federation provided information for the first time on housing conditions throughout the country. Using these data, GFWC was successful in having "homemaker" included as an occupation in the 1930 census. Finally, and most consequentially, the Federation's survey represented a first attempt at determining and assessing those factors relevant to housing quality.[68] The Federation's home equipment survey formulated a notable portion of the questions that were replicated later in the property inventories that in turn played a role, independent of BHA's activities, in establishing home mortgage redlining.

BHA's Creation of *The Better Homes Manual*

BHA was largely an educational enterprise, and one that thrived on publicity. On these counts, it was a stunning success. The consummation of the program was the 1931 publication of the *Better Homes Manual*.[69] This *Manual* was exhaustive, covering most feasible pertinent topics relevant to home construction and home ownership. Intended as a comprehensive text and resource for all potential homeowners, it was nearly 800 pages long. The *Manual* was written by over seventy authors, including BHA director James Ford, Herbert Hoover (president of the BHA board), John Gries and James Taylor from the Commerce Department, and housing and planning luminaries such as Lewis Mumford, the architectural writer and future author of *The City in History*; Lawrence Veiller, perhaps the best-known housing reform activist in New York City from the turn of the century, Edith Elmer Wood, and many others. Compiled from this deep reservoir of housing experts active in BHA programs, the *Manual* included the full range of topics relevant to home building and ownership. It covered responsible financing of home purchase and mortgages, the importance of architecture, building materials and techniques, local planning and zoning issues, and, in extraordinary detail, the structural prerequisites of an acceptable standard American home.

The specifics of the underwriting standards assembled by the FHA and BHA's recommendations provided in the *Better Homes Manual* are strikingly similar. Indeed, on many critical features (especially having to do with the basic structural features of the home), the language between the two is nearly identical, and definitive. The home had to have a continuous supply of pure, fresh water and an internal plumbing system that brings and returns water from the bathrooms and kitchens.[70] Bathrooms were critically important and should be furnished with the best and most up-to-date fixtures.[71] Sewage disposal was critical for the health and safety of the family and toilets and plumbing in the home (along with connection to the public sewer system) were mandatory.[72] Indeed, a high-quality and well-maintained plumbing system was imperative for the home.[73] Equally important, for all areas of the country a central heating system was necessary, as was a system of constant and adequate hot water.[74]

Table 3. Comparing FHA Underwriting Criteria and Standards in *Better Homes Manual*

*Federal Housing Administration**	*Better Homes in America***
Water, sewer, heating, and electrical systems	
Water Supply: a supply of pure water shall be available to all housing units (sec 527)	Water supply. Running water is required (p. 528)
A sufficient supply of pure water is essential (sec 207a)	All homes need a bounteous supply of water (p.177)
Shut off valves are critical (sec 207c)	Shut off valves recommended (p. 342)
All piping materials should be of high quality to assure their successful utility over a long period of time (sec 207c)	Use the best quality plumbing fixtures (p. 342)
Hot water heater and storage tanks should be of adequate quality and capacity to provide hot water to the home (sec 207d)	An ample supply of hot water is essential (p. 525)
Heating: every dwelling shall have an adequate heating system (sec 533)	A central heating system is a necessity (pp. 310ff.)
Publicly provided sewerage systems are strongly preferred (sec 207f)	Location of home should take account of provisions for water and gas mains and sewage disposal (p. 358)
Electrical wiring: where publicly accessible electricity is available all dwellings shall be wired for electrical service (sec 534)	Installation of additional convenience outlets, such as floor and base plugs (p. 487)
Suitable outlets should be provided in adequate numbers in suitable locations to permit the convenient use of electrical appliances and household electrical equipment (sec 209a, c)	All new homes should be generously wired (pp. 306–7)
Property location, zoning, and restrictive covenants	
Property should through zoning, deed restrictions be used as "security against decline in desirability for residential purposes due to the encroachment of inharmonious elements" (sec 201a)	Protection offered to homes: (a) private restrictions, (b) zoning ordinances and city planning (p. 88)
Property should be located "as to be free from unusual danger[s]" such as from "conflagrations, flood, subsidence, [or] erosion" (sec 201b)	Residences should not be located on land that is frequently flooded or so low that it is damp or subject to difficulties in sewage disposal (p. 519)
Property should be accessible to suitable employment areas, market centers, schools, and recreational facilities." (sec 201c)	Reasonable proximity to places of employment for each of the working members of the household should also be taken into consideration (p. 518)

"It is preferable to be on a minor or less used street." (sec 201d)	There should be a minor street serving the dwelling (p. 651)

Internal arrangement of the home

Preference should be given to designs that are "simple and direct" (sec 204c)	The key to home design is to create a simple, dignified architecture (p. 125)
Ample light is critical [natural light] in the placement of the home on the lot (sec 201e)	Every room is afforded an abundance not only of light but of sunshine (pp. 45, 68, 513)
Kitchen should have adequate windows and their placement is critical for natural ventilation (sec 203)	The kitchen should have cross ventilation at all costs (p. 174)
Immediate access to the kitchen is critical (sec 203)	The relation of the kitchen to other rooms in the home is essential (pp. 456–57)
Bedrooms should be arranged "with special consideration as to privacy"; bedrooms should open onto a common hallway (sec 203d)	Plan bedrooms for privacy and with direct access from the hall (p. 181)
Bathroom should be located conveniently to the bedrooms (203d)	Plan for easy access to bathrooms (p. 181)
Basements are "rarely essential" (sec 203l)	A full basement is not an absolute necessity (p. 77)
Basement rooms: no habitable room will have a portion of its height below adjoining ground level (sec 515)	No living quarters to be in basement (p. 527)

Construction and materials

Quality of building materials and construction standards should exceed local building codes which are primarily concerned with safety (sec 205a)	Building code[s are] an important factor in good housing; they assure the proper use and development of private property (pp. 639–40)
Construction materials should be chosen for their suitability of use and their ability to stand up to use over a long period of time (sec 205b)	It is important to use good, quality building materials (p. 204)

*Federal Housing Administration, *Property Standards: Requirements for Mortgage Insurance Under Title II of the National Housing Act* (Washington, D.C.: GPO, 1936).
** Blanche Halbert, ed., *Better Homes Manual* (Chicago: University of Chicago Press, 1931).

One last structural element was critical for the modern home: an electrical system with outlets in all rooms to power all necessary appliances.[75] In addition, homes were to be constructed with the highest quality materials available, utilizing the most up-to-date and efficient building techniques and following (hopefully exceeding) established building and zoning codes.[76]

FHA underwriting and the standards articulated in the *Manual* agreed also on neighborhood, architectural, and a host of other issues. Echoing concerns that would have resonated with earlier housing reformers, both dictated that the home should have ample natural light, enjoy fresh air, and be arranged attractively on a small individual plot of land.[77] Privacy was paramount: bedrooms must be arranged to assure privacy, especially for the parents. The number of bathrooms must be adequate; indeed both the FHA and BHA recommend at least one full and one half bath for a three-bedroom home.[78] The *Manual*, reflecting the preferences of housing experts at that time, recommended simple, indeed plain, home designs (as well as decorations); FHA standards followed suit.[79] Also included were dictates regarding the neighborhood. Homes were best located in a community that hosted a plethora of amenities—recreational facilities, shopping, and access to all modes of transportation.[80] Protecting the character of a residential community was considered crucial. Zoning was mandatory and deed restrictions primarily aimed to assure that all properties in a single neighborhood would be racially segregated were highly recommended.[81]

FHA Underwriting and the Origins of Mortgage Redlining

BHA's contribution to American housing policy in the early 1930s resulted from a process that was disjointed, developed from numerous sources (some public, many private), and forged in a dire economic and financial crisis. One of the centerpieces of the federal response to the crisis was the Banking Act of 1933, legislation that included the well-known Glass-Steagall provisions and the adoption of a national deposit insurance program. The act also created the Federal Deposit Insurance Corporation (FDIC) to implement this program. This was the most contentious part of the bill because such programs had been implemented in numerous states across the country and all had proven to be abject failures. They failed, most contemporaries concluded, because of "moral hazard"; the public guarantee on deposits had led state-chartered banks to engage in highly risky loans and investments because the banks would not incur any possible losses. With these states' experiences in

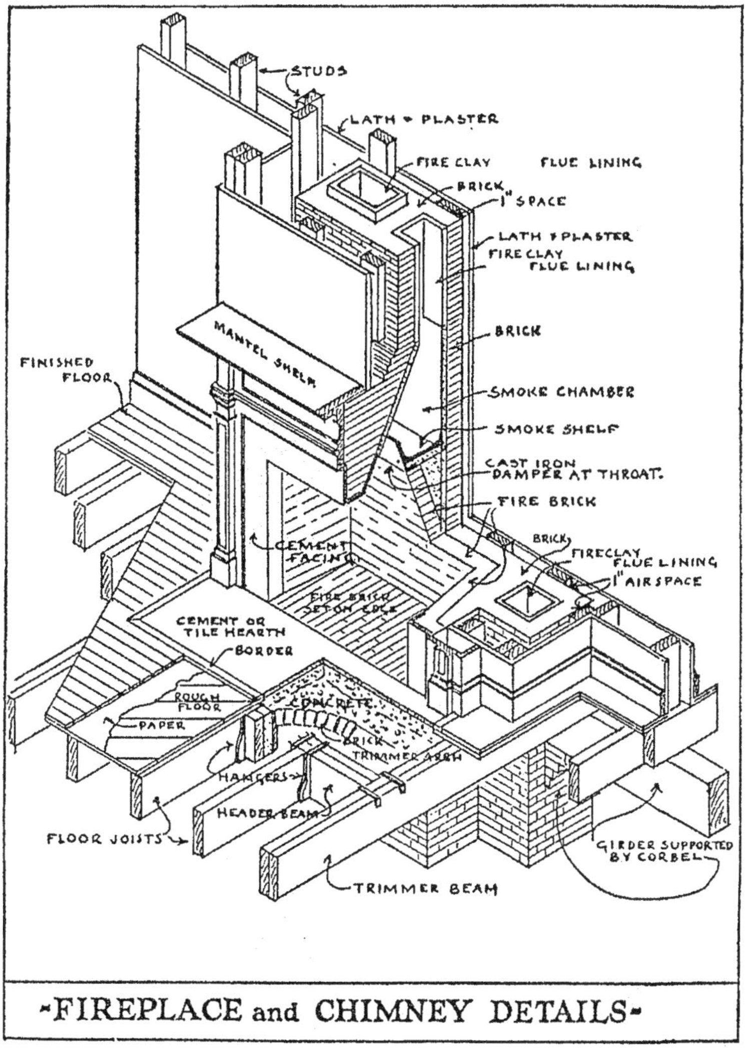

Fig. 40.—The size of the fireplace opening depends upon the size of the individual flue which serves the fireplace. Where damper and smoke chamber are wrongly placed there is likely to be trouble with the drafts.

Figure 3. "Fireplace and Chimney Details," *Better Housing Manual*, 264.

mind, the federal government put in place a strict and thorough regulatory system to administer the deposit insurance program implemented by the FDIC. FDIC regulation was heavy-handed and predicated on the basic principle that no financial institution should be allowed to make loans and investments that were so risky as to threaten the viability of that bank.

The same year of BHA's demise brought passage of the National Housing Act of 1934. Title II of the Act created a mortgage insurance program and established the FHA to implement this new initiative. Mortgage insurance, another centerpiece equal in importance to deposit insurance in the New Deal response to the economic crisis, revolutionized the way in which homes were financed in the United States. Designed starkly in contrast to the home finance system that prevailed throughout the 1920s, the 1934 Housing Act stipulated that the only type of mortgage—long term, with a low interest rate, and fully amortized—would be eligible for mortgage insurance. Immediately, the calculus for financing homes changed. Only homes that could retain or increase their value over a lengthy time frame (up to 20 years as explicitly spelled out in the legislation) could quality for these mortgages.[82] This rendered the majority of American housing units obsolete and ineligible for mortgage insurance.[83] As was typical of legislation formulated in the New Deal, the Housing Act of 1934 was a short and concise piece of legislation that created a new agency and assigned to this bureaucratic agency all responsibilities, including elaborating the administrative law. Congress permitted the FHA substantial leeway in writing and promulgating the underwriting standards the agency would use to implement the law. The well-known, public, fully elaborated, and articulated criteria of a standard well-built American home developed and published by BHA in its *Better Homes Manual* represented a resource available to the FHA that the agency exploited when, in less than a year (a bare nanosecond in bureaucratic time), it wrote its first incarnation of its *Underwriting Manual.*

The creation of a mortgage insurance program again raised the specter of moral hazard. By insuring home mortgages, the full faith and authority of the finances of the national state were potentially in jeopardy. The newly minted FHA had a strong motivation to establish a set of cautious and inflexible underwriting standards, standards that would dictate the use of high-quality materials and the construction of well-built homes. Doing so would assure that homes financed using federally insured mortgages would maintain their value over the long run. Given the need for rapid promulgation of standards, it is hardly surprising that the underwriting standards used by the FHA to administer the nation's mortgage insurance program closely approximated all the basic criteria articulated by the BHA's *Better Homes Manual.* The FHA adopted and codified the substantial work of the BHA, a private, civic organization.

It is difficult to overstate the importance of the creation and implementation of the mortgage insurance program. With the immediate coupling of the program to the stringent dictates of banking regulations adopted with the creation of a deposit guaranty program, only mortgages insured by the FHA would be approved by regulators. The interaction of banking regulations and the creation of mortgage insurance brought about the practice of governmentally sanctioned home mortgage redlining.[84]

The prerequisites articulated for an adequate home by BHA and adopted by the FHA focus almost exclusively on the physical attributes of the home and the property. Little mention is provided in these formative documents of the social structure of the community. Although the endorsement of property covenants reveals that BHA experts and FHA bureaucrats expressed their concern with the social class and race of a community's population, the standards they established were nonetheless overwhelmingly focused on the physical attributes of a home. When mortgage insurance was first implemented, the physical characteristics of the housing unit were of paramount importance; the social class and race of the community were treated with less gravity. Janet Hutchinson, a historian who has studied BHA, provides an apt summary: "the FHA codified the Better Homes standards and tastes."[85]

BHA, a private civic organization, albeit one with intimate links to, and support from, key institutions and individuals within both the federal and state governments, forged the content of the most important and consequential component of American housing policy outside of, and independently of, government. In this era when American statebuilding was in flux, the appropriate role of a civic association such as BHA was hardly fixed or stable. What was in the public realm could expand or contract and the relationship between Hoover's Commerce Department and the BHA reflects this. Hoover allowed BHA to craft its elaborate framework for the adequate American home, to set standards on the location, physical structure, and basic structural amenities of a house, and conduct the activities of a public agency because these boundaries had yet to be established. BHA's work—its comprehensive elaboration of the components of not the ideal, but the median, American home—was conducted largely in the private, civic sphere. Only later, once the administrative structure (and tasks) of a national public agency came into existence through the creation of mortgage insurance and the FHA, did these standards come to be adopted by the FHA in a way that was already articulated and formed.

In part this occurred because the BHA's work conformed to Hoover's ideas of the proper role of the "associative state." The powerful commerce secretary was all too willing to cede these ostensibly public, government activities to private, civic associations such as BHA. to serve as conduits and intermediaries between government and the profit-seeking, private real estate and finance industry, as well as with the public writ large. BHA's objectives, furthermore, fit nicely with the explicit program of the Division of Building and Housing in the Commerce Department. BHA strongly supported uniform and consistent building and zoning codes, as well as the use of high-quality building materials and efficient construction methods—all objectives of the division.[86]

Independent from government (and therefore not subject to the cluttered voices of competing interest groups), BHA was able to select the civic organizations it wished to work with and which private interests it wanted to advance, and decide how to articulate the content of its program, coordinate publicity, and organize the demonstrations. BHA's autonomy and its insulation from unwanted or competing interests allowed it to formulate a clear and well-articulated vision of the American home, to exercise top down control over its local chapters (which were in large part GFWC chapters as well), and to assemble a set of experts over the array of topics they identified as critical to the home and publish the *Better Homes Manual.*

This independence relied upon external resources. At its inception and throughout its history, BHA had neither substantial material nor administrative resources of its own. However, BHA derived most of its financial support from a single philanthropic source, the Laura Spelman Rockefeller Foundation, which placed few restrictions on BHA for the decade that it provided funding. Additionally, BHA borrowed the administrative backbone of the GFWC, along with, to a lesser degree, Red Cross and 4-H chapters, to conduct its annual local activities. While hardly without some differences (GFWC frequently complained that BHA took all credit for the work of chapters that were in fact affiliated with the Federation), BHA maintained access to the GFWC's considerable administrative network, and its vast store of organizing capacity, and indeed the human capital of its members.

BHA was one of several responses to the nation's housing crisis, recognized as a lack of housing especially in urban areas, with overpriced and overcrowded homes, deteriorated or physically deficient homes, and unsanitary conditions. BHA's objective was to spur the revitalization of the American home, to create a self-conscious identity of wives as homemakers, and to increase the number of quality homes.[87] The tactic BHA chose to achieve these goals was to formulate a model of the basic adequate American home. Through the development of demonstration homes annually in thousands of localities throughout the country, with tens of thousands of volunteers and millions of visitors, using both local and national publicity, and finally arranging the publication of a housing primer, BHA advanced a clear, well-articulated, and comprehensive model of the basic American home. This tactic was successful.

BHA's primary approach was to create and engage extensive participation around a clear, palpable, and unchallenged construct of the standard American house. It was a single-family detached dwelling with a small lot located in a suburban setting. This home had all the required structural amenities—water, sewer, and electricity—and was generally a six-room house with a bath and a half and individual bedrooms for each child. Reflecting the long-standing concerns of American housing reformers, the very design of this house prevented a whole host of possible housing ills: inadequate light or fresh air, unsanitary conditions, overcrowding, or lack of privacy. The BHA model home was socially constructed, a haven premised on a gendered division of labor: the wife-homemaker organized the household and created a nurturing environment for child rearing, while the father was responsible for providing the material means of support.

BHA played an instrumental role in providing a solution to the nation's perceived housing problems, but this solution was both unintentional and deferred temporally. BHA's cultural model of the adequate home was widely publicized, fully documented, and widely embraced. This view of the American home was comprehensive, detailed, and compelling. No alternative was available to define the makings of a standard American home. When the need for a fully articulated, comprehensive, and detailed set of housing standards arose as a result of the passage of the Housing Act, officials at the newly formed FHA found an already available and sufficiently specific set of fully elaborated standards to judge housing quality, value, and the likelihood that housing units built to these standards would retain a market value at or above the original appraisal or sales price. The work of the BHA, and especially the composition of its *Manual*, had been developed from the combined expertise of architects and engineers, public regulators, and all segments of the real estate industry. BHA's decade-long programs and the *Manual* that it produced provided not simply a culturally constructed, palpable, complete, and administratively compelling model that an agency of the national state, the FHA, could readily and productively adopt (and adapt) for its own purposes. The work of forming a complete set of basic housing standards was completed by Better Homes in America, and augmented by the independent housing surveys conducted by the General Federation of Women's Clubs, well before the financial crisis and electoral upheaval that brought the policies and programs of the New Deal into creation.

Better Homes in America found a new and ultimately extraordinarily potent program to improve the quality of American homes. It inherited from earlier housing reform movements a focus on the physical environment of the home and a clearly articulated belief that overcrowded, unsanitary, poorly constructed housing densely developed in slums bred crime and disease and undermined the ability of the nation to create and secure the loyalty of its citizens. Previous housing reform movements had engaged in the political process through lobbying city councils and state legislators for modifications to the law. These changes were typically negative and restrictive, creating a set of regulations on private landowners levying penalties for noncompliance. BHA, in contrast, did not overtly attempt to influence legislation. Rather it constructed a well-articulated and compelling vision rooted literally in a home's soil, design, foundations, building materials, arrangement of rooms, and a skeletal structure including not only the frame and walls of the home but also plumbing, heating, and electrical systems. In contrast to previous housing reform movements that sought restrictive, regulatory restrictions on landlords and developers to achieve their objectives, BHA provided a fully articulated affirmative view of the physical structure of the American home. Unwittingly, by doing so, BHA created an elaborated set of prescriptive standards that were positive but not subject to compromise. These standards were both inflexible and incorporated an entire set of physical requirements that had to be achieved for a home to be sufficient and acceptable. The home standards so clearly articulated by BHA, and the housing principles that BHA had forged into a consensus among private experts and the real estate industry, and widely popularized in the annual demonstration projects, were both available to the newly minted FHA bureaucracy that faced the challenging task of creating underwriting standards de novo. The standards developed by

BHA, and its housing principles, represented substantial administrative assets; both were compelling and, given their comprehensiveness and inflexibility, perfectly (if unintentionally) crafted for a bureaucracy.

Ironically, this now largely forgotten housing movement, Better Homes in America, created and sustained by women and an extensive women's organization, had a lasting effect on housing markets in the United States. Much scholarly and journalist ink has been devoted to the struggle by the other arm of the progressive housing movement to bring public housing to the forefront of American housing policy. Their advocacy resulted in the creation of the all-too-typical large-scale public housing projects that slowly descended, managed by short-sighted and thoroughly segregationist housing authorities, into the urban disasters epitomized by Pruitt-Igoe in St. Louis or the Robert Taylor Homes in Chicago. Notably, these specific projects and nearly all high-density public housing projects have been removed from America's urban built environment. At the same time, tens of millions of private, primarily single-family, homes have been built, financed, and occupied by an equal number of middle and lower-middle class, and large portions of the working-class people, the result of a stunningly successful national policy of housing development (with admittedly starkly different outcomes for white and non-white Americans) that is in turn based on underwriting standards directly conveyed and adopted from the work of Better Homes in America.

Notes

Introduction. Statebuilding in the Progressive Era: A Continuing Dilemma in American Political Development

1. Paula Baker, "The Domestication of Politics: Women and American Political Society, 1780–1920," *American Historical Review* 89, 3 (1984): 620–47, 633.

2. Pamela Brandwein, "Law and American Political Development," *Annual Review of Law and Social Science* 7 (2011): 210–11.

3. Robert H. Wiebe, *The Search for Order, 1877–1920* (New York: Hill and Wang, 1967), esp. chaps. 1–2.

4. See the discussion of this point in Theda Skocpol, *Protecting Soldiers and Mothers: The Political Origins of Social Policy in the United States* (Cambridge, Mass.: Belknap Press of Harvard University Press, 1992), 42–43, pointing out that the United States has always had a state; 3–5, 15–23, on received "truths" about the American past.

5. Louis Hartz, *The Liberal Tradition in America* (New York: Harcourt, Brace, 1955); on a "notorious 80-year time out" from political development in the Jim Crow South following Reconstruction, see Karen Orren and Stephen Skowronek, *The Search for American Political Development* (Cambridge: Cambridge University Press, 2004), 179.

6. Peter B. Evans, Dietrich Rueschemeyer, and Theda Skocpol, *Bringing the State Back In* (Cambridge: Cambridge University Press, 1985).

7. Daniel Carpenter, *The Forging of Bureaucratic Autonomy: Reputations, Networks, and Policy Innovation in Executive Agencies, 1862–1928* (Oxford: Oxford University Press, 2001), 3–4, 6–7, 30–31, quote 30.

8. Skocpol, *Protecting Soldiers and Mothers*, 41.

9. Skocpol, *Protecting Soldiers and Mothers*, 47–48.

10. Skocpol, *Protecting Soldiers and Mothers*, 39, 41.

11. Baker, "Domestication of Politics," 641, 647.

12. Stephen Skowronek, *Building a New American State: The Expansion of National Administrative Capacities 1877–1920* (Cambridge: Cambridge University Press, 1982), 16–17.

13. Skowronek, *Building a New American State*, 10–11.

14. Skowronek, *Building a New American State*, 285–86.

15. Skowronek, *Building a New American State*, 42–43.

16. Skowronek, *Building a New American State*, 166.

17. See Brandwein, "Law and American Political Development."

18. Baker, "Domestication of Politics," 626–31.

19. In the juvenile court movement, there was some backlash at the state level by the second decade of the twentieth century, but for the most part courts upheld key provisions of juvenile court laws. See Nackenoff and Sullivan, this volume.

20. Brian Balogh, *A Government Out of Sight: The Mystery of National Authority in Nineteenth-Century America* (Cambridge: Cambridge University Press, 2009), 354–55, 354.

21. For example, Jane Addams, *Democracy and Social Ethics* (1902), ed. and intro. Anne Firor Scott (Cambridge, Mass: Belknap Press of Harvard University Press, 1964); Jane Addams, "If Men Were Seeking the Franchise," *Ladies' Home Journal* 30 (June 1913): 21. Carol Nackenoff, "Gendered Citizenship: Alternative Narratives of Political Incorporation in the United States, 1875–1925," in *The Liberal Tradition in America: Reassessing the Legacy of American Liberalism*, ed. David Ericson and Louisa Bertch Green (New York: Routledge, 1999), 137–69. See also Balogh, *A Government Out of Sight*, chap. 9.

22. William J. Novak, "The Myth of the 'Weak' American State," *American Historical Review* 113 (June 2008): 752–72, 760.

23. Novak, "The Myth of the 'Weak' American State," 770.

24. Elisabeth S. Clemens, "Lineages of the Rube Goldberg State: Building and Blurring Public Programs, 1900–1940," in *Rethinking Political Institutions*, ed. Ian Shapiro, Stephen Skowronek, and Daniel Galvin (New York: New York University Press, 2006), 187–215, 187.

25. Clemens, "Lineages of the Rube Goldberg State," 195.

26. Clemens, "Lineages of the Rube Goldberg State," 187–88, 188.

27. Clemens, "Lineages of the Rube Goldberg State," 190.

28. Clemens, "Lineages of the Rube Goldberg State," 191.

29. Clemens, "Lineages of the Rube Goldberg State," 191.

30. Clemens, "Lineages of the Rube Goldberg State," 192–93, 192.

31. Clemens, "Lineages of the Rube Goldberg State," 192–93

32. Clemens, "Lineages of the Rube Goldberg State," 193.

33. Clemens, "Lineages of the Rube Goldberg State," 194.

34. Clemens, "Lineages of the Rube Goldberg State," 194.

35. Baker, "The Domestication of Politics," 635.

36. Baker, "The Domestication of Politics," 636.

37. Baker, "The Domestication of Politics," 641.

38. See also Carol Nackenoff, "Gendered Citizenship: Alternative Narratives of Political Incorporation in the United States, 1875–1925," in Ericson and Green, *Liberal Tradition in America*, 137–69.

39. Baker, "The Domestication of Politics," 641, 647.

40. Brandwein, "Law and American Political Development," 210–11.

41. See Richard Bensel, *Yankee Leviathan: The Origins of Central State Authority in America, 1859–1877* (New York: Cambridge University Press, 1991).

42. Novak, "The Myth of the 'Weak' American State," 752–72, 765.

43. Stephen Skowronek and Matthew Glassman, "Formative Acts," in *Formative Acts: American Politics in the Making*, ed. Skowronek and Glassman (Philadelphia: University of Pennsylvania Press, 2007), 1.

44. Novak, "The Myth of the 'Weak' American State," 763.

45. Orren and Skowronek, *The Search for American Political Development*, 123.

46. This insight, present across several chapters, supplements Victoria Hattam and Joseph Lowndes's caution that accounts of development that fail to address culture are deficient. Hattam and Lowndes, however, do not account as much for the conscious efforts many of these external actors made to create institutions and change policy. Victoria Hattam and Joseph Lowndes, "The Ground Beneath Our Feet: Language, Culture, and Political Change," in Skowronek and Glassman, *Formative Acts*, 199–222.

47. Adam Sheingate, "The Terrain of the Political Entrepreneur," in Skowronek and Glassman, *Formative Acts*, 13–31, 13.

48. Novak, "The Myth of the 'Weak' American State," 765–66.

49. Novak, "The Myth of the 'Weak' American State," 770.

50. Baker, "The Domestication of Politics," 641.

51. See Novak, "The Myth of the 'Weak' American State."

52. Baker, "The Domestication of Politics," 637.

53. Baker, "The Domestication of Politics," 641.

54. Richard Bensel, "A Calculated Enhancement of Passion: Bryan and the 'Cross of Gold' in the 1896 Democratic National Convention," in Skowronek and Glassman, *Formative Acts*, 77–104.

55. Novak, "The Myth of the 'Weak' American State," 768.

56. William Novak, *The People's Welfare: Law and Regulation in Nineteenth-Century America* (Chapel Hill: University of North Carolina Press, 1996); Howard Gillman, *The Constitution Besieged: The Rise and Demise of Lochner Era Police Powers Jurisprudence* (Durham, N.C.: Duke University Press, 1992).

57. Novak, "The Myth of the 'Weak' American State," 768.

58. Skocpol, *Protecting Soldiers and Mothers*.

59. Baker, "The Domestication of Politics."

60. See Richard Valelly, "Partisan Entrepreneurship and Policy Windows: George Frisbie Hoar and the 1890 Federal Election Bill," in Skowronek and Glassman, *Formative Acts*, 126–52.

61. Novak, "The Myth of the 'Weak' American State," 770–71.

Chapter 1. Making Citizens of Freedmen and Polygamists

The author thanks her colleagues in Rockefeller College, particularly Bruce Miroff and Patricia Strach, for their comments on an earlier version of this project. She also thanks Pamela Brandwein and the anonymous reviewer for the manuscript for their helpful guidance, and Carol Nackenoff for her assistance in developing the chapter. The idea for this chapter came out of a brief paper composed for the Maryland Conference on Constitutional Law (better known as Mark Graber's Schmooze); as always, he knows how to ask the right questions.

1. Sarah Barringer Gordon, *The Mormon Question: Polygamy and Constitutional Conflict in Nineteenth-Century America* (Chapel Hill: University of North Carolina Press, 2002), 155–56.

2. In particular, elite whites' anxiety about Chinese immigration continued to rise, and national policymakers struggled over how to handle western tribes of Native Americans who occupied desirable lands.

3. See, e.g., Garrett Epps's description of the struggle between advocates for black and woman suffrage; he highlights the arguments black men made about the need for the vote to protect their families. Garrett Epps, *Democracy Reborn: The Fourteenth Amendment and the Fight for Civil Rights in Post-Civil War America* (New York: Henry Holt, 2006).

4. Bartholomew Sparrow, *The Insular Cases and the Emergence of American Empire* (Lawrence: University of Kansas Press, 2006).

5. Eric Foner, *Reconstruction: America's Unfinished Revolution* (New York: HarperCollins, 2002), 371.

6. John Bickers, "The Power to Do What Manifestly Must Be Done: Congress, the Freedmen's Bureau, and Constitutional Imagination," *Roger Williams University Law Review* 12 (2006): 70–120, 81.

7. Epps, *Democracy Reborn*, 150.

8. Epps, *Democracy Reborn*, 152.

9. Epps, *Democracy Reborn*, 152.

10. The Sea Island land distribution resulted from a field order General William Sherman issued in early 1865, which formally confiscated approximately 400,000 acres of coastal land and laid the groundwork for parceling it out in 40-acre increments to freedmen as heads of household. The Sea Island emancipated blacks were ultimately unable to retain legal possession of the lands after President Johnson rescinded Sherman's order. See Katherine Franke, "Becoming a Citizen: Reconstruction Era Regulation of African American Marriages," *Yale Journal of Law and the Humanities* 11 (1999): 251–310.

11. Foner, *Reconstruction*, 158–59

12. Foner, *Reconstruction*, 159–61.

13. Angela Onwuachi-Willig, "Return of the Ring: Welfare Reform's Marriage Cure as the Revival of Post-Bellum Control," *California Law Review* 93 (2005): 1647–96; Priscilla Yamin, *American Marriage: A Political Institution* (Philadelphia: University of Pennsylvania Press, 2012).

14. The abstract model of a contractual agreement assumes two contractors who have equal bargaining power and no particular relationship with each other.

15. *Williams v. Waters*, 36 Ga. 454, 454 (1867).

16. *Williams v. Waters*, 454.

17. *Williams v. Waters*, 458. Nonetheless, the court allowed the defendant to ask for mitigation on the basis that the freedmen had not worked hard enough to maximize the plantation's profits.

18. *Hunt v. Wing*, 57 Tenn. 139, 144 (1872).

19. *Hunt v. Wing*, 146.

20. See Franke, "Becoming a Citizen."

21. See Yamin, *American Marriage*, chap. 1. But note also that several states either created new legal bans on interracial intimacy or strengthened the penalties for it in the years immediately after the Civil War.

22. As Peggy Pascoe notes, the Fourteenth Amendment, along with the Civil Rights Act, generated the possibility that southern states that had not reconstituted bans on interracial intimate relationships had to recognize such relationships as marriages. In some states, courts found common-law marriages to the advantages of the partners and children of deceased white men. Peggy Pascoe, *What Comes Naturally: Miscegenation Law and the Making of Race in America* (New York: Oxford University Press, 2009), 40–46. While this outcome was continuous with a handful of antebellum cases, in Mississippi the high court's 1873 ruling rested on the state's policy choice to "put a stop to meretricious cohabitation, and to introduce all, or as many as possible, of this class [of freedmen and freedwomen], as well as those 'cohabiting as man and wife,' without formal marriage, to enter formally and publicly into the marital status; a consummation of incalculable importance to the welfare of the State" (*Dickerson v. Brown*, 49 Miss. 357, 374 (1873)). As Pascoe explains, southerners in other states also doubted the legitimacy of policies barring interracial marriage, repealing laws in Louisiana, South Carolina, and Mississippi, and striking them down judicially in Alabama and Texas. Pascoe argues that these doubts "ultimately rested on the connections between marriage, civil rights, and political equality in nineteenth-century thinking about the rights of free White men" (Pascoe, *What Comes Naturally*, 41). As southern intransigence gained momentum, a legal struggle eventually settled that, despite the Civil Rights Act protection for contract rights, the marriage contract did not fall under the ordinary rules for interpreting contractual equality, thereby closing the door to any configuration of interracial marriage as a basic right for black men. Julie Novkov, *Racial Union: Law, Intimacy, and the White State in Alabama, 1865–1954* (Ann Arbor: University of Michigan Press, 2008).

23. *McMillan v. State*, 35 Ga. 54 (1866).

24. *Robinson v. Commonwealth*, 69 Ky. 309 (1869).

25. *Robinson v. Commonwealth*, 309.

26. *Robinson v. Commonwealth*, 312.

27. *Johnson and Crow v. Perkins*, 60 Tenn. 367, 368 (1872).

28. Richard Valelly, "Partisan Entrepreneurship and Policy Windows," in *Formative Acts: American Politics in the Making*, ed. Stephen Skowronek and Matthew Glassman (Philadelphia: University of Pennsylvania Press, 2007), 126–49.

29. Barbara Welke, *Recasting American Liberty: Gender, Race, Law and the Railroad Revolution, 1865–1920* (New York: Cambridge University Press, 2001).

30. Lou Falkner Williams, *The Great South Carolina Ku Klux Klan Trials, 1871–1872* (Athens: University of Georgia Press, 1996), 5.

31. Pamela Brandwein, *Rethinking the Judicial Settlement of Reconstruction* (Cambridge: Cambridge University Press, 2011); Pamela Brandwein, "A Judicial Abandonment of Blacks? Rethinking the 'State Action' Cases of the Waite Court," *Law and Society Review* 40 (2008): 343–86.

32. *United States v. Rhodes*, 27 F. Cas. 785, 788 (C.C. D. Ky. 1866). Associate Supreme Court Justice Noah Swayne heard the case sitting as a circuit judge. As Pamela Brandwein explains, the involvement of a Supreme Court justice in the case rendered the opinion particularly noteworthy in the legal context of the time. Brandwein, "A Judicial Abandonment of Blacks?"

33. *United States v. Rhodes*, 792–93.

34. As best I can tell on review of the case, the men actually killed four people. Three were found dead at the scene: a black male, Jack Foster, head of the household and owner of the cabin in which the murders occurred, his wife Sallie, and Lucy Armstrong. The fourth was the Fosters's seventeen-year-old son, who crawled to a nearby house mortally injured. Of the four killings, the murder for which the men were convicted and sentenced was characterized as having been "one of peculiar atrocity" because Lucy Armstrong, Sallie Foster's mother, over ninety, had her head hacked open with a broadaxe. Two girls aged ten and thirteen survived the attack, unnoticed by Blyew and Kennard as they slept or hid in their trundle bed. The older girl testified against the two white men at the trial. *Blyew v. United States*, 80 U.S. 581 (1872).

35. The solicitor general was a new player at this time. The 1870 Act to Establish the Department of Justice (discussed below) created both the DOJ and the position of solicitor general. Samuel F. Phillips of North Carolina, who held the position until 1885, would go on to serve as a member of Homer Plessy's legal term in *Plessy v. Ferguson*. See U.S. Department of Justice, "Samuel Phillips Biography," 2010, http://www.justice.gov/osg/aboutosg/samuelphillipsbio.htm.

36. *Blyew v. United States*, 581, 589.

37. *Blyew v. United States*, 589.

38. Williams, *The Klan Trials*, 5.

39. Williams, *The Klan Trials*, 5.

40. The Klan had by this time spread to several states and engaged in an organized and coordinated campaign of political violence and intimidation that affected elections across the South. See, e.g., Glenn Feldman's discussion of the Klan in Alabama, *Politics, Society, and the Klan in Alabama, 1915–1949* (Tuscaloosa: University of Alabama Press, 1999).

41. Williams, *The Klan Trials*, 10–24.

42. Williams, *The Klan Trials*, 24–39. Eric Foner, among others, provides a comprehensive discussion of Klan violence, the congressional investigations into it, and Congress's choice to pass legislation targeting night riders. Foner, *Reconstruction*.

43. The Enforcement Acts of 1870 and 1871 are often referred to collectively and pejoratively as the Force Acts. Like the "force acts" passed during Andrew Jackson's presidency, these laws sought to bring a recalcitrant South into line with national agendas. Because the term, like so many other terms commonly used to describe Reconstruction's acts and actors (e.g., carpetbaggers and scalawags, Redemption), implicitly criticizes the North and reinforces a Dunning school narrative, I avoid it.

44. Williams, *The Klan Trials*, 40–43; see also Foner, *Reconstruction*.

45. Williams, *The Klan Trials*, 43.

46. Richard Valelly, *The Two Reconstructions: The Struggle for Black Enfranchisement* (Chicago: University of Chicago Press, 2004).

47. Williams, *The Klan Trials*, 43–46.

48. Valelly, *The Two Reconstructions*, 100.

49. Williams, *The Klan Trials*, 53.

50. Williams, *The Klan Trials*, 53–55.

51. Williams, *The Klan Trials*, 55–57.

52. Williams, *The Klan Trials*, 49–57.

53. Williams, *The Klan Trials*, 70–80.

54. Williams, *The Klan Trials*, 63.

55. Foner, *Reconstruction*, 458.

56. Williams, *The Klan Trials*, 101.

57. Williams, *The Klan Trials*, 112.

58. Stephen Cresswell, *Mormons and Cowboys, Moonshiners and Klansmen: Federal Law Enforcement in the South and West, 1870–1893* (Tuscaloosa: University of Alabama Press, 1991), 42.

59. Cresswell, *Mormons and Cowboys*, 33–34.

60. Cresswell, *Mormons and Cowboys*, 39.

61. *Ex parte Yarbrough*, 110 U.S. 651, 656–657 (1884). *Yarbrough* has largely been overshadowed in common understandings of constitutional history by the *Civil Rights Cases*, decided a year earlier. As Brandwein has shown, however, overlooking *Yarbrough* is a mistake. Brandwein, *Rethinking Judicial Settlement*, 148-53.

62. *Ex parte Yarbrough*. The U.S. attorney who handled the prosecutions, Emory Speer, would later go on to serve as a federal judge, where he would use his authority to rule against Alabama's system of racially based peonage in a series of cases in the early twentieth century.

63. *Ex parte Yarbrough*, 663–64.

64. *Ex parte Yarbrough*, 666.

65. *Ex parte Yarbrough*, 667.

66. See Cresswell, *Mormons and Cowboys*, 36; William Warren Rogers, *The One-Gallused Rebellion: Agrarianism in Alabama, 1865–1896* (Tuscaloosa: University of Alabama Press, 2001).

67. See Cresswell, *Mormons and Cowboys*, 76.

68. See, e.g., Welke, *Recasting American Liberty*.

69. See Cresswell, *Mormons and Cowboys*. Concerns about polygamy in this era were not limited to the Saints. The practices of polygamy and prostitution among Chinese were significant rhetorical factors behind congressional legislation strictly limiting Chinese immigration and policies targeting Chinese women seeking entrance to the United States.

70. Gordon, *The Mormon Question*.

71. Martha Ertman, "Race Treason: The Untold Story of America's Ban on Polygamy," *Columbia Journal of Gender and Law* 19 (2010): 287–366, 299–300.

72. Gordon, *The Mormon Question*, 87.

73. Cresswell, *Mormons and Cowboys*, 81–82.

74. Ertman, "Race Treason," 296–97.

75. Gordon, *The Mormon Question*, 110–12.

76. Cresswell, *Mormons and Cowboys*, 82–84.

77. Gordon, *The Mormon Question*, 112.

78. Gordon, *The Mormon Question*, 119. The reader is reminded that politically prominent Democrats also argued against the Enforcement Acts targeting the Klan.

79. *Reynolds v. United States*, 98 U.S. 145, 145 (1879).

80. Gordon, *The Mormon Question*, 123.

81. *Bradwell v. Illinois*, 83 U.S. 130 (1873).

82. Gordon, *The Mormon Question*, 126.

83. Ertman, "Race Treason," 300–302.

84. Gordon, *The Mormon Question*, 126.

85. Gordon, *The Mormon Question*, 127. The massacre, described briefly by Gordon and Cresswell and discussed extensively in Jon Krakauer's *Under the Banner of Heaven*, took place in 1857. A group of Mormons assisted by a band of Paiute Indians, most likely acting on the direct orders of Brigham Young, murdered 125 Arkansans traveling west in a wagon train. While Young eventually allowed the leader of the Mormon assailants to be tried, convicted, and executed in 1873 for his role in the massacre, the memory of this event still generated simmering outrage. Jon Krakauer, *Under the Banner of Heaven: A Story of Violent Faith* (New York: Doubleday, 2003); Gordon, *The Mormon Question*; Cresswell, *Mormons and Cowboys*.

86. Ertman, "Race Treason," 308. Christine Talbot argues that viewing the attack on Mormonism as a purely Orientalist project is misleading because of the complex position of the Mormons themselves as colonizers and targets of federal authority. Christine Talbot, "'Turkey Is in Our Midst': Orientalism and Contagion in Nineteenth Century Anti-Mormonism," *Journal of Law and Family Studies* 8 (2006): 363–88.

87. *Reynolds v. United States*, 158–60. The Court dealt with the procedural issues through the ordinary principles of trusting the judgment of the trial court concerning the empaneling of grand and petit jurors and allowing the introduction of well-grounded secondary evidence procured through a previous criminal proceeding. Justice Stephen Johnson Field, however, wrote separately to indicate his belief that the admission of Amelia Reynolds's testimony was improper (*Reynolds v. United States*, 169).

88. *Reynolds v. United States*, 166.

89. *Reynolds v. United States*, 165.

90. This argument had been developed extensively in the 1870s to support the constitutionality of laws banning interracial marriage. See Novkov, *Racial Union*; Pascoe, *What Comes Naturally*.

91. *Reynolds v. United States*, 165.

92. *Reynolds v. United States*, 165–66.

93. *Reynolds v. United States*, 166.

94. Gordon, *The Mormon Question*, 144–45.

95. See Ertman, "Race Treason."

96. Gordon, *The Mormon Question*, 147.

97. *Miles v. United States*, 103 U.S. 304, 310 (1881).

98. *Miles v. United States*, 313.

99. *Miles v. United States*, 315. In a later case, Chief Justice Zane attempted to craft a judicial workaround to this problem by citing a revision in the Utah criminal code and declaring that polygamy constituted the kind of crime against the dignity of a wife that lifted the usual common-law principle of marital privilege. The Supreme Court disagreed, reaffirming the common-law principle and reversing the conviction of the alleged polygamist. *Bassett v. United States*, 137 U.S. 496 (1890).

100. Cresswell, *Mormons and Cowboys*, 96–97.

101. Gordon, *The Mormon Question*, 153. Senator George Edmunds of Vermont also tried to convince his congressional colleagues to withhold the franchise from admitted polygamists, which would have silenced George Cannon, Utah's territorial representative to Congress. Although the denial of franchise was not ultimately part of the Edmunds Act, it passed separately in 1882. Note, too, that Congress never made this tactic available to prosecutors during the Klan trials.

102. Cresswell, *Mormons and Cowboys*, 99.

103. Gordon, *The Mormon Question*, 155–56.

104. *Clawson v. United States*, 112 U.S. 143 (1885).

105. *Clawson v. United States*.

106. *Murphy v. Ramsey*, 114 U.S. 15 (1885).

107. *Cannon v. United States*, 116 U.S. 55 (1885).

108. *Ex parte Nielsen*, 131 U.S. 176 (1889).

109. *Ex parte Nielsen*, 181.

110. *Ex parte Nielsen*, 182–91.

111. Edmunds-Tucker Act, 24 Stat. 635 (1887). See Cresswell for a discussion of the implications.

112. *Mormon Church v. United States*, 136 U.S. 1 (1890).

113. Gordon, *The Mormon Question*, 220.

114. Brandwein explains that the Reconstruction Amendments and rulings interpreting them incorporated the idea that the federal government could act if it could show that the states were refusing to fulfill their responsibilities to protect and enforce

rights for their citizens. See Brandwein, *Rethinking the Judicial Settlement of Reconstruction.*

115. See Yamin, *American Marriage.*

116. See *Modern Polygamy in the United States*, ed. Cardell Jacobson and Lara Burton (New York: Oxford University Press, 2006).

117. Mary Dudziak, *Cold War Civil Rights: Race and the Image of American Democracy* (Princeton, N.J.: Princeton University Press, 2009); Christopher S. Parker, *Fighting for Democracy: Black Veterans and the Struggle Against White Supremacy in the Postwar South* (Princeton, N.J.: Princeton University Press, 2009); Philip Klinkner and Rogers Smith, *The Unsteady March: The Rise and Decline of Racial Equality in the United States* (Chicago: University of Chicago Press, 1999).

118. Initially, the National Woman Suffrage Association supported polygamous wives and woman suffrage in Utah while the American Woman Suffrage Association was skeptical, but after 1882 the NWSA pulled back its support as well. Ertman, "Race Treason," 329–30.

119. Gordon, *The Mormon Question.*

120. On the racial transformation of "ethnic" immigrants, see Victoria Hattam, *In the Shadow of Race: Jews, Latinos, and Immigrant Politics in the United States* (Chicago: University of Chicago Press, 2007).

121. Racialized constructions of Mormons did not disappear as soon as the LDS Church renounced polygamy. See Ertman, "Race Treason," 351.

122. See Ertman, "Race Treason."

Chapter 2. Demagogues and the Demon Drink: Newspapers and the Revival of Prohibition in Georgia

The author would like to thank Pamela Brandwein, Carol Nackenoff, Julie Novkov, Ann-Marie Szymanski, and an anonymous reviewer for the University of Pennsylvania Press for critical comments and suggestions on earlier drafts of the chapter.

Epigraphs: Booker T. Washington, "Extracts from an Address in Brooklyn," December 8, 1907, in *Booker T. Washington Papers*, vol. 9, *1906–08*, ed. Lewis R. Harland and Raymond W. Smock (Urbana: University of Illinois Press, 1989), 418–19, quoted in Ann-Marie Szymanski, "Beyond Parochialism: Southern Progressivism, Prohibition, and Statebuilding," *Journal of Southern History* 69, 1 (2003): 120; Max Weber, "The Profession and Vocation of Politics," in *Weber: Political Writings*, ed. Peter Lassman and Ronald Spiers (Cambridge: Cambridge University Press, 1994), 331.

1. J. J. Ansley, *History of the Georgia Woman's Christian Temperance Union from Its Organization, 1883–1907* (Columbus, Ga.: Gilbert Printing, 1914), 239.

2. Timothy E. Cook, *Governing with the News: The News Media as a Political Institution* (Chicago: University of Chicago Press, 1998).

3. Cook, *Governing*. See also, Timothy E. Cook, "The News Media as a Political Institution: Looking Backward and Looking Forward," *Political Communication* 23

(2006): 159–71, and Diana Owen, "The Institution of the Media: Tim Cook's Legacy to Scholars and Students of American Government," *Political Communication* 24 (2007): 239–44. The understanding of "institution" here is influenced by Richard M. Valelly, *The Two Reconstructions: The Struggle for Black Enfranchisement* (Chicago: University of Chicago Press, 2004), esp. 225–50.

4. E. H. Cherrington, ed., *The Anti-Saloon League Year Book: An Encyclopedia of Facts and Figures Dealing with the Liquor Traffic and the Temperance Reform* (Westerville, Ohio: American Issue Press, 1917).

5. Where Szymanski finds linear development, and Nackenoff and Sullivan, this volume, find nonlinear development, my chapter describes a linear institutional development (prohibition) rooted in conditions marked by nonlinearity (state and local state-press relations).

6. Thanks to Carol Nackenoff for this formulation. Generally the relation between state and press matches Elisabeth Clemens's "political-dependence explanation" of the Rube Goldberg state (see the Introduction to this volume). I am suggesting a "window of opportunity" in the Progressive Era, at the state and municipal level, during which newspaper editors had sufficient institutional autonomy to exercise independent influence on policy development.

7. Ted Curtis Smythe, *The Gilded Age Press, 1865–1900* (Westport, Conn.: Praeger, 2003), 20–22; George H. Douglas, *The Golden Age of the Newspaper* (Westport, Conn.: Greenwood, 1999), 35–44.

8. Carl R. Osthaus, *Partisans of the Southern Press: Editorial Spokesmen of the Nineteenth Century* (Lexington: University Press of Kentucky, 1994); Daniel S. Margolies, *Henry Watterson and the New South: The Politics of Empire, Free Trade, and Globalization* (Lexington: University Press of Kentucky, 2006).

9. On Harding, see Randolphe C. Downes, *The Rise of Warren Gamaliel Harding, 1865–1920* (Columbus: Ohio State University Press, 1970), esp. chap. 2; on James M. Cox, see Irving Stone, *They Also Ran: The Story of the Men Who Were Defeated for the Presidency* (Garden City, N.Y.: Doubleday, 1966), 19–34.

10. Weber, "Profession and Vocation."

11. Fred Fedler, *Lessons from the Past: Journalists' Lives and Work, 1850–1950* (Prospect Heights, Ill.: Waveland, 2000).

12. Cook, *Governing.*

13. Thomas C. Leonard, *The Power of the Press: The Birth of American Political Reporting* (New York: Oxford University Press, 1986). The literature here is vast. Of especial importance to shaping my own understanding, in addition to those cited elsewhere, are Gerald J. Baldasty, *The Commercialization of News in the Nineteenth Century* (Madison: University of Wisconsin Press, 1992); Michael Schudson, *Discovering the News: A Social History of American Newspapers* (New York: Basic Books, 1978); Richard L. Kaplan, *Politics and the American Press: The Rise of Objectivity, 1865–1920* (Cambridge: Cambridge University Press, 2002); Michael E. McGerr, *The Decline of Popular Politics: The American North, 1865–1928* (New York: Oxford University Press,

1986); David Paul Nord, *Communities of Journalism: A History of American Newspapers and Their Readers* (Urbana: University of Illinois Press, 2001).

14. Betty Houchin Winfield, "1908: A Very Political Year for the Press," in *Journalism 1908: Birth of a Profession*, ed. Betty Houchin Winfield (Columbia: University of Missouri Press, 2008), 18–19.

15. Louis T. Griffith and John E. Talmadge, *Georgia Journalism, 1763–1950* (Athens: University of Georgia Press, 1951).

16. Richard Hofstadter, *The Age of Reform* (New York: Knopf, 1955), 185.

17. Osthaus, *Partisans.*

18. Griffith and Talmadge, *Journalism.*

19. Osthaus, *Partisans*, 181.

20. Griffith and Talmadge, *Journalism*, 103; Osthaus, *Partisans*, 183.

21. Griffith and Talmadge, *Journalism*, 103

22. Dewey W. Grantham, Jr., *Hoke Smith and the Politics of the New South* (Baton Rouge: Louisiana State University Press, 1967), Mark Bauerlein, *Negrophobia: A Race Riot in Atlanta, 1906* (San Francisco: Encounter Books, 2001).

23. Franklin M. Garrett, *Atlanta and Environs: A Chronicle of Its People and Events*, vol. 2 (Athens: University of Georgia Press, 1954).

24. Grantham, *Hoke Smith*; Bauerlein, *Negrophobia*; David Fort Godshalk, *Veiled Visions: The 1906 Atlanta Race Riot and the Reshaping of American Race Relations* (Chapel Hill: University of North Carolina Press, 2005).

25. Garrett, *Atlanta and Environs*; Grantham, *Hoke Smith.*

26. Grantham, *Hoke Smith.*

27. Griffith and Talmadge, *Journalism.*

28. Bauerlein, *Negrophobia*, 119.

29. *Constitution*, November 24, 1899; *Journal of the Senate of the State of Georgia, for the Annual Session of the General Assembly, 1899*, 717.

30. Daniel Jay Whitener, *Prohibition in North Carolina, 1715–1945* (Chapel Hill: University of North Carolina Press, 1945), 153.

31. For various accounts of the Jim Crow racial order, see Julie Novkov, *Racial Union: Law, Intimacy, and the White State in Alabama, 1865–1954* (Ann Arbor: University of Michigan Press, 2008); Kimberley Johnson, *Reforming Jim Crow: Southern Politics and State in the Age Before* Brown (Oxford: University of Oxford Press, 2010); Marek D. Steedman, *Jim Crow Citizenship: Liberalism and the Southern Defense of Racial Hierarchy* (New York: Routledge, 2012).

32. General accounts of prohibition at the national level include Jack S. Blocker, Jr., *Retreat from Reform: The Prohibition Movement in the United States 1890–1913* (Westport, Conn.: Greenwood, 1976); Jack S. Blocker, Jr., *American Temperance Movements: Cycles of Reform* (Boston: Twayne, 1989); Norman H. Clark, *Deliver Us from Evil: An Interpretation of American Prohibition* (New York: Norton, 1976); Richard F. Hamm, *Shaping the Eighteenth Amendment: Temperance Reform, Legal Culture, and the Polity, 1880–1920* (Chapel Hill: University of North Carolina Press, 1995); Thomas R.

Pegram, *Battling Demon Rum: The Struggle for a Dry America, 1800–1933* (Chicago: Ivan Dee, 1998); Andrew Sinclair, *Era of Excess: A Social History of the Prohibition Movement* (New York: Harper & Row, 1964); Ann-Marie E. Szymanski, *Pathways to Prohibition: Radicals, Moderates, and Social Movement Outcomes* (Durham, N.C.: Duke University Press, 2003); James H. Timberlake, *Prohibition and the Progressive Movement 1900–1920* (Cambridge, Mass.: Harvard University Press, 1963).

33. K. Austin Kerr, *Organized for Prohibition: A New History of the Anti-Saloon League* (New Haven, Conn.: Yale University Press, 1985); James Morone, *Hellfire Nation: The Politics of Sin in American History* (New Haven, Conn.: Yale University Press, 2003), 300–301, Hamm, *Shaping*, 228.

34. Desmond S. King and Rogers M. Smith, "Racial Orders in American Political Development," *American Political Science Review* 99, 1 (February 2005): 75–92.

35. Joe L. Coker, *Liquor in the Land of the Lost Cause: Southern White Evangelicals and the Prohibition Movement* (Lexington: University Press of Kentucky, 2007). More generally, see Gaines M. Foster, *Moral Reconstruction: Christian Lobbyists and the Federal Legislation of Morality, 1865–1920* (Chapel Hill: University of North Carolina Press, 2002).

36. Hamm, *Shaping*.

37. *Constitution*, December 9, 1899, 9.

38. Inspired by Maine's adoption of statewide prohibition in 1851, a Prohibition Party did field a candidate for governor in Georgia in 1855 (Garrett, *Atlanta and Environs*, 393–94).

39. William A. Link, *The Paradox of Southern Progressivism* (Chapel Hill: University of North Carolina Press, 1993).

40. Link, *Paradox*, 42–48.

41. Robert H. Wiebe, *The Search for Order, 1877–1920* (New York: Hill and Wang, 1967). Richard Bensel documented the alacrity with which the South turned to statebuilding under the Confederacy. It is worth noting, however, that Bensel finds the Confederacy less enthusiastic in its statebuilding efforts precisely in the area of citizenship rights. Richard Franklin Bensel, *Yankee Leviathan: The Origins of Central State Authority in America, 1859–1877* (Cambridge: Cambridge University Press, 1990).

42. Ansley, *History*, 216.

43. Szymanski, *Pathways*.

44. Had seven of the eleven senators representing "dry" counties switched their votes, the Willingham bill would have passed the Georgia Senate in 1899. The figures come from cross-referencing the vote on the Willingham bill as reported in the *Constitution*, November 24, 1899, with the *Journal of the Georgia Senate*, 717, as well as the results of the 1898 election for the Georgia General Assembly, reported in the *Constitution*, with the counties listed as "dry" and "wet" in Ansley, *History*. The number may be higher for members of the Georgia House of Representatives, as precise identification of representatives with districts was not always possible. I assumed the

same twenty counties were "wet" in 1899 and 1907. For county maps of Georgia in 1899, see Georgia Department of Agriculture, *Georgia Historical and Industrial* (Atlanta: Franklin Printing, 1901). In fact, 90 counties had been "dry or partially so" by 1884, before the local option law was formally adopted, Garrett, *Atlanta and Environs*, 95–96.

45. *Constitution*, November 22, 1899, 3.

46. *Constitution*, November 21, 1899, 2.

47. The law was responsive to the rhetoric emerging from Georgia in other ways: it segregated saloons by race and gender, banned musical instruments and performances from saloons, and sought to end the rather common saloon/grocery store combination in New Orleans. Alecia Long, *The Great Southern Babylon: Sex, Race, and Respectability in New Orleans 1865–1920* (Baton Rouge,: Louisiana State University Press, 2004), 181–82; Jared Y. Sanders, "Inaugural Address, May 18, 1908," *Official Journal of the Proceedings of the Senate of the State of Louisiana*, 1st sess. (Baton Rouge, 1908).

48. Ansley, *History*, 178.

49. Godshalk, *Veiled Visions*, 52.

50. Morton Keller, *Regulating a New Society: Public Policy and Social Change in America, 1900–1933* (Cambridge, Mass.: Harvard University Press, 1998), 127.

51. Keller, *Regulating*, 130; Morone, *Hellfire*, 300.

52. Morone, *Hellfire*.

53. George Frederickson, *The Black Image in the White Mind: The Debate on Afro-American Character and Destiny, 1817–1914* (New York: Harper Torchbooks, 1971); Robert Jeffrey Young, *Domesticating Slavery: The Master Class in Georgia and South Carolina, 1670–1837* (Chapel Hill: University of North Carolina Press, 1999).

54. The number of dead is disputed. For various accounts of the Wilmington riot, see David S. Cecelski and Timothy B. Tyson, eds., *Democracy Betrayed: The Wilmington Race Riot of 1898 and Its Legacy* (Chapel Hill: University of North Carolina Press, 1998); Glenda Elizabeth Gilmore, *Gender and Jim Crow: Women and the Politics of the White Supremacy in North Carolina, 1896–1920* (Chapel Hill: University of North Carolina Press, 1996); H. Leon Prather, Sr., *We Have Taken a City: Wilmington Racial Massacre and Coup of 1898* (Cranberry, N.J.: Associated University Presses, 1984). The events surrounding the riot are fictionalized in Charles W. Chesnutt, *The Marrow of Tradition*, ed. Nancy Bentley and Sandra Gunning (Boston: Bedford/St. Martin's, 2002).

55. William Ivy Hair, *Carnival of Fury: Robert Charles and the New Orleans Race Riot of 1900* (Baton Rouge: Louisiana State University Press, 1976), 141.

56. Long, *Great Southern Babylon*, 200–203.

57. *Constitution*, November 20, 1899, 5 (the identical phrase was used by the *Georgian* in 1907).

58. The disfranchisement bill also failed in 1899, although Georgia would institute a white primary in 1900.

59. *Constitution*, December 8, 1899, 12.

60. Szymanski; Greer; Nackenoff and Sullivan, this volume.

61. On "sequencing" arguments in American political development, see Paul

Pierson, *Politics in Time: History, Institutions, and Social Analysis* (Princeton, N.J.: Princeton University Press, 2004), esp. chap. 2.

62. Grantham, *Hoke Smith*, 139–40.

63. N. W. Ayer and Son, *American Newspaper Annual*, part 1 (Philadelphia: Ayer and Son, 1906), 119–20.

64. Ayer and Son, *American Newspaper Annual*, 119–20.

65. Grantham, *Hoke Smith*, 150–51.

66. Godshalk, *Veiled Visions*, 50–51.

67. Godshalk, *Veiled Visions*, 51.

68. For black responses to the campaign, see Godshalk, *Veiled Visions*.

69. Bauerlein, *Negrophobia*; Godshalk, *Veiled Visions*.

70. Ayer and Son, *American Newspaper Annual*, 119–20.

71. The account relies on Bauerlein, *Negrophobia*; Godshalk *Veiled Visions*. Still the best brief articles on the event and its significance are Charles Crowe, "Racial Violence and Social Reform—Origins of the Atlanta Race Riot of 1906," *Journal of Negro History* 53, 3 (July 1968): 234–56, and Charles Crowe, "Racial Massacre in Atlanta September 22, 1906," *Journal of Negro History* 54, 2 (April 1969): 150–73. Larger cultural and political context for the riot can be found in Gregory Mixon, *The Atlanta Riot: Race, Class, and Violence in a New South City* (Gainesville: University Press of Florida, 2005); John Dittmer, *Black Georgia in the Progressive Era 1900–1920* (Urbana: University of Illinois Press, 1977); Allison Dorsey, *To Build Our Lives Together: Community Formation in Black Atlanta, 1875–1906* (Athens: University of Georgia Press, 2004); Steve Goodson, *Highbrows, Hillbillies, and Hellfire: Public Entertainment in Atlanta 1880–1930* (Athens: University of Georgia Press, 2002); and Georgina Hickey, *Hope and Danger in the New South City: Working-Class Women and Urban Development in Atlanta, 1890–1940* (Athens: University of Georgia Press, 2003).

72. Ray Stannard Baker, *The Atlanta Riot* (New York: Phillips, 1907); J. Max Barber, "The Atlanta Tragedy," *The Voice* 3 (November 1906): 473–79. For Du Bois's response to the riot, see Godshalk *Veiled Visions*, 121–24.

73. Bauerlein, *Negrophobia*, 118.

74. Bauerlein, *Negrophobia*, 117.

75. Bauerlein, *Negrophobia*, 129, 118.

76. Bauerlein, *Negrophobia*, 101.

77. *The Voice* (or *Voice of the Negro*) was a monthly magazine aimed at middle-class black professionals, with a national circulation of around 13,000. My focus here is on the white press, and Atlanta did not yet have a black-owned daily paper. It did have three black weekly papers, the largest of which reached more than 7,000 homes.

78. It would seem that the *Georgian* largely inherited the readership of the *News*: compare Ayer and Son, *American Newspaper Annual*, part 1, 119–20, to 118–19.

79. Marek D. Steedman, "'Walk with Me in White': Autonomy in a Herrenvolk Democracy," *Du Bois Review* 8, 2 (2011): 329–57; Mixon, *Atlanta Riot*.

80. *Georgian*, July 2, 1907.

81. *Georgian*, July 4, 1907.

82. *Georgian*, June 29, 1907.

83. *Georgian*, June 29, 1907, 6.

84. *Georgian*, July 6, 1907.

85. *Georgian*, July 9, 1907.

86. *Georgian*, July 8, 1907; *Constitution*, July 8, 1907.

87. *Georgian*, July 8, 1907, 13. On *American Express Company v. Iowa*, see Keller, *Regulating*, 136.

88. *Georgian*, July 8, 1907.

89. *Georgian*, July 6, 1907. Tellingly, Seely refused Mary Armor's offer to publicly shame advertisers threatening the *Georgian*. He politely declined her request for names but explained it as a point of principle, *Georgian*, July 15, 1907.

90. The differing strategies of the *Georgian* and *Constitution* can be seen by reviewing their July 8–14 issues. The *Georgian* filled its pages with pro-prohibition letters; the *Constitution* printed relatively few, with a mix of pro and anti views.

91. John Temple Graves, "Georgia Pioneers in the Prohibition Crusade," *Cosmopolitan* 45 (June 1908): 83–90.

92. *Georgian*, July 6, 1907, 11.

93. *Georgian*, July 15, 1907, 2.

94. *Constitution*, July 9, 1907. The *Constitution*, for its part, omits to mention the presence of copies of the *Georgian* on the same desks: the coverage quite explicitly follows the interests of the parties as rivals for political influence.

95. The success of prohibition allowed many leaders of the WCTU to take a more open stand in favor of woman suffrage: Armor herself was a member of the Georgia Woman Suffrage Association by 1910. On the tension between masculine assumptions about women's domestic role and prosuffrage sentiment within the Georgia WCTU, see Stacey Horstmann Gatti, "'To Do Her Duty Nobly and Well': White Women's Organizations Debate Woman Suffrage, 1910–1920," in *Entering the Fray: Gender, Politics, and Culture in the New South*, ed. Jonathan Daniel Wells and Sheila R. Phipps (Columbia: University of Missouri Press, 2009).

96. Paula Baker, "The Domestication of Politics: Women and American Political Society, 1780–1920," *American Historical Review* 89, 3 (June 1984): 620–47; see also Catherine Gilbert Murdock, *Domesticating Drink: Women, Men, and Alcohol in America, 1870–1940* (Baltimore: Johns Hopkins University Press, 1998).

97. See Pearson and Smith and Nackenoff and Sullivan, both this volume. The contrast to male attempts to mold the language of chivalry to the cause of animal welfare makes a particularly instructive comparison; see Pearson and Smith

98. South Carolina was probably insulated from immediate impact by its preexisting state-controlled dispensary system. Oklahoma was clearly part of the Jim Crow South, and adopted disfranchisement along with constitutional prohibition prior to joining the Union. Some would also allow West Virginia as a southern state, but its internal politics (the strength of the Republican Party and the general circumstances under which

prohibition was adopted) are quite distinctive: I am not claiming prohibition had no independent appeal outside the South.

99. The discussion here is not meant to be definitive. A keyword search was conducted on newspapers available in the Library of Congress Chronicling America digital database (as of October 26, 2012), for Florida, Louisiana, Oklahoma, South Carolina, Tennessee, Texas, and Virginia. The total number of newspapers searched was around 98. Dates are defined in the text, but searches were conducted separately for the year prior and following each riot. Newspaper pages were identified matching searches for "'prohibition' AND 'race problem'"; "'saloon OR liquor OR whiskey' AND 'race problem'"; "'negro OR race OR colored' AND 'low dives.'" Those pages were then examined for individual articles substantively linking race and alcohol or race and prohibition. Thanks to Ann-Marie Szymanski for suggesting the possibility.

100. *Sumter* (South Carolina) *Watchman and Southron*, June 7, 1899.

101. *Keowee* (South Carolina) *Courier*, August 22, 1906.

102. *Pensacola Journal*, July 18, 1907, September 11, 1907.

103. *Panama City Pilot*, September 5, 1907, 2.

104. *Pensacola Journal*, September 10, 11, 22, 1907; *Ocala Banner*, September 20, 27, 1907; *Pensacola Journal*, September 15, 1907.

105. *Pensacola Journal*, September 15, 1907; Tom Watson's *Weekly Jeffersonian* cast the fight as one between "manhood and whiskey" and stood "squarely for manhood," quoted in Edgefield *Advertiser*, July 24, 1907.

106. *Jackson Daily News*, quoted in *Ocala Banner*, September 6, 1907.

107. *Pensacola Journal*, September 22, 1907.

108. Alexander J. McKelway, "State Prohibition in Georgia and in the South," *Outlook* 86 (1907): 947–49.

109. Steedman, *Jim Crow Citizenship*. The South was not alone in developing institutions to effect what Julie Novkov calls "cultural tutelage." See Novkov, this volume.

110. Johnson, *Reforming*.

111. See especially Novkov, this volume, and Pearson and Smith, this volume.

112. On the relation between institutions and ideas, see Robert C. Lieberman, "Ideas, Institutions, and Political Order: Explaining Political Change," *American Political Science Review* 96 (2002): 697–712, and Pamela Brandwein, "Law and American Political Development," *American Review of Law and Social Science* 7 (2011): 187–216.

Chapter 3. Statebuilding through Corruption: Graft and Trash in Pittsburgh and New Orleans

We thank Joel Tarr, David C. W. Parker, Carol Nackenoff, Julie Novkov, Laura Jensen and the two anonymous reviewers from University of Pennsylvania Press for their contributions to this project.

1. Irwin Osborn, "Disposal of Garbage by the Reduction Method," *American Journal of Public Health* 3 (1912): 356.

2. William Francis Morse, *The Collection and Disposal of Municipal Waste* (New York: Municipal Journal and Engineer, 1908), 412.

3. Though political scientists define machines by their successful hold on political power, historians refer to New Orleans during this period as a machine city because of the tactics political actors used to gain and maintain power. City leaders were able to consolidate power (and become a political machine in every sense of the word) after 1904. See Brian Gary Ettinger, "John Fitzpatrick and the Limits of Working-Class Politics in New Orleans, 1892–1896," *Louisiana History* 26, 4 (1985); Edward Haas, "John Fitzpatrick and Political Continuity in New Orleans, 1896–1899," *Louisiana History* 22 (Winter 1981); Raymond Nussbaum, "'The Ring Is Smashed!': The New Orleans Municipal Election of 1896," *Louisiana History* 17 (Summer 1976).

4. Nathaniel H. Neff, "Economic Development Through Bureaucratic Corruption," *American Behavioral Scientist* 8, 3 (1964).

5. Eric McKitrick, "The Study of Corruption," *Political Science Quarterly* 72, 4 (1957); John D. Buenker, *Urban Liberalism and Progressive Reform* (New York: Scribner's, 1973); Jon Teaford, "Finis for Tweed and Steffens: Rewriting the History of Urban Rule," *Reviews in American History* 10, 4 (1982); Philip J. Ethington, "Recasting Urban Political History: Gender, the Public, the Household, and Political Participation in Boston and San Francisco During the Progressive Era," *Social Science History* 16 (Summer 1992).

6. Teaford, "Finis for Tweed and Steffens," 139.

7. Jessica Trounstine, *Political Monopolies in American Cities: The Rise and Fall of Bosses and Reformers* (Chicago: University of Chicago Press, 2008).

8. Neff, "Economic Development Through Bureaucratic Corruption," 11.

9. Patricia Strach and Kathleen S. Sullivan, "The State's Relations: What the Institution of Family Tells Us About Governance," *Political Research Quarterly* 64, 1 (2011).

10. Lawrence Larsen, "Nineteenth-Century Sanitation: A Study in Filth and Frustration," *Wisconsin Magazine of History* (1969): 246; George Albert Soper, *Modern Methods of Street Cleaning* (New York: Engineering News, 1909), 174.

11. William McGowan, "America's Wasteland: A History of America's Garbage Industry, 1880–1989," *Business and Economic History* 24 (1995): 157; Rudolph Hering and Samuel A. Greeley, *Collection and Disposal of Municipal Refuse* (New York: McGraw-Hill, 1921), 1.

12. Martin V. Melosi, *Garbage in the Cities: Refuse, Reform, and the Environment* (Pittsburgh: University of Pittsburgh Press, 2005), 17.

13. Yellow fever could have devastating effects. For example, in the outbreak of 1853, 8,000 people died. See Jo Ann Carrigan, "Yellow Fever in New Orleans, 1853: Abstractions and Realities," *Journal of Southern History* 25, 3 (1959): 342.

14. Carrigan, "Yellow Fever in New Orleans."

15. *Report of the Sanitary Commission of New Orleans on the Epidemic Yellow Fever* (New Orleans: City Council of New Orleans, 1854), 390.

16. Margaret Humphreys, *Yellow Fever and the South* (Baltimore: Johns Hopkins University Press, 1992), 54.

17. *Annual Report of the Board of Health of the State of Louisiana to the General Assembly for the Year 1877*, 10, Historic New Orleans Collection (hereafter THNOC).

18. Dennis East, Jr., "Health and Wealth: Goals of the New Orleans Public Health Movement, 1879–1884," *Louisiana History* 9 (1968): 249.

19. Melosi, *Garbage in the Cities*, 18.

20. Edward Fenner, "Annual Address of Edward Fenner, Vice President, at the Regular Meeting of the New Orleans Auxiliary Sanitary Association, November 23, 1880," 3–4, THNOC.

21. Fenner, "Annual Address."

22. John Ellis, *Yellow Fever and Public Health* (Lexington: University of Kentucky Press), 354.; George E. Waring, *Report on the Social Statistics of Cities* (Washington, D.C.: Government Printing Office, 1887), 287; Joy Jackson, *New Orleans in the Gilded Age: Politics and Urban Progress, 1880–1896* (New Orleans: Louisiana State University Press, 1969), 173.

23. Authors' calculations of data collected from Payroll, Department of Public Works 1883, City Archives, New Orleans Public Library (hereafter NOPL).

24. *Yellow Fever and Public Health*, 87–94.

25. Eric Arensen, *Waterfront Workers of New Orleans: Race, Class and Politics, 1863–1923* (New York: Oxford University Press, 1994), 81. The Ring's garbage boat was soon declared a nuisance. "The Barracks Street Garbage Boat," *Daily Picayune*, July 27, 1887, 4; "A Garbage Nuisance," *Daily Picayune*, July 23, 1887, 4.

26. Robert Williams, "Martin Behrman and New Orleans Civic Development, 1904–1920," *Louisiana History* 2 (1961): 394.

27. Nussbaum, "'The Ring Is Smashed!'," 285.

28. Ettinger, "John Fitzpatrick and the Limits of Working-Class Politics."

29. Ettinger, "John Fitzpatrick and the Limits of Working-Class Politics," 346.

30. Ettinger, "John Fitzpatrick and the Limits of Working-Class Politics," 344.

31. "A Digest of the Acts of Assembly Relating to, and the General Ordinances of the City of Pittsburgh, from 1804 to September 1, 1886" (Harrisburg, Pa.: B. K. Meyers, 1886), 30.

32. *Municipal Record Minutes of the Proceedings of the Select and Common Councils of the City of Pittsburgh for the year 1875* (Pittsburgh: Herald Printing Co., 1876), 199, Historical Society of Western Pennsylvania (hereafter HSWP).

33. "A Digest of the Acts of Assembly," 30.

34. "A Digest of the Acts of Assembly," 40–41. Reliance on private scavengers was common practice in cities. See Charles V. Chapin, *Municipal Sanitation in the United States* (Providence, R.I.: Snow & Farnham, 1901), 691.

35. Carl A. Zimring, *Cash for Your Trash: Scrap Recycling in America* (New Brunswick: Rutgers University Press, 2009), 34.

36. "Fever Epidemic: South Siders Suffering from Typhoid Fever," *Pittsburgh Post*, April 2, 1880, 4.

37. "Fever Epidemic." The swampy ground in the upper wards of the South Side was

caused by the accumulation of filth under houses, making the ground soft and boggy when ashes, filth, and garbage were used as fillings. "The South Side Scourge," *Pittsburgh Post*, April 5, 1880, 4.

38. "Sanitarians' Council," *Pittsburgh Post*, May 1, 1880, 4; "The South Side Scourge"; "South Side Health," *Pittsburgh Post*, June 1, 1880, 4.

39. "Fever Epidemic."

40. Francis G. Couvares, *The Remaking of Pittsburgh: Class and Culture in an Industrializing City* (Albany: State University of New York Press, 1984), 64.

41. John F. Bauman and Edward K. Muller, *Before Renaissance: Planning in Pittsburgh, 1889–1943* (Pittsburgh: University of Pittsburgh Press, 2006), 21.

42. Lincoln Steffens, *The Shame of the Cities* (New York: Sagamore Press, 1904/1957), 115.

43. *Annual Report of the Department of Public Works for the City of Pittsburgh for the Year 1897* (Pittsburgh: Herald Publishing, 1898), 57.

44. Quoted in Steffens, *The Shame of the Cities*, 119.

45. Bauman and Muller, *Before Renaissance*, 23.

46. "Taxpayers Growling," *Pittsburgh Post*, January 2, 1895, 2.

47. "Taxpayers Growling."

48. "Questions of Sanitation," *Pittsburgh Post*, January 3, 1895, 8.

49. Works Progress Administration Project 665-64-3-112, *Biographies of the Mayors of New Orleans* (New Orleans: City Hall Archives, 1939), 142, NOPL.

50. *Committee on Public Health, Reports and Actions* (1892–1896), 18, 20, NOPL.

51. "Garbage Disposal: The Board of Health Wants Immediate Action Taken," *Daily Picayune*, April 21, 1893, 6.

52. "The Handling of Garbage," *Daily Picayune*, April 21, 1893, 4.

53. "Garbage Removal," *New Orleans Times Democrat*, April 13, 1893, A4. New Orleans' unfiltered water and mere twenty-two miles of paved streets likewise attested to the failure of public works. See Ettinger, "John Fitzpatrick and the Limits of Working-Class Politics," 342.

54. They learned about the latest technology, and they learned what not to do, as a New York contingent found when it "visited Boston, Montreal, Chicago, St. Louis, Atlanta, Cincinnati, and then Pittsburgh. . . . [W]hen informed that the Pittsburgh plant consisted of a 30-ton furnace 7 years old, they returned to their car." "Looking into Garbage," *Pittsburgh Post*, October 27, 1894, 4.

55. "The Fouling of Beaches," *Harper's Weekly* (July 2, 1898), 663, cited in Melosi, *Garbage in the Cities*, 70 n47; Dona Brown, ed., *A Tourist's New England: Travel Fiction, 1820–1920* (Hanover, N.H.: University Press of New England,1999), 8–9.

56. Hering and Greeley, *Collection and Disposal of Municipal Refuse*, 241.

57. Hering and Greeley, *Collection and Disposal of Municipal Refuse*, 248–57.

58. Hering and Greeley, *Collection and Disposal of Municipal Refuse*, 258–61.

59. Hering and Greeley, *Collection and Disposal of Municipal Refuse*, 2; "Report on the Committee on Disposal of Waste and Garbage," *Public Health Papers and Reports*

1891, 102–3; "Refuse Disposal in America," *Surveyor and Municipal and County Engineer*, January 21, 1898: 47.

60. Frank Moore Colby, ed., *The New International Yearbook: A Compendium of the World's Progress for the Year 1914* (New York: Dodd, Mead, 1915), 280.

61. Colby, ed., *New International Yearbook*, 280.

62. The reduction process also produced unwanted by-products, namely, odor. Reduction processes produced a distinctive stench, likened to a "strong caramel odor, approximately described as the odor of sweetish burnt coffee, and which is very objectionable to many nostrils." Paul Hansen, *City Wastes Disposal and Street Cleaning, Proceedings of the Annual Meeting of the Ohio Society of Engineers* (Columbus, Ohio: Trauger, 1908), 111. This particular problem was not only technical but political. Understandably, local residents did not want reduction facilities to be built near their homes. Because of this problem, experts recommended that plants be built away from residential areas. Hering and Greeley, *Collection and Disposal of Municipal Refuse*, 444.

63. Hansen, *City Wastes Disposal and Street Cleaning*, 110–11.

64. Colby, *The New International Yearbook*, 280.

65. Hering and Greeley, *Collection and Disposal of Municipal Refuse*, 2.

66. Hering and Greeley, *Collection and Disposal of Municipal Refuse*, 477; "American Refuse Disposal Plants," *Municipal Journal* 33 (September 5, 1912): 319.

67. "American Refuse Disposal Plants," 322.

68. M. N. Baker, ed., *Municipal Yearbook: 1902* (New York: Engineering News, 1902), xxii.

69. Daniel Zarin, "Searching for Pennies in Piles of Trash: Municipal Refuse Utilization in the United States, 1870–1930," *Environmental Review* 11 (1987): 213.

70. Hering and Greeley, *Collection and Disposal of Municipal Refuse*, 513.

71. Data from C.-E. A. Winslow and P. Hansen, "Some Statistics of Garbage Disposal for the Larger American Cities in 1902," *Public Health Papers and Reports* 29 (1903): 141–65.

72. Morse, *The Collection and Disposal of Municipal Waste*, 412.The correlations between reduction and population (.47, $p < .001$) and reduction and manufacturing capital in a given city (.52, $p < .001$) suggest that large commercial centers have resources necessary to create and maintain reduction facilities. Though we cannot separate out the independent effect of population and of manufacturing, this is a problem of history (how cities actually developed) and not an artifact of data.

73. Cleveland and Milwaukee were the only two cities with publicly owned and operated reduction facilities. Milwaukee's plant was used only for processing dead animals. Department of Commerce, Bureau of the Census, "General Statistics of Cities: 1909" (Washington, D.C.: Government Printing Office, 1913), 49. Cleveland had started out with a reduction plant run by a contractor, but it bought the plant in 1905. Its facilities were well regarded. Morse, *Collection and Disposal of Municipal Waste*, 397; Colby, *The New International Yearbook*, 272.

74. "Method and Cost of Garbage Disposal at Columbus, Ohio," *Engineering and Contracting* 36 (September 27, 2011): 328; Morse, *The Collection and Disposal of Municipal Waste*, 290; "Garbage Disposal," *Municipal Engineering* 14 (1898): 44.

75. William Francis Morse, "Disposal of Garbage and Waste of World's Columbian Exposition," *Medical Record* (October 28, 1893): 569; "Garbage Disposal," *Municipal Engineering* 14 (1898): 44; Chapin, *Municipal Sanitation in the United States*, 701–2.

76. William Francis Morse, "The Disposal of Municipal Waste," *American Municipalities* (1897).

77. Hansen, *City Wastes Disposal and Street Cleaning*, 111.

78. Bureau of Health, "Report of Superintendent," *Eighth Annual Report of the Department of Public Safety, City of Pittsburgh for the Year 1895*, 313, Library and Services Division, HSWP.

79. Bureau of Health, "Report of Superintendent," *Eighth Annual Report*, 765.

80. Department of Public Safety, "Report of the Director, Contracts Awarded by the Director of the Department of Public Safety during the Fiscal Year ending Jan 31, 1900," *12th Annual Report of the Department of Public Safety, City of Pittsburgh, 1899*, 22, HSWP.

81. *Fisher et al. v. American Reduction Co.*, 42 A.36 (Pa. 1899).

82. By the mid-nineteenth century, Americans turned to ward politicians or even private groups or individuals for such vital urban services as water supply, street sanitation, and fire protection. Stanley K. Schultz and Clay McShane, "To Engineer the Metropolis: Sewers, Sanitation, and City Planning in Late-Nineteenth Century America," *Journal of American History* 65, 2 (1978); "Letting Plans Made and Contracts Awarded," *Annual Report of the Department of Public Works of the City of Pittsburgh for the Fiscal Year 1897* (Pittsburgh: Herald, 1898), 54–59, HSWP. There was plenty of business for Flinn. The mazelike organization of subterranean pipes for water, sewage, gas, steam, pneumatic mail delivery, and conduits for telegraph, telephone, electric light, and power purposes, meant that streets had to be dug up (and repaved) to locate them. Soper, *Modern Methods of Street Cleaning*, 5–6. Through an arrangement with E. M. Bigelow, director of the Department of Public Works, some contracts required a very specialized asphalt from a pitch lake on the island of Trinidad in the Caribbean; conveniently, Booth & Flinn controlled that pitch lake. *Thomas Loughrey et al. v. City of Pittsburgh, Controller, and Booth & Flinn, Ltd.*, Court of Common Pleas, 1898, from Flinn letterbook, Papers of William Flinn, Archives Service Center, University of Pittsburgh (hereafter ACS). See also Letter dated Feb. 12, 1898, to S. E. Taylor, Secretary, Trinidad Asp. Paving Company from William Flinn, ACS.

83. Colby, *The New International Yearbook*, 280.

84. Bureau of Health, "Report of Superintendent," *Eighth Annual Report*, 307.

85. Letter dated April 21, 1898, to John Fredericks, Esq., from George Flinn, Flinn letterbook; Letter dated April 23, 1898, from George Flinn to William Flinn, Flinn letterbook. Flinn was so pleased that he struck deals with agents in Rochester, New York, and Washington, D.C., to contract for the construction of, and/or investment in, new plants there. Letter dated Jan. 13, 1898, to F. G. Lauer, President, Rochester Vulcanite

Pavement Co., from William Flinn, Flinn letterbook; Letter dated Feb. 2, 1898, to F. C. Lauer, Esq., from William Flinn, Flinn letterbook; Letter dated Feb. 12. 1898, to F. C. Lauer, Esq., from William Flinn, Flinn letterbook; Letter dated March 1, 1898, to A. W. Dow, Esq., from William Flinn, Flinn letterbook; Letter dated March 7, 1898, to A. W. Dow, Esq., from William Flinn, Flinn letterbook, ACS.

86. "City Garbage: The Question of Its Collection and Final Disposition," *Daily Picayune*, May 30, 1892, 3.

87. "City Garbage," 3.

88. "Garbage Disposal," *Daily Picayune*, April 21, 1893.

89. "News Gathered at the City Hall," *Daily Picayune*, August 3, 1893, 12.

90. "The Garbage Job," *Daily Picayune*, August 15, 1893, 4; "The Cost of the Garbage Service," *Daily Picayune*, August 18, 1893, 7.

91. Letter dated May 27, 1898, to John Fredericks, Esq., from William Flinn, Flinn letterbook, ACS.

92. Letter dated March 5, 1898, to T.F. Van Kirk, Esq., from William Flinn, Flinn letterbook, ACS.

93. Letter dated Jan. 31, 1898, to Mr. C. Gray, from William Flinn, Flinn letterbook, ACS.

94. *Fisher et al. v. American Reduction Co.*, 42 Atl. 36 (Pa. 1899): 38–39.

95. *Fisher et al. v. American Reduction Co.*, 42 Atl. 36, 38.

96. Bauman and Muller, *Before Renaissance*, 40. The Ladies Protective Health Association had formed in 1889 to combat impure water, inadequate garbage disposal, and smoke. See Angela Gugliotta, "How, When, and for Whom Was Smoke a Problem for Pittsburgh?" in *Devastation and Renewal: An Environmental History of Pittsburgh and Its Region*, ed. Joel Tarr (Pittsburgh: University of Pittsburgh Press, 2003), 116.

97. "The Index: Celebrated Twentieth Anniversary Has Accomplished Much," November 13, 1915, Civic Club of Allegheny County Records, ACS.

98. Minutes, November 5, 1897, 147–48, Board of Director Minutes, Civic Club of Allegheny County Records, ACS.

99. See 1903 Sanitary Complaints; 1903 Alley Complaints; both Civic Club of Allegheny County Records, ACS.

100. Neighboring residents complained of foul odors. Department of Public Health Report, *Annual Reports of Mayor for Year Ending January 31, 1912*, 767, HSWP.

101. *A Digest of the Acts of Assembly Relating to the General Ordinances and Laws of the City of Allegheny from 1840 to April 1st 1897*, 140. Historic Pittsburgh Digital Research Library, http://digital.library.pitt.edu/cgi-bin/t/text/text-idx?idno=00hc13553m;view=toc;c=pitttext.

102. New York Bureau of Municipal Research, *The City of Pittsburgh, Pennsylvania: Report on a Survey of Public Health* (Pittsburgh: Pittsburgh Printing, 1913), 24.

103. New York Bureau of Municipal Research, *The City of Pittsburgh*, 30.

104. Joel A. Tarr, "Building the Urban Infrastructure in the Nineteenth Century: An Introduction," *Essays in Public Works History* 14 (1985): 64.

105. Department of Public Health Report, *Annual Reports of Mayor for Year Ending January 31, 1912*, 480, HSWP.

106. Craig Colten, *An Unnatural Metropolis: Wresting New Orleans from Nature* (Baton Rouge: Louisiana State University Press, 2005), 59–60.

107. Ettinger, "John Fitzpatrick and the Limits of Working-Class Politics," 355.

108. "News Gathered at City Hall," *Daily Picayune*, August 3, 1893, 12; "News Gathered at City Hall," *Daily Picayune*, August 19, 1893, 7; "The Cost of the Garbage Service"; "That Garbage Contract," *Daily Picayune*, August 19, 1893, 4; "The Garbage Business," *Daily Picayune*, August 21, 1893, 4.

109. "The Garbage Business," *Daily Picayune*, August 21, 1893, 4.

110. Joy Jackson, *New Orleans in the Gilded Age*, 137–60.

111. Ettinger, "John Fitzpatrick and the Limits of Working-Class Politics," 355–56.

112. "City Hall: Get Your Garbage Boxes," *Daily Picayune*, March 4, 1894; "A Lady's Plan to Bring About a Better System of Garbage Gathering," *Daily Picayune*, March 10, 1894, 3; "The Garbage Job and Garbage Boxes," *Daily Picayune*, March 15, 1894, 4.

113. Jackson, *New Orleans in the Gilded Age*, 138.

114. Haas, "John Fitzpatrick and Political Continuity in New Orleans."

115. Ettinger, "John Fitzpatrick and the Limits of Working-Class Politics," 356.

116. Ettinger, "John Fitzpatrick and the Limits of Working-Class Politics," 344.

117. "Mayor Shakespeare [*sic*] Firm," *New York Times*, November 22, 1891, 1.

118. "Mayor Shakespeare Firm," 1.

119. "History of Major Burke's Frauds," *New York Times*, March 22, 1894, 7; "Stuck the Company $480,000," *Worcester Daily Spy*, June 10, 1895.

120. "M. J. Hart Indicted," *St. Louis Republic*, August 14, 1895. "Maurice J. Hart Indicted," *New York Times*, August 14, 1895.

121. Colten, *An Unnatural Metropolis*, 59–60; Morse, *The Collection and Disposal of Municipal Waste*.

122. Hering and Greeley, *Collection and Disposal of Municipal Refuse*, 558.

123. "Garbage Collection and Disposal Plans in New Orleans," *Municipal Engineering* 37 (1909): 49.

124. Steffens, *The Shame of the Cities*, 109.

125. Ettinger, "John Fitzpatrick and the Limits of Working-Class Politics," 343.

126. Flinn, however, influenced city politics until 1911, when a new city charter was passed: "Who Was William Flinn?" *Pittsburgh City Paper* (March 4–10, 2004): 8, HSWP.

127. "Annual Report of the Department of Public Health," *Annual Reports of the Departments and Offices of the City of Pittsburgh, 1912*, 480, HSWP.

128. "Annual Report of the Department of Public Health," *Annual Reports of the Departments and Offices of the City of Pittsburgh, 1914*, 287, HSWP.

129. Ettinger, "John Fitzpatrick and the Limits of Working-Class Politics."

130. Ettinger, "John Fitzpatrick and the Limits of Working-Class Politics."

131. *Notes on Municipal Progress in New Orleans During 1897 and 1898—Charter*

Reform, Proceedings of the Indianapolis Conference for Good City Government and Fourth Annual Meeting of the National Municipal League (Philadelphia: National Municipal League, 1898), 267.

132. George Reynolds, *Machine Politics in New Orleans, 1897–1926* (New York: Columbia University Press, 1936), 15.

133. Mary Lou Widmer, *New Orleans, 1900–1920* (Gretna, La.: Pelican, 2007), 59.

134. John Kemp, *Martin Berhman of New Orleans: Memoirs of a City Boss* (Baton Rouge: Louisiana State University Press, 1977), xxi.

135. Williams, "Martin Behrman and New Orleans Civic Development," 373–74; Matthew Schott, "The New Orleans Machine and Progressivism," *Louisiana History* 2 (Spring 1983): 141–53.

136. Williams, "Martin Behrman and New Orleans Civic Development, " 394.

137. "From the Commissioner of Public Works—Being a Detailed Statement of the Working of His Department for December 1904," January 17, 1905. NOPL.

138. George Smith, "Report of the Commissioner of Public Works of his Department," February 9, 1907; August 6, 1907; March 10, 1908; June 8, 1908, NOPL.

139. *Martin Behrman Administration Biography, 1904–1916*, 33, NOPL.

140. "Report of the Working Forces of the Department of Public Works," January 10, 1908, NOPL.

141. George Smith, "Systems of Collection and Disposal of Garbage in the City of New Orleans," *American Journal of Public Health* 2, 12 (1912): 924.

142. Williams, "Martin Behrman and New Orleans Civic Development," 395.

143. "Annual Report of the Surgeon General of the Public Health Service of the United States for the Fiscal Year 1922" (Washington, D.C.: Government Printing Office, 1922), 87.

144. "Refuse Collection in New Orleans," *Public Works* 52 (June 10, 1922): 419–20. Municipal Survey Commisstion, *Administrative Survey of the Government and City of New Orleans* (New Orleans: Louisiana Printing, 1922), 174.

145. Steffens, *The Shame of the Cities*, 114.

146. Trounstine, *Political Monopolies in American Cities*; Teaford, "Finis for Tweed and Steffens."

Chapter 4. Developing the Animal Welfare State

1. Stephen Skowronek, *Building a New American State: The Expansion of National Administrative Capacities, 1877–1920* (New York: Cambridge University Press, 1982).

2. William Novak, "The Myth of the 'Weak' American State," *American Historical Review* 113 (2008): 752–72; William Novak, "The Pluralist State: The Convergence of Public and Private Power in America," in *American Public Life and the Historical Imagination*, ed. Wendy Gamber, Michael Grossberg, and Hendrik Hartog (Notre Dame, Ind.: University of Notre Dame Press, 2003), 27–48.

3. Richard Andrews, *Managing the Environment, Managing Ourselves* (New Haven: Yale University Press, 1999), 46–49; William Cronon, *Changes in the Land* (New York:

Hill & Wang, 1983), 92–98, 101; Jon T. Coleman, *Vicious: Wolves and Men in America* (New Haven, Conn.: Yale University Press, 2004).

4. Cronon, *Changes in the Land*, 134–37; Virginia DeJohn Anderson, *Creatures of Empire: How Domestic Animals Transformed Early America* (Oxford: Oxford University Press, 2002), 142, 158–63.

5. Percy Bidwell and John Falconer, *History of Agriculture in the Northern United States, 1620–1860* (Washington, D.C.: Carnegie Institution, 1925), 23–24.

6. Quoted in Diane Beers, *For the Prevention of Cruelty: The History and Legacy of Animal Rights Activism in the United States* (Athens: Ohio University Press, 2006), 19.

7. Anderson, *Creatures of Empire*, 114, 124.

8. Terry Jordan, *North American Cattle-Ranching Frontiers* (Albuquerque: University of New Mexico Press, 1993), 113, 118.

9. Karen Orren and Stephen Skowronek, *The Search for American Political Development* (Cambridge: Cambridge University Press, 2004), 22–23.

10. William Novak, *The People's Welfare: Law and Regulation in Nineteenth-Century America* (Chapel Hill: University of North Carolina Press, 1996), 12.

11. Clay McShane, "Gelded Age Boston," *New England Quarterly* 74 (June 2001): 274–302, 276.

12. Novak, *The People's Welfare*, 3–5.

13. McShane, "Gelded Age Boston," 279; Jason Hribal, "Animals Are Part of the Working Class: A Challenge to Labor History," *Labor History* 4 (2003): 435–53.

14. Novak, *The People's Welfare*, 228–29; Andrews, *Managing the Environment*, 110.

15. Novak, *The People's Welfare*, 229.

16. James Jasper and Dorothy Nelkin, *The Animal Rights Crusade* (New York: Free Press, 1992), 57.

17. Anderson, *Creatures of Empire*, 93.

18. New York Rev. Stat., Ch. 374, sec. 1–10 (1867).

19. New York Rev. Stat., Ch. 374, sec. 1–10 (1867), 77–78; Joel Prentiss Bishop, *Commentaries on the Law of Statutory Crimes* (Boston: Little, Brown, 1873), 693.

20. Bishop, *Commentaries on the Law of Statutory Crimes*, 79, 99–101. For a fuller examination of the rights-talk of animal protectionists, see Susan J. Pearson, *The Rights of the Defenseless: Protecting Animals and Children in Gilded Age America* (Chicago: University of Chicago Press, 2011), chap. 3.

21. Pearson, *The Rights of the Defenseless*, 111–14

22. Pearson, *The Rights of the Defenseless*, 99.

23. *Broadway etc. Stage Co. v. ASPCA*, 15 Abbott 51 (New York, 1873).

24. Ernst Freund, *The Police Power, Public Power and Constitutional Rights* (Chicago: Callaghan and Co., 1904); Pearson, *Rights of the Defenseless*, 81–82; 164.

25. Pearson, *The Rights of the Defenseless*, 81–82; 164.

26. Pearson, *The Rights of the Defenseless*, 58–59, 76.

27. "Man's Brutality to Brutes," *New York Times*, August 27, 1870.

28. For more on the slippery slope theory of violence, see Pearson, *The Rights of the Defenseless*, chap. 2.

29. McShane, "Gelded Age Boston," 274–302, 294.

30. Clay McShane and Joel Tarr, *The Horse in the City* (Baltimore: Johns Hopkins University Press, 2007), 47–48.

31. Henry Bergh, "The Cost of Cruelty," *North American Review* 133 (July 1882): 75–81. Bergh doesn't address why government regulation is needed to protect the owners of the livestock from these losses, but it's likely that he and his audience saw the railroads as far too powerful to be restrained through private actions in tort or contract.

32. Katherine C. Grier, *Pets in America: A History* (Chapel Hill: University of North Carolina Press), 21–26.

33. The following account is based largely on Eric Stoykovich, "Of a Predatory Nature? Dogs and the Protection of Sheep in the Eastern United States," paper presented at American Society for Environmental History conference, Baton Rouge, Louisiana, 2007.

34. Similar laws were passed in England and France in the late eighteenth century. Harriet Ritvo, *The Animal Estate: The English and Other Creatures in the Victorian Age* (Cambridge, Mass.: Harvard University Press, 1987), 188–90; Kathleen Kete, *The Beast in the Boudoir: Petkeeping in Nineteenth-Century Paris* (Berkeley: University of California Press, 1994), 40–54.

35. Stoykovich, "Of a Predatory Nature?" 8, quoting "Dogs and Dog Laws," Report of the Commissioner of Agriculture for the Year 1863 (Washington, D.C.: Government Printing Office, 1863), 454–55.

36. Kete, *The Beast in the Boudoir*, 54. A similar debate over dog taxes in England began with an effort to discourage people, and especially the poor, from owning dogs. But it resulted in a tax that fell less heavily on the poor, acknowledging their right to own dogs for work or companionship. Ingrid Tague, "Eighteenth-Century English Debate on a Dog Tax," *Historical Journal* 51, 4 (2008): 901–20.

37. Stoykovich, "Of a Predatory Nature?" 8, quoting Fifth Annual Report of the Secretary of the Maine Board of Agriculture (Augusta: Stevens and Sayward, 1860), 41–43.

38. Grier, *Pets in America*, 163.

39. Stoykovich, "Of a Predatory Nature?" 7, 10.

40. Grier, *Pets in America*, 214, 217; Beers, *For the Prevention of Cruelty*, 71.

41. Elisabeth Clemens, "Lineages of the Rube Goldberg State," in *Rethinking Political Institutions*, ed. Ian Shapiro, Stephen Skowronek, and Daniel Galvin (New York: New York University Press, 2006), 197.

42. Brian Harrison, *Peaceable Kingdom: Stability and Change in Modern Britain* (Oxford: Clarendon, 1982), 91–97.

43. The following is based on David Slansky, "The Private Police," *UCLA Law Review* 46 (1999): 1165.

44. *Davis et al. v. The American Society for the Prevention of Cruelty to Animals*, 1878 N.Y. Lexis 872.

45. Pearson, *The Rights of the Defenseless*, 180. Dog taxation was particularly troublesome because dog licensure laws were often enforced by SPCAs or Humane Societies and usually authorized such organizations to confiscate and destroy unlicensed dogs. Once dogs were recognized as property this raised issues about due process and the authority of apparently private organizations. See also *Fagin v. Ohio Humane Society*, 1898 Ohio Misc. Lexis 186.

46. *Pearson, The Rights of the Defenseless*, , 152–54.

47. Beers. *For the Prevention of Cruelty*, 61.

48. Pearson, *The Rights of the Defenseless*, 1–4.

49. Pearson, *The Rights of the Defenseless*, 144.

50. Pearson, *The Rights of the Defenseless*, 137–38, 91–92; Bernard Unti, "Cruelty Indivisible," in *The International Handbook of Animal Abuse and Cruelty*, ed. Frank Ascione (West Lafayette, Ind.: Purdue University Press, 2008), 10–11.

51. Pearson, *The Rights of the Defenseless*, 182.

52. Pearson, *The Rights of the Defenseless*, 182–83.

53. Theda Skocpol, *Protecting Soldiers and Mothers: The Political Origins of Social Policy in the United States* (Cambridge, Mass. : Harvard University Press, 1992).

54. Skocpol, *Protecting Soldiers and Mothers*, 145–47.

55. Illinois Humane Society, *Fourteenth Annual Report* (Chicago: Humane Society, 1884), 12.

56. NYSPCC, *Fourteenth Annual Report*, 10.

57. NYSPCC, *Forty-Third Annual Report, December 31, 1917* (New York, 1918), 11.

58. NYSPCC, *Fifteenth Annual Report, December 31, 1889* (New York, 1890), 7; *Twenty-Fourth Annual Report, December 31, 1898* (New York, 1899), 7.

59. Pearson, *The Rights of the Defenseless*, 154–55.

60. Beers, *For the Prevention of Cruelty*, 55–56, 75.

61. Willard Cochrane, *The Development of American Agriculture* (Minneapolis: University of Minnesota Press, 1979), 244–45.

62. Andrews, *Managing the Environment*, 132.

63. Beers, *For the Prevention of Cruelty*, 94–95.

64. 7 USC sec. 1901; Jasper and Nelkin, *Animal Rights Crusade*, 140. The law did not criminalize inhumane slaughter; rather, it provided that federal agencies could buy meat only from companies that complied with the law. This created considerable financial pressure on the large meat processing companies to comply.

65. Pearson, *The Rights of the Defenseless*, 195.

66. Pearson, *The Rights of the Defenseless*, 198.

67. Orren and Skowronek, *In Search of American Political Development*, 106.

68. Grier, *Pets in America*, 89–90, 151, 214–17.

Chapter 5. Wildlife Protection and the Development of Centralized Governance in the Progressive Era

1. Elisabeth Clemens, "Lineages of the Rube Goldberg State: Building and Blurring Public Programs, 1900–1940," in *Rethinking Political Institutions: The Art of the State*, ed. Ian Shapiro, Stephen Skowronek, and Daniel Galvin, (New York: New York University Press, 2006), 380–43.

2. George Cameron Coggins and Sebastian T. Patti, "The Resurrection and Expansion of the Migratory Bird Treaty Act," *University of Colorado Law Review* 50 (1978–1979): 165–206; Conrad A. Fjetland, "Possibilities for Expansion of the Migratory Bird Treaty Act for the Protection of Birds," *Natural Resources Journal* 40 (2000): 47–68.

3. Marge Davis, *Sportsmen United: The Story of the Tennessee Conservation League* (Mt. Juliet, Tenn.: Bench Top Books, 1997), 15–16.

4. Reformers opposed to the smoke nuisance recognized that smoke traveled across jurisdictional boundaries, but they typically promoted voluntary cooperation between localities during the Progressive Era. See, for instance, "Address of Welcome—Hon. Frederick S. Spiegal, Mayor," *Proceedings, Tenth Annual Convention of the Smoke Prevention Association, Hotel Sinton, Cincinnati, Ohio, September 8–10, 1915* (Chicago: Smoke Prevention Association, 1915), 7. Meanwhile, some conservationists supported the development of comprehensive waterways planning, but their ambitions were thwarted by opponents in Congress and government agencies such as the U.S. Army Corps of Engineers. See Samuel P. Hays, *Conservation and the Gospel of Efficiency: The Progressive Conservation Movement, 1890–1920* (Cambridge: Cambridge University Press, 1959), chap. 6; Donald J. Pisani, "Water Planning in the Progressive Era: The Inland Waterways Commission Reconsidered," *Journal of Policy History* 18 (2006): 389–418.

5. For a recent account of the influence of urban progressives, see John Louis Recchiuti, *Civic Engagement: Social Science and Progressive-Era Reform in New York City* (Philadelphia: University of Pennsylvania Press, 2007).

6. For rural America's support for the good roads movement and prohibition, see respectively Christopher H. Wells, "The Changing Nature of Country Roads: Farmers, Reformers, and the Shifting Uses of Rural Space, 1880–1905," *Agricultural History* 80 (2006): 143–66, and Ann-Marie Szymanski, "Beyond Parochialism: Southern Progressivism, Prohibition, and State-Building," *Journal of Southern History* 69 (2003): 107–36. For rural opposition to the anti-child labor movement and the country life movement's quest for agricultural efficiency, see William A. Link, *The Paradox of Southern Progressivism, 1880–1930* (Chapel Hill: University of North Carolina Press, 1992), 304–11; for the country life movement, see David B. Danbom, "Rural Education Reform and the Country Life Movement, 1900–1920," *Agricultural History* 53 (1979): 463–74, and William L. Bowers, "Country Life Reform, 1900–1920: A Neglected Aspect of Progressive Era History," *Agricultural History* 45 (1971): 211–21.

7. Daniel P. Carpenter, *The Forging of Bureaucratic Autonomy: Reputations, Networks, and Policy Innovation in Executive Agencies, 1862–1928* (Princeton, N.J.: Princeton University Press, 2001).

8. Eugene T. Peterson, "The History of Wild Life Conservation in Michigan, 1859–1921," Ph.D. dissertation, University of Michigan, 1952, 16. In addition to bolstering wildlife protection efforts, private action helped to uphold laws against theft, robbery, trespassing, counterfeiting, child abuse, cruelty to animals, pornography, abortion, prostitution, gambling, illicit alcohol sales, and air pollution. See Ann-Marie Szymanski, "Dry Compulsions: Prohibition and the Creation of State-Level Enforcement Agencies," *Journal of Policy History* 11 (1999): 115–46; Szymanski, "Stop Thief! Private Protective Societies in Nineteenth-Century New England," *New England Quarterly* 78 (2005): 405–43; Szymanski, "From Private Policing to Administrative Regulation: The Shift from 'Regulation Without Bureaucracies' to Centralized Agencies in the United States, 1890–1930," paper presented at annual meeting of the American Political Science Association, Washington, D.C., September 3, 2005.

9. John F. Reiger, *American Sportsmen and the Origins of Conservation*, 3rd ed. (Corvallis: Oregon State University Press, 2001), 87–89.

10. Reiger, *American Sportsmen and the Origins of Conservation*, chaps. 2–7; Thomas R. Dunlap, "Sport Hunting and Conservation, 1880–1920," *Environmental Review* 12 (1988): 51–60; James B. Trefethen, *An American Crusade for Wildlife* (New York: Winchester Press, 1975), chaps. 9, 11; Thomas R. Dunlap, *Saving America's Wildlife* (Princeton, N.J.: Princeton University Press, 1988), chap. 1; Peterson, "The History of Wild Life Conservation in Michigan," chaps. 1, 2.

11. Andrea L. Smalley, "'Our Lady Sportsmen': Gender, Class, and Conservation in Sport Hunting Magazines," *Journal of the Gilded Age and Progressive Era* 4 (2005): 355–80; Kathy S. Mason, "Out of Fashion: Harriet Hemenway and the Audubon Society, 1896–1905," *Historian* 65 (Fall 2002): 1–14; Leslie Kemp Poole, "The Women of the Early Florida Audubon Society: Agents of History in the Fight to Save State Birds," *Florida Historical Quarterly* 85 (2007): 297–323; Carolyn Merchant, "Women of the Progressive Conservation Movement, 1900–1916," *Environmental Review* 8 (1984): 69–73.

12. Davis, *Sportsmen United*, 13. For examples of state cases that upheld state wildlife regulation, see *Gentile v. State*, 29 Ind. 409 (1868); *Phelps v. Racey*, 60 N.Y. 10 (1875); *Magner v. People*, 97 Ill. 320 (1881); *Commonwealth v. Gilbert*, 160 Mass. 157 (1893); *Minnesota v. Rodman*, 58 Minn. 393 (1894).

13. *Geer v. Connecticut*, 161 U.S. 519 (1896). More controversially, the *Geer* decision also confirmed the states' capacity to ban the transport or shipping of illegally acquired animals out of state. As Justice Stephen Field wrote in his dissent (at 541), this position challenged the "absolute control of Congress in the regulation of interstate commerce, unimpeded by any state authority" (at 541).

14. T. S. Palmer, *Chronology and Index of the More Important Events in American Game Protection 1776–1911* (Washington, D.C.: Government Printing Office, 1912); T.

S. Palmer, *Legislation for the Protection of Birds Other Than Game Birds* (Washington, D.C.: Government Printing Office, 1902); Davis, *Sportsmen United*, 13–15.

15. For the establishment of the first fish commissions, see John T. Cumbler, "The Early Making of an Environmental Consciousness: Fish, Fisheries Commissions, and the Connecticut River," *Environmental History Review* 15 (1991): 73–91; William D. Bryan, "Piscatorial Politics: Fishery Regulation and the Economic Future of Rhode Island, 1869–1872," *New England Quarterly* 84 (2011): 444–72; Richard R. Wescott, "Early Conservation Programs and the Development of the Vacation Industry in Maine, 1865–1900," *Maine Historical Quarterly* 27 (1987): 3–7.

16. Trefethen, *American Crusade for Wildlife*, 107.

17. For some accounts of New England town-meeting governments, see Lyndon Oak, *History of Garland, Maine* (Dover, Me.: Observer Publishing, 1912); C. O. Parmenter, *History of Pelham, Massachusetts* (Amherst, Mass.: Carpenter and Morehouse, 1898); William A. Benedict and Hiram A. Tracy, *History of the Town of Sutton, Massachusetts* (Worcester, Mass.: Sanford, 1878); Evan W. Woollacott, *The Gavel and the Book: The Simsbury Town Meeting, 1670–1986* (Canaan, N.H.: Phoenix, 1987). For the relative powers of town-meeting governments and counties elsewhere in the North, see Philip L. White, *Beekmantown, New York: Forest Frontier to Farm Community* (Austin: University of Texas Press, 1979), chaps. 9–12; Merle Curti et al., *The Making of an American Community: A Case Study of Democracy in a Frontier County* (Stanford, Calif.: Stanford University Press, 1959), chaps. 10–13; James Bryce, *The American Commonwealth*, ed. Gary L. McDowell (Indianapolis: Liberty Fund, 1995), 1: 538–48; Albert Shaw, *Local Government in Illinois*, Johns Hopkins University Studies in Historical and Political Science, ed. Herbert B. Adams, 1st ser. (Baltimore: Press of the Friedenwald Co., 1883), 1, no. 3, 5–19; Edward W. Bemis, *Local Government in Michigan and the Northwest*, Johns Hopkins University Studies in Historical and Political Science 1st ser., 1, 5 (Baltimore: Johns Hopkins University Press, 1883), 5–25. It should be noted, however, that in some states rural townships lacked town-meeting government, and instead elected township officers. See, for example, Albert Shaw, *Local Government in Pennsylvania*, Johns Hopkins University Studies in Historical and Political Science, ed. Herbert B. Adams, 1st ser. 1, 3 (Baltimore: Johns Hopkins University Press, 1893), 20–37.

18. For an overview of local government in the South, see Charles S. Sydnor, *The Development of Southern Sectionalism, 1819–1848* (Baton Rouge: Louisiana State University Press, 1948), chap. 2; Bryce, *The American Commonwealth*, 1: 531–32, 537–38. For more detailed examinations of how southern county government functioned, see Robert M. Ireland, *The County Courts in Antebellum Kentucky* (Lexington: University Press of Kentucky, 1972); Robert M. Ireland, *Little Kingdoms: The Counties of Kentucky, 1850–1891* (Lexington: University Press of Kentucky, 1977), chaps. 1, 2; Steven Hahn, *The Roots of Southern Populism: Yeoman Farmers and the Transformation of the Georgia Upcountry, 1850–1890* (New York: Oxford University Press, 1983), 91–99.

19. Reiger, *American Sportsmen and the Origins of Conservation*, chaps. 2–7; Davis, *Sportsmen United*, 1–8.

20. Peterson, "The History of Wild Life Conservation in Michigan," 73–74; "The Michigan Association," *Forest and Stream*, 2 February 1882, 8. See also "Meetings of Game Societies," *Forest and Stream*, February 3, 1881, 10.

21. "Game Protection: The Game Law Problem Solved," *Forest and Stream*, November 20, 1879, 831; "Trespass and Game Laws," *Forest and Stream*, May 7, 1874, 195; "Central Pennsylvania," *Forest and Stream*, May 7, 1885, 290.

22. "Response to a Would-Be Game Protector," *Forest and Stream*, July 31, 1879, 510.

23. Stanley D. Casto, "Texas Sportsmen and the Conservation of Bird Life, 1890–1915," *East Texas Historical Journal* 44, 1 (2006): 10.

24. Evadene Burris Swanson, "The Use and Conservation of Minnesota Game, 1850–1900," Ph.D. dissertation, University of Minnesota, 1940, 243–51; *The Virginia Fish and Game Protective Association to the People of Virginia* (Richmond, Va.: Clemmit and Jones, 1878), 9; "The Connecticut Association," *Forest and Stream*, September 27, 1888; "Fish Protection in Connecticut," *Forest and Stream*, June 13, 1889, 423; "Connecticut Law Breakers," *Forest and Stream*, April 24, 1890, 273; "Protecting Connecticut Trout," *Forest and Stream*, June 26, 1890, 455; "Grouse Chokers," *Forest and Stream*, April 23, 1891, 271. It is unclear from the CAFSPGF accounts as to the source of its detectives' power to arrest. However, it would not have been unusual for local sheriffs to deputize their detectives for this purpose.

25. Stuart McIver, *Death in the Everglades* (Gainesville: University Press of Florida, 2003), 144–47; Stuart McIver, "Death of a Bird Warden," *South Florida History* 29 (Fall 2001): 20–27.

26. "Trespass and Game Laws," *Forest and Stream*, May 7, 1874, 195; Edwyn Sandys, "The Game Field," *Outing* (March 1902): 738; "The Delaware Game Outlook," *Forest and Stream*, October 14, 1905, 313; Oliver H. Orr, *Saving American Birds: T. Gilbert Pearson and the Founding of the Audubon Movement* (Gainesville: University Press of Florida, 1992), 109, 113–14, 119–32, 173, 179. For more on the development of humane societies and juvenile courts in providing for animal and child welfare, see Pearson and Smith, and Nackenoff and Sullivan, this volume.

27. S. A. Goodwin (?), *Prohibition Impossible Through a Separate Party and Why*, undated pamphlet, box 3, Howard Hyde Russell Papers, Bentley Historical Library, University of Michigan, 14–15.

28. McIver, *Death in the Everglades*, 163–64; McIver, "Death of a Bird Warden," 26–27. Of course, not every private regulator risked life and limb; many associations hired private detectives to do their dirty work. Detectives cost money, however, and needed to be closely monitored to ensure they didn't undermine the group's mission.

29. Clemens, "Lineages of the Rube Goldberg State," 194–200.

30. "Trespass and Game Laws," *Forest and Stream*, May 7, 1874, 195.

31. Swanson, "The Use and Conservation of Minnesota Game," 244–50; "Winter

Talks on Summer Pastimes," *Forest and Stream*, January 25, 1883, 509; "Snap Shots," *Forest and Stream*, November 29, 1888, 361.

32. "Game Protection," *Forest and Stream*, March 2, 1876, 57; "Trespass and Game Laws," *Forest and Stream*, May 7, 1874, 195.

33. Peterson, "The History of Wild Life Conservation in Michigan," 81–85. See also Swanson, "The Use and Conservation of Minnesota Game," 208–17, 222–26.

34. See, e.g., "Salmon Breeding," *Hartford Daily Courant*, February 7, 1871, 2; "The Influx of Shad into the Connecticut and Hudson," *New London Democrat*, June 24, 1871, 2; "Fish Culture: The Work of the Connecticut Commission," *New Haven Register*, July 31, 1880, 1; "Cannot Be Done," *New Haven Register*, July 26, 1881, 4.

35. "Game Laws to be Enforced," *New Haven Register*, September 7, 1887, 4; "Letter 5," *Forest and Stream*, August 30, 1888, 106; "Connecticut Farmers and Sportsmen," *Forest and Stream*, August 16, 1888, 65; "The Connecticut Association," *Forest and Stream*, September 6, 1888, 125; A. C. Collins, "Game Protection," *Outing* (December 1889): 203; "Drop a Dollar in the Slot," *Forest and Stream*, December 5, 1889, 389; "The Fishery Quarrel," *New Haven Register*, April 25, 1890, 4; "Fishculture: More About Connecticut Shad," *Forest and Stream*, February 12, 1891, 69; "Connecticut Birds," *Forest and Stream*, August 6, 1891, 44; "The Shad Bone of Contention," *New Haven Register*, January 10, 1895, 2; "Mr. Follett's Romance," *New Haven Register*, May 2, 1894, 1; "No Trace of Follett," *New Haven Register*, May 4, 1894, 1; "Advice to a Fish Commissioner," *New Haven Register*, May 5, 1994, 2; "For Netting Trout," *Boston Daily Journal*, January 30, 1895, 2; "Five Minutes Enough," *New Haven Register*, March 29, 1895, 1; "The Connecticut Fish Commission," *Forest and Stream*, May 13, 1899, 372; "Connecticut's Misfortune," *Forest and Stream*, May 13, 1899, 1.

36. Joe Kosack, *The Pennsylvania Game Commission: 200 Years of Wildlife Conservation* (Harrisburg: Pennsylvania Game Commission, 1995), chap. 3; Wescott, "Early Conservation Programs and the Development of the Vacation Industry in Maine," 7–8.

37. Louis S. Warren, *The Hunter's Game: Poachers and Conservationists in Twentieth-Century America* (New Haven, Conn.: Yale University Press, 1997), chap. 1, 49; *Annual Report of the Game Commissioners of the State of Pennsylvania, 1906* (Harrisburg, Pa.: Harrisburg Publishing, 1907), 11–12; *Annual Report of the Game Commissioners of the State of Pennsylvania, 1908* (Harrisburg, Pa.: Harrisburg Publishing, 1909), 25–27; Kosack, *The Pennsylvania Game Commission*, 32. Apparently the Game Commission was later able to secure public funds to reimburse the costs accrued from the Houk case. See *Annual Report of the Game Commissioners of the State of Pennsylvania, 1908*, 31.

38. *Seventh Annual Meeting of the West Virginia Forest, Fish and Game Protective Association Held at Minnehaha Springs, W.VA., November 5th and 6th, 1913* (Charleston, W.Va.: Union Publishing, 1913), 100–102.

39. Henry Chase, *Game Protection and Propagation in America* (Philadelphia: Lippincott, 1913), 97–100; T. S. Palmer, *Federal Game Protection: A Five Years' Retrospect* (Washington, D.C.: USDA, 1906), 552; Kosack, *Pennsylvania Game Commission*, 23–44;

Warren, *Hunter's Game*, 56–57; *Annual Report of the Game Commissioners of the State of Pennsylvania, 1913* (Harrisburg, Pa.: William Stanley Ray, 1914), 13; *Annual Report of the Game Commissioners of the State of Pennsylvania, 1914* (Harrisburg, Pa:. William Stanley Ray, 1915), 14–16.

40. H. Kenneth Bechtel, *State Police in the United States: A Socio-Historical Analysis* (Westport, Conn.: Greenwood Press), chaps. 2–8; *Annual Report of the Game Commissioners of the State of Pennsylvania, 1907* (Harrisburg, Pa.: Harrisburg Publishing, 1907), 14–16.

41. Peterson, "The History of Wild Life Conservation in Michigan," chaps. 1–3; Wescott, "Early Conservation Programs and the Development of the Vacation Industry in Maine," 2–13; Mark H. Davis, "Market Hunters vs. Sportsmen on the Prairie: The Case of William Kerr and Robert Poole," *Minnesota History* 60 (2006): 52; Swanson, "The Use and Conservation of Minnesota Game," 205.

42. Warren, *The Hunter's Game*, chap. 2; Kosack, *The Pennsylvania Game Commission*, 35–37, 44–49, 58–63, chap. 12; "Endorse the Migratory Bill," *Forest and Stream*, August 1917, 370; Kurkpatrick Dorsey, *The Dawn of Conservation Diplomacy: U.S.-Canadian Wildlife Protection Treaties in the Progressive Era* (Seattle: University of Washington Press, 1998), 222; Trefethen, *An American Crusade for Wildlife*, 157–58.

43. Trefethen, *An American Crusade for Wildlife*, 145–48; Dorsey, *The Dawn of Conservation Diplomacy*, 169–72; Davis, *Sportsmen United*, 16; Karel Bicha, "Spring Shooting: An Issue in the Mississippi Flyway, 1887–1913," *Journal of Sport History* 5 (1978): 65–74.

44. Dorsey, *The Dawn of Conservation Diplomacy*, chaps. 1–3 (quotation on p. 77).

45. Dean C. Allard, *Spencer Fullerton Baird and the U.S. Fish Commission* (New York: Arno, 1978), 64–131; Jennifer Corinne Browne, "'The Gamest Fish That Swims': Management of the Big Hole River Fishery in Montana," *Pacific Northwest Quarterly* 97 (2006): 251–70; Reiger, *American Sportsmen and the Origins of Conservation*, 79–87.

46. Carpenter, *The Forging of Bureaucratic Autonomy*, chaps. 2, 6. Julian Zelizer points out this weakness in his review of Carpenter's book. See his "Entrepreneurial Bureaucrats," *Reviews in American History* 31 (2003): 63.

47. Keir B. Sterling, "Builders of the U.S. Biological Survey, 1885–1890," *Journal of Forest History* 33 (1989): 180–87; Keir B. Sterling, *Last of the Naturalists: The Career of C. Hart Merriam* (New York: Arno, 1977), chaps. 3–8; Jenks Cameron, *The Bureau of Biological Survey: Its History, Activities and Operations* (Baltimore: Johns Hopkins University Press, 1929), 19–35.

48. Sterling, "Builders of the U.S. Biological Survey," 180–87; Sterling, *Last of the Naturalists*, 66, 280–82; Cameron, *The Bureau of Biological Survey*, 38–43; Wilfred H. Osgood, *Biographical Memoir of Clinton Hart Merriam* (Washington, D.C.: National Academy of Sciences, 1945), 15–16.

49. Although Merriam was not particularly successful at securing financial support for the Survey and eventually lost control of its mission, it should be noted that he had enough support in Congress to guide the agency from an office in a division to its own

division, and finally to status as a bureau. In that sense, Merriam could be construed as successful in expanding his department's autonomy in the long run. See Sterling, *Last of the Naturalists*, chaps. 6–8.

50. W. L. McAtee, "In Memoriam: Theodore Sherman Palmer," *The Auk* (July 1956): 366–77; Sterling, "Builders of the U.S. Biological Survey," 182–83.

51. Dorsey, *The Dawn of Conservation Diplomacy,* chaps. 6, 7.

52. Mason, "Out of Fashion," 1–14; Poole, "The Women of the Early Florida Audubon Society," 297–323; Merchant, "Women of the Progressive Conservation Movement," 69–73; Dorsey, *The Dawn of Conservation Diplomacy*, 180–83, 222.

53. "A New Game Protective Association," *Forest and Stream*, September 30, 1911, 518; "American Game Protective and Propagation Association," *Forest and Stream*, December 23, 1911, 1904; "Work of the New Protective Association," *Forest and Stream*, January 13, 1912, 48; "Migratory Game Birds," *Forest and Stream*, March 9, 1912, 308; T. S. Palmer, "Game Bills Now Pending in Congress," *Forest and Stream*, December 21, 1912, 786; "McClean Bill Passes," *Forest and Stream*, March 8, 1913, 304; "Vermont Fish and Game League," *Forest and Stream*, February 28, 1914; Dorsey, *The Dawn of Conservation Diplomacy*, 185–88, 194–212, 218–30; Trefethen, *An American Crusade for Wildlife*, 151–52.

54. *Colman's Rural World*, July 3, 1913, 8. Other examples include "Bird Protection Law," *Colman's Rural World*, April 15, 1915, 14; "When the Cream Test Varies," *Indiana's Farmer Guide*, February 16, 1918, 16; "Effect of Bird Law," *Indiana's Farmer Guide*, May 10, 1919, 6.

55. Dorsey, *Dawn of Conservation Diplomacy*, 221–24, 228; Poole, "Women of the Early Florida Audubon Society," 297–323.

56. See Walter Wheeler Cook, "What Is the Police Power?" *Columbia Law Review* 7 (1907): 322–36; *U.S. v. DeWitt*, 76 U.S. (9 Wall) 41 (1869); *U. S. v. E. C. Knight Co.*, 156 U.S. 1 (1895).

57. Dorsey, *The Dawn of Conservation Diplomacy*, 198–201. For cases where states argued that they had the sole power to control the animals within their borders, see *State v. Sawyer*, 113 Me. 458 (1915); *State v. McCullagh*, 96 Kan. 786 (1915); *State v. Carey*, 39 S.D. 524 (1917).

58. Trefethen, *An American Crusade for Wildlife*, 131.

59. Palmer, *Federal Game Protection*, 541–48; Orr, *Saving American Birds*, 25, 84, 238; "The Lacey Act," *Forest and Stream*, January 25, 1902, 68; "Protection of Birds and Game," *Forest and Stream*, January 17, 1903, 52; Trefethen, *An American Crusade for Wildlife*, 131–36; "The Audubon Bird Law," *Forest and Stream*, July 15, 1905, 1; William Dutcher et al., "The Protection of Birds," *The Friend: A Religious and Literary Journal*, December 16, 1905, 182.

60. "The Lacey Act," *Forest and Stream*, January 25, 1902, 68.

61. Dorsey, *Dawn of Conservation Diplomacy*, 183–88; Palmer, *Federal Game Protection*, 554–56; Trefethen, *An American Crusade for Wildlife*, 148–53. The Weeks-McLean Act also prohibited importation of wild bird feathers for use in women's fashion.

62. "A Federal Game Law," *Forest and Stream*, December 10, 1904, 492; George Shiras III, "Federal Protection of Wildfowl," *Forest and Stream*, November 24, 1906, 815; Dorsey, *Dawn of Conservation Diplomacy*, 183–88.

63. "A Long Step Forward," *Forest and Stream*, February 1, 1913, 144; "McClean Bill Passes," *Forest and Stream*, March 8, 1913, 304; T. S. Palmer, "Game Legislation of the 62nd Congress," *Forest and Stream*, March 22, 1913, 367; N. L. Chapin, "Live Notes from the Field," *Forest and Stream*, June 13, 1914, 791; Dorsey, *The Dawn of Conservation Diplomacy*, 185–88; Trefethen, *An American Crusade for Wildlife*, 151–53.

64. *U.S. v. Shauver*, District Court, E.D., Arkansas Jonesboro Division 214 F. 154 (1914); Woodrow Wilson, "Regulations for the Protection of Migratory Birds," *Forest and Stream*, October 11, 1913, 463; "Two Decisions on the Migratory Bird Law," *Forest and Stream*, July 11, 1914, 46; "Letter from William T. Hornaday," *Forest and Stream*, July 11, 1914, 46; Dorsey, *The Dawn of Conservation Diplomacy*, 198–201; Bicha, "Spring Shooting: An Issue in the Mississippi Flyway," 65–74; Mark Cioc, *The Game of Conservation: International Treaties to Protect the World's Migratory Animals* (Columbus: University of Ohio Press, 2009), 70–71.

65. For the perspective that a constitutional amendment might be necessary to impose national bird regulations, see Sydney G. Fisher, "An Open Letter to Congressman Lacey," *Forest and Stream*, June 30, 1906, 1032; "Conservation in New York State," *Forest and Stream*, December 27, 1913; Herbert K. Job, "The Problem of the Wildfowl," *Forest and Stream*, February 21, 1914, 240; "Address of Senator George P. McLean," *Forest and Stream*, October 24, 1914, 528; "Protecting Migratory Birds," *Forest and Stream*, September 1915, 544.

66. Progressive reformers would ultimately secure four amendments to the U.S. Constitution: the Sixteenth Amendment (authorizing the income tax), the Seventeenth Amendment (direct election of U.S. senators) the Eighteenth Amendment (national prohibition), and the Nineteenth Amendment (women's suffrage).

67. Dorsey, *The Dawn of Conservation Diplomacy*, chaps. 2, 5, 187–88, 191–98, 201; Cioc, *The Game of Conservation*, 71; "A World-Wide Campaign," *Youth's Companion*, April 24, 1913, 218; Chandler P. Anderson, "The Extent and Limitations of the Treaty-Making Power Under the Constitution," *American Journal of International Law* 1 (1907): 636–70; Chase, *Game Protection and Propagation*, chap. 8; "Validity of the Migratory Bird Treaty," *Central Law Journal* 90 (January 1919): 19; Chandler P. Anderson, "The Extension of Congressional Jurisdiction by the Treaty-Making Power," *American Journal of International Law* 14 (1920): 400–402.

68. Chase, *Game Protection and Propagation*, chap. 8; "Fact and Comment," *Youth's Companion*, March 19, 1914, 150; "No Spring Slaughter," *Forest and Stream*, October 1916, 1192; William T. Hornaday, *The Statement of the Permanent Wildlife Protection Fund, Volume 2, 1915–1916* (New York: Permanent Wildlife Protection Fund, 1917), 2, 127–43; Dorsey, *The Dawn of Conservation Diplomacy*, 234–35.

69. George A. Lawyer, *Federal Protection of Migratory Birds* (Washington, D.C.: U.S. Department of Agriculture, 1918), 7–10; Chase, *Game Protection and Propagation*, chap.

8 (quotation on pp. 73–74); Hornaday, *The Statement of the Permanent Wildlife Protection Fund*, 130–38 (quotation on p. 138); Dorsey, *The Dawn of Conservation Diplomacy*, chap. 8; Cioc, *The Game of Conservation*, 73–78.

70. *Missouri v. Holland*, 252 U.S. 416 (1920); G. Edward White, *The New Deal and the Constitution* (Cambridge, Mass.: Harvard University Press, 2002), 53–60.

71. *Missouri v. Holland*, 252 U.S. 416 (1920); White, *The New Deal and the Constitution*, 53–60.

72. R. Alton Lee, "The Eradication of Phossy Jaw: A Unique Development of Federal Police Power," *The Historian* 29 (November 1966): 1–28; Kathleen S. Sullivan, "Marriage and Federal Police Power," *Studies in American Political Development* 20 (2006): 45–56.

73. Julie Novkov, "Historicizing the Figure of the Child in Legal Discourse: The Battle over the Regulation of Child Labor," *American Journal of Legal History* 44 (2000): 369–404.

74. Dorsey, *The Dawn of Conservation Diplomacy*, 234–36.

75. Barry Cushman, *Rethinking the New Deal Court: The Structure of a Constitutional Revolution* (New York: Oxford University Press, 1998), 139–54; *Swift and Co. v. United States*, 196 U.S. 375 (1905).

76. *Missouri v. Holland*, 252 U.S. 416 (1920).

77. Many thanks to Jeremy Rabkin for suggesting this as a possible way of understanding Holmes's jurisprudence.

78. See, for example, *Lincoln v. United States/Warner, Barnes and Co., Ltd. v. United States*, 197 U.S. 419 (1905); *Kawananakoa v. Polyblank*, 205 U.S. 349 (1907); *Maria Francisca O'Reilly de Camara, Countess of Buena Vista, v. Brooke, Major General, U.S.A.*, 209 U.S. 45 (1907); *Reavis v. Fianza*, 215 U.S. 16 (1909); *Carino v. Insular Government of the Philippine Islands*, 212 U.S. 449 (1909); *Tiaco v. Forbes*, 228 U.S. 549 (1913); *Panama Railroad Co. v. Bosse*, 249 U.S.41 (1918).

79. In *American Banana Co. v. United Fruit Co.*, 213 U.S. 347 (1909), for instance, Holmes refused to expand the jurisdiction of the U.S. courts to hear a case that arose out of a controversy in which the alleged events occurred on Panamanian soil.

80. G. Edward White, "The Transformation of the Constitutional Regime of Foreign Relations," *Virginia Law Review* 85 (1999): 62–76.

81. Sterling, "Builders of the U.S. Biological Survey," 184–85; Dorsey, *The Dawn of Conservation Diplomacy*, 192–98.

Chapter 6. The House That Julia (and Friends) Built: Networking the Chicago Juvenile Court

The authors would like to thank Linnet Davis-Stermitz '12 from Swarthmore College, who assisted with archival work in Chicago and with additional aspects of this research, and Swarthmore student Minh-Duyen Nguyen '13 for research assistance. We would also like to thank Kristi Andersen, Pamela Brandwein, Eileen McDonagh, Julie Novkov, Patricia Strach, Dara Strolovitch, and the anonymous reviewers from the University of Pennsylvania Press for comments on earlier versions of this chapter.

Finally, we would like to thank Michael Kappeler, Web UI specialist with Swarthmore College's Information Technology Services, and Swarthmore graduate David Selassie Bampo Opoku '12 for preparation of the figure that appears in this chapter.

1. The phrase is Stephen Skowronek's from *Building a New American State: The Expansion of National Administrative Capacities 1877–1920* (Cambridge: Cambridge University Press, 1982); Theda Skocpol's *Protecting Soldiers and Mothers* is an exception to the characterization of the literature as state-centered: *Protecting Soldiers and Mothers: The Political Origins of Social Policy in the United States* (Cambridge, Mass.: Belknap Press of Harvard University Press, 1992).

2. Daniel P. Carpenter, *The Forging of Bureaucratic Autonomy: Reputations, Networks, and Policy Innovation in Executive Agencies, 1862–1928* (Princeton, N.J.: Princeton University Press, 2001), 6.

3. Brian Balogh, *A Government Out of Sight: The Mystery of National Authority in Nineteenth-Century America* (Cambridge: Cambridge University Press, 2009), 354–55, 354.

4. Carpenter, *The Forging of Bureaucratic Autonomy*; Anne Meis Knupfer, "Professionalizing Probation Work in Chicago, 1900–1935," *Social Service Review* 73 (December 1999): 478–95.

5. David Tanenhaus, *Juvenile Justice in the Making* (New York: Oxford University Press, 2004); Michael Willrich, *City of Courts: Socializing Justice in Progressive Chicago* (New York: Cambridge University Press, 2003), Elizabeth Clapp, *Mothers of All Children: Women Reformers and the Rise of Juvenile Courts in Progressive Era America* (University Park: Pennsylvania State University Press, 1998); Victoria Getis, *The Juvenile Court and the Progressives* (Urbana: University of Illinois Press, 2000).

6. Elisabeth S. Clemens, "Lineages of the Rube Goldberg State: Building and Blurring Public Programs, 1900–1940," in *Rethinking Political Institutions*, ed. Ian Shapiro, Stephen Skowronek, and Daniel Galvin (New York: NYU Press, 2006), 193.

7. Paula Baker, "The Domestication of Politics: Women in American Political Society, 1780–1920," *American Historical Review* 89, 3 (June 1984): 620–47.

8. Clemens, "Lineages of the Rube Goldberg State," 190.

9. Carol Nackenoff, "Gendered Citizenship: Alternative Narratives of Political Incorporation in the United States, 1875–1925," in *The Liberal Tradition in America*, ed. David F. Ericson and Louisa Bertch Green (New York: Routledge, 1999), 146 and passim; Jane Addams, "Philanthropy and Politics" (January 1913), 2140, Jane Addams Collection, Papers 1838–date, Series 3: Speeches and Publications by Jane Addams, 1878–1935, Box 5, Friends Historical Library, Swarthmore College.

10. Theda Skocpol, *Protecting Soldiers and Mothers*; David Beito, *From Mutual Aid to the Welfare State: Fraternal Societies and Social Services, 1890–1967* (Chapel Hill: University of North Carolina Press, 2000); Jennifer Klein, *For All These Rights: Business, Labor, and the Shaping of America's Public-Private Welfare State* (Princeton, N.J.: Princeton University Press, 2003); Robert Buroker, "From Voluntary Association to Welfare

State: The Illinois Immigrants' Protective League, 1908–1926," *Journal of American History* 58 (December 1971): 643–60; Patricia Strach and Kathleen S. Sullivan, "The State's Relations: What the Institution of Family Tells Us About Governance," *Political Research Quarterly* 64 (March 2011): 94–106.

11. Deborah A. Stone, "Causal Stories and the Formation of Policy Agendas," *Political Science Quarterly* 104 (Summer 1989): 281–300.

12. Kent Baxter, *The Modern Age: Turn-of-the-Century American Culture and the Invention of Adolescence* (Tuscaloosa: University of Alabama Press, 2008), 29; Tanenhaus, *Juvenile Justice in the Making*, 6.

13. "The President's Address," *Annual Report of the Illinois Humane Society. 1879–80*, Annual Reports, 1879–1899, Illinois Humane Society Records, Daley Library Special Collections, University of Illinois at Chicago (hereafter UIC).

14. Letter from Thomas Barrett, Lieut., Cottage Grove Station, City of Chicago Police Department, to Officer Dudley, Esq. Dated November 11, 1879, and Letter from Edward Ryan, City of Chicago Police Department, to Humane Society, dated September 29, 1879, Illinois Humane Society. Case Records, Children, dated 1879. Illinois Humane Society Records, UIC; Case Report dated July 27, 1888. Case Records, Children, July 1888. Illinois Humane Society Records, UIC; *Thirtieth Annual Report of The Illinois Humane Society*, 1899, 14, Illinois Humane Society Annual Reports, UIC.

15. *Annual Meeting of the Illinois Humane Society. Twelfth Annual Report. 1882*, 36. Annual Reports, 1879–1899, Illinois Humane Society Records, UIC. Nighttime employment worried reformers, who feared that stage children (especially girls) could become lured by the immorality and prostitution they encountered there. See Julie Novkov, "Historicizing the Figure of the Child in Legal Discourse: The Battle over the Regulation of Child Labor," *American Journal of Legal History* 44 (October 2000): 377.

16. Letter to Mr. Dudley dated Oct 2, 1879, Case Records, Children, dated 1879, Illinois Humane Society Records, UIC; *Annual Meeting of the Illinois Humane Society. Twelfth Annual Report. 1882*, 36–37.

17. Letter from Office of the Society for the Prevention of Cruelty to Children & Animals, Cincinnati, to President of the Illinois Humane Society. Dated August 11, 1879. Case Records, Children, dated 1879; Letters from the New York Society for the Prevention of Cruelty to Children to Secretary, Chicago P.C.C. dated January 31, 1886 and April 15, 1886. Case Records, Children, January 1886–September 1886; Case Report dated July 28, 1888. Case Records, Children, July 1888; Letter from Samuel Davidson, Western Pennsylvania Humane Society, to H.W. Clark, Esq., dated July 30, 1888. Case Records, Children, July 1888.

18. Susan J. Pearson and Kimberly K. Smith, "Developing the Animal Welfare State," this volume.

19. *Annual Meeting of the Illinois Humane Society. Fourteenth Annual Report. 1884*, 6. Annual Reports, 1879–1899, Illinois Humane Society Records, UIC.

20. *Annual Report of the Illinois Humane Society. Fourteenth Annual Report, 1884*, 15.

21. Elizabeth S. Scott, "The Legal Construction of Adolescence," *Hofstra Law Review* 29 (Winter 2000): 582; Grace Abbott, "Topical Abstract of Laws Governing the Trial and Disposition of Juvenile Offenders," quoting the language of the laws in Colorado (1903), Missouri (1909), Tennessee (1905) and Buffalo (1909), in Hastings H. Hart, Thomas Johnson Homer, and Grace Abbott, *Juvenile Court Laws in the United States: A Summary by States* (New York: Charities Publication Committee/Russell Sage, 1910), 122.

22. In *Ex parte Crouse*, 4 Whart. 9 (Pa. 1838), the Supreme Court of Pennsylvania argued that the public has an interest in the knowledge and virtue of its members.

23. Joan Gittens, *Poor Relations: The Children of the State of Illinois, 1818–1900* (Urbana: University of Illinois Press, 1994), 97–98, 107–9. The case, *People ex rel. O'Connell v. Turner*, 55 Ill. 280 (1870), was unusual in its rejection of the logic of *parens patriae* and had been largely circumvented in practice.

24. *Fourth Biennial Report of the Board of State Commissioners of Public Charities of the State of Illinois* (Springfield: D.W. Lusk, 1877), 151–53.

25. Gittens, *Poor Relations*, 98–99.

26. Kathleen S. Sullivan and Carol Nackenoff, "Bringing Courts Back In: Rethinking the Place of Courts in Progressive Era American Political Development," in process.

27. History from http://www.childrenshomeandaid.org/page.aspx?pid=251; http://www.childrenshomeandaid.org/ document.doc?id=53, accessed February 7, 2012.

28. Patricia Susan Hart, *A Home for Every Child: The Washington Children's Home Society in the Progressive Era* (Seattle: University of Washington Press, 2010), 21.

29. Paul Gerard Anderson, "Juvenile Justice: A Progressive Paradox," introduction to the New Edition of Timothy D. Hurley, *Origin of the Illinois Juvenile Court Law* (New York: AMS Press, 1977), n.p.

30. Suronda Gonzales, "Immigrants in Our Midst: Grace Abbott, the Immigrants' Protective League of Chicago, and the New American Citizenship, 1908–1924," Ph.D. dissertation, State University of New York at Binghamton, 2004, 18–19.

31. Michael Feldberg, ed., *Blessings of Freedom: Chapters in American Jewish History*. (American Jewish Historical Society, 2002, distr. KTAV Publishing House), 186. Low became director of the 7th Ward Bureau of the National Council of Jewish Women; this would be renamed the Bureau of Personal Service.

32. Michael Feldberg, ed., *Blessings of Freedom*. Mack and Addams were joined by Minnie Low. Entry on Minnie Low, 186–87.

33. Addams taught, did club work, and kept a hand in managing everything. See Louise W. Knight, *Citizen: Jane Addams and the Struggle for Democracy* (Chicago: University of Chicago Press, 2005), 238.

34. Knight, *Citizen*, 237–38. Dewey would become a member of the Hull-House Association board of trustees in 1897 and serve until 1903 (Knight, 478n30).

35. Willrich, *City of Courts*, 80; Clapp, *Mothers of All Children*, 21.

36. See Sophonisba Preston Breckinridge and Edith Abbott, *The Delinquent Child and the Home*, into Julia Lathrop (New York: Charities Publication Committee, 1912).

37. *Annals*, IV, 127–28. The recollection in January 1911 is by Mrs. Edith C.

Hancock. Florence Haythorn, the teacher, later became Mrs. Charles Jewell. The statement that the Reform Department "took charge of the Cook County Jail School in February, 1892" is made in a recollection by Mrs. Bradford Hancock on March 1, 1916. *Annals*, V, 178; Julia Lathrop, Memorandum, May 3, 1917, Lathrop, Julia, Correspondence and Memoranda, 1917, JPA Records Supplement I, UIC; Getis, *Juvenile Court*, 32–33.

38. Lathrop, Memorandum, May 3, 1917; Hon. Richard S. Tuthill, "The Juvenile Court Law in Cook County: What It Is, and What It Is Doing," speech to Chicago Congregational Club, March 19, 1900, 30, Research Center, Chicago History Museum (hereafter CHM); *First Annual Report of the John Worthy School of the City of Chicago for the Period ending Dec 31, 1900* (Chicago: Ryan & Hart, 1901).

39. Meeting Minutes, Chicago Woman's Club, 1896–1897, 118, CHM.

40. The Protective Agency for Women and Children, sponsored by the Chicago Woman's Club and founded in 1885, was the only agency that protected wives subjected to domestic violence and rape victims. It merged with the Bureau of Justice in 1896, and in 1905 became part of the Legal Aid Society of Chicago. Elizabeth Pleck, "Feminist Responses to 'Crimes against Women,' 1868–1896," *Signs* 8 (Spring 1983): 465–66. Meeting Minutes, Chicago Woman's Club, 1896–1897, 118, CHM.

41. *Annals*, V, 158, January 8, 1896. On the appeal, see Clapp, *Mothers of All Children*, 38–39, citing the Lucy Flower scrapbooks. *Annals*, V, 164–65.

42. *Annals*, VI, 190, notes dated November 15, 1899, and V, 177, referring to a decision made in April, 1898; Clapp, *Mothers of All Children*, 41.

43. Melanie Gustafson, *Women and the Republican Party, 1854–1924* (Urbana: University of Illinois Press: 2001), 99. Her appointment was part of a wave of appointments of women by Governor Altgeld.

44. Jane Addams, *My Friend, Julia Lathrop* (Urbana: University of Illinois Press, 2004), 48–61, 94.

45. Recollection of Edith C. Hancock dated January 1911. *Annals*, IV, 127.

46. Addams, *Twenty Years at Hull-House* (1910; New York: Macmillan, 1925), 323.

47. *Annals*, VI, 188. On Kelsey, see also Getis, *Juvenile Court and the Progressives*, 110.

48. *Annals*, V, 177.

49. Getis, *Juvenile Court and the Progressives,* 35; David S. Tanenhaus, "The Evolution of Juvenile Courts in the Early Twentieth Century: Beyond the Myth of Immaculate Construction," 42–74 in *Juvenile Justice in the Making,* ed. Margaret K. Rosenheim, Franklin E. Zimring, David S. Tanenhaus, and Bernardine Dohrn; Bernardine Dohrn, "The School, The Child, and the Court, 267–310 in *Juvenile Justice in the Making*; and Addams, *My Friend Julia Lathrop*, 95.

50. Addams, *My Friend, Julia Lathrop*, 95; Clapp, *Mothers of All Children*, 71.

51. Getis, *Juvenile Court and the Progressives*, 28; Florence Kelley, "Women and Social Legislation in the United States," *Annals of the American Academy of Political and Social Science* 56 (November 1914): 62–70; Letter from Mrs. Lucy L. Flower to Mrs.

Bowen, dated May 1917, and Lathrop, Memorandum in Lathrop, Julia, Correspondence and Memoranda, 1917, JPA Records Supplement I, UIC.

52. Anthony Platt, *The Child Savers: The Invention of Delinquency* (1969; Chicago: University of Chicago Press, 1977), 133; Getis, *Juvenile Court and the Progressives*, 38; Hastings Hart, *Preventive Treatment of Neglected Children* (New York: Charities Publication Committee, 1910), 252.

53. Harvey B. Hurd, *The revised statutes of the state of Illinois, 1901 comprising the "revised statutes of 1874," and all amendments thereto, together with the general acts of 1875, 1877, 1879, 1881, 1882, 1883, 1885, 1887, 1889, 1891, 1893, 1895, 1897, 1898, 1899 and 1901, being all the general statutes of the state in force on the first day of January, 1902* (Chicago: Chicago Legal News, 1901), 256, 171 §3. Cook County was the only county with a city meeting the population threshold, deliberately set so that this would be the case. Chicago activists wanted the court; other, smaller cities would not be compelled to organize one.

54. Helen Jeter, *The Chicago Juvenile Court* (Chicago: University of Chicago Libraries; reprinted from U.S. Department of Labor, Children's Bureau, Publication 104, 1922), 5.

55. "Resignations from the Ill. State Board of Charities," *Charities* 7 (August 17, 1901): 152–54.

56. Gustafson, *Women and the Republican Party*, 99; Addams, "Julia Lathrop's Services to the State of Illinois," *Social Service Review* 9 (June 1935): 191–211.

57. *Annual Report of the Illinois Humane Society. 1900*, 12–13; Annual Reports, 1900–1910, Illinois Humane Society Records, UIC. They also reported a decline in children begging on the streets.

58. On this last, and on Tuthill's inclusion of the CWC in an early organizational meeting of judicial and political officials, see Clapp, *Mothers of All Children*, 169.

59. Letter from Mrs. Lucy L. Flower to Mrs. Bowen dated May 1917; Lathrop, Julia, Correspondence and Memoranda, 1917, JPA Records Supplement I, UIC. Flower points out that Tuthill had the last laugh; while his colleagues were reluctant to accept the Juvenile Court position, he was the only Republican reelected in 1900, because, she says, of his work on the Juvenile Court.

60. Tuthill, "The Juvenile Court Law," in "Proceedings of the Illinois Conference of Charities at the State University at Champaign, November 14–15, 1900," in *Sixteenth Biennial Report of the Board of State Commissioners of Public Charities of the State of Illinois* (Springfield: Phillips, 1900), 336–37.

61. *Fifteenth Annual Report of the Juvenile Protective Association of Chicago. 1915*, 11; Annual Reports, 1907–1939, Supplement 1–4, Juvenile Protective Association Records, UIC.

62. *Fifteenth Annual Report of the Juvenile Protective Association of Chicago. 1915*, 11.

63. Jane Addams, *Twenty Years*, 324.

64. Gwenn Hoerr McNamee, "The Origin of the Cook County Juvenile Court," in *A Noble Social Experiment?: The First 100 Years of the Cook County Juvenile Court 1899–1999*, ed. Gwenn Hoerr McNamee (Chicago Bar Association, 1999), 20.

65. Addams, *Twenty Years*, 324.

66. Organization records pinpoint the founding as the moment when Stevens offered her services, though Bowen dates it a bit earlier: *Fifteenth Annual Report of the Juvenile Protective Association of Chicago. 1915*, 11. Bowen indicates Mrs. Flower as founder and Julia Lathrop as first president, saying she succeeded Lathrop in what she believes was 1900. Louise de Koven Bowen, *Growing Up with a City*, intro. Maureen A. Flanagan (1926; Urbana: University of Illinois Press, 2002), 104; *Annals*, VI, 192: "An account of the establishment of the Juvenile Court appears in William Hard's 'The Woman of Tomorrow,' which was first published in 1910, and dedicated 'To the Mothers of the World.' The chapter entitled 'Chicago Women as Citizens' was reprinted in pamphlet form by Mrs. Wilmarth and widely distributed." The quote, reprinted in the *Annals*, is from this source.

67. Articles of Association of the Juvenile Court Committee, March 26, 1904, Series I, Juvenile Court Committee-Organization and Purpose, 1904–1909, Juvenile Protective Association Papers, UIC. Other child-helping agencies with which they cooperated included the Compulsory Education Department and the state factory inspector.

68. Hart, *Preventive Treatment*, 210; Bowen, *Growing Up with a City*, 107; *Annual Report of the Juvenile Court Committee. 1906*, Annual Reports, 1907–1939, Supplement 1–4, Juvenile Protective Association Records, UIC. Its leadership included Mrs. Joseph Tilton Bowen as president; Julia Lathrop, vice-president; Mrs. Charles Henrotin, 2nd vice-president; Mrs. George Dean, 3rd vice-president. Its board of directors was comprised of Mrs. Bowen, Mrs. Tracy, Mrs. Henry Hooper, Miss Lathrop, Mrs. Walker, Mrs. George Bass, Mrs. Henrotin, Mrs. Dean, and Mrs. Harry Hart.

69. Bowen, *Growing Up with a City*, 113, 104–5 (hyphenation original).

70. Quotes from Julian W. Mack, "The Juvenile Court," *Harvard Law Review* 23, 104 (1909–10): 116, 119, 120.

71. Thomas Eliot, *The Juvenile Court and the Community* (New York: Macmillan, 1914), 173–75.

72. Knupfer, "Professionalizing Probation Work in Chicago," 480, 481 Later African American probation officers included Irene McCoy Gaines, prominent in the Federation of Women's Clubs, and industrial secretary of the Chicago YWCA. Ida B. Wells Barnett was among those calling attention to the problem of African American youth hanging out on street corners and in front of saloons at night and she, too, served as a probation officer for the Juvenile Court. A number of homes for dependent or needy children were established by the Colored Women's Clubs. The Phyllis Wheatley Home was first established in 1908. Its purpose was "to solve the problem of the colored girl or woman of good character who come [*sic*] to Chicago for the purpose of advancement, often without relatives, friends or money; to surround them with Christian influences, to elevate the standard of employment and to provide a social or community center." Gareth Canaan, "The Economic and Class Dimensions of Juvenile Delinquency in Black Chicago during the 1920s," in McNamee, *A Noble Social Experiment?* 41–42.

73. Canaan, "Economic and Class Dimensions of Juvenile Delinquency," 41–42, citing Anne Meis Knupfer, *Toward a Tenderer Humanity and a Nobler Womanhood: African American Women's Clubs in Turn-of-the-Century Chicago* (New York: NYU Press, 1996), 66, 173.

74. Julia Lathrop, "Development of the Probation System in a Large City," *Charities* 13, 15 (January 7, 1905): 345.

75. Anderson, "Juvenile Justice: a Progressive Paradox," introduction to Hurley, *Origin of the Juvenile Court Law*. Both Catholic and Protestant reformers wanted legal leverage over those lacking proper parental guardianship: "The key to the Bill was its unstated premise: approved placement corporations would be denominational." While an Illinois Supreme Court decision of 1888 had thwarted denominational transfer and care of such children, the premise that religious organizations would be involved in child placement remained part of reformers' efforts.

76. Hurley, *Origin of the Illinois Juvenile Court Law*, 38, sec. 18. This amendment was proposed by Timothy D. Hurley and Hastings H. Hart; Tanenhaus, *Juvenile Justice in the Making*, 22.

77. *Sixteenth Biennial Report of the Board of State Commissioners of Public Charities of the State of Ill*inois (Springfield: Phillips, 1900), 353. On the Court's responsibility for administration of the compulsory school attendance law, see "Report of Hon. Merritt W. Pinckney, Judge of Juvenile Court, Covering the Work of the Court from the Date its Organization to Dec. 1, 1913" (Cook County, Illinois, n.p.).

78. "Jetsam and Flotsam: Illinois Juvenile Court," *Central Law Journal* 54 (1902): 112.

79. Jeter, *Chicago Juvenile Court*, 6.

80. "Hope Hall," *The Church at Home and Abroad, by The General Assembly of the Presbyterian Church* 21 (1897), 160.

81. Dodds resigned from his position as family instructor at the parental school, and it is likely that he moved soon after. By 1906, California officials were praising the work he did as chief probation officer of the Los Angeles Juvenile Court. *School Journal* 64 (January 1902): 78; Judge H. H. Klamroth, "Probation Work," *Proceedings of the Fourth California State Conference Charities and Corrections* (1906): 116.

82. Sara Hart explains how she got involved: "One day, as Julia Lathrop and I were attending a court session, she whispered to me, 'How would you like to take care of the detention home?' I shrugged, 'I know nothing about it.' She retorted, 'Neither does anyone else!' I decided to do it." Sara Hart, *The Pleasure Is Mine: An Autobiography* (Chicago: Valentine-Newman, 1947), 99. Hart and her husband (a founder of clothier Hart, Schaffner and Marx) were also part of the leadership at Sinai Temple.

83. *Cook County Charity Service. Fiscal Year 1907*, 33, CHM; Letter from Detention Home Committee to Board of Commissioners, dated March 7, 1904, *Official Proceedings of the Board of Commissioners of Cook County for the Year 1903–1904* (Chicago: Henry Shepherd, 1904), 220.

84. Proceedings, Chicago Board of Education, January 31, 1906, 453.

85. Bowen, *Growing Up with a City*, 109–11.

86. Bowen, *Growing Up with a City*, 107. The JCC was once called before the court when accused of serving worms in the childrens' soup; it was vermicelli, unfamiliar to those who brought the charges (107).

87. Addams, *Twenty Years*, 355–56.

88. *Annual Report of the Juvenile Court Committee. 1906*, 1–5.

89. *Annual Report of the Juvenile Court Committee. 1906*, 1.

90. *Annual Report of the Juvenile Court Committee. 1906*, 1–5.

91. Tanenhaus, *Juvenile Justice in the Making*, 32–33. The JCC incorporated in 1904.

92. Bowen, *Growing Up with a City*, 115 (for $100,000 figure for JCC spending to 1907). *Annual Report of the Juvenile Protective Association, 1915–1916*; Annual Reports, 1907–1939, Juvenile Protective Association Records, UIC.

93. *Cook County Charity Service. Fiscal Year 1908*, 174; CHM. Cook County officers earned $85 a month (plus expenses) in comparison to $100 a month in many other court systems. Even in the early 1920s, probation officers earned a salary of $1,788 per year, and their field expenses needed to come out of their salary.

94. Jeter, *Chicago Juvenile Court,* 30.

95. Savilla Millis, *The Juvenile Detention Home In Relation to Juvenile Court Policy* (Chicago: 1927), 18.

96. *Cook County Charity Service. Fiscal Year 1905*, 13; CHM.

97. *Cook County Charity Service, Fiscal Year 1906*, 110–12; CHM.

98. *Cook County Charity Service. Fiscal Year 1907*, 29; CHM.

99. *Cook County Charity Service. Fiscal Year 1907*, 30.

100. Cook County, Illinois Juvenile Court, Report of Hon. Merritt W. Pinckney, Judge of Juvenile Court, Covering the Work of the Court from the Date of its Organization to Dec. 1, 1913. No publisher data. Provided by the University of Illinois Library at Urbana-Champaign.

101. Millis, *Juvenile Detention Home*, 18.

102. Jeter, *Chicago Juvenile Court*, 47.

103. Kathleen Jones, *Taming the Troublesome Child: American Families, Child Guidance, and the Limits of Psychiatric Authority* (Cambridge, Mass.: Harvard University Press, 1999), 41; William Healy, *The Individual Delinquent* (Boston: Little, Brown, 1918), 809.

104. Clapp, *Mothers of All Children*, 193.

105. Horace Kallen, intro.to Harry Barnard, *The Forging of an American Jew: The Life and Times of Judge Julian W. Mack* (New York: Herzl Press, 1974), xiv. The introduction is reprinted from Kallen's entry on Julian William Mack in the *American Jewish Year Book* 46 (1944).

106. *Chicago City Manual 1914* prepared by Francis Eastman (Chicago: Bureau of Statistics, 1914), 165. Cook County Juvenile Court, "Report of Hon. Merritt W. Pinckney, Judge of the Juvenile Court, Covering the Work of the Court from the Date of its Organization to Dec. 1, 1913" (n.p.).

107. Jeter, *Chicago Juvenile Court*, 48n14.

108. Herman Adler, "Organization of Psychopathic Work in the Criminal Courts," *Journal of the American Institute of Criminal Law and Criminology* 8 (September 1917): 373.

109. Jeter, *Chicago Juvenile Court*, 47. The name was changed to Institute for Juvenile Research in 1920.

110. Healy, *Individual Delinquent*, 810.

111. Paula Baker, "The Domestication of Politics," 620–47.

112. Articles of Incorporation, Juvenile Protective League, dated April 16, 1906, Series I, Juvenile Court Committee—Organization and Purpose, 1904–1909, Juvenile Protective Association Papers, UIC; Announcement, signed by Judge Mack and Henry Thurston, dated February 29, 1906. Executive Committee minutes, Feb. 1906–Dec. 1913, Supplement I, Juvenile Protective Association Records, UIC.

113. Minutes, March 10, 1906, Juvenile Protective Association, Supplement I, Executive Committee minutes, Feb. 1906–Dec. 1913, UIC.

114. Minutes, July 10, 1907, Executive Committee minutes, Feb. 1906–Dec. 1913. Supplement I, Juvenile Protective Association Records, UIC.

115. See Paul P. Van Riper, *History of the United States Civil Service* (Evanston, Ill.: Row, Peterson, 1958).

116. Jane Addams, "Julia Lathrop's Services to the State of Illinois," 200–201.

117. Julia Lathrop, "Development of the Probation System in a Large City," 346; Jane Addams, *Twenty Years*, 324–25; Bowen, *Growing Up with a City*, 115–17.

118. Examination for Chief Probation Officer held Jan. 1913, Evelina Belden Paulson Papers, Juvenile Court of Cook County, Illinois, case studies and reports, Feb. 1908–July 1918, Juvenile Protective Association Records, UIC.

119. Bowen, *Growing Up with a City*, 104–5; Knupfer, "Professionalizing Probation Work in Chicago," 480–81.

120. Joan Gittens, *Poor Relations*, 111. Gittens shows how certain responses (cited in Bowen, *Growing Up with a City*) made perfect sense from Catholic candidates. Figures from San Francisco, April 1–December 1, 1906, indicate that, of delinquents whose religion was known, 69 percent were Roman Catholic: "The Juvenile Court, City and County of San Francisco. A report" (San Francisco, 1906), calculated from raw data, 11.

121. Gittens, *Poor Relations*, 111.

122. Jeter, *Juvenile Court*, 7n33.

123. This assault on the court is covered fully by Tanenhaus, *Juvenile Justice in the Making*. Issues included abrogation of parental rights, whether the Juvenile Court was legal at all, giving probation officers improper authority, and violation of separation of church and state via county payments to religiously based orphan homes and industrial schools to which some of the court's children had been sent.

124. Jeter, *Chicago Juvenile Court*, 8; *Cook County Charity Service. Fiscal Year 1917*, 301, CHM.

125. "Women to Assist Court," ProQuest Historical Newspapers, *Chicago Tribune*, Feb. 14, 1906, 7.

126. "Women to Assist Court," 7. In 1906, 238 people volunteered to serve as friendly visitors; 76 withdrew their names, and the remaining volunteers handled 150 cases. Of these, 88 followed through with the tasks assigned. *Annual Report of the Juvenile Court Committee. 1906,* 17, Annual Reports, 1907–1939, Juvenile Protective Association Records, UIC.

127. Willrich, *City of Courts*, 120–22, 133–35; Bowen, *Growing Up with a City*, 126–29.

128. From Jean Norris, "A New Future for Women at Law," *Association Monthly* (June 1920): 287. By 1920, Georgiana Bullock was judge of the Children's Court in Los Angeles.

129. http://www.uic.edu/depts/lib/specialcoll/services/rjd/findingaids/MBartelmeb.html.

130. Another lawyer, Nellie Carlin, was appointed as her replacement as public guardian. Bartelme would go on to be elected to the Circuit Court of Cook County in 1923.

131. Gwen Hoerr McNamee, "The Bartelme Years," in McNamee, *A Noble Social Experiment?*, 67.

132. Kendall Burton, "Mother Knows Best: Mary Margaret Bartelme and the Chicago Juvenile Reform Movement," 23, Prepared for Women in the Legal Profession, Autumn 2002, Professor Barbara Babcock, http://www.docstoc.com/docs/30202422/MOTHER-KNOWS-BEST-MARY-MARGARET-BARTELME-AND-THE-CHICAGO, accessed May 11, 2013.

133. McNamee, "Bartelme Years," 66.

134. Burton, "Mother Knows Best," 25–26.

135. Jeter, *Chicago Juvenile Court*, 31.

136. *Annual Report of the Juvenile Court Committee, 1906*, 1, Annual Reports, 1907–1939, Juvenile Protective Association Records, UIC.

137. Clapp, *Mothers of All Children*, 141.

138. *Charities* 13, 11 (December 10, 1904): 275.

139. Judge Julian Mack and Judge Richard Tuthill from the Chicago Juvenile Court, and Robert Wilkin of the Brooklyn Juvenile Court, along with a number of other Juvenile Court judges, were on the subcommittee, as was Timothy Hurley. Clapp, *Mothers of All Children*, 143.

140. Gayle Gullet, *Becoming Citizens: The Emergence and Development of the California Women's Movement, 1880–1911* (Urbana: University of Illinois Press, 2000), 142.

141. "Probation Work," by Judge H. H. Klamroth, Pasadena, Proceedings of the Third California State Conference Charities and Correction (1904), 116.

142. Clapp, *Mothers of All Children*, 141–42.

143. Barnard, *Forging of an American Jew*, 70.

144. Thomas D. Eliot, "The Trend of the Juvenile Court," *Annals of the American Academy of Political and Social Science* 52 (March 1914): 149.

145. Grace Abbott, "A Topical Abstract of State Laws Governing the Trial and Disposition of Juvenile Offenders," in *Juvenile Court Laws in the United States*, part 2, 122.

146. *The Progress of Probation: Annual Report and Proceedings of the Eighth Annual Conference of the National Probation Association* (Albany: National Probation Association, 1916), 8. See also Horace Greeley, *The Tribune Almanac and Political Register* (New York: Tribune Association, 1914), 447.

147. *Progress of Probation*, 84–85.

148. *Proceedings of the Conference on the Care of Dependent Children Held at Washington, D.C. January 25, 26, 1909* (Washington, D.C.: Government Printing Office, 1909), 20–31.

149. Juvenile Court Standards (Washington, D.C., May 18, 1923), U.S. Department of Labor, Children's Bureau publication 121 (Washington: Government Printing Office, 1923), mchlibrary.info/history/chbu/20531-1923.PDF. See also Gilbert Geis, "Publicity and Juvenile Court Proceedings," *Crime & Delinquency* 4 (October 1958): 344–45.

150. Clapp, *Mothers of All Children*, 135–40, 137n17. Clapp states that at first Hurley advocated adoption of only certain aspects of the Illinois legislation, but by 1903 his publication was advocating adopting the same legislation.

151. Lincoln Steffens, "Ben B. Lindsey: The Just Judge," *McClure's Magazine* 27, 6 (October 1906): 563–82; 28, 1 (November 1906): 74–88; and 28, 2 (December 1906): 162–76.

152. Clapp, *Mothers of All Children*, 140.

153. *Charities* 13, 15 (January 7, 1905), esp. 323–59.

154. *Charities* 13, 15 (January 7, 1905), 329–37. Bates found that there were nineteen states with a system of probation in place, though not all of these states had separate juvenile courts.

155. Clarke A. Chambers, *Paul U. Kellogg and the Survey: Voices for Social Welfare and Social Justice* (Minneapolis: University of Minnesota Press, 1971), 53. On the history of these journals see also the Social Welfare History Project online, http://www.socialwelfarehistory.com/people/kellogg-paul-underwood/.

156. *The Child, the Clinic, and the Court: A Group of Papers*, by Jane Addams et al. (New York: New Republic, 1925). Published in cooperation with the Wieboldt Foundation. Addams notes (Introduction, 1) that the commemorative event was also the fifteenth anniversary of the first Psychopathic Institute.

157. *The Survey* 32 (April–September 1914). Survey Associates, Inc., was incorporated in October 1912. On the history, see also the Online Finding Aids for the Survey Associates Records, University of Minnesota Libraries, http://discover.lib.umn.edu/cgi/f/findaid/findaid-idx?c=umfa;cc=umfa;rgn=main;view=text;didno=sw0001.

158. Barnard, *Forging of an American Jew*, 70.

159. Julian Mack, "The Juvenile Court," 104–22. The Warren Court decision in *In re Gault et al.*, 387 U.S. 1 (1967), quoted Mack's view of *parens patriae* from this article at the same time the Court rejected some practices of the juvenile court reformers.

160. Northwestern's Dean Wigmore wrote about "Roscoe Pound's St. Paul Address of 1906: The Spark That Kindled the White Flame of Progress," in *Journal of the American Judicature Society* 20 (1937): 176. The insurgent law professors rallied to Pound's admonition that courts not act like miniature legislatures and to his attack on the judicial activism of the U.S. Supreme Court under chief justices Melville Fuller and Edward White; he said that "our administration of justice is not decadent. It is simply behind the times," quoted in N. E. H. Hull, *Roscoe Pound and Karl Llewellyn: Searching for an American Jurisprudence* (Chicago: University of Chicago Press, 1997), 65.

161. Willrich, *City of Courts*, 106–7, 107.

162. On Roscoe Pound's association with the Juvenile Court Committee and Hull-House, see Hull, *Roscoe Pound and Karl Llewellyn*, 72. For Pound's quote, Paul W. Alexander, "A Brief Reintroduction to the Juvenile Court," *American Bar Association Journal* 50 (1964): 353–56, 353.

163. Mary Jo Deegan, *Race, Hull-House, and the University of Chicago* (Westport, Conn.: Praeger, 2002), table 2.3, 36–37. On Emil Hirsch, see magazine.uchicago .edu/0004/ features/levi2.html.

164. Roscoe Pound, "Legislation as a Social Function," *American Journal of Sociology* 18 (May 1913): 767–68.

165. Before the School of Civics and Philanthropy was established as an independent school in 1908, Addams, Lathrop, and other reformers participated in the School of Social Economics created by Chicago Commons Settlement director Graham Taylor, and in the Extension Program of the University, which became the Social Science Center for Practical Training in Philanthropy and Social Work, with Lathrop becoming director of research in 1907. www.ssa.uchicago.edu/timeline.

166. Ssacentennial.uchicago.edu/history/. See also Barnard, *Forging of an American Jew*, 71, for Mack's membership on the board.

167. According to the SSA Centennial web page, Ssacentennial.uchicago.edu/ history, the board helped bring the school to Chicago. Barnard suggests Mack played a role: *Forging of an American Jew*, 71.

168. See Barnard, *Forging of an American Jew*, 71.

169. Edith Abbott, "Julia Lathrop and the Public Social Services," *Social Service Review*, quoted in Addams, *My Friend, Julia Lathrop*, 113; manuscript found in Jane Addams's papers after her 1935 death and copyrighted 1935, renewed 1963, introduction by Anne Firor Scott. On Lathrop's networks and the use she made of them in the Children's Bureau, see Jacqueline K. Parker and Edward M. Carpenter, "Julia Lathrop and the Children's Bureau: The Emergence of an Institution," *Social Service Review* 55, 1 (1981): 61–62.

170. Skocpol, *Protecting Soldiers and Mothers*, 495.

171. Breckinridge and Abbott, *The Delinquent Child and the Home.*

172. Sessions of National Conference of Charities and Correction, http://www.archive.org/ search.php?query=creator%3A%22National+Conference+of+Charities+and+Correction+%28U.S+.%29.+Session%22.

173. *Cook County Charity Service. Fiscal Year 1924*, 263–66. CHM

174. Gittens, *Poor Relations*, 123.

175. See Frank R. Baumgartner and Bryan D. Jones, *Agendas and Instability in American Politics* (Chicago: University of Chicago Press, 1993); John W. Kingdon, *Agendas, Alternatives, and Public Policies* (Boston: Little, Brown, 1984).

Chapter 7. Housing Reform and the Origins of Mortgage Redlining in the United States

The author is indebted to Carol Nackenoff, Julie Novkov, Marty Abravenel, Joe Valenti, Oscar Gonzales, Jessica Wang, Pamela Brandwein, and an anonymous reviewer for their comments on earlier drafts of this chapter. A version of this chapter was presented at the Policy History Conference, June 6–9, 2012. The views expressed here are mine alone and do not reflect those of the Department of the Treasury.

1. Marriner S. Eccles, *Beckoning Frontiers: Public and Personal Recollections* (New York: Knopf, 1951), 147–48.

2. Gertrude Sipperly Fish, "Housing Policy During the Great Depression," in *The Story of Housing*, ed. Gertrude S. Fish (New York: Macmillan, 1979), 201–2; see also David L. Mason, *From Building and Loans to Bail Outs: A History of the American Savings and Loan Industry 1831–1995* (Cambridge: Cambridge University Press, 2004), 94–97.

3. John M. Gaus and Leonard D. White, "Public Administration in 1934," *American Political Science Review* 29, 3 (June 1935): 443; C. Herman Pritchett, "The Paradox of the Government Corporation," *Public Administrative Review* 1, 4 (Summer 1941): 384–86.

4. Kenneth T. Jackson, *Crabgrass Frontier: The Suburbanization of the United States* (New York: Oxford University Press, 1984), 203; Richard Harris, *Building a Market: The Rise of the Home Improvement Industry, 1914–1960* (Chicago: University of Chicago Press, 2012), 190–91.

5. Charles Abrams, *Forbidden Neighbors: A Study of Prejudice in Housing* (New York: Harper, 1955), 155. In 1922, Ernest Fisher, the first FHA director of research, wrote in a book sponsored by the National Association of Real Estate Boards (NAREB) that "It is a matter of common observation that purchase of property by certain racial types is very likely to diminish the value of other property in the section."

6. Antero Pietila, *Not in My Neighborhood: How Bigotry Shaped a Great American City* (Chicago: Ivan R. Dee, 2010), 72–73; Jackson, *Crabgrass Frontier*, 208–9.

7. FHA, *Property Standards: Requirements for Mortgage Insurance Under Title II of*

the National Housing Act (Washington, FHA, 1936), 4: "*Mortgage insurance, therefore, may be made available only when a property is of a character which will not induce neighborhood blight or threaten to influence adversely the mortgage security in neighboring properties*" (emphasis original); racially restrictive covenants are explicitly endorsed in the *Underwriting Manual* (in the initial 1935 version), part 2, secs. 305, 309, 310, 312, 341.

8. Michael Jones-Correa, "The Origins and Diffusion of Racial Restrictive Covenants," *Political Science Quarterly* 115, 4 (Winter 2000–2001): 543–44.

9. My use of redlining differs somewhat from most other scholars who have assessed the role of the Home Owners' Loan Corporation (HOLC) and its numerous Residential Security Maps; see National Archives and Records Administration (NARA), RG 195, and the one remaining FHA Mortgage Security Map of Chicago, Ernest Burgess papers in the Archives of Regenstein Library at the University of Chicago. The FHA Chicago map was reproduced in the *Journal of Urban History*: see Jennifer Light, "Nationality and Neighborhood Risk and the Origins of FHA Underwriting," *Journal of Urban History* 36 (2010): 634–71. Indeed, Light emphasizes, as do most scholars, the ethnicity and racial composition of a neighborhood as the primary determinant of, in this case, FHA underwriting standards. See also Kevin Fox Gotham, *Race, Real Estate, and Uneven Development: The Kansas City Experience, 1900–2000* (Albany: State University of New York Press, 2002); Lizabeth Cohen, *Making a New Deal: Industrial Workers in Chicago, 1919–1939* (New York: Cambridge University Press, 1990), 276; Thomas J. Sugrue, *The Origins of the Urban Crisis: Race and Inequality in Postwar Detroit* (Princeton, N.J.: Princeton University Press, 1996), 43–44. Robert K. Nelson, "Race and Redlining in Richmond," http://americanpast.richmond.edu/holc/pages/intro, accessed March 25, 2011, writes: "There is little nuance to be found among the assessment surveys and the residential security map of Richmond, Virginia, produced for the Home Owners' Loan Corporation (HOLC) in 1937: in them race is everywhere and everywhere a determining factor." Other scholars—such as Jackson, *Crabgrass Frontier*, and Colin Gordon, *Mapping Decline: St. Louis and the Fate of the American City* (Philadelphia: University of Pennsylvania Press, 2010), and many others—take care to emphasize that HOLC's Residential Security Maps take many factors into account when they established their mortgage risk standards including the age, quality, upkeep, and amenities of the home as well as the race and ethnicity of residents. My use of redlining is more in concert with the approach by Jackson and Gordon—there was an array of reasons a neighborhood was redlined including race and ethnicity but the fundamental factor was the availability of mortgage insurance. As such, by redlining I mean the inability to secure conventional mortgage loans in specific communities, and the underlying cause, FHA unwillingness to extend mortgage insurance.

10. Gotham, *Race, Real Estate, and Uneven Development*, 64; Charles L. Nier, III, "The Shadow of Credit: The Historical Origins of Racial Predatory Lending and Its Impact upon African-American Wealth Accumulation," *University of Pennsylvania Journal of Law and Social Change* 2, 1 (2007–2008): 177–83; Abrams, *Forbidden Neighbors*,

159–66; Guy Stuart, *Discriminating Risk: The U.S. Mortgage Lending Industry in the Twentieth Century* (Ithaca, N.Y.: Cornell University Press, 2003), 79.

11. FHA, *Underwriting Manual: Underwriting and Valuation Procedure Under Title II of the National Housing Act* (Washington: Government Printing Office, 1935, 1936, 1938).

12. Robert D. Putnam, *Bowling Alone: The Collapse and Revival of American Community* (New York: Simon & Schuster, 2000); Theda Skocpol, "How Americans Became Civic," in Theda Skocpol and Morris. P. Fiorina (eds.), *Civic Engagement in American Democracy* (Washington, DC: Brookings Institution Press, 1999); Theda Skocpol, *Diminished Democracy: From Membership to Management in American Civic Life* (Norman: University of Oklahoma Press, 2003).

13. Ervin Miller, "The Character of Deposit Insurance in the United States," *Review of Insurance Studies*, vol. 1, 3 (Fall 1954): 80; FDIC, *A Brief History of Deposit Insurance in the United States* (Washington, D.C.: FDIC, 1998), 12–19; Linda M. Hooks and Kenneth J. Robinson, "Deposit Insurance and Moral Hazard," *Journal of Economic History* 62 (September 2002): 833; Eugene White, "Deposit Insurance," in *Reforming Financial Systems*, ed. Gerard Caprio Jr. and Dimitri Vittas (Cambridge: Cambridge University Press, 1997), 88–91.

14. Lendol Calder, *Financing the American Dream: A Cultural History of Consumer Credit* (Princeton: Princeton University Press, 1999), 184–206; Louis Hyman, *Debtor Nation* (Princeton, N.J.: Princeton University Press, 2011), 27–42.

15. James Ford, *Slums and Housing* (Cambridge, Mass.: Harvard University Press, 1936), esp. chaps. 14–17; Ford was executive director of Better Homes in America, Inc.; James Borchert, *Alley Life in Washington: Family, Community, Religion, and Folklife in the City, 1850–1970* (Urbana: University of Illinois Press, 1982); Carroll D. Wright, *The Slums of Baltimore, Chicago, New York, and Philadelphia* (Washington: Government Printing Office, 1894).

16. Lawrence Veiller, "Housing and Health," *Annals of the American Academy of Political and Social Science* 37 (March 1911): 13–15; Catherine Bauer, *Modern Housing* (Boston: Houghton Mifflin, 1934), 56–62, 141–46.

17. Roy Lubove, *The Progressives and the Slum* (Pittsburgh: University of Pittsburgh Press, 1963), 82–94.

18. Theda Skocpol, *Protecting Soldiers and Mothers: The Political Origins of Social Policy in the United States* (Cambridge, Mass.: Harvard University Press, 1992), 328–33, 432–45.

19. See Theodore M. Porter, *Trust in Numbers: The Pursuit of Objectivity in Science and Public Life* (Princeton, N.J.: Princeton University Press, 1995).

20. Ernest T. Trigg, "Housing and Building Conditions," *Annals of the American Academy of Political and Social Science* 89 (May 1920): 74; Herbert Hoover, "The Home as an Investment," in *Better Homes in America Plan Book for Demonstration Week October 9 to 14, 1922*, ed. Marie Meloney (Washington, D.C.: Better Homes for America).

21. Homer Hoyt, "The Housing Shortage and the Supply of Building Materials," *Annals of the American Academy of Political and Social Science* 89 (May 1920): 67–68.

22. George E. Roberts, "The Cause and Process of Inflation," *Annals of the American Academy of Political and Social Science* 89 (May 1920): 247–49; Columbia Law Review Association, "Statutes Relating to the Housing Shortage," *Columbia Law Review* 23 (June 1923): 583–84.

23. James R. Grossman, *Land of Hope: Chicago, Black Southerners, and the Great Migration* (Chicago: University of Chicago Press, 1989), 135–39; Abrams, *Forbidden Neighbors*, 20–26, 84–90; T. J. Woofter, Jr., *Negro Problems in Cities* (New York, Doubleday, Doran & Co., 1928), 28–30, 37–39; Otis Dudley Duncan and Beverly Duncan, *The Negro Population of Chicago* (Chicago: University of Chicago Press, 1957), 88–93, see especially the maps between 92–93.

24. William M. Tuttle, Jr., *Race Riot: Chicago in the Red Summer of 1919* (New York: Atheneum, 1972); Adam Cohen and Elizabeth Taylor, *American Pharaoh: Mayor Richard J. Daley, His Battle for Chicago and the Nation* (Boston, Little, Brown, 2000), 32–36.

25. James Ford, "Housing for War Workers Engaged on Army and Navy Contracts," *Annals of American Academy of Political and Social Science* 79 (September 1918): 270–74; William H. Ledbetter, "Public Housing: A Social Experiment Seeks Acceptance," *Law and Contemporary Problems* 32 (Summer 1967): 491–92.

26. Homer Hoyt, *100 Years of Land Values in Chicago* (Chicago: University of Chicago Press, 1933).

27. Kendrick A. Clements, *The Life of Herbert Hoover: Imperfect Visionary 1918–1928* (New York: Palgrave, 2010), 221–22; Trigg, "Housing and Building Conditions"; Herbert Hoover, "Memorandum on the Economic Situation, *Annals of the American Academy of Political and Social Science* 87 (January 1920): 106–11.

28. Steven E. Andrachek, "Housing in the United States: 1890–1929," in Fish, ed., *The Story of Housing*, 135.

29. Carol Aronovici, "United States Housing Corporation," *Journal of Sociology* 26 (May 1921): 788.

30. Steven E. Andrachek, "Housing in the United States: 1890–1929," 125–28; a similar split occurred among city planners, see Mel Scott, *American City Planning* (Berkeley: University of California Press, 1969), 316–27.

31. Carol Aronovici, *Housing the Masses* (New York: J. Wiley & Son, 1939), and *Housing and the Housing Problem* (Chicago: A. C. McClurg, 1920); Edith Elmer Wood, *Housing the Unskilled Wage Earner* (New York: Macmillan, 1919); Bauer, *Modern Housing*.

32. Mark I. Gelfand, *A Nation of Cities: The Federal Government and Urban America, 1933–1965* (New York: Oxford University Press, 1975), 107–12.

33. Peter Dreier, John Mollenkopf, and Todd Swanstrom, *Place Matters: Metropolitics for the Twenty-First Century* (Lawrence: University of Kansas Press, 2001), 102–20;

Douglas W. Rae, *City: Urbanism and Its End* (New Haven, Conn.: Yale University Press, 2003), 274–80; Gordon, *Mapping Decline*; Mark Gottdiener, *Planned Sprawl: Private and Public Interests in Suburbia* (Beverly Hills, Calif.: Sage, 1977).

34. Lawrence J. Vale, "The Ideological Origins of Affordable Homeownership Efforts," in *Chasing the American Dream: New Perspectives on Affordable Homeownership*, ed. William M. Rohe and Harry L. Watson (Ithaca, N.Y.: Cornell University Press, 2007) 20; Marc Weiss, "Marketing and Financing Home Ownership: Mortgage Lending and Public Policy in the United States," *Business and Economic History* 2nd ser. 18 (1987): 112.

35. Vale, "The Ideological Origins of Affordable Homeownership Efforts," 20.

36. Herbert Hoover, *The Memoirs of Herbert Hoover: The Cabinet and the Presidency* (New York: Macmillan, 1952), 92.

37. Hoover, *Memoirs*, 93–96.

38. David M. P. Freund, *Colored Property: State Policy and White Racial Politics in Suburban America* (Chicago: University of Chicago Press, 2007), 72–81.

39. Janet A. Hutchinson, "American Housing, Gender, and the Better Homes in America, 1922–1935" (Ph.D. dissertation, University of Delaware, 1989), 23–24, 31–32; Ellis W. Hawley, "Herbert Hoover, the Commerce Secretariat, and the Vision of the Associative State," *Journal of American History* 61 (June 1974): 117–18; Jean Hoff Wilson, *Herbert Hoover: Forgotten Progressive* (Boston: Little, Brown, 1975), 86–90.

40. Hutchinson, "American Housing," 22–23.

41. Hutchinson, "American Housing," 32–33, 50–51.

42. Marie Meloney, "The New Woman," *Delineator*, 1 November 1922, quoted in Karen E. Altman, "Consuming Ideology: The Better Homes in America Campaign," *Critical Studies in Mass Communication* 7 (1990): 288.

43. Vale, "The Ideological Origins of Affordable Homeownership Efforts," 20; Hutchinson, "American Housing," 32, 163–67.

44. Wilson, *Herbert Hoover: Forgotten Progressive*, 209–13.

45. Janet Hutchinson, "Building for Babbitt," *Journal of Policy History* 9 (April 1997): 187; Hawley, "Herbert Hoover, the Commerce Secretariat, and the Vision of the Associative State"; Gail Radford, *Modern Housing in America* (Chicago, University of Chicago Press, 1996), 51–52.

46. Calder, *Financing the American Dream*, 199–208; Butterick Publishing Company, *Midas Gold: A Study of Family Incomes, "Overselling" and Time-Payments as a Broadener of the Market* (New York: Butterick, 1925). The Introductory Essay is by Christine Frederick, a colleague of Meloney's at the *Delineator*.

47. Theda Skocpol, Marjorie Abend-Wein, Christopher Howard, and Susan Goodrich, "Women's Associations and the Enactment of Mothers' Pensions in the United State," *American Political Science Review* 87 (September 1993): 687. Women's magazines, including the *Delineator* and *Good Housekeeping* published emotional and detailed stories supporting the passage of mothers' pensions.

48. Hutchinson, "American Housing," 59–60.

49. "40,000 People Visit GFWC Model Home," *General Federation News* 4, 1–2 (August–September 1923): 1, 16.

50. Hutchinson, "American Housing," 101–4.

51. Mrs. W. B. (Marie) Meloney, *Better Homes in America*, 12–24.

52. Hutchinson, "American Housing," 101–3.

53. Mason, *From Buildings and Loans to Bail Outs*, 45–46.

54. Hutchinson, "American Housing," 62, 90.

55. Mary Bell Dickson Sherman, "President's Report," January 12, 1926, Mary Bell King Sherman Papers, 1924–1928 (Washington: GFWC):12. The GFWC committee conducting this project included representatives from the Commerce, Interior, and Agriculture Departments along with private interest groups including the Farm Bureau, Grange, National Electrical Light Association, and manufacturers' groups. Secretary Hoover was repeatedly consulted.

56. Mary Bell Dickinson Sherman, "Report of the Better Equipped Homes Campaign," Nineteenth Biennial Convention, General Federal of Women's Clubs, May 28 to June 7, 1928, 67–70.

57. Skocpol, *Protecting Soldiers and Mothers*, 328–33, 432–45.

58. Porter, *Trust in Numbers*, 33–37, 74–77 notes that quantification is especially fitting in the modern democratic society: "reliance on numbers and quantitative manipulation minimizes the need for intimate knowledge and trust." He continues to note—and this is a theme in his book—that "all manner of social scientists, those in our society that have access to and mastery of the method of data analysis have been singularly unsuccessful in affecting public opinion. Rather, the mathematician or economist has found a receptive audience among those (frequently similarly trained) holding positions of authority in public bureaucracies."

59. "National Survey of American Home is Launched by General Federation and Approved by President Coolidge," *General Federation News* 5 (May 1925): 2, 15; GFWC, *Outline Handbook, 1926–1928, Departments of Work* (Washington, D.C.: GFWC, 1926), 7.

60. General Federal of Women's Clubs, Thirteenth Biennial Council, June 27 to July 1, 1929, Swapscott, Massachusetts, 141.

61. Edith Elmer Wood, *Introduction to Housing: Facts and Principles* (Washington, D.C.: U.S. Housing Authority, 1940), 148, 17.

62. Mary Bell Dickson Sherman, "The Home Equipment Survey," speech before Central Supply Association, October 21, 1926, Hotel Sherman, Chicago.

63. Edith Elmer Wood, *Recent Trends in American Housing* (New York: Macmillan, 1931), 26.

64. Coleman Woodbury, "Housing and Housing Research," *American Economic Review* 27, 1, Supplement: Papers and Proceedings (March 1937); see remarks by Homer Hoyt at 229; Homer Hoyt, *The Structure and Growth of Residential Neighborhoods in American Cities* (Washington, D.C.: FHA, 1939), 124–28.

65. Edith Elmer Wood, *Slums and Blighted Areas* (Washington, D.C.: Federal Emergency Administration, 1935), 6.

66. Homer Hoyt, "Instructions as to Procedure in Rating Neighborhoods," memo to Dr. Ernest Fisher, July 22, 1935, NARA, RG, 31, Box 18; Woodbury, "Housing and Housing Research"; , Hoyt, *Structure and Growth of Residential Neighborhoods*, 35–47.

67. Illinois State Housing Board, *Annual Report*, 1937, Ernest W. Burgess Papers, University of Chicago Library, Box 9, Folder 1.

68. Porter, *Trust in Numbers*, 33–37: defining and counting elements is, as Porter points out, both an exercise of power and "good public relations," at which the GFWC excelled.

69. Blanche Halbert, ed., *The Better Homes Manual* (hereafter BHM) (Chicago, University of Chicago Press, 1931).

70. Federal Housing Administration, *Property Standards: Requirements for Mortgage Insurance Under Title II of the National Housing Act* (hereafter FHAPS) (Washington, D.C.: Government Printing Office, 1936), sec. 207a–207c; BHM, 273, 348.

71. FHAPS, sec 203e; BHM, 355–56.

72. FHAPS sec 207a; BHM, 115.

73. FHAPS, sec 525–26; BHM, 348.

74. FHAPS, sec 208a–b, 207d; BHM, 248, 525.

75. FHAPS, sec 209a–c; BHM, 306–7.

76. FHAPS, sec 516, 205a; BHM, 639–40.

77. FHAPS, sec 203a–b; BHM, 174.

78. FHAPS, sec. 203d–e; BHM, 181, 355–56.

79. FHAPS, sec 204a; BHM, 125.

80. FHAPS, sec. 201c, BHM, 518.

81. FHAPS, sec 201a; BHM, ix, 8, 88.

82. Stuart, *Discriminating Risk*, 25, 46–50; National Housing Act of 1934, Sec 203 (b).

83. Adam Gordon, "The Creation of Homeownership: How New Deal Changes in Banking Regulation Simultaneously Made Homeownership Accessible to Whites and Out of Reach for Blacks," *Yale Law Journal* 115 (October 2005): 193–94. Gordon argues that the creation of the FHA and the mortgage insurance program it administered transformed the American home financing industry. However, more important, because the program was so indelibly inscribed by institutional racism, the substantial benefits that accrued to a wide swath of social strata of the country were denied to nonwhites, because housing was, by fiat of the national state, transformed into a financial instrument. The primary way Americans accumulated wealth was denied especially to African Americans and Latinos, a difference that could permanently be present in the American political economy.

84. See James Greer, "The Home Owners' Loan Corporation and the Development of the Residential Security Maps," *Journal of Urban History* 39, 2 (March 2013): 278–79.

85. Janet Hutchinson, "Shaping Housing and Enhancing Consumption: Hoover's Interwar Housing Policy," in *From Tenements to the Taylor Homes*, ed. John F. Bauman, Roger Biles, and Kristin M. Sylvian (University Park: Pennsylvania State University Press, 2000), 94.

86. Freund, *Colored Property*.

87. Hutchinson, "American Housing," 13.

Contributors

James Greer is an independent scholar. He is a senior analyst at the U.S. Department of the Treasury. He holds a Ph.D. in Political Science from the University of Chicago and is writing a book on the historical development of home mortgage redlining in the United States. His articles have appeared in *Politics & Society* and the *Journal of Urban History*.

Carol Nackenoff is Richter Professor of Political Science at Swarthmore College. She received her Ph.D. from the University of Chicago and is currently writing a monograph on the contested meaning of citizenship in the United States in 1875-1925, having authored articles on gendered citizenship and Native American citizenship related to this project. She is author of *The Fictional Republic: Horatio Alger and American Political Discourse* and coeditor (with Marilyn Fischer and Wendy Chmielewski) and contributor to *Jane Addams and the Practice of Democracy*. She teaches courses in constitutional law, American politics, and environmental politics and policy and serves on the editorial board of *Polity*.

Julie Novkov is Professor of Political Science and Women's Studies at the University at Albany, SUNY and chairs the Department of Political Science. She received her Ph.D. from the University of Michigan and her J.D. from New York University and is writing a book on citizenship and civic membership in the context of military service. She is author of the prize-winning *Racial Union* and *Constituting Workers, Protecting Women*. She also coedited and contributed to *Race and American Political Development* (with Joseph Lowndes and Dorian Warren), and *Security Disarmed* (with Barbara Sutton and Sandra Morgen). Her research and teaching address the intersections of law, history, U.S. political development, and subordinated identity.

Susan Pearson teaches history at Northwestern University. She received her Ph.D. in history from the University of North Carolina. She is the author of *The Rights of the Defenseless: Protecting Animals and Children in the Gilded Age* and is currently working on a project examining the spread of compulsory and universal birth registration in the United States. She is a founding editor of H-Animal, the H-Net Network on Animal Studies. Her prize-winning article on the origins of baby contests in the United States appeared in *Journal of Social History*.

Kimberly Smith is Professor of Political Science and Environmental Studies at Carleton College, teaching courses in political theory, constitutional law, environmental ethics, and environmental politics. She earned her Ph.D. in political science from the University of Michigan and her J.D. from the Boalt School of Law, University of California at Berkeley. In 2009, she Smith was appointed to the editorial board of *Environmental Ethics* and served as the first elected President of the Association for Environmental Studies and Sciences. She is the author of *The Dominion of Voice: Riot, Reason, and Romance in Antebellum Politics*, winner of the Merle Curti Prize in Intellectual History from the Organization of American Historians; *Wendell Berry and the Agrarian Tradition*; and *African American Environmental Thought*.

Marek D. Steedman is Associate Professor of Political Science at the University of Southern Mississippi, with a Ph.D. in political theory from the University of Michigan. His book, *Jim Crow Citizenship*, examines the relation between race and the liberal and republican traditions in American political thought. His work has appeared in *Du Bois Review* and *Historical Reflections*, and the edited volumes *Lotman and Cultural Studies* and *Gender and Slave Emancipation in the Atlantic World*.

Patricia Strach is Associate Professor in the Departments of Political Science and Public Administration and Policy at the University at Albany. She received her Ph.D. in Political Science from the University of Wisconsin, Madison. She is the author of *All in the Family: The Private Roots of American Public Policy* and articles in *Political Research Quarterly*, *Journal of Policy History*, *Polity*, and *American Politics Research*. In 2008–2010, she was a Robert Wood Johnson Scholar in Health Policy Research at Harvard University. She is working on a book on Americans' participation in market activism.

Kathleen Sullivan is Associate Professor of Political Science at Ohio University and works in the fields of constitutional law and American political development. She received her Ph.D. in Government from the University of Texas at Austin. She is author of *Constitutional Context: Women and Rights Discourse in Nineteenth-Century America*. She was a fellow at the NEH Munson Institute, "The American Maritime People," and is currently studying the treatment of seamen in port cities in the nineteenth century.

Ann-Marie Szymanski is Associate Professor of Political Science at the University of Oklahoma. She holds a Ph.D. in Government from Cornell University. She is the author of *Pathways to Prohibition: Radicals, Moderates, and Social Movement Outcomes*, as well as several articles and papers that explore the interplay between associations, state structure, and policymaking. She is currently working on a book manuscript that examines the role of private groups in the creation and enforcement of American regulatory policy.

Index

Acknowledgments

In addition to the scholars whose chapters appear in this volume, many of whom have read and astutely commented on each other's work at various points, we acknowledge the many others who have been part of the long-term conversation. Priscilla Yamin's considerations of marriage politics have helped us to attend to broader understandings of what constitutes an institution. Eileen McDonagh's creative engagements with gender and feminine discourses of power have helped us to look for political authority in a variety of places. Pamela Brandwein's considerations of the role of racial struggles and the relationship between constitutional and political change along with her elegant means of tracing change have contributed to our understandings of the relationship between law and policy.

In seeking a home for our collaboration, we found a warm welcome from Peter Agree, Richard Valelly, and fellow-traveler Pamela Brandwein at the University of Pennsylvania Press, and we thank them for their enthusiasm and support.